AFTER COLONIALISM

EDITORS

Sherry B. Ortner, Nicholas B. Dirks, Geoff Eley

A LIST OF TITLES

IN THIS SERIES APPEARS

AT THE BACK OF

THE BOOK

PRINCETON STUDIES IN
CULTURE / POWER / HISTORY

AFTER COLONIALISM

IMPERIAL HISTORIES AND POSTCOLONIAL DISPLACEMENTS

Edited by Gyan Prakash

PRINCETON UNIVERSITY PRESS

PRINCETON, NEW JERSEY

Library of Congress Cataloging-in-Publication Data

After colonialism : imperial histories and postcolonial
displacements / edited by Gyan Prakash.
p.   cm. — (Princeton studies in culture/power/history)
Includes index.
ISBN 0-691-03743-4 (CL)
ISBN 0-691-03742-6 (PA)
1. Colonies—History.   2. Imperialism—History.
I. Prakash, Gyan, 1952–   .   II. Series.
JV105.A35   1994
325'.32—dc20   94-21310   CIP

The following essays have been published previously in slightly
different form: Homi K. Bhabha, "In a Spirit of Calm Violence,"
as "By Bread Alone," in his *The Location of Culture* (London:
Routledge, 1994), reprinted with permission; Steven Feierman,
"Africa in History: The End of Universal Narratives," as "African
History and World History," in *Africa and the Disciplines*, ed. Robert
H. Bates, V. Y. Mudimbe, and Jean O'Barr (Chicago: University of
Chicago Press, 1993) © 1993 by The University of Chicago. All rights
reserved; J. Jorge Klor de Alva, "The Postcolonization of the (Latin)
American Experience; A Reconsideration of 'Colonialism,' 'Post-
colonialism,' and 'Mestizaje,'" as "Colonialism and Post-Colonialism
as (Latin) American Mirages," *Colonial Latin American Review* 1, nos.
1–2 (1992): 3–23; and Edward Said, "Secular Intrepretation, the
Geographical Element, and the Methodology of Imperialism,"
reprinted by permission from his *Culture and Imperialism* (New York:
Alfred A. Knopf, Inc., 1993), copyright © 1993 by Edward W. Said.

Contents

Preface

IN RECENT YEARS, the study of colonialism has witnessed a resurgence of scholarly interest and attracted a great deal of valuable research and rethinking across several disciplines. With a view to advance the study and reconsideration of the colonial experience and its effects, the Shelby Cullom Davis Center for Historical Studies, Princeton University, organized a series of seminars and colloquia over two years (1990–92) on the theme, "Imperialism, Colonialism, and the Colonial Aftermath." The Center appointed visiting fellows and invited scholars, representing a variety of disciplines and approaches, to present their research at its weekly seminars, colloquia, and luncheon discussions. The fellows and their areas of research ranged from India, North and sub-Saharan Africa, the Caribbean, and Latin America to Europe and North America. The topics were similarly varied and extended from ancient to modern imperialism; from medical history to vodou to race and slavery to literary genres to museums to urbanization. Interpretive approaches encompassed the analysis of political economy, social history, literary analysis, and cultural criticism. Papers were drawn from different disciplines—history, anthropology, literature—and discussions often crossed disciplinary boundaries to explore issues of evidence, knowability, methods, and possibilities of other forms of knowledge and agency.

This volume represents a selection from the two years of wide-ranging and stimulating presentations. Its objective is to display a range of approaches currently employed to offer a fresh understanding of modern colonial history and reflect on the forms of identities and knowledges it produced. Many papers could not be included because they were either committed elsewhere for publication or did not fit the themes of this volume. But the present selection owes a great deal to the work of other fellows and papers not included here, as it does to the discussions that started on Friday mornings at the seminar, spilled over to the lunches, and continued into and surfaced in the next gathering.

All the participants, including the regulars from the history department and other departments at Princeton, deserve thanks for making the two years invigorating and productively contentious. But, most of all, thanks are due to Natalie Zemon Davis, the director of the Davis Center. It was her intelligence, enthusiasm, and inspiring leadership that provided the essential continuity from one week to the next. She kept discussions focused on important issues, reminded the seminar of convergences and differences in interpretations and methods, and offered constructive criticisms. Natalie's characteristic leadership put its stamp on discussions, and the participants waited with anticipation for her summaries at the end of Friday seminars. The volume has benefited a great deal from her leadership during those two years, and I was fortunate to receive her advice in fulfilling my editorial responsibilities.

I am grateful to Kari Hoover, the secretary of the Davis Center, who cheerfully handled various chores related to the preparation of this volume, and to Random House for allowing us to reprint Edward Said's essay, which was presented originally at the Davis Center and published in his *Culture and Imperialism*. I am also grateful to my editor, Mary Murrell, at Princeton University Press, who saw potential in this volume and whose support and insights were invaluable.

AFTER COLONIALISM

After Colonialism

GYAN PRAKASH

MODERN COLONIALISM, it is now widely recognized, instituted enduring hierarchies of subjects and knowledges—the colonizer and the colonized, the Occidental and the Oriental, the civilized and the primitive,
the scientific and the superstitious, the developed and the underdeveloped. The scholarship in different disciplines has made us all too aware
that such dichotomies reduced complex differences and interactions to
the binary (self/other) logic of colonial power. But if the colonial rulers
enacted their authority by constituting the "native" as their inverse
image, then surely the "native" exercised a pressure on the identification
of the colonizer. I refer here not to the dialectic but to the dissemination
of the self and the other that ensued as the identity and authority of the
colonizer were instituted in the language and the figure of the "native."
Compelled to mix with, work upon, and express their authority in re-
pressed knowledges and subjects, the colonial categories were never instituted without their dislocation and transformation. The writ of rationality and order was always overwritten by its denial in the colonies,
the pieties of progress always violated irreverently in practice, the assertion of the universality of Western ideals always qualified drastically. Paradoxes and ironies abounded, as did the justification of the gap between
rhetoric and practice on the grounds of expediency and the exceptional
circumstances of the colonies. These contortions of the discourse were
endemic to colonialism not because of the colonizer's bad faith but due
to the functioning of colonial power as a form of transaction and translation between incommensurable cultures and positions. The establishment of colonial power in the figure of the "native," therefore, was also
a displacement and relocation of colonial oppositions. For as the authority of the "civilized" was articulated in the speech of the "uncivilized,"
colonial oppositions were crossed and hybridized. It is on this liminal
site of mixtures and crossings produced by the exercise of colonial
power that boundaries were redrawn and the colonizer/colonized divide was reordered.

Placed against the background of colonialism's functioning as a form
of relocation and renegotiation of oppositions and boundaries, the colo-

nial aftermath does not appear as a narrative framed by the hierarchical knowledges and subjects instituted by Western domination. There is another story in that Western domination that, in fact, surfaces precisely at the point where the encounter with cultural difference is organized into the colonizer/colonized polarity, where the historicist notion of history gathers "people without history" into its fold, and where the metropolitan culture speaks to the marginalized in the language of its supremacist myths. There emerges in these constitutive processes of colonial power an estrangement and displacement of colonial constructions. Consider, for example, the "civilizing mission" in Africa performed in the establishment of "tribes" as "traditional" sources of power and authority; or the British role as the "unconscious tool of history" in India acted out in the archaic Mughal rituals emptied of their traditional meanings; or the doctrine of liberty and freedom elaborated in the exploitation of black slaves in the Americas. In these performances, as the myths of the civilizing mission and historical progress find perverse expressions in caricatures of indigenous traditions and racist stereotyping and exploitation of blacks, the colonial reality appears in its estranged representation.

In these performances the artful lie of colonialism emerges as its alienated and artless truth: the paradoxes reveal a fundamental instability and division in the functioning of colonial power. This perspective of colonialism's functioning offers another vision of the aftermath of colonial conquest. Societies and knowledges come into view only after having been worked over by colonialism, but the texture of their transformation exhibits fissures covered over flimsily by colonial categories. After all, the mission to spread civic virtue with military power, or propagate the text of the "Rights of Man" in the context of slave and indentured labor, could not but introduce rifts and tensions in the structure of Western power. This tenuousness of colonial power bears testimony to the pressure exercised silently by the subordinated and enables another view of colonial change. The fragile alignment of discrepant histories and knowledges after colonialism emerges with possibilities for a postcolonial realignment. In this realignment there appears another form of "after colonialism"—one that seizes on colonialism's contingent arrangement of values and social identification and rearranges them to reveal sources of knowledge and agency simmering beneath the calm surface of colonial history and historiography.

It is this dynamic and double sense of the colonial aftermath that animates this volume of essays. While individual contributions are written from a range of perspectives and address specific concerns of different disciplinary fields, they can be read to question the leaden understanding of colonialism as History: history with a clear trajectory originating in the early modern European expansions and ending with the postwar anticolonial nationalism and decolonization. This view is complicit with Western domination, but offers itself nonetheless as a clear lens through which we can understand colonialism. It sequesters colonialism tightly in the airless container of History, and casts postcoloniality as a new beginning, one in which certain old modes of domination may persist and acquire new forms of sustenance but one that marks the end of an era. To pry open the reading of colonialism from this prison-house of historicism requires more than the concept of neocolonialism. For at stake is not simply the issue as to whether or not former colonies have become free from domination, but also the question as to how the history of colonialism and colonialism's disciplining of history can be shaken loose from the domination of categories and ideas it produced—colonizer and colonized; white, black, and brown; civilized and uncivilized; modern and archaic; cultural identity; tribe and nation.

Such categories and ideas have not gone unchallenged. The history of scholarship on colonialism abounds with examples of the questioning of the idea of history as History, the interrogation of the concepts of race and tribe. Scholars have frequently noted and highlighted the contradictions and impasses in the exercise of colonial power, and there exist many descriptions of how the colonized resisted the imposition of the "civilizing mission" as History. More recently, Orientalism, the Oriental, the native, the nation-state, and other such categories have been subjected to close scrutiny to reveal their location in the colonial discourse of power. Burdened with the weight of power, these categories have been shown to owe their origin and life to another time; if they survive into the present, they do so as forms of a past whose time has passed—they are history.

It would be wrong, and arrogant, to understate the importance of such previous critiques of colonial history. Indeed, it would be contrary to the spirit of this volume to deny the troubled life of colonialism in scholarship. Yet it should be recognized that while there are many examples of critiques of liberal historiography and of its complicity with imperialism, the revision of the discipline from the place of "otherness" is yet to occur.[1] We have several accounts of the resistance of the colonized, but few treatments of their resistance as theoretical events; there exist fine descriptions of the "people without history," but their conceptions are frequently treated as myths and "ethnohistories" left for anthropologists to decode and interpret; and while there are scrupulous accounts of Western domination, we have yet to fully recognize another history of agency and knowledge alive in the dead weight of the colonial past.

It is in this respect that the present volume can be read differently from previous critiques: it provides material to move beyond marking the contradictions and impasses in the history of colonialism, to proceed further than the description of the construction of power-laden categories. The essays enable us to return to the history of colonialism without rehearsing the naturalization of colonialism as History. By this I mean a project of understanding that delves into the history of colonialism not only to document its record of domination but also to track the failures, silences, displacements, and transformations produced by its functioning; not only to chronicle the functioning of Western dominance and resistances to it, but to mark those (subaltern) positions and knowledges that could not be properly recognized and named, only "normalized," by colonial discourses. Quite simply, the essays in this volume should be read to revisit the historical record, to push at the edges, to unsettle the calmness with which colonial categories and knowledges were instituted as the facts of history. This is to shake colonialism loose from the stillness of the past; it is to throw open for realignment the conflictual, discrepant, and even violent processes that formed the precipitous basis of colonial power. + processes y its continuation.

Something of this sense of the realignment of the colonial record can be observed in Gandhi's text, *Hind Swaraj*.[2] Written in 1908 as he traveled from London to South Africa by sea, this text is a severe indictment of modern civilization. Attacking, with a certain recklessness, lawyers, doctors, parliaments, machinery, railways, and mills for having created illusions of freedom in an unhindered pursuit of material satisfaction, Gandhi projects nonviolent self-control over passion, greed, and hatred as the basis for India's freedom. The specific content of his criticisms is less relevant than the mode in which the creed of a nonmodern and nonviolent Indian struggle for freedom is crafted out of a violent denunciation of the modern civilization. There is more to this mode, however, than the irony that the philosophy of nonviolence is overwritten by a language bristling with violent criticism. Indeed, the ironic juxtaposition of violence and nonviolence highlights how an encounter with colonialism could produce a program for the dislocation of its violence. Thus, as the *Hind Swaraj* directs its bitter, violent criticism at the British rule in India, the violence of colonialism emerges as the central truth of the modern capitalist civilization, not its peripheral and unnecessary sideshow. Unlike other nationalists, who spoke of the "Un-British rule" in India and demanded, in Gandhi's words, "English rule without the Englishman,"[3] he sees colonization as the alienated local image of the modern English nation: "Civilization is not an incurable disease, but it should never be forgotten that the English people are at present afflicted by it."[4] After offering this biting criticism of the modern civilization and parliamentary government (which is compared to a sterile woman and a prostitute), Gandhi turns to India's ancient "village communities" as an alternative model, but he does not do so as a nativist. Indeed, this notion of premodern India as a collection of village communities was derived from colonial sociology, most notably from Henry Maine (who is cited as an authority in the text). Gandhi's concept of a nonmodern civilization drew on Tolstoy, Thoreau, and Ruskin, who are also cited as authorities.[5] Again, the content of his vision is not the issue here, but the fact that it emerged from a rereading of the colonial archive. It was by rescuing the premodern from its assigned space as history, from its designation as colonialism's self-confirming other, and by inserting it in the same time as the modern that Gandhi was able to formulate his concept of the nonmodern. By such a reinterpretation of the premodern as the nonmodern, by realigning categories aligned by colonialism, Gandhi was able to produce a postcolonial text that made the violent critique of the colonial discourse speak with nonviolent meanings.

In a different location and with an acute phenomenological imagination, Fanon's memorable essays also tug insistently at the seams of the fabric of colonial truths. Consider this remarkable passage in his essay "The Fact of Blackness," which forms part of that extraordinary analysis of colonial identities, *Black Skin, White Masks*:

'Understand, my dear boy, color prejudice is something I find utterly foreign. . . . But of course, come in, sir, there is no color prejudice among us. . . . Quite, the Negro is a man like ourselves. . . . It is not because he is black that he is less intelligent than we are. . . . I had a Senegalese buddy in the army who was really clever. . . .'

Where am I to be classified? Or, if you prefer, tucked away?

'A Martinican, a native of "our" old colonies.'

Where shall I hide?

'Look at the nigger! . . . Mama, a Negro! . . . Hell, he's getting mad. . . . Take no notice, sir, he does not know that you are as civilized as we. . . .'

My body was given back to me sprawled out, clad in mourning in that white winter day. The Negro is an animal, the Negro is bad, the Negro is mean; look, a nigger, it's cold, the nigger is shivering, the nigger is shivering because he is cold, the little boy is trembling because he is afraid of the nigger, the nigger is shivering with cold, that cold that goes through your bones, the handsome little boy is trembling because he thinks that the nigger is quivering with rage, the little white boy throws himself into his mother's arms: Mama, the nigger's going to eat me up.[6]

I have quoted this passage at length because it stages a stunning displacement of the "Rights of Man." But it does so not as a form of unmasking, not to reveal the "reality" lurking under the "myth" of the colonial discourse; its ambition is greater, and its effect more devastating. Fanon represents racism as the phantasmic truth of colonialism in which the disavowal of racial difference produces a racist double-speak:

"But of course, come in, sir, there is no color prejudice among us. . . . Quite, the Negro is a man like ourselves. . . . It is not because he is black that he is less intelligent than we are." The rationality of this fantasy is articulated in the delirium of "The Negro is an animal, the Negro is bad, the Negro is mean; look, a nigger, it's cold"; and the meaningfulness of the racist fantasy is expressed in the broken nonsense of "the little boy is trembling because he is afraid of the nigger, the nigger is shivering with cold." Caught in between reality and fantasy, rationality and delirium, originary colonial identities take shape in the uncertain moment of the fearful gaze: "Look at the nigger! . . . Mama, a Negro!"

Performed here is a wholescale dislocation, not demystification, of the racist discourse. It is not that a "real" black man emerges from Fanon's allusion to the racist fear; instead, as we see him through the fearful eyes of the French child, the black identity appears anew, as a product of historical relations and racist anxiety, not origin. In pursuing such a strategy, Fanon neither calls for a more consistent application of European humanism (a color-blind humanity extended to everyone) nor does he uncover the "real" history of European colonialism; rather, his account transgresses and undermines the terms of the discourse. As Homi Bhabha writes:

> It is one of the original and disturbing qualities of *Black Skin, White Masks* that it rarely historicizes the colonial experience. There is no master narrative or realist perspective that provide a background of social and historical facts against which emerge problems of the individual or collective psyche. . . . It is through image and fantasy—those orders that figure transgressively on the borders of history and the unconscious—that Fanon profoundly evokes the colonial condition.[7]

It is not that Fanon replaces history with psychoanalysis in order to place colonialism in its "true" register; rather, he locates psychic desire and fantasy at the heart of the rationalist discourse of history and thus foregrounds the fissured formation of the colonial society. There emerges a constitutive relationship between the order of the military barracks and the command of civic authority, between the profusion of racist fears and fantasies and the articulation of the "Rights of Man," between the brute exploitation of slave labor and the development of the rational capitalist enterprise. As the French Revolution appears cross-cut by Haiti, it is not that one negates the other; instead, the confrontation and entanglement of the lofty and universalist rhetoric of equality, liberty, and fraternity with the degrading practices of slavery reveal the limits of the ideology invisible in France itself. As military might, slavery, racism, and political domination in the colonies become the medium for the articulation of the "civilizing mission," there emerges another vision of colonialism, another possibility for the revision of colonial power and knowledge.

Such a theory of colonialism, or a discourse on colonial history, should be considered as an event, a significant occurrence, in the history of colonization. Gandhi and Fanon are only two well-known names among the nameless whose practices and resistance transformed colonialism's theory of history and produced new forms of historical imagination. From Latin America to India, the colonized shifted the terrain of engagement by occupying and carving out positions placed in between the powerful command of authority and the powerless silence of the victim. Consider, for example, the conversion of the Tagalog to Christianity in seventeenth-century Philippines. As Vincent Rafael shows, the Tagalog responded to Spanish proselytization with subterfuges and subversive compliances, offering "confession without sin, submission without translation."[8] The Tagalog "submitted" to the Spanish missionaries, but they also hollowed out the meaning of submission; they infused the penitent-priest relationship with meanings drawn from the unequal reciprocity of debt transactions, and turned the confession of sins into an occasion for boasting and protesting their innocence. With such a strategy, the Tagalog forged positions for themselves that were partial and conditional because they brought together traditions and strategies from different registers contingently. But as partial, hybrid, and contingent as they may have been, these positions were no less radically transformative for these reasons. On the contrary, by taking perspectives and strategies out of their "proper" domains and combining them, the position of the penitent in relation to the priest was relocated by the Tagalog, transgressing and redrawing colonial boundaries.

Even anticolonial nationalism was compelled to transgress colonial polarities as it sought to articulate an essentialized nation. The nationalists, to be sure, believed that the colonized formed a unity; that they constituted a national essence opposed to that of the colonizers. But the production of this unity required the invocation of difference. The nationalist intellectuals spoke of "unity in diversity"; they claimed that the colonized formed a nation in spite of social, regional, and ethnic differences. Such assertions were not merely polemical responses to the colonial rulers who resisted the nationalist demands; instead, they underscored the necessity of the stage of difference for the performance of the nation's unity.[9] Thus, the demand for a modern nationhood was anchored in appeals to a "lost" ancient belonging, and the unity of the national subject was forged in the space of difference and conflicts.

But if nationalism achieved its authority from the transgression of boundaries, it disavowed the ambivalence of the nation's process of emergence. It normalized and contained the space of difference that it invoked in performing the nation's unity. Movements, perspectives, and groups that stood in between boundaries and polarities were reappropriated to advance the nation's dominance. Take, for example, anticolonial peasant uprisings in India. As Ranajit Guha's study shows, neither the position of the peasant subalterns nor their religious ideology and modes of resistance could be accommodated easily in the nationalist discourse. The subalterns' social location defied the identities of nation and class, and their insurgent consciousness, religiosity, mythic visions, and notions of political community were at odds with the model of causality and rational action advanced by the nationalist elites.[10] These other visions, whether articulated in subaltern insurgency or in Gandhi's utopia of a nonmodern India, arose at the intersection of political, social, and cultural differences and sought to renegotiate a more democratic postcolonial order. The elite discourse was compelled to engage the subalterns and Gandhi; it cited peasant "unrest" and the ideas of nonviolence to authorize the demand for a nation-state, but it did not treat them as sources of knowledge and agency. The subalterns were regarded as incapable of articulating the demands of the nation and Gandhi was dismissed as outmoded by the disciplines of history instituted by colonialism and rearticulated by nationalism.[11]

The subaltern sources of knowledge and agency were major historical events, yet they had no place in the fields of knowledge that grew in an incestuous relationship with colonialism. These disciplines offered a "prose of counterinsurgency" to comprehend and contain an insurgent reality—notions of peoples without history, and race and culture types developed to reorder and reappropriate irreducible heterogeneity into power-laden polarities. In recent years, scholarship in different disciplines has vigorously traced the relationship between the formation of authoritative knowledges and the exercise of colonial power that denied other people knowledge and agency. Edward Said's *Orientalism* is a pioneering example of the growing trend in scholarly work that documents the ties between knowledge and power; and his recent *Culture and Imperialism* extends this work further through an exploration of the cultural relationship of power between the metropolitan West and the rest.[12] Homi Bhabha's essays on the ambivalent, hybrid enunciation of metropolitan discourses have foregrounded the uncertain and unstable status and functioning of colonial disciplines in both its senses.[13] Consider also the combative essays in the *Subaltern Studies* project that have fastened on the figure of the subaltern to lay bare the relationship between disciplinary knowledges and the colonial and elite-nationalist strategies of power.[14] In literature, history, and anthropology, there has been a rapid proliferation of studies that question their disciplinary foundations; concepts and methods developed seemingly within enclosed fields of knowledge, geography, culture, history, and institutions have been shown to spill into one another.[15]

The disturbance of colonial categories and disciplines extends beyond scholarship. One can observe it in Tayib Salih's novel, *Season of Migration to the North*, which recounts the experience of the narrator, a Western-educated Sudanese, who returns from Europe to his village on the Nile, to discover in the story of another Western-educated compatriot, that the colonized identity was a lie, a fabrication.[16] In a brilliant literary reenactment of Fanon, Salih unravels the process of the racist identity-formation instituted under colonialism, upsetting notions of cultural wholeness, essences, and origin. One can witness a similar dismantling of the stable self/other construct of colonialism in the emergence of the marginal in the very bosom of the metropolitan as we hear Whisky Sisodia declare in Salman Rushdie's *Satanic Verses*: "The trouble with the English is that their history happened overseas, so they don't know what it means."[17] In a different context, Toni Morrison's *Beloved* achieves a startling representation of the historical meaning of the racist exploitation under slavery in North America as it remembers the lives of the survivors of slavery with the uncanny afterlife of the ghosts of racial violence from the past.[18] From the irruption of the dead in the living, there arises the haunting agency and knowledge of the victims that torment the narrative of slavery recounted by history.

In these writings, assembled from widely different contexts to illustrate the range of reformulations of disciplinary knowledge, there is a reenactment of history that reproduces the old but also goes beyond it; there is an immersion and intervention into the historical record that is also profoundly transformative. These writings reinterpret identity as a process of ambivalent identification, reopen theories of enclosed histories with accounts of entangled, hierarchical engagements, and resituate historical antagonisms in the agonistic process of narrating and rememorizing. In the aftermath of decolonization, their return to the scene after colonialism breaches open categories of identity and history universalized by Western expansion and releases other sources of knowledge and agency.

It is fitting that such refashionings of history and theory emerge from that other place, the site of colonialism, because it was there that the disciplines both reached for mastery and were undone. It was in British India, for instance, as I have shown elsewhere, that scientific knowledge was placed in a position of undisputed cultural authority and where its "inappropriate" mixture with superstition exposed and realigned the process of its authorization.[19] To return to the colonial scene, therefore, is to release histories and knowledges from their disciplining as area-studies; as imperial and overseas history; as the study of the exotic other that seals metropolitan structures from the contagion of the record of their own formation elsewhere—in fantasy and fear, in cultural difference and uneven and entangled histories, in contingency and contention.

The alternative sources of knowledge and agency released by the return to the cracks of colonial disciplines are heterogeneous: they cannot be classified into some global postcolonial other. This is because postcolonial knowledge takes shape at the specific and local points of disciplinary failures; it arises at certain conjunctures and affiliates with particular traditions of thought. Therefore, while returns to the interpellation of different regions, cultures, and histories undo colonial disciplining, they do not use the heterogeneous colonial sites to fabricate a homogeneous account of colonial history. Thus, as scholars, activists, and intellectuals have fastened on the tensions, anxieties, and intermixtures in colonial discourses to split apart the categories of identity and history associated with racism and western domination, the new sources of knowledge that they have offered remain contextual and contingent. This is true from Fanon's destabilization of colonial identities to Toni Morrison's exploration of the memory of the racist violence of slavery in the constitution of the contemporary North American identities. This is not to say that such texts are insular and nativist. Far from it. Migrancy, hybridity, and imbrication mark Gandhi's nonmodern utopia as much as they appear in Salman Rushdie's novels. But they remain particular and partial knowledges located in contingent constellations of the local and the extralocal, and cannot be emblematized as instances of a global other.

It is in this spirit of releasing heterogeneous sources of knowledge and agency from the grip of the disciplines of colonialism that this volume resists disciplinary boundaries and geographical enclosures. The contributions range from literary studies to historical accounts and from Latin America to India. They cross historical analysis of texts with textual examination of historical records, and they situate metropolitan cultural practices in engagements with nonmetropolitan locations. Interdisciplinarity here means exploring and realigning disciplinary boundaries. This may frustrate conventional expectations of analysis and evidence, but the historical analysis of disciplines cannot but disorient disciplinary expectations shaped in the history of colonialism. It is this difficult and disorienting task that the essays in this volume perform. Organized in three thematic sections with overlapping concerns, they open received knowledges to historical examination from different angles and with a variety of approaches, repeatedly broaching and breaching the colonial archive and exploring other sources of knowledge and agency.

The opening section turns the marginalized and the silenced in modern disciplines into the stirring presence that disturbs the colonial constitution of knowledge. Edward Said's wide-ranging essay on the institution of comparative literature highlights the discipline's hidden "geographical notation," its fleeting reference to empire. He pinpoints precisely this incidental notation to reveal its central function in the constitution of metropolitan culture. Thus, in his acute reading of Jane Austen's *Mansfield Park*, the passing reference to the distant slave-plantation of Antigua becomes the critical basis for the representation of the intimacy and grace of Mansfield Park. To disclose such intimacy of empire and culture, Said argues, we must reread the cultural archive "not univocally but contrapuntally," reading Jane Austen and John Stuart Mill alongside Frantz Fanon and Amilcar Cabral. Similarly, Steven Feierman's essay focuses on the disturbing presence of Africa in historiography to highlight the provinciality of the universalizing concepts of world history. Showing that historiographical schemes based on such ideas as civilization, material life, and commodities run up against processes that cannot be assimilated, he makes a case for multiple narratives faithful to historical interconnections and discrepant histories.

Joan Dayan's essay on the history and the historiography of the Haitian revolution also focuses on the troubling legends, traditions, and figures from which historians have sought to seal the revolution. She rereads the practice of vodou, the legends of Dessalines' resurrection and his possession by the Black Virgin, to offer another view of the revolution that breaks from the homogeneity of what can be and has been said about it. The Haitian revolution is reopened to the world of vodou, but the "French" meaning attributed to the revolution by history and historiography is not simply reversed. In fact, rather like Dessalines' strategy of "blackening" that eliminated the stain of color from racial identification and remarked it with economic and political signs, Dayan's rereading of the revolution displaces the black/white polarity with uncontainable hybridity. Similarly, Ruth Phillips' study finds that the silence of the North American museums on native American "tourist art" speaks the unspeakable. There emerges a pulsating history of the native Americans' encounter and negotiation with Western economic and artistic systems that, though unequal, could not be contained in the stillness of the premodern/modern dichotomy upon which colonial power was founded. In producing objects that looked "too white," the native Americans, she suggests, threatened the colonial notions of identity. Thus, their "white" objects had to be classified as "tourist art" and disciplined out of museums.

The next section moves from foregrounding the disturbing presence of difference in disciplinary knowledge to an analysis of strategies to contain the anxieties it produced. For Diderot and Herder, as Anthony Pagden's account shows, colonization was an anxious encounter with cultural difference: colonial conquests revealed the universal values of reason and free agency (Diderot) to be particular and contingent; or they undermined the "natural" separation of cultures (Herder). Diderot and Herder contained this threatening encounter, however, by regarding colonialism as an effacement of cultural difference. This became possible when difference was conceived as diversity, according to which each culture was an atomistic whole with separate origins and essences. Such a notion of difference as diversity opposed colonization, but Diderot's expansive vision of universal values nourished by miscegenated societies and Herder's restrictive view of an atomistic separation of cultures were two sides of the same coin; neither of them could renegotiate the cultural difference that assailed the European self but was displaced and dichotomized as the non-Western other in colonial discourse.

The threat that cultural difference posed to Dutch colonialism burst forcefully upon Formosa where, as Leonard Blussé's account details, the missionary project ended in a slaughter of the local population. As the drive to convert the Formosans required that they recognize the authority of Christianity, the binary logic of colonialism forced the missionaries to choose either the indigenization of the gospel or its coercive imposition. In the savage slaughter unleashed by the Dutch, colonialism revealed its truth in the violent suppression of the contagion of difference. As we move from seventeenth-century Formosa to nineteenth-century India, conversion once again exposes colonialism's confrontation with cultural difference. Gauri Viswanathan's study carefully traces the complicity of conversion and colonialism that produced a silencing of the converted. Analyzing court cases dealing with the denial of the civic rights of Hindu converts by their communities, Viswanathan documents the priority that the British accorded to the legislated identity as Hindus over the converts' adopted identity. In this process, as the "private" sphere of belief was rewritten in the "public" language of social identity and customary practices, the truth of the liberal doctrine of free individuality appeared in its disavowal and displacement. This left no room for the expression of the colonized's experience of conversion, for private, "autonomous" subjectivity: they could not speak.

Zachary Lockman's sober analysis of labor-Zionism's history in Palestine also broaches the question of the breach opened and closed in colonial discourse as it confronted the disturbing presence of the Arab workers. Their presence could be literally thought out of existence, as it was in the slogan, "A land without a people for a people without land." The process of "emptying" the land, however, was complex and contentious; it was accomplished only when the socialist-Zionists, faced with the task of negotiating the relationship between socialism and nationalism, between class and culture, gave in to a colonialist solution. Arab workers became simply "the Arabs" in discourse, laying the basis for decades of a still-unresolved conflict. J. Jorge Klor de Alva's provocative essay also presents Latin America as an area where indigenous inhabitants are yet to experience decolonization. His account shows that, because colonialism organized cultural difference in the colonizer/colonized polarity, there arose an ideology of nativism that was used by the Europeanized mestizos to proclaim national "independence" in the nineteenth century as decolonization when, in fact, they were never colonized. Indeed, the mestizos used, and continue to do so, the ideology of nativism to establish their rule on behalf of the native Americans, who remain the only group yet to experience decolonization. Similarly, the European immigrants in North America, he suggests, employed the nativist ideology to kill or effectively marginalize the local population and establish themselves as natives ranged against British colonialism.

This volume concludes with three essays that sketch forms of knowledge and agency that emerge from the displacements produced by the very functioning of the colonial discourse. Irene Silverblatt describes how an "Indian" identity appeared in sixteenth-century Peru first in a movement that asked the Andeans to "return" their huacas (sacred place, deity). This "return" to the colonial binary of the Spanish/Indian, repeated in the seventeenth century, unraveled it through an "inappropriate" mixture of categories taken out of their "appropriate" contexts. Thus, as "Indianness" was articulated in the return to the past, in the restaging of old bonds in new contexts, Andean symbols and rituals acquired another signification that ran counter to the christianizing mission. Heretics and witches became the normalized forms in which the colonial panic encountered subaltern agency and knowledge produced in the functioning of colonial categories.

Emily Apter's essay moves from the concept of return to the notion of parodic repetition to chart the displacement of colonial norms. This parodic repetition occurs in the writings and readings of Elissa Rhaïs's novels as they invoke and reinvoke Orientalist stereotypes, thereby draining them of meanings that these are expected to articulate. Thus, the figure of the Oriental woman appears as a masquerade, as an identity staged before and for Western eyes. The real, as a result, is travestied as a colonial image-making split between fantasy and reality. Sketched here is an undoing of colonial realism that produced a collision of realisms, opening the possibility for the recognition of alternative agency and identity in the functioning of colonial categories.

Homi Bhabha brings together several of the volume's principal concerns as he locates subaltern agency in the interstices of colonialism's disciplinary knowledge and in the ambivalent functioning of its disciplines. He begins with Michel Foucault's account of the rise of history and anthropology in *The Order of Things* which, Bhabha argues, re-enacts the indeterminate and disturbing eruption of the colonies in the nineteenth-century emergence of disciplines. Bhabha then moves to the 1857 rebellion in India to locate a similar outbreak of subaltern agency that also seizes and shifts the terrain of disciplinary engagement. His purpose is to outline an agency that is not individualistic, deterministic, and homogeneous but partial, contingent, and ambivalent; not prior to and subsumed by the social but intersubjective and emergent as an effect of enactment and articulation. He outlines this form of agency in the indeterminacy of meaning unleashed by rumors about the circulation of chapatis (unleavened flat bread) during the rebellion. This indeterminacy not only caused panic in the colonizers but also circulated the contagion of ambivalence in the sensible, serial narrative of historians. As the Indian chapati's symbolic meaning was turned inside out and became a sign of an "English" panic, there arose an agency in between the sahib and the sepoy, interposed between history and its repetition in fear and fantasy.

Once again, we are brought to a notion of an "after colonialism," a reinscriptive colonial aftermath, which arises neither inside nor outside colonial norms but in the interstitial space cracked open by the uncertain process of their normalization. It is there that this collection of essays finds its place and explores another history.

NOTES

1. The argument here is analagous to that of Dipesh Chakrabarty, who writes that "insofar as the academic discourse of history—that is, 'history' as a discourse produced at the institutional site of the university—is concerned, 'Europe' remains the sovereign, theoretical subject of all histories, including the one we call 'Indian,' 'Chinese,' 'Kenyan,' and so on " ("Postcoloniality and the Artifice of History: Who Speaks for 'Indian' Pasts," *Representations* 37 [Winter 1992]: 1).

2. *Hind Swaraj or Indian Home Rule* (Ahmedabad: Navjivan, 1938).

3. Ibid., 30.

4. Ibid., 38.

5. Ibid., 105.

6. Frantz Fanon, *Black Skin, White Masks*, with a foreword by Homi Bhabha (London and Sydney: Pluto, 1986), 113–14.

7. Homi Bhabha, foreword to *Black Skin, White Masks*, xii–xiii.

8. "Confession, Conversion, and Reciprocity in Early Tagalog Colonial Society," in *Colonialism and Culture*, ed. Nicholas Dirks (Ann Arbor: University of Michigan Press, 1992), 85.

9. On the narration of nation in the interstitial space of social and cultural difference, see Homi Bhabha, "DissemiNation: Time, Narrative, and the Mar-

gins of the Modern Nation," in *Nation and Narration*, ed. Homi Bhabha (London and New York: Routledge, 1990), 291–322.

10. Ranajit Guha, *Elementary Aspects of Peasant Insurgency in Colonial India* (Delhi: Oxford University Press, 1983).

11. On this point, see Ashis Nandy, *The Intimate Enemy: Loss and Recovery of Self under Colonialism* (Delhi: Oxford University Press, 1983); and Partha Chatterjee, *Nationalist Thought and the Colonial World: A Derivative Discourse?* (London: Zed Books, 1986).

12. *Orientalism* (New York: Random House, 1978); and *Culture and Imperialism* (New York: Alfred A. Knopf, 1993).

13. See his "Of Mimicry and Man: The Ambivalence of Colonial Discourse," *October* 28 (1984): 125–33; "Sly Civility," *October* 34 (1985): 71–80; and "The Other Question: Difference, Discrimination and the Discourse of Colonialism," in *Literature, Politics, and Theory*, ed. Francis Barker et al. (London, 1986), 148–72.

14. See, for example, *Selected Subaltern Studies*, ed. Ranajit Guha (New York: Oxford University Press, 1988), particularly Ranajit Guha's "The Prose of Counter-Insurgency," 45–84; Chatterjee, *Nationalist Thought and the Colonial World*; and idem, *Nation and Its Fragments* (Princeton: Princeton University Press, 1993).

15. Some examples are: *Anthropology & the Colonial Encounter*, ed. Talal Asad (London and Atlantic Highlands, N.J.: Ithaca Press and Humanities Press, 1973); *Writing Culture: The Poetics and Politics of Ethnography*, ed. James Clifford and George Marcus (Berkeley: University of California Press, 1986); Bernard S. Cohn, *An Anthropologist among the Historians and Other Essays* (Delhi: Oxford University Press, 1987); Gayatri Chakravorty Spivak, *In Other Worlds: Essays in Cultural Politics* (New York: Methuen, 1987); Robert Young, *White Mythologies: Writing History and the West* (London and New York: Routledge, 1990); Gauri Viswanathan, *Masks of Conquest: Literary Study and British Rule in India* (New York: Columbia University Press, 1989); and Nicholas Dirks, ed., *Colonialism and Culture*.

16. Tayib Salih, *Season of Migration to the North*, trans. Denys Johnson-Davies (Washington, D.C.: Three Continents Press, 1980).

17. Salman Rushdie, *Satanic Verses* (New York: Viking, 1988), 337.

18. Toni Morrison, *Beloved* (New York: Vintage, 1981). See also Bhabha's reading of the novel in his essay in this volume.

19. Gyan Prakash, "Science 'Gone Native' in Colonial India," *Representations* 40 (Fall 1992): 153–78. This essay was originally presented at the Davis Center seminar.

Part One

COLONIALISM AND THE DISCIPLINES

CHAPTER 1

Secular Interpretation,
the Geographical Element,
and the Methodology of Imperialism

EDWARD SAID

FROM LONG BEFORE World War Two until the early 1970s, the main tradition of comparative-literature studies in Europe and the United States was heavily dominated by a style of scholarship that has now almost disappeared. The main feature of this older style was that it was scholarship principally, and not what we have come to call criticism. No one today is trained as were Erich Auerbach and Leo Spitzer, two of the greatest German comparatists who found refuge in the United States as a result of fascism: this is as much a quantitative as a qualitative fact. Whereas today's comparatist will present his or her qualifications in Romanticism between 1795 and 1830 in France, England, and Germany, yesterday's comparatist was more likely, first, to have studied an earlier period; second, to have done a long apprenticeship with various philological and scholarly experts in various universities in various fields over many years; third, to have a secure grounding in all or most of the classical languages, the early European vernaculars, and their literatures. The early-twentieth-century comparatist was a *philolog* who, as Francis Fergusson put it in a review of Auerbach's *Mimesis*, was so learned and had so much stamina as to make "our most intransigent 'scholars'—those who pretend with the straightest faces to scientific rigor and exhaustiveness—[appear to be] timid and relaxed."[1]

Behind such scholars was an even longer tradition of humanistic learning that derived from that efflorescence of secular anthropology—which included a revolution in the philological disciplines—we associate with the late eighteenth century and with such figures as Vico, Herder, Rousseau, and the brothers Schlegel. And underlying *their* work was the belief that mankind formed a marvelous, almost symphonic whole whose progress and formations, again as a whole, could be studied exclusively as a concerted and secular historical experience, not as an exemplification of the divine. Because "man" has made history, there was a special hermeneutical way of studying history that differed in intent as well as method from the natural sciences. These great Enlightenment insights became widespread, and were accepted in Germany, France, Italy, Russia, Switzerland, and, subsequently, England.

It is not a vulgarization of history to remark that a major reason why such a view of human culture became current in Europe and America in several forms during the two centuries between 1745 and 1945 was the striking rise of nationalism during the same period. The interrelations between scholarship (or literature, for that matter) and the institutions of nationalism have not been as seriously studied as they should, but it is nevertheless evident that when most European thinkers celebrated humanity or culture they were principally celebrating ideas and values they ascribed to their own national culture, or to Europe as distinct from the Orient, Africa, and even the Americas. What partly animated my study of Orientalism was my critique of the way in which the alleged universalism of fields such as the classics (not to mention historiography, anthropology, and sociology) was Eurocentric in the extreme, as if other literatures and societies had either an inferior or transcended value. (Even the comparatists trained in the dignified tradition that produced Curtius and Auerbach showed little interest in Asian, African, or Latin American texts.) And as the national and international competition between European countries increased during the nineteenth century, so too did the level of intensity in competition between one national scholarly interpretative tradition and another. Ernest Renan's polemics on Germany and the Jewish tradition are a well-known example of this.

Yet this narrow, often strident nationalism was in fact counteracted by a more generous cultural vision represented by the intellectual ancestors of Curtius and Auerbach, scholars whose ideas emerged in pre-imperial Germany (perhaps as compensation for the political unification eluding the country), and, a little later, in France. These thinkers took nationalism to be a transitory, finally secondary matter: what mattered far more was the concert of peoples and spirits that transcended the shabby political realm of bureaucracy, armies, customs barriers, and xenophobia. Out of this catholic tradition, to which European (as opposed to national) thinkers appealed in times of severe conflict, came the idea that the comparative study of literature could furnish a trans-national, even trans-human perspective on literary performance. Thus the idea of comparative literature not only expressed universality and the kind of understanding gained by philologists about language families, but also symbolized the crisis-free serenity of an almost ideal realm. Standing above small-minded political affairs were both a kind of anthropological Eden in which men and women happily produced something called literature, and a world that Matthew Arnold and his disciples designated as that of "culture," where only "the best that is thought and known" could be admitted.

Goethe's idea of *Weltliteratur*—a concept that waffled between the notion of "great books" and a vague synthesis of *all* the world's literatures—was very important to professional scholars of comparative literature in the early twentieth century. But still, as I have suggested, its practical meaning and operating ideology were that, so far as literature and culture were concerned, Europe led the way and was the main subject of interest. In the world of great scholars such as Karl Vossler and De Sanctis, it is most specifically Romania that makes intelligible and provides a center for the enormous grouping of literatures produced world-wide; Romania underpins Europe, just as (in a curiously regressive way) the Church and the Holy Roman Empire guarantee the integrity of the core European literatures. At a still deeper level, it is from the Christian Incarnation that Western realistic literature as we know it emerges. This tenaciously advanced thesis explained Dante's supreme importance to Auerbach, Curtius, Vossler, and Spitzer.

To speak of comparative literature therefore was to speak of the interaction of world literatures with one another, but the field was epistemologically organized as a sort of hierarchy, with Europe and its Latin Christian literatures at its center and top. When Auerbach, in a justly famous essay entitled "Philologie der *Weltliteratur*," written after World War Two, takes note of how many "other" literary languages and literatures seemed to have emerged (as if from nowhere: he makes no mention of either colonialism or decolonization), he expresses more anguish and fear than pleasure at the prospect of what he seems so reluctant to acknowledge. Romania is under threat.[2]

Certainly American practitioners and academic departments found this European pattern a congenial one to emulate. The first American department of comparative literature was established in 1891 at Columbia University, as was the first journal of comparative literature. Consider what George Edward Woodberry—the department's first chaired professor—had to say about his field:

> The parts of the world draw together, and with them the parts of knowledge, slowly knitting into that one intellectual state which, above the sphere of politics and with no more institutional machinery than tribunals of jurists and congresses of gentlemen, will be at last the true bond of all the world. The modern scholar shares more than other citizens in the benefits of this enlargement and intercommunication, this age equally of expansion and concentration on the vast scale, this infinitely extended and intimate commingling of nations with one another and with the past; his

ordinary mental experience includes more of race-memory and of race-imagination than belonged to his predecessors, and his outlook before and after is on greater horizons; he lives in a larger world—is, in fact, born no longer to the freedom of a city merely, however noble, but to that new citizenship in the rising state which—the obscurer or brighter dream of all great scholars from Plato to Goethe—is without frontiers or race or force, but there is reason supreme. The emergence and growth of the new study known as Comparative Literature are incidental to the coming of this larger world and the entrance of scholars upon its work: the study will run its course, and together with other converging elements goes to its goal in the unity of mankind found in the spiritual unities of science, art and love.[3]

Such rhetoric uncomplicatedly and naively resonates with the influence of Croce and De Sanctis, and also with the earlier ideas of Wilhelm von Humboldt. But there is a certain quaintness in Woodberry's "tribunals of jurists and congresses of gentlemen," more than a little belied by the actualities of life in the "larger world" he speaks of. In a time of the greatest Western imperial hegemony in history, Woodberry manages to overlook that dominating form of political unity in order to celebrate a still higher, strictly ideal unity. He is unclear about how "the spiritual unities of science, art and love" are to deal with less pleasant realities, much less how "spiritual unities" can be expected to overcome the facts of materiality, power, and political division.

Academic work in comparative literature carried with it the notion that Europe and the United States together were the center of the world, not simply by virtue of their political positions, but also because their literatures were the ones most worth studying. When Europe succumbed to fascism and when the United States benefited so richly from the many emigré scholars who came to it, understandably little of their sense of crisis took root with them. *Mimesis*, for example, written while Auerbach was in exile from Nazi Europe in Istanbul, was not simply an exercise in textual explication, but—he says in his 1952 essay to which I have just referred—an act of civilizational survival. It had seemed to him that his mission as a comparatist was to present, perhaps for the last time, the complex evolution of European literature in all its variety from Homer to Virginia Woolf. Curtius's book on the Latin Middle Ages was composed out of the same driven fear. Yet how little of that spirit survived in the thousands of academic literary scholars who were influenced by these two books! *Mimesis* was praised for being a remarkable work of rich analysis, but the sense of its mission died in the often trivial uses made of it.[4] Finally in the late 1950s *Sputnik* came along, and transformed the study of foreign languages—and of comparative literature—into fields directly affecting national security. The National Defense

Education Act[5] promoted the field and, with it, alas, an even more complacent ethnocentrism and covert Cold Warriorism than Woodberry could have imagined.

As *Mimesis* immediately reveals, however, the notion of Western literature that lies at the very core of comparative study centrally highlights, dramatizes, and celebrates a certain idea of history, and at the same time obscures the fundamental geographical and political reality empowering that idea. The idea of European or Western literary history contained in it and the other scholarly works of comparative literature is essentially idealistic and, in an unsystematic way, Hegelian. Thus the principle of development by which Romania is said to have acquired dominance is incorporative and synthetic. More and more reality is included in a literature that expands and elaborates from the medieval chronicles to the great edifices of nineteenth-century narrative fiction—in the works of Stendhal, Balzac, Zola, Dickens, Proust. Each work in the progression represents a synthesis of problematic elements that disturb the basic Christian order so memorably laid out in the *Divine Comedy*. Class, political upheavals, shifts in economic patterns and organization, war: all these subjects, for great authors like Cervantes, Shakespeare, Montaigne, as well as a host of lesser writers, are enfolded within recurringly renewed structures, visions, stabilities, all of them attesting to the abiding dialectical order represented by Europe itself.

The salutary vision of a "world literature" that acquired a redemptive status in the twentieth century coincides with what theorists of colonial geography also articulated. In the writings of Halford Mackinder, George Chisolm, Georges Hardy, Leroy-Beaulieu, and Lucien Fevre, a much franker appraisal of the world system appears, equally metrocentric and imperial; but instead of history alone, now both empire and actual geographical space collaborate to produce a "world-empire" commanded by Europe. But in this geographically articulated vision (much of it based, as Paul Carter shows in *The Road to Botany Bay*, on the cartographic results of actual geographical exploration and conquest) there is no less strong a commitment to the belief that European pre-eminence is natural, the culmination of what Chisolm calls various "historical advantages" that allowed Europe to override the "natural advantages" of the more fertile, wealthy, and accessible regions it controlled.[6] Fevre's *La Terre et l'évolution humaine* (1922), a vigorous and integral encyclopedia, matches Woodberry for its scope and utopianism.

To their audience in the late nineteenth and early twentieth centuries, the great geographical synthesizers offered technical explanations for ready political actualities. Europe *did* command the world; the imperial map *did* license the cultural vision. To us, a century later, the coincidence or similarity between one vision of a world system and the other, between geography and literary history, seems interesting but problematic. What should we do with this similarity?

First of all, I believe, it needs *articulation* and *activation*, which can only come about if we take serious account of the present, and notably of the dismantling of the classical empires and the new independence of dozens of formerly colonized peoples and territories. We need to see that the contemporary global setting—overlapping territories, intertwined histories—was already prefigured and inscribed in the coincidences and convergences among geography, culture, and history that were so important to the pioneers of comparative literature. Then we can grasp in a new and more dynamic way both the idealist historicism which fuelled the comparatist "world literature" scheme and the concretely imperial world map of the same moment.

But that cannot be done without accepting that what is common to both is an elaboration of power. The genuinely profound scholarship of the people who believed in and practiced *Weltliteratur* implied the extraordinary privilege of an observer located in the West who could actually survey the world's literary output with a kind of sovereign detachment. Orientalists and other specialists about the non-European world—anthropologists, historians, philologists—had that power, and, as I have tried to show elsewhere, it often went hand in glove with a consciously undertaken imperial enterprise. We must articulate these various sovereign dispositions and see their common methodology.

An explicitly geographical model is provided in Gramsci's essay *Some Aspects of the Southern Question*. Under-read and under-analyzed, this study is the only sustained piece of political and cultural analysis Gramsci wrote (although he never finished it); it addresses the geographical conundrum posed for action and analysis by his comrades as to how to think about, plan for, and study southern Italy, given that its social disintegration made it seem incomprehensible yet paradoxically crucial to an understanding of the north. Gramsci's brilliant analysis goes, I think, beyond its tactical relevance to Italian politics in 1926, for it provides a culmination to his journalism before 1926 and also a prelude to *The Prison Notebooks*, in which he gave, as his towering counterpart Lukacs did not, paramount focus to the territorial, spatial, geographical foundations of social life.

Lukacs belongs to the Hegelian tradition of Marxism, Gramsci to a Vichian, Crocean departure from it. For Lukacs the central problematic in his major work through *History and Class Consciousness* (1923) is temporality; for Gramsci, as even a cursory examination of his conceptual vocabulary immediately reveals, social history and actuality are grasped in geographical terms—such words as "terrain," "territory," "blocks," and "region" predominate. In *The Southern Question*,

Gramsci not only is at pains to show that the division between the northern and southern regions of Italy is basic to the challenge of what to do politically about the national working-class movement at a moment of impasse, but also is fastidious in describing the peculiar topography of the south, remarkable, as he says, for the striking contrast between the large undifferentiated mass of peasants on the one hand, and the presence of "big" landowners, important publishing houses, and distinguished cultural formations on the other. Croce himself, a most impressive and notable figure in Italy, is seen by Gramsci with characteristic shrewdness as a southern philosopher who finds it easier to relate to Europe and to Plato than to his own crumbling meridional environment.

The problem therefore is how to connect the south, whose poverty and vast labor pool are inertly vulnerable to northern economic policies and powers, with a north that is dependent on it. Gramsci formulates the answer in ways that forecast his celebrated animadversions on the intellectual in the *Quaderni*: he considers Piero Gobetti, who as an intellectual understood the need for connecting the northern proletariat with the southern peasantry, a strategy that stood in stark contrast with the careers of Croce and Guistino Fortunato, and who linked north and south by virtue of his capacity for organizing culture. His work "posed the Southern question on a terrain different from the traditional one [which regarded the south simply as a backward region of Italy] by introducing into it the proletariat of the North."[7] But this introduction could not occur, Gramsci continues, unless one remembered that intellectual work is slower, works according to more extended calendars than that of any other social group. Culture cannot be looked at as an immediate fact but has to be seen (as he was to say in the *Quaderni*) *sub specie aeternitatis*. Much time elapses before new cultural formations emerge, and intellectuals, who depend on long years of preparation, action, and tradition, are necessary to the process.

Gramsci also understands that in the extended time span during which the coral-like formation of a culture occurs, one needs "breaks of an organic kind." Gobetti represents one such break, a fissure that opened up within the cultural structures that supported and occluded the north-south discrepancy for so long in Italian history. Gramsci regards Gobetti with evident warmth, appreciation, and cordiality as an individual, but his political and social significance for Gramsci's analysis of the southern question—and it is appropriate that the unfinished essay ends abruptly with this consideration of Gobetti—is that he accentuates the need for a social formation to develop, elaborate, build upon the break instituted by his work, and by his insistence that intellectual effort itself furnishes the link between disparate, apparently autonomous regions of human history.

What we might call the Gobetti factor functions like an animating connective that expresses and represents the relationship between the development of comparative literature and the emergence of imperial geography, and does so dynamically and organically. To say of both discourses merely that they are imperialist is to say little about where and how they take place. Above all it leaves out what makes it possible for us to articulate them *together*, as an ensemble, as having a relationship that is more than coincidental, conjunctural, mechanical. For this we must look at the domination of the non-European world from the perspective of a resisting, gradually more and more challenging alternative.

Without significant exception the universalizing discourses of modern Europe and the United States assume the silence, willing or otherwise, of the non-European world. There is incorporation; there is inclusion; there is direct rule; there is coercion. But there is only infrequently an acknowledgement that the colonized people should be heard from, their ideas known.

It is possible to argue that the continued production and interpretation of Western culture itself made exactly the same assumption well on into the twentieth century, even as political resistance grew to the West's power in the "peripheral" world. Because of that, and because of where it led, it becomes possible now to reinterpret the Western cultural archive as if fractured geographically by the activated imperial divide, to do a rather different kind of reading and interpretation. In the first place, the history of fields like comparative literature, English studies, cultural analysis, anthropology can be seen as affiliated with the empire and, in a manner of speaking, even contributing to its methods for maintaining Western ascendancy over non-Western natives, especially if we are aware of the spatial consciousness exemplified in Gramsci's "southern question." And in the second place our interpretative change of perspective allows us to challenge the sovereign and unchallenged authority of the allegedly detached Western observer.

Western cultural forms can be taken out of the autonomous enclosures in which they have been protected, and placed instead in the dynamic global environment created by imperialism, itself revised as an ongoing contest between north and south, metropolis and periphery, white and native. We may thus consider imperialism as a process occurring as part of the metropolitan culture, which at times acknowledges, at other times obscures the sustained business of the empire itself. The important point—a very Gramscian one—is how the national British, French, and American cultures maintain hegemony over the peripheries. How within them was consent gained and continuously consolidated for the distant rule of native peoples and territories?

As we look back at the cultural archive, we begin to reread it not uni-vocally but *contrapuntally*, with a simultaneous awareness both of the metropolitan history that is narrated and of those other histories against which (and together with which) the dominating discourse acts. In the counterpoint of Western classical music, various themes play off one an-other, with only a provisional privilege being given to any particular one; yet in the resulting polyphony there is concert and order, an organized interplay that derives from the themes, not from a rigorous melodic or formal principle outside the work. In the same way, I believe, we can read and interpret English novels, for example, whose engagement (usu-ally suppressed for the most part) with the West Indies or India, say, is shaped and perhaps even determined by the specific history of coloniza-tion, resistance, and finally native nationalism. At this point alternative or new narratives emerge, and they become institutionalized or discur-sively stable entities.

It should be evident that no one overarching theoretical principle governs the whole imperialist ensemble, and it should be just as evident that the principle of domination and resistance based on the division between the West and the rest of the world—to adapt freely from the African critic Chinweizu—runs like a fissure throughout. That fissure affected all the many local engagements, overlappings, interdependen-cies in Africa, India, and elsewhere in the peripheries, each different, each with its own density of associations and forms, its own motifs, works, institutions, and—most important from our point of view as re-readers—its own possibilities and conditions of knowledge. For each lo-cale in which the engagement occurs, and the imperialist model is disas-sembled, its incorporative, universalizing, and totalizing codes rendered ineffective and inapplicable, a particular type of research and knowledge begins to build up.

An example of the new knowledge would be the study of Orientalism or Africanism and, to take a related set, the study of Englishness and Frenchness. These identities are today analyzed not as god-given es-sences, but as results of collaboration between the African history and the history of Africa in England, for instance, or between the study of French history and the reorganization of knowledge during the First Empire. In an important sense, we are dealing with the formation of cultural identities understood not as essentializations (although part of their enduring appeal is that they seem and are considered to be like essentializations) but as contrapuntal ensembles, for it is the case that no identity can ever exist by itself and without an array of opposites, nega-tives, oppositions: Greeks always require barbarians, and Europeans Af-ricans, Orientals, etc. The opposite is certainly true as well. Even the mammoth engagements in our own time over such essentializations as "Islam," the "West," the "Orient," "Japan," or "Europe" admit to a particular knowledge and structures of attitude and reference, and those require careful analysis and research.

If one studies some of the major metropolitan cultures—England's, France's, and the United States', for instance—in the geographical context of their struggles for (and over) empires, a distinctive cultural topography becomes apparent. In using the phrase "structures of attitude and reference" I have this topography in mind, as I also have in mind Raymond Williams's seminal phrase "structures of feeling." I am talking about the way in which structures of location and geographical reference appear in the cultural languages of literature, history, or ethnography, sometimes allusively and sometimes carefully plotted, across several individual works that are not otherwise connected to one another or to an official ideology of "empire."

In British culture, for instance, one may discover a consistency of concern in Spenser, Shakespeare, Defoe, and Austen that fixes socially desirable, empowered space in metropolitan England or Europe and connects it by design, motive, and development to distant or peripheral worlds (Ireland, Venice, Africa, Jamaica), conceived of as desirable but subordinate. And with these meticulously maintained references come attitudes—about rule, control, profit and enhancement, and suitability—that grow with astonishing power from the seventeenth to the end of the nineteenth century. These structures do not arise from some pre-existing (semi-conspiratorial) design that the writers then manipulate, but are bound up with the development of Britain's cultural identity, as that identity imagines itself in a geographically conceived world. Similar structures may be remarked in French and American cultures, growing for different reasons and obviously in different ways. We are not yet at the stage where we can say whether these globally integral structures are preparations for imperial control and conquest, or whether they accompany such enterprises, or whether in some reflective or careless way they are a result of empire. We are only at a stage where we must look at the astonishing frequency of geographical articulations in the three Western cultures that most dominated far-flung territories.

To the best of my ability to have read and understood these "structures of attitude and reference," there was scarcely any dissent, any departure, any demurral from them: there was virtual unanimity that subject races should be ruled, that they *are* subject races, that one race deserves and has consistently earned the right to be considered the race whose main mission is to expand beyond its own domain. (Indeed, as Seeley was to put it in 1883, about Britain—France and the United

States had their own theorists—the British could only be understood as such.) It is perhaps embarrassing that sectors of the metropolitan cultures that have since become vanguards in the social contests of our time were uncomplaining members of this imperial consensus. With few exceptions, the women's as well as the working-class movement was pro-empire. And, while one must always be at great pains to show that different imaginations, sensibilities, ideas, and philosophies were at work, and that each work of literature or art is special, there was virtual unity of purpose on this score: the empire must be maintained, and it *was* maintained.

Reading and interpreting the major metropolitan cultural texts in this newly activated, reinformed way could not have been possible without the movements of resistance that occurred everywhere in the peripheries against the empire. And today writers and scholars from the formerly colonized world have imposed their diverse histories on, have mapped their local geographies in, the great canonical texts of the European center. And from these overlapping yet discrepant interactions the new readings and knowledges are beginning to appear. One need only think of the tremendously powerful upheavals that occurred at the end of the 1980s—the breaking down of barriers, the popular insurgencies, the drift across borders, the looming problems of immigrant, refugee, and minority rights in the West—to see how obsolete are the old categories, the tight separations, and the comfortable autonomies.

It is very important, though, to assess how these entities were built, and to understand how patiently the idea of an unencumbered English culture, for example, acquired its authority and its power to impose itself across the seas. This is a tremendous task for any individual, but a whole new generation of scholars and intellectuals from the Third World is engaged on just such an undertaking.

Here a word of caution and prudence is required. Consider the uneasy relationship between nationalism and liberation, two ideals or goals for people engaged against imperialism. In the main it is true that the creation of very many newly independent nation-states in the post-colonial world has succeeded in re-establishing the primacy of what has been called imagined communities, parodied and mocked by writers like V. S. Naipaul and Conor Cruise O'Brien, hijacked by a host of dictators and petty tyrants, enshrined in various state nationalisms. Nevertheless in general there is an oppositional quality to the consciousness of many Third World scholars and intellectuals, particularly (but not exclusively) those who are exiles, expatriates, or refugees and immigrants in the West, many of them inheritors of the work done by earlier twentieth-century expatriates like George Antonius and C.L.R. James. Their work in trying to connect experiences across the imperial divide, in re-examining the great canons, in producing what in effect is a critical literature cannot be, and generally has not been, co-opted by the resurgent nationalisms, despotisms, and ungenerous ideologies that betrayed the liberationist ideal in favor of the nationalist independence actuality.

Moreover their work should be seen as sharing important concerns with minority and "suppressed" voices within the metropolis itself: feminists, African-American writers, intellectuals, artists, among others. But here too vigilance and self-criticism are crucial, since there is an inherent danger to oppositional effort of becoming institutionalized, marginality turning into separatism, and resistance hardening into dogma. Surely the activism that reposits and reformulates the political challenges in intellectual life is safe-guarded against orthodoxy. But there is always a need to keep community before coercion, criticism before mere solidarity, and vigilance ahead of assent.

Since my themes here are sort of a sequel to *Orientalism,* which like this essay was written in the United States, some consideration of America's cultural and political environment is warranted. The United States is no ordinary large country. The United States is the last superpower, an enormously influential, frequently interventionary power nearly everywhere in the world. Citizens and intellectuals of the United States have a particular responsibility for what goes on between the United States and the rest of the world, a responsibility that is in no way discharged or fulfilled by saying that the Soviet Union, Britain, France, or China were, or are, worse. The fact is that we are indeed responsible for, and therefore most capable of, influencing *this* country in ways that we were not for the pre-Gorbachev Soviet Union, or other countries. So we should first take scrupulous note of how in Central and Latin America—to mention the most obvious—as well as in the Middle East, Africa, and Asia, the United States has replaced the great earlier empires and is *the* dominant outside force.

Looked at honestly, the record is not a good one. United States military interventions since World War Two have occurred (and are still occurring) on nearly every continent, many of great complexity and extent, with tremendous national investment, as we are now only beginning to understand. All of this is, in William Appleman Williams's phrase, empire as a way of life. The continuing disclosures about the war in Vietnam, about the United States' support of "contras" in Nicaragua, about the crisis in the Persian Gulf, are only part of the story of this complex of interventions. Insufficient attention is paid to the fact that United States Middle Eastern and Central American policies—whether exploiting a geo-political opening among Iranian so-called moderates, or aiding the so-called Contra Freedom Fighters in overthrowing the elected, legal government of Nicaragua, or coming to the aid of the Saudi and Kuwaiti royal families—can only be described as imperialist.

Even if we were to allow, as many have, that United States foreign policy is principally altruistic and dedicated to such unimpeachable goals as freedom and democracy, there is considerable room for skepticism. The relevance of T. S. Eliot's remarks in "Tradition and the Individual Talent" about the historical sense are demonstrably important. Are we not as a nation repeating what France and Britain, Spain and Portugal, Holland and Germany, did before us? And yet do we not tend to regard ourselves as somehow exempt from the more sordid imperial adventures that preceded ours? Besides, is there not an unquestioned assumption on our part that our destiny is to rule and lead the world, a destiny that we have assigned ourselves as part of our errand into the wilderness?

In short, we face as a nation the deep, profoundly perturbed and perturbing question of our relationship to others—other cultures, states, histories, experiences, traditions, peoples, and destinies. There is no Archimedean point beyond the question from which to answer it; there is no vantage outside the actuality of relationships among cultures, among unequal imperial and non-imperial powers, among us and others; no one has the epistemological privilege of somehow judging, evaluating, and interpreting the world free from the encumbering interests and engagements of the ongoing relationships themselves. We are, so to speak, *of* the connections, not outside and beyond them. And it behooves us as intellectuals and humanists and secular critics to understand the United States in the world of nations and power from *within* the actuality, as participants in it, not detached outside observers who, like Oliver Goldsmith, in Yeats's perfect phrase, deliberately sip at the honeypots of our minds.

Contemporary travails in recent European and American anthropology reflect these conundrums and embroilments in a symptomatic and interesting way. That cultural practice and intellectual activity carry, as a major constitutive element, an unequal relationship of force between the outside Western ethnographer-observer and the primitive, or at least different, but certainly weaker and less developed non-European, non-Western person. In the extraordinarily rich text of *Kim*, Kipling extrapolates the political meaning of that relationship and embodies it in the figure of Colonel Creighton, an ethnographer in charge of the Survey of India, also the head of British intelligence services in India, the "Great Game" to which young Kim belongs. Modern Western anthropology frequently repeated that problematic relationship, and in recent works of a number of theoreticians deals with the almost insuperable contradiction between a political actuality based on force, and a scientific and humane desire to understand the Other hermeneutically and sympathetically in modes not influenced by force.

Whether these efforts succeed or fail is a less interesting matter than what distinguishes them, what makes them possible: an acute and embarrassed awareness of the all-pervasive, unavoidable imperial setting. In fact, there is no way that I know of apprehending the world from within American culture (with a whole history of exterminism and incorporation behind it) without also apprehending the imperial contest itself. This, I would say, is a cultural fact of extraordinary political as well as interpretive importance, yet it has not been recognized as such in cultural and literary theory, and is routinely circumvented or occluded in cultural discourses. To read most cultural deconstructionists, or Marxists, or new historicists is to read writers whose political horizon, whose historical location is within a society and culture deeply enmeshed in imperial domination. Yet little notice is taken of this horizon, few acknowledgements of the setting are advanced, little realization of the imperial closure itself is allowed for. Instead, one has the impression that interpretation of other cultures, texts, and people—which at bottom is what all interpretation is about—occurs in a timeless vacuum, so forgiving and permissive as to deliver the interpretation directly into a universalism free from attachment, inhibition, and interest.

We live of course in a world not only of commodities but also of representation, and representations—their production, circulation, history, and interpretation—are the very element of culture. In much recent theory the problem of representation is deemed to be central, yet rarely is it put in its full political context, a context that is primarily imperial. Instead we have on the one hand an isolated cultural sphere, believed to be freely and unconditionally available to weightless theoretical speculation and investigation, and, on the other, a debased political sphere, where the real struggle between interests is supposed to occur. To the professional student of culture—the humanist, the critic, the scholar—only one sphere is relevant, and, more to the point, it is accepted that the two spheres are separated, whereas the two are not only connected but ultimately the same.

A radical falsification has become established in this separation. Culture is exonerated of any entanglements with power, representations are considered only as apolitical images to be parsed and construed as so many grammars of exchange, and the divorce of the present from the past is assumed to be complete. And yet, far from this separation of spheres being a neutral or accidental choice, its real meaning is an act of complicity, the humanist's choice of a disguised, denuded, systematically purged textual model over a more embattled model, whose principal features would inevitably coalesce around the continuing struggle over the question of empire itself.

Let me put this differently, using examples that will be familiar to everyone. For at least a decade, there has been a decently earnest debate in the United States over the meaning, contents, and goals of liberal education. Much but not all this debate was stimulated in the university after the upheavals of the 1960s, when it appeared for the first time in this century that the structure, authority, and tradition of American education were challenged by marauding energies, released by socially and intellectually inspired provocations. The newer currents in the academy, and the force of what is called theory (a rubric under which were herded many new disciplines like psychoanalysis, linguistics, and Nietzschean philosophy, unhoused from the traditional fields such as philology, moral philosophy, and the natural sciences), acquired prestige and interest; they appeared to undermine the authority and the stability of established canons, well-capitalized fields, long-standing procedures of accreditation, research, and the division of intellectual labor. That all this occurred in the modest and circumscribed terrain of cultural-academic praxis simultaneously with the great wave of anti-war, anti-imperialist protest was not fortuitous but, rather, a genuine political and intellectual conjuncture.

There is considerable irony that our search in the metropolis for a newly invigorated, reclaimed tradition follows the exhaustion of modernism and is expressed variously as post-modernism or, as I said earlier, citing Lyotard, as the loss of the legitimizing power of the narratives of Western emancipation and enlightenment; simultaneously, modernism is rediscovered in the formerly colonized, peripheral world, where resistance, the logic of daring, and various investigations of age-old tradition (al-Turath, in the Islamic world) together set the tone.

One response in the West to the new conjectures, then, has been profoundly reactionary: the effort to reassert old authorities and canons, the effort to reinstate ten or twenty or thirty essential Western books without which a Westerner would not be educated—these efforts are couched in the rhetoric of embattled patriotism.

But there can be another response, worth returning to here, for it offers an important theoretical opportunity. Cultural experience or indeed every cultural form is radically, quintessentially hybrid, and if it has been the practice in the West since Immanuel Kant to isolate cultural and aesthetic realms from the worldly domain, it is now time to rejoin them. This is by no means a simple matter, since—I believe—it has been the essence of experience in the West at least since the late eighteenth century not only to acquire distant domination and reinforce hegemony, but also to divide the realms of culture and experience into apparently separate spheres. Entities such as races and nations, essences such as Englishness or Orientalism, modes of production such as the Asiatic or Occidental, all of these in my opinion testify to an ideology whose cultural correlatives well precede the actual accumulation of imperial territories world-wide.

Most historians of empire speak of the "age of empire" as formally beginning around 1878, with the "scramble for Africa." A closer look at the cultural actuality reveals a much earlier, more deeply and stubbornly held view about overseas European hegemony; we can locate a coherent, fully mobilized system of ideas near the end of the eighteenth century, and there follows the set of integral developments such as the first great systematic conquests under Napoleon, the rise of nationalism and the European nation-state, the advent of large-scale industrialization, and the consolidation of power in the bourgeoisie. This is also the period in which the novel form and the new historical narrative become pre-eminent, and in which the importance of subjectivity to historical time takes firm hold.

Yet most cultural historians, and certainly all literary scholars, have failed to remark the *geographical* notation, the theoretical mapping and charting of territory that underlies Western fiction, historical writing, and philosophical discourse of the time. There is first the authority of the European observer—traveler, merchant, scholar, historian, novelist. Then there is the hierarchy of spaces by which the metropolitan center and, gradually, the metropolitan economy are seen as dependent upon an overseas system of territorial control, economic exploitation, and a socio-cultural vision; without these stability and prosperity at home— "home" being a word with extremely potent resonances—would not be possible. The perfect example of what I mean is to be found in Jane Austen's *Mansfield Park*, in which Thomas Bertram's slave plantation in Antigua is mysteriously necessary to the poise and beauty of Mansfield Park, a place described in moral and aesthetic terms well before the scramble for Africa, or before the age of empire officially began. As John Stuart Mill puts it in the *Principles of Political Economy*:

> These [outlying possessions of ours] are hardly to be looked upon as countries, . . . but more properly as outlying agricultural or manufacturing estates belonging to a larger community. Our West Indian colonies, for example, cannot be regarded as countries with a productive capital of their own . . . [but are rather] the place where England finds it convenient to carry on the production of sugar, coffee and a few other tropical commodities.[8]

Read this extraordinary passage together with Jane Austen, and a much less benign picture stands forth than the usual one of cultural formations in the pre-imperialist age. In Mill we have the ruthless proprietary tones of the white master used to effacing the reality, work, and suffering of millions of slaves, transported across the middle passage, reduced only to an incorporated status "for the benefit of the proprietors." These colonies are, Mill says, to be considered as hardly anything more than a convenience, an attitude confirmed by Austen, who in *Mansfield Park* sublimates the agonies of Caribbean existence to a mere half dozen passing references to Antigua. And much the same processes occur in other canonical writers of Britain and France; in short, the metropolis gets its authority to a considerable extent from the devaluation as well as the exploitation of the outlying colonial possession. (Not for nothing, then, did Walter Rodney entitle his great decolonizing treatise of 1972 *How Europe Underdeveloped Africa.*) *Sel*

Lastly, the authority of the observer, and of European geographical centrality, is buttressed by a cultural discourse relegating and confining the non-European to a secondary racial, cultural, ontological status. Yet this secondariness is, paradoxically, essential to the primariness of the European; this of course is the paradox explored by Césaire, Fanon, and Memmi, and it is but one among many of the ironies of modern critical theory that it has rarely been explored by investigators of the aporias and impossibilities of reading. Perhaps that is because it places emphasis not so much on *how* to read, but rather on *what* is read and *where* it is written about and represented. It is to Conrad's enormous credit to have sounded in such a complex and riven prose the authentic imperialist tone—how you supply the forces of world-wide accumulation and rule with a self-confirming ideological motor (what Marlow in *Heart of Darkness* calls efficiency with devotion to an idea at the back of it, "it" being the taking away of the earth from those with darker complexions and flatter noses) and simultaneously draw a screen across the process, saying that art and culture have nothing to do with "it."

What to read and what to do with that reading, that is the full form of the question. All the energies poured into critical theory, into novel and demystifying theoretical praxes like the new historicism and deconstruction and Marxism have avoided the major, I would say determining, political horizon of modern Western culture, namely imperialism. This massive avoidance has sustained a canonical inclusion and exclusion: you include the Rousseaus, the Nietzsches, the Wordsworths, the Dickenses, the Flauberts, and so on, and at the same you exclude their relationships with the protracted, complex, and striated work of empire. But why is this a matter of what to read and about where? Very simply, because critical discourse has taken no cognizance of the enormously exciting, varied post-colonial literature produced in resistance to the imperialist expansion of Europe and the United States in the past two centuries. To read Austen without also reading Fanon and Cabral—and so on and on—is to disaffiliate modern culture from its engagements and attachments. That is a process that should be reversed.

But there is more to be done. Critical theory and literary historical scholarship have reinterpreted and revalidated major swatches of Western literature, art, and philosophy. Much of this has been exciting and powerful work, even though one often senses more an energy of elaboration and refinement than a committed engagement to what I would call secular and affiliated criticism; such criticism cannot be undertaken without a fairly strong sense of how consciously chosen historical models are relevant to social and intellectual change. Yet if you read and interpret modern European and American culture as having had something to do with imperialism, it becomes incumbent upon you also to reinterpret the canon in the light of texts whose place there has been insufficiently linked to, insufficiently weighted toward the expansion of Europe. Put differently, this procedure entails reading the canon as a polyphonic accompaniment to the expansion of Europe, giving a revised direction and valence to writers such as Conrad and Kipling, who have always been read as sports, not as writers whose manifestly imperialist subject matter has a long subterranean or implicit and proleptic life in the earlier work of writers like, say, Austen or Chateaubriand.

Second, theoretical work must begin to formulate the relationship between empire and culture. There have been a few milestones—Kiernan's work, for instance, and Martin Green's—but concern with the issue has not been intense. Things, however, are beginning to change, as I noted earlier. A whole range of work in other disciplines, a new group of often younger scholars and critics—here, in the Third World, in Europe—are beginning to embark on the theoretical and historical enterprises; many of them seem in one way or another to be converging on questions of imperialist discourse, colonialist practice, and so forth. Theoretically we are only at the stage of trying to inventory the *interpellation* of culture by empire, but the efforts so far made are only slightly more than rudimentary. And as the study of culture extends into the mass media, popular culture, micro-politics, and so forth, the focus of modes of power and hegemony grows sharper.

Third, we should keep before us the prerogatives of the present as signposts and paradigms for the study of the past. If I have insisted on integration and connections between the past and the present, between imperializer and imperialized, between culture and imperialism, I have done so not to level or reduce differences, but rather to convey a more urgent sense of the interdependence between things. So vast and yet so detailed is imperialism as an experience with crucial cultural dimensions, that we must speak of overlapping territories, intertwined histories common to men and women, whites and non-whites, dwellers in the metropolis and on the peripheries, past as well as present and future; these territories and histories can only be seen from the perspective of the whole of secular human history.

NOTES

1. Francis Fergusson, *The Human Image in Dramatic Literature* (New York: Doubleday, Anchor, 1957), pp. 205–6.

2. Erich Auerbach, "Philology and *Weltliteratur*," trans. M. and E. W. Said, *Centennial Review* 13 (Winter 1969); see my discussion of this work in *The World, the Text, and the Critic* (Cambridge, Mass.: Harvard University Press, 1983), pp. 1–9.

3. George E. Woodberry, "Editorial" (1903), in *Comparative Literature: The Early Years, An Anthology of Essays*, ed. Hans Joachim Schulz and Phillip K. Rein (Chapel Hill: University of North Carolina Press, 1973), p. 211. See also Harry Levin, *Grounds for Comparison* (Cambridge, Mass.: Harvard University Press, 1972), pp. 57–130; Claudio Guillérn, *Entre lo uno y lo diverso: Introducción a la literatura comparada* (Barcelona: Editorial Critica, 1985), pp. 54–121.

4. Erich Auerbach, *Mimesis: The Representation of Reality in Western Literature*, trans. Willard Trask (Princeton: Princeton University Press, 1953). See also Said, "Secular Criticism," in *The World, the Text, and the Critic*, pp. 31–53, 148–49.

5. An act of the United States Congress passed in 1958, the National Defense Eduacation Act (NDEA) authorized the expenditure of $295 million for science and languages, both deemed important for national security. Departments of comparative literature were among the beneficiaries of this act.

6. Cited in Smith, *Uneven Development*, pp. 101–2.

7. Antonio Gramsci, "Some Aspects of the Southern Question," in *Selections from Political Writings, 1921–1926*, trans. and ed. Quintin Hoare (London: Lawrence and Wishart, 1978), p. 461. For an unusual application of Gramsci's theories about "Southernism," see Timothy Brennan, "Literary Criticism and the Southern Question," *Cultural Critique* 11 (Winter 1988–89): 89–114.

8. John Stuart Mill, *Principles of Political Economy*, ed. J. M. Robson (Toronto: University of Toronto Press, 1965), 3:693.

CHAPTER 2

Africa in History: The End of
Universal Narratives

STEVEN FEIERMAN

THE STORY of "African history," its recent emergence as a field of scholarly knowledge, shows that the expansion of the historian's world to new subject areas cannot be pictured only as a process of addition—as the growth of a fund of knowledge. The expansion of Africanist knowledge in the years since 1960 has had profoundly subversive effects on general historical learning. One of the first effects of the appearance of African history (and of other histories like it) in the world of established scholarship was to dissolve world history, to make it impossible to write clear and coherent narratives tying together the world's parts. But this was only the most obvious and superficial effect of the incorporation of new knowledge. Much more important has been the tension between the accustomed language in which historians construct their explanations, and the historical experience of Africans, which cannot be encompassed by that language. Because African history breaks the bounds of historical language it undermines general historical thought and, in the end, cuts beneath even its own foundations. But this is a later part of the story.

African history was largely ignored by the established historical profession of the United States until relatively recently. In the mid-1950s graduate students of history at Harvard, Princeton, Chicago, Berkeley, Columbia, and almost all of America's other historically white universities lived in a world where the field did not exist. None of these major postgraduate institutions offered courses in the subject. In 1958–59 the American Historical Association surveyed department chairs on the major fields of their graduate students. The total number of graduate students was 1,735; the number reported as concentrating in African history was one.[1]

By the late 1970s there were six hundred professional African historians in the United States, and the number has continued to grow.[2] Most of these wrote Ph.D. dissertations in African history and many continue to do research after the doctorate. The growth in numbers has therefore

led to an enormous expansion in knowledge. The most obvious consequence of this expansion has been to show that what was once thought
to be a universal history was in fact very partial and very selective. The
narrative of human history that many Western historians held at that
time could no longer stand.

We can trace the process by which history undermined itself from
within, by which knowledge grew and brought itself into doubt, by examining a number of books about history on a world scale, all of them
published during the years of African history's growth. Some of these
cover all the ages of human history, others cover only a brief period, but
all of them attempt to integrate the history of every part of the world in
a single narrative.

In the early 1960s it was still possible to describe human history in
terms of a story with a single narrative thread, from the earliest periods
until modern times. Now that possibility is gone. It is difficult for us to
remember how profoundly our historical vision has changed unless we
return to examine important works of that time. For example, William
McNeill's *The Rise of the West*, published in 1963 when African history
was just beginning to emerge, presented a unicentric and unidirectional
narrative, of a kind that would not be acceptable today.

The Rise of the West divided the ancient world between "civilizations"
and the land of "barbarians." The book focused on the diffusion of the
techniques of civilization, originally from Mesopotamia, and then
within the area McNeill calls the "ecumene," as opposed to the land of
the barbarians. The ecumene was an intercommunicating zone within
which the basic techniques of civilization were created, and within
which they spread. The zone's boundaries shifted with time, but its early
core was in the ancient Near East.

The origin of civilization, in McNeill's narrative, grows out of the introduction of agriculture, which diffused from its center in a relatively
unified process. He acknowledges in the introduction[3] that agriculture
was introduced more than once, but he tries in the body of the work to
maintain a single narrative thread, with only a partial exception for the
introduction of agriculture in China. About the Americas, McNeill
wrote, "Seeds or cuttings must have been carried across the ocean by
human agency at a very early time."[4] And on Africa he saw no possibility
that domestication had independent beginnings. He wrote that agriculture came to eastern and southern Africa only within the past five centuries. Until then, "primitive hunters roamed as their forefathers had done
for untold millennia."[5]

This statement is itself incorrect by millennia. We now know, as
scholars of that generation did not, that animal domestication came very
early to Africa (possibly earlier than to Southwest Asia), and that there

were autonomous centers of crop domestication in Africa south of the Sahara.[6]

McNeill saw the great African empires—states like Ghana, Mali, and Songhay—as borrowings. The more advanced of Africa's societies, he wrote, "were never independent of the main civilizations of Eurasia."[7] Islam played a central role in the diffusion of civilization's techniques. Recent archaeological research has shown that this vision is flawed. Urbanism based on commerce, for example, was not brought to West Africa by Islam; it came before Islam. By about A.D. 500 Jenne-jeno, on the Niger River, emerged as a town built on local trade in agricultural surpluses drawn from lands flooded by the river. In this case, West Africans had built their own town, which then grew further when Islam became important.[8] The evidence points to the growth of locally rooted centers that came ultimately to participate in long-distance trade. In southern Africa, also, historians have learned that the great state of Zimbabwe grew out of local roots.[9]

During the postwar years, even before the accumulation of significant Africanist knowledge, new historical approaches were appearing that would make it easier to deal with the challenge of evidence from beyond Europe. On the definition of historical space, as on many other problems, the development of the *Annales* school of history writing in France interacted in creative ways with the development of African history. Fernand Braudel, the great leader of second-generation *Annales* historians, opened up the boundaries of historical space in a way that made it easier to understand Africa in world history. Many earlier scholars had limited themselves to national histories, of France, or of Italy, or of Spain. Others moved beyond national boundaries to continental ones. Braudel in his masterpiece saw the Mediterranean, with its palms and olive trees, as a significant historical unit, even though it took in parts of Europe and parts of Africa and Asia. It was tied together by its sea routes, but then extended wherever human communication took it: "We should imagine a hundred frontiers, not one," he wrote, "some political, some economic, and some cultural."[10]

A flexible approach to spatial boundaries gives historians a tool with which to break out of narrow definitions of core and periphery in world history. We do not need to see West African Muslims in a narrow framework that casts them only as bearers of culture from the center of civilization to the periphery. We can see them as West Africans, in economy, in language, and in many elements of discursive practice, and yet at the same time as Muslims. We do not read from a single historical map that inevitably separates Africans from Middle Easterners. We read many maps overlaid, one upon the other, some for language, some for economy, some for religion. Similarly, when historians define the boundaries of African healing practices they do not need to stop at the continent's edge; their history can extend to the Americas. If historians adopt a flexible and situationally specific understanding of historical space the plantation complex, which is often seen as narrowly American, as a phenomenon of the Caribbean, Brazil, and the southern United States, can now be understood as extending to the east coast of Africa and to northern Nigeria.[11]

Yet Braudel himself could not break out of a unidirectional history of the world with Europe at its center. *Civilisation matérielle, économie et capitalisme*, his three-volume history of the world between the fifteenth and eighteenth centuries, is driven by a tension between Braudel's disciplined attempt to find the correct spatial frame for each phenomenon (to explain the eighteenth-century rise of population on a worldwide basis, for example) and his definition of modern world history as the rise of a dominant Europe. The problematic character of Europe's role emerges with special clarity in volume 3, which draws heavily on the thought of Immanuel Wallerstein. It asks about the process by which a dominant capitalist world emerged, with its core in the West. In 1750, he says, the countries that were later to become industrialized produced 22.5 percent of the world's gross product. In 1976 the same countries produced 75 percent of that product. What were the origins of this movement from the relative economic parity of the world's parts to the dominance of the capitalist core?[12]

Braudel was concerned with the systematic character of inequality between the people he called "les *have* et les *have not*."[13] He was interested in how the dominance of the capitalist center grew out of developments within Europe, and out of relations among local world-economies. He tried to make a serious assessment of the degree to which wealth drawn from outside Europe contributed to the rise of capitalism, but he treated Africans, and to a lesser extent people of the Americas, as historical actors only to the extent that they met European needs:

> While we might have preferred to see this 'Non-Europe' on its own terms, it cannot properly be understood, even before the eighteenth century, except in terms of the mighty shadow cast over it by western Europe. . . . It was from all over the world . . . that Europe was now drawing a substantial part of her strength and substance. And it was this extra share which enabled Europeans to reach superhuman heights in tackling the tasks encountered on the path to progress.[14]

This is a rather strange statement, lumping together much of the world simply on the basis that it is not Europe, and proposing to ignore non-Europe on its own terms.

Braudel describes African developments, in particular, in terms of racial essences. In his view all civilization originated from the north, radiating southward. He writes, "I should like now to concentrate on the heartland of Black Africa, leaving aside the countries of the Maghreb—a 'White Africa' contained within the orbit of Islam."[15] Braudel's understanding of historical space is usually a subtle one in which each spatial frame is carefully differentiated. Here, however, he merges several frames in an inflexible and inaccurate way. First, he merges race ("White" or "Black") with religion (Islamic or non-Islamic), even though many of the Muslims were people he would otherwise have described as "Black."

Second, he characterizes "Black Africa" as passive and inert. He writes that European ships on the west coast met "neither resistance nor surveillance" and that the same thing happened on the shores of the desert: "Islam's camel-trains were as free to choose their entry-points as Europe's ships."[16] This is demonstrably incorrect. A very large body of historical literature explores the complex interactions between West African kings or traders and those who came across the desert from the north. The spread of Islam and of the trans-Saharan trade was shaped by initiatives taken on both sides of the desert.[17]

According to Braudel, all movement was in a single direction. "Curiously, no black explorers ever undertook any of the voyages across either the desert or the ocean which lay on their doorstep. . . .To the African, the Atlantic was, like the Sahara, an impenetrable obstacle."[18] He writes this despite the knowledge (with which he was certainly acquainted) that many Muslims who traded across the desert, or who went on the pilgrimage to Mecca from the West African Sudan, were Africans he would describe as black, carrying the cultural heritage of West Africa with them. African rulers are reported as having made the pilgrimage to Mecca as early as the eleventh century.[19] Mansa Musa of Mali traveled from West Africa to Cairo and then to Mecca in the fourteenth century with a retinue reported as numbering sixty thousand.[20] Even though the correct number is likely to be smaller, there is no question that thousands of Africans crossed the desert to visit the world of the Mediterranean and the Red Sea, and others (from the east coast) crossed the Indian Ocean to reach the Persian Gulf and India.

Finally, it appears to be the case that Braudel's characterization of the difference between "Black Africa" and "White Africa" is based on his understanding of race. In *Grammaire des civilisations* he acknowledges that Ethiopia (in this case Christian) was a civilization, explaining that it "undeniably possesses white ethnic elements, and is founded on a *metisse* population, very different, however, from those of the true Melano-Africans."[21] At times he denies the existence of facts in order to preserve the clear distinction between a black Africa that is uncivilized and a white Africa that is civilized. In 1963 he acknowledges that the region near the Gulf of Guinea was urbanized very early.[22] But later he argues that towns were one of the distinguishing marks of civilization, and that there were no towns on the fringes of the Gulf of Guinea.[23]

The core of the problem, in this instance, is not a vision of the historical process as originating in Europe; it is the unproblematized use of a word—"civilization"—with deep European roots. The word is then carried over into a narrative that is firmly centered in Africa, and it shapes the narrative in ways that are profound but largely implicit. The same problem is evident in the work of Pierre Chaunu and Bartolome Bennassar, members of the third generation of *Annales* historians. In their history of the world between the fourteenth and sixteenth centuries the central process is the merging of local historical spaces into a single interconnected worldwide space. Bennassar took care to read the new Africanist work, but then built his narrative around the impact of "civilizations" on the world. He explains, for example, that many of the Muslim merchants of West Africa were black West Africans but then also, in an argument entirely without foundation, attributes the development of East Africa's great lakes kingdoms to the impact of Muslims.[24]

Despite the centrality of "civilizations" to Bennassar and Chaunu, to Braudel, and to McNeill, the term is not always the subject of careful discussion. McNeill, who wrote that "civilized society had much to impart and relatively little to learn from peoples not yet civilized," defined civilization as "a style of human life characterized by a complexity, wealth, and general impressiveness that justify the epithet 'civilized.' "[25]

"Civilization" in its usage over the centuries in the English language has carried connotations of self and other, or of the proper and improper ordering of society. To "civilize," in the *Oxford English Dictionary* (1933), is "to polish what is rude or uncouth . . . to domesticate, tame (wild animals) . . . to make 'civil' " in the sense of "having proper public or social order." "Civilization" is a civilized condition or state in these senses, but then also "a developed or advanced state of human society."

Braudel makes a distinction between "civilizations" and "cultures," with the societies of black Africa counted among the cultures. In *The Structures of Everyday Life* he writes that "a culture is a civilization that has not yet achieved maturity,"[26] but then in *Grammaire des civilisations* he borrows from Levi-Strauss's division of societies between clocks and steam-engines, to argue that

> The societies which correspond to cultures are those . . . which have a tendency to maintain themselves indefinitely in their initial state, which explains furthermore why they appear to us as societies without history and without progress. . . . In brief primitive cultures will be the fruit of egalitarian societies, for whom relations between groups are regulated once and for all and repeat themselves, whereas civilizations are founded on hierarchical

societies, with . . . changing tensions, social conflicts, political struggle, and perpetual evolution.[27]

African cultures, according to this argument, are egalitarian and static; European civilizations, hierarchical and dynamic.

The strongest external sign of civilization, according to Braudel, is the presence of towns,[28] but these in turn are indicators of the existence of hierarchized space, divided between rich centers and poor peripheries.[29] Spatial inequalities emerge where intercommunication and commerce are well developed, and where agriculture is productive. The productivity of civilized society is the fruit of farming with a plow; cultures usually rely on the hoe.[30] Chaunu is clear on the reason for the importance of agricultural change: increased productivity leads to rising population densities, which are accompanied in turn by the emergence of hierarchy.[31] One of the central elements in the emergence of civilization is the existence of writing. Chaunu writes that he follows Braudel on the importance of writing for civilization: "The arts of memory are situated at the heart of accumulation" and writing is "the most efficacious" of the arts of memory.[32]

We have here a complex of elements that together form a coherent configuration: political and economic hierarchy, towns, commerce and intercommunication, writing, the plow, high densities of population, and historical dynamism.

The problem with this complex when applied to Africa, in the context of world histories like Braudel's or Bennassar and Chaunu's, is that the interrelations do not hold. In much of sub-Saharan Africa plows are not used because they are damaging to tropical soils. Some areas boasted thriving commerce, considerable intercommunication, and high population densities, but without political hierarchy.

The Igbo-speaking areas of southeastern Nigeria, for example, had very high population densities; in recent times some parts of the region have reached eight hundred per square mile. People cultivated the land with hoes, had a very dense network of periodic markets (in which markets took turns with one another on four- or eight-day cycles to make it easy for merchants to move from one to another), and had a network of long-distance trade fairs. By late in the first millennium A.D. the region was importing substantial quantities of trade goods overland from the Mediterranean—all this without writing and, in most parts of Igboland, without clear forms of political hierarchy. Egalitarian councils maintained the market peace, and the agents of religious oracles communicated over long distances. Many different kinds of ritual functionaries coexisted in Igboland, each preserving one or another form of knowledge, to be transmitted orally to the next generation. Artisans practiced numerous crafts. The region was economically dynamic both internally and in relation to export trade; when demand for palm oil grew in the early nineteenth century, Igboland and the area to the south of it rose to the challenge, and by 1853 were exporting thirty thousand tons of palm oil a year, using indigenous forms of organization.[33] It did not by any means belong in the set of societies to which Braudel would assign it—those with a "tendency to maintain themselves indefinitely in their initial state . . . for whom relations between groups are regulated once and for all and repeat themselves."

The point of this is important: the historical experience of southeastern Nigeria followed a pattern for which the historians' category of "civilization" was largely irrelevant. The region had high population densities in the absence of hierarchical states, commerce without literacy, and productive agriculture without plows. "Civilization's" characteristics—high population density, commerce, hierarchy, and so on—are meaningful only insofar as the separate elements have relational significance for one another: to the extent that the plow, political hierarchy, and mercantile activity are interrelated, for example. The elements have no explanatory significance if treated simply as a check list. In this part of Nigeria, it is clear, a different set of interrelations was at work. Taking account of them makes it impossible for historians to write in their accustomed way about the history of "civilizations."

The problem is a much more fundamental one, however. Braudel, and Bennassar and Chaunu, were in fact interested in finding terms that were less culturally encrusted than "civilization," more value-neutral, in which to explain change in African societies. Bennassar, for example, explored the principles of African social organization in his search for an answer to the central question asked also by Braudel: Why was Africa not the place where economic change took off? Why was it not Africa where the great breakthrough to capitalism occurred? In order to answer this question, Bennassar began from an understanding of the social factors that led to the breakthrough in Europe. The central factor, in his view, was the partial freedom of merchants from political control, and their capacity to accumulate wealth in their own right. He looked for the same factors in Africa, beginning with what seem to him the most advanced of the African kingdoms. In the kingdom of Kongo, he argued, merchants were closely controlled by the king. Land reverted to the king at the owner's death, thus cutting off the possibility of accumulation. The king was the source of poverty and prosperity, merchants lacked autonomy, and economic growth was restricted.[34]

The analysis falls down, however, not only because of the wide diversity of state structures in Africa, but also because of the incorrectness of its more basic assumption that autonomous merchants require a state structure in order to carry on their business. John Janzen has written the history of a set of institutions with mercantile functions that cut across regions occupied by states and regions of acephalous political organization. It is an area extending beyond the northern edge of the Kongo kingdom, mostly to the north of the Congo River as it descends to the Atlantic Ocean. This was a region of intense activity among merchants, who traded locally and contributed to the export trade. The seventeenth-century ivory trade was fed by an annual kill of three thousand to four thousand elephants. Estimates, also in the seventeenth century, had it that the region was capable of exporting up to forty tons of copper a year.[35] Yet a crucial part of the region's economy was outside the borders of any kingdom. It was an area in which a number of important governmental functions were borne by Lemba—a healing association or, in Janzen's (and Victor Turner's) term, a "drum of affliction."

People were initiated into Lemba as a way of treating their illnesses, yet it was also a form of commercial organization. Initiates played an essential role in maintaining free passage across an entire network of four-day markets. Lemba was a form of religious expression, a consecrated medicine, in which the highest levels of initiation were very expensive. The richest merchants were most likely to rise to the top of Lemba, and they used ritual networks to advance their economic interests. It is an example of exactly the sort of mercantile autonomy for which Bennassar was searching. He did not find it (or other similar institutions), however, because the world historian does not normally search for mercantile activity in "'the sacred medicine of governing'; . . . 'the government of multiplication and reproduction'; . . . and 'sacred medicine integrating people, villages and markets.'"[36]

The problem here is that the categories of historical analysis, even though ostensibly value-neutral, are drawn from Europe, and therefore the historian looks in Africa for a familiar constellation of king, nobles, church, and merchants. "The sacred medicine of governing" is alien to the analysis. Valentin Mudimbe has explained that functional analyses depend on a contrast between the normal and the pathological. If what is European is defined as normal, then the non-European appears to be disordered, abnormal, primitive.[37]

How, then, do we construct an account of world history within a single framework, if the principles of social organization of Lemba, or in Igboland, are different from principles in Europe? One further possibility is to build a narrative of world history around a historical process that is undeniably world-encompassing, like the development of a worldwide trade in commodities. Eric Wolf tries to do this while giving full weight to non-Europeans in *Europe and the People without History*.[38] Because he works so hard to reverse the balance of emphasis from Europe to "the people without history," we can see the limits and the difficulties of the enterprise.

The early parts of Wolf's book make no attempt to picture a unified process in world history. Wolf orients this description around three "modes of production," but he does so without reducing diverse experience to a few simple types—without doing violence to the specificity of local forms. The modes are not types of societies, he writes, but rather "constructs in which to envisage certain strategic relationships."[39]

It is for the capitalist period that Wolf aims to construct a universal history, based on regularities in the historical process and not only in the historian's frame of analysis. The rise of the world market leads to the emergence of money (and of prices) as a universal language. Goods everywhere in the world become commodities, and these "can be compared and exchanged without reference to the social matrix in which they were produced."[40] Each commodity has a quantitative value in relation to all other commodities because of the existence of market institutions. For the period when a world market exists, the historian can write a universal history of the way commodities are produced and exchanged. This is Wolf's project. He sketches the political and economic consequences of the fur trade for the peoples of North America, and of the slave trade for Africa. Later in the book he tours the world, showing the effects of commodity production—explaining the impact of rubber production, for example, on the Amazon basin and on southern Asia.

Wolf's focus on non-Europeans in world history is especially useful in revealing how difficult it is to construct a single master-narrative, for there must necessarily be levels of experience he does not describe—levels at which people struggle to create new ways of giving cultural form to social action, levels at which local experience escapes from the regularity of "universal" processes.

Recent work by Arjun Appadurai and Igor Kopytoff shows, for example, that objects become commodities in culturally specific ways.[41] Objects, in this view, have a life history during which they move into and out of commodity status, as in the case of an heirloom that family members will not sell until a particular point in the family's life cycle when it becomes available for sale. The pattern by which objects move into and out of commodity status varies from one society to another.

Sharon Hutchinson, writing on the Nuer of the southern Sudan, shows that money and commodities are culturally constructed in ways radically different from the expected ones. The culture of commodities is locally constructed, not a universal pattern. Nor can one "predict how money will be conceptualized and incorporated by other cultures."[42]

Nuer these days work for wages, become active as merchants, and engage in the trade in cattle and other commodities as buyers and sellers.

They can therefore be said to have entered the capitalist world of commodity exchange; they speak the universal language of money and price. Nevertheless, cattle are commodities in relatively circumscribed contexts; they are unlike the commodities described by Wolf, or the commodities found in Marx, for whom capitalist exchange breaks down boundaries and opens free movement. Nuer sell cattle for money, but they may not exchange the money thus earned in all the ways they might have exchanged cattle. The crucial difference between money and cattle is that "cattle have blood," which people equate with procreative force; "money has no blood." For this reason money cannot be used in contexts in which the blood of cattle is relevant: for bloodwealth, or sacrifice, or (except to a limited extent) for bridewealth. Even when cattle are used in social transactions, distinctions are made between the uses of animals bought with money ("cattle of money") and animals that came as bridewealth ("cattle of girls").

Money itself is not a homogeneous medium of exchange for people in Nuerland. Money earned emptying latrines or doing domestic work is called "money of shit," and it cannot be used to purchase cows. "Cattle bought with the money of shit cannot live."[43] Other wages are called "money of sweat," and earnings from the sale of livestock are "money of cattle." For the Nuer, money is not universally fluid. There are several kinds of it, with several uses.[44]

Nuer have constructed a new synthesis of market and community, a new set of exchange categories, to meet their own particular needs. It is this sort of creative process that is not accounted for in a narrative of the spread of commodities in world history. To say this is not to deny the existence of commodities, nor of their commensurability on a worldwide basis, nor of the significance of the emergence of a world market. It is simply to say that the history of commodities is not a total history, that there are realms of experience beyond its reach.

The sense that we can no longer tell history as a single story, from a single consistent point of view or from a unified perspective, strikes deep resonances in recent social and cultural thought. Michel Foucault wrote, in *Language, Countermemory, Practice*, that the idea of the whole of society "arose in the Western world, in this highly individualized historical development that culminates in capitalism. To speak of the 'whole of society' apart from the only form it has ever taken is to transform our past into a dream."[45] The very categories by which we understand universal experience originate in the particular experience of the core of the capitalist world.

This is the same lesson taught by an examination of African history: the categories that are ostensibly universal are in fact particular, and they refer to the experience of modern Europe. That we have learned this lesson in two different ways—through philosophically based writings on Europe and through histories of non-Europeans—forces us to ask about the relationship between the two sets of developments. A central question that has not yet been fully addressed is about the relationship between the crisis of historical representation that came about when historians began to hear the voices of those who had been voiceless, and the more general epistemological crisis affecting all the social sciences and humanities.

To answer this question one would need to write a general political and intellectual history of the years since World War II. It is only possible, in the scope of a few paragraphs, to make tentative suggestions.

In the decades after 1945 the politics of race turned in a decisively new direction in the European colonial empires and in the United States. The struggles that led to decolonization—wars in Indochina, Algeria, and Kenya, and less violent independence movements in innumerable other territories—led to a reconsideration among European intellectuals of the qualities and values that had been defined as European. The loss of empire happened at a time when some thinkers were questioning whether historians and others in the human sciences were at all capable of describing the Other, or whether by doing so they were engaging in what Emmanuel Levinas called "ontological imperialism," in which otherness vanishes and becomes part of the same.[46]

Some thinkers argued that descriptions of the native, the colonial other, were embedded in a discourse in which Europeans defined themselves. In Edward Said's words, "The Orient was . . . not Europe's interlocutor, but its silent other."[47] How was it possible to define freedom unless one could contrast it with bondage, autonomy except in contrast to slavery, or civilization (itself at the heart of world history, as we have seen) except in contrast to barbarism? Without the native, without the slave, the bondsman, or the barbarian, the central values of the West are difficult to imagine. The slave and the barbarian were not incidental to civilization, aberrant conditions at the margins; they were constitutive of civilization, a way civilization defined itself. With the civil rights movement in the United States similar perceptions began to emerge, that slavery and later forms of racial oppression were not errors at the margins of American society; they had, in some fundamental way, defined American society. The relationship between race and America's central egalitarian values was, in Gunnar Myrdal's term, "An American Dilemma."

The decline of the colonial empires and the end of official segregation in the United States brought increasing numbers of nonwhites into the world's historical profession and into the audiences that historians addressed. In the 1960s many newly independent African nations founded their own universities. The Africans who staffed the new history departments had a compelling interest in reconstructing the autonomous history of Africans within the national borders. British, or French, or American historians, who were now looking at the history of nations in a very different way than they had the history of colonies, were influenced also by the expanded presence of Africans and African-Americans as colleagues and as students. The result of all these developments was that a growing group of historians began to work seriously in Africa, in Europe, and in North America, to reconstruct and recover the African past.

There were other forces at work in the wider intellectual transformation—the rise of women in academia and of feminism, and radical shifts in the history of science that influenced thinking about history as a science. Nevertheless, two of the most central ones grew out of the racial politics of the postwar decades: a sense of the defining place of the subordinated other in European discourses, and the opening up of non-Western histories as legitimate subjects of historical research.

The specialist work of historical reconstruction served to take the people about whom anthropologists had always written and to insist that they be placed within the larger historical narrative. The change in context required a change in how historians understood agency. Previously mute people had now to be seen as authors and actors. Exotic cultures were not new to the academic imagination, but the style of description was new. The new knowledge broke with a long intellectual tradition that treated exotic cultures as though they existed at a different time from the rest of humanity, stone age, or bronze age, or iron age peoples, remnants of the past, not living in the same world where historians live, not subject to the same political and economic forces.[48]

Once historians of Africa took exotic cultures out of their "culture gardens" and into their own world, that world no longer existed in the same form. Treating Africans and women, peasants and slaves as historical actors presented a fundamental challenge to general historical understanding. It challenged the notion that history told from the point of view of a narrower and less representative population was value-neutral or universal.

The challenge it presents to African history is just as fundamental. The historian, whether African or outsider, must struggle to understand the place of the historical actor within a complex web of local cultural understandings and at the same time avoid seeing that action only in local terms. Local actors were, at one and the same time, orienting their actions to the local context and playing on a world stage, influencing worldwide historical processes. A childless Igbo woman, for example, was concerned with her practical alternatives when she went before the

Aro oracle to learn the causes of her childlessness. At the same time her interaction with oracle agents and with the oracle itself (together with the interactions of others like her) shaped the course of the Atlantic slave trade, for the oracle was important to the process of enslavement. The problem for the historian is how to capture all different levels at the same time, how to do justice to the local, the regional, and the international in a single description or a single framework of analysis.

It is worth making a brief exploration of the history of the place of Africans in the Atlantic slave trade to understand some of the problems of multilayered interpretation. The slave trade was a set of actions that articulated with one another on an enormous scale, reaching across several continents. Individual slaves might have been torn from their homes hundreds of miles into the interior of Nigeria, or of Angola, or of some other part of the continent. If we can imagine a brother and sister taken together, then perhaps the brother found himself walking to the coast to embark on a ship, while his sister stopped along the way to toil as an unfree worker nearer to home. Once the brother crossed the ocean he would forge bonds with other slaves, perhaps from the Gold Coast or the Guinea Coast. He might well have worked on a sugar plantation owned by a capitalist in the north of England. Defined as a spatial system, in Braudelian terms, a system of slavery extended to the Caribbean, to North, South, and Central America, to Europe, and to the Indian Ocean.

Within an imagined system, understood in this way, there were many other boundaries: local and subsystem boundaries. Each local area had its own patterns of custom and of language, its own characteristic forms of social interaction. People spoke to one another in local languages; they consulted local oracles or spirit mediums. Yet they also participated in a coordinated metasystem of meaning and action reaching from the interior of Africa to the Americas and to Europe.

The problem of interpretation, in this palimpsest of social forms, is evident from the many meanings of the word "slave." A man who was sold to traders in Central Africa and who ultimately crossed the Atlantic to work on a plantation in Jamaica was clearly a slave. But it is doubtful that his original owner in Africa knew the English word "slave," and doubtful also that the local term defining the person's form of dependency was the precise equivalent of "slave." The major associations of "slavery" in English are with the plantation slavery of the American south, the Caribbean, and Latin America. Yet historians also use the word for statuses within Africa that seem very much unlike plantation slavery.

In Shambaai, in the mountains of northern Tanzania where I did ethnographic research and collected oral narratives, poor men who could not feed their children during famines relied in precolonial times on the food stores of the chief. A man who could not feed his daughter would leave her at the chief's court where she ate and where she worked. At famine's end the father would come bringing goats to redeem his daughter from the chief's control, and he would take her home. The girl, while at the court, might be called an *mtung'wa*, the same as the word for "slave"; she was also called an *mndee* of the chief—the chief's "girl," an ambiguous term that might at times be translated as "slave." An American would not be likely to think of her as a slave, but if her father did not return to reclaim his daughter she remained in servitude.[49]

In the late 1960s I interviewed a man whose mother, born in a part of East Africa distant from Shambaai, had been a "slave" (*mtung'wa*) at a chief's court. Soon after German conquest the chief sold her to a commoner and she became a wife. My informant described his mother as an unhappy woman who had been abused by her co-wife and by her husband because she had no birth-family to insist on her rights. The other woman in the household, the co-wife, had a greater level of protection because her husband had made a bridewealth payment to her male relatives. The woman could therefore ask them for help when she needed it.

In the period when all this was happening, Arab plantation owners on the Tanzania coast, and on the islands of Zanzibar and Pemba just off the coast, employed slave labor to grow cloves, sugar, and grain. A few years earlier the woman without a family, my informant's mother, might have been sold as a plantation slave if the chief had chosen to do so. Instead she became a wife without full rights.

The case illustrates that slavery was only one in a range of related statuses. The woman in question was a wife, not a slave, but a wife without full rights. She might easily have become a plantation slave, and she might also have been a wife with full rights if she had been married at home, and if her brothers or father had received a bridewealth payment. An omniscient social observer would be able to place these different statuses within a total range of women's statuses, as a social map. But if the statuses are seen instead from the point of view of the woman at the time, for whom they were possible life choices, it is clear that they presented a challenge: how to negotiate so as to become a wife without rights rather than a slave, or, better still, to become a wife with full rights.

The woman of the period understood that her life chances were defined by the constellation of relationships of dependency. If her negotiations were unsuccessful, if she was taken in the intercontinental slave trade, she experienced a disastrous simplification of her possibilities.

Now only the slave status was relevant. Historians find it difficult to characterize the status of a woman in the process of becoming enslaved. If they treat her as a slave they appear to be denying the importance of locally based forms of dependency; if they treat her status in local terms they are denying the importance of the intercontinental process.

Scholars who write about slavery in Africa tend to choose one or the other of these positions. Some emphasize the violent process by which people are enslaved through kidnapping or warfare, leading to the radical kinlessness ("natal alienation") of the slave, who was then treated as chattel. Others place their central emphasis on 'slavery' in African societies as a transitional status for people who were on their way toward being incorporated into new kinship groups.[50] The interpretation of slavery as radical kinlessness growing out of violence is weak because it is difficult to see, within this framework, how people might have become enslaved through a subtle process of social negotiation, or how they might have negotiated an end to their slave status. On the other hand, the interpretations that focus on reincorporation have their own weaknesses, for they leave little space for radically kinless plantation slaves, whether they were sent off to the Americas or whether they were put to work on plantations that grew up in Africa.

To understand why both reincorporation and radical kinlessness were a part of the story, and to see the relationship between the local cultures of dependency and the worldwide trade in slaves, I would like to look briefly at the life of a single "slave," as reported to us in her own words and as brought to the attention of historians by Marcia Wright.[51] Narwimba lived in the region between Lake Tanganyika and Lake Nyasa, near the border between what are now Tanzania and Zambia. The time of Narwimba's story, the 1880s and early 1890s, was a time of great upheaval in the region, a time when slaves were captured and used locally, and when some were sent off to plantations of the East African coast.

This was a period of great difficulty for Narwimba, beginning with her husband's death in about 1880. At one point Narwimba was taken captive by soldiers of a foreign chief and offered for sale to slave traders. She escaped, but lived to see her granddaughter taken captive and released on two separate occasions. Narwimba lived through the transition to colonial rule, and ultimately came to live with her son, who had been converted by Christian missionaries.

The period was one of intense danger and intense struggle for Narwimba, much of it engendered by the violent theft of people for the slave trade. Narwimba's own strategies all show how important she thought it was to avoid being made marginal in kinship terms, and to retain an attachment to a protective male, preferably in a marriage relationship marked by the payment of bridewealth. We can see this at several important moments.

After Narwimba's husband died one of his relations came to visit and to decide whether to marry her. Narwimba, in her own account, said, "And I, on my part, begged him to take me to wife so that we might be protected."[52] Lacking his protection, she would become much more vulnerable. Narwimba's daughter took up residence with a man who paid no bridewealth. It is possible that she felt it necessary to accept this irregular liaison because of the weakness of her mother's position. At any rate, the daughter born to this union belonged to the household of the chief. Her father held no rights in her, because he had paid no bridewealth for her mother. The result of this was that Narwimba's granddaughter Musamarire was a vulnerable member of the chief's household. On one occasion, when diplomacy required the chief to give up a person in order to make peace, he proposed to give up Musamarire. Narwimba fled with her instead. On another occasion the granddaughter was seized again, in a dispute over a debt.

In Narwimba's time enslavement as violent theft was taking place; the scholars who describe forms of radical kinlessness are correct. But it was taking place within a context in which there was room for Narwimba to maneuver. The way she could protect herself over the long term was by negotiating a place for herself within a male-dominated kinship system.

Slavery may have been antikinship, but it existed within a context in which the alternatives to enslavement were kinship alternatives and the character of slave capturing and slave trading was shaped by their relation to networks of kinship. The character of relationships between master and slave, in this case, was shaped by the existence of other forms of dependency alongside slavery. The existence of kinship and gender alternatives to slavery shaped the struggle between Narwimba and the potential slave-masters who would have taken control of her or of her granddaughter.

The case of Narwimba shows, in addition, that just as local traditions of dependency had an effect on African plantation slavery, the introduction of slavery had a profound impact on other forms of dependency. Narwimba was clearly willing to accept the possibility of extreme and relatively brutal subordination in marriage because a marriage, even of this kind, was protection against enslavement. A woman's capacity to resist a brutal husband would undoubtedly have been greater in the generation of Narwimba's mother, before the slave trade presented extreme dangers. To understand the slave trade in this particular context, we need to understand local traditions of dependency, their place in shaping the internal dynamics of slavery, and the place of slavery in shaping local patterns of kinship.

Describing Narwimba's struggle as precipitated by the development of the international slave trade but rooted in local social forms does not entirely break out of the structure of the European master-narrative. The problem, of course, is that in this account the central thrusting forces that shaped Narwimba's life originated on the international scene and with the history of capitalism. This is not at all how Narwimba's contemporaries in Central Africa would have seen things. They would have placed the events of her life within the context of the narratives of individual language groups, or narratives of general distribution among the region's Bantu-speaking peoples. Quite possibly these narratives would not have assigned a major role to international trade or to a Europe-centered economy.

As a child, Narwimba fled with her family from attacks by Ngoni soldiers and found refuge with the Kyungu (the paramount chief) of the Ngonde polity. It was the Kyungu who later instructed a relative of her dead husband to marry her. Ngonde narratives from the Kyungu's land (or Ngoni ones, or others of the region) offer the historian alternatives to the Europe-centered ones, alternatives closer to Narwimba's own life and language.

Ngonde histories would have remained true to their own principles in their construction of Narwimba's story. Their political histories were built on the understanding that the Kyungu's wholeness and social health shaped the basic conditions of health and prosperity for the whole of his land. There was an identity between the Kyungu's physical health and the well-being of his domains. If a drop of his blood fell to the ground it was a sign that the whole land would suffer famine or disease unless he was killed. There was an identity also between the Kyungu's uncontested sexual dominance within his household and his life-giving dominance within the polity. According to some traditions, in early generations most of the Kyungu's sons were killed because the people of Ngonde "feared that, if the Kyungu had many [living] sons, they might seduce his wives and so bring sickness on himself and on his country."[53] In Ngonde, as in other parts of the region, adultery with a chief's wife was an act of war or of treason. At the level of the nobles, also, rank found its expression in marriage practice. A chief paid and received higher bridewealth than a commoner.[54]

A local person, trying to make sense of Narwimba's life, might well have understood it within the context of marriage as a range of forms that express degrees of political dominance. Narwimba and her close relatives would, for much of their lives, have practiced forms of marriage that were very humble when seen within the larger hierarchy. The size of bridewealth payments expressed rank, and Narwimba's daughter married entirely without bridewealth.

Most university historians would focus on an entirely different context for Narwimba's life, as we have seen. They would pay significant attention to the history of trade. From this viewpoint, a major event would be the opening up of Ngonde's trade with the Indian Ocean. This important change came as a result of the reorientation of the Kyungu's ivory trade toward the east (across Lake Malawi). The shift to the east was associated with fundamental change in the constitution of the polity, toward the growth of secular authority. The Ngonde narratives themselves, however, do not assign a central place to the history of trade as university historians do. Godfrey Wilson, who studied these oral traditions in the 1930s, complained that they gave him only glimpses of the important commercial changes.[55] Instead, the traditions recounted by senior Ngonde men described constitutional changes as precipitated by crucial political marriages.[56] According to the Kyungu's own narrative, as told to Wilson, the eastward shift in trade took place when an early Kyungu "struck the lake and walked over to Mwela [the land of Mwela boatmen] to marry a woman, Mapunda."[57]

Ngonde historians, then, might well have understood Narwimba's story as a very humble and minor part of a much larger story in which rank and political change are marked by marriage. To these historians the Atlantic slave trade would have appeared to be distant, and indeed largely irrelevant. The world historian who chooses to focus on the Atlantic slave trade or the rise of capitalism needs to explain why this context is privileged, why Narwimba's life ought to be explained in this way and not in relation to the personal history of the Kyungus and their marriages.

The European or American historian might well argue that Ngonde history is local and the history of capitalism global—that if we want to understand events on a wide scale, we must stick to the European narrative. In fact, African historical processes are not so narrowly localized. Some interrelations among gender, descent, and rank are broadly distributed, and they can be studied by historians using the tools of historical linguistics and comparative historical ethnography. Some of the events in Narwimba's own life were embedded in historical movements of enormous sweep. At the very beginning of her story, for example, came the Ngoni raid that dispossessed her family. The Ngoni, at this time, were a new presence in Central African society. Each Ngoni state was organized by a ruling group that originated in South Africa, over a thousand miles away, in the wars surrounding the creation of the Zulu kingdom. The small bands of armed Ngoni men took wives and children as captives in order to build snowball states. They, too, like the Kyungu, were operating within the regional politics of marriage and dependency, which they were using for new forms of state building.[58]

The study of African history presses us to move beyond forms of historical representation in which the energy driving the story originates in Europe, while African history (or Latin American) provides local color, a picturesque setting for the central drama. There is no way to understand Narwimba's story without sinking roots into the longer story of the development of social forms in Africa. What was the range of paths by which people established relations of dependency? How was authority instituted? What were the idioms of power in the regional histories of Africa? Everything we know about the study of history tells us that we cannot understand something as complex as the idioms of power without studying their variation in space and their history in time. African narratives must carry their full weight.

The search for African narratives reveals that they are multiple narratives. It would be a mistake to give a privileged place to Ngoni royal narratives, or to the Kyungu's narrative, or to those of Ngonde nobles. There is no reason these should carry greater weight, or be accorded greater privilege, than Narwimba's own account, no reason the words of the Kyungu's rituals should count more than the words of subject women's rituals.

Each of the many African narratives carries the marks of its own history, including the history of relations with Europe. In Rwanda, for example, Joseph Rwabukumba and Alexis Kagame, Rwandan scholars, have written histories of the kingdom based on extensive collections of local oral traditions. They take varieties of local knowledge that were meant to be secret and separate—*ubwiiru* as a dynastic ritual code, for example—make a written record of them, and compare them with other traditions in order to construct a general narrative. Rwandan oral historians of the nineteenth century had methods for making critical comparisons of traditions, but they were not the same as Kagame's techniques. Nor would the oral histories have found an easy place, as do Kagame's, within a general framework of historical knowledge created among academics outside Rwanda.[59] Kagame and Rwabukumba are Rwandan historians, using Rwandan materials, writing within a genre created in Europe.

The task of finding purely African narratives is no easier if we shift our attention from university scholars to the peasantry. In Rwanda under the Belgians and Tanganyika under the British the colonial authorities ruled through African chiefs so as to build on what, in the words of one British governor, was the "loyalty and 'free awe'" of subjects for their chiefs. The effect was to cast peasant debates on colonial policy in terms of ancient forms of political discourse. When the oral histories of the dynasties took on marks of colonial domination, dissident oral historians responded by searching out antidynastic histories in their own past, and (in the case of Tanganyika) stories of regicide from textbooks of English history.[60]

We are left, then, with an enormously expanded subject matter, with historical narratives originating in Africa that must be given full weight alongside those originating in Europe. We have seen, however, that this is not a simple process of adding one more body of knowledge to our fund, of increasing the balance in the account. The need for historians to hear African voices originates with the same impulse as the need to hear the voices that had been silent within European history. Since that is so, it hardly feels satisfying to listen to a single authoritative African voice, leaving others silent, or to read African texts without seeing marks of power, or without asking about the authority of the historian (African or American, European or Asian) who presumes to represent history. Historians have no choice but to open up world history to African history, but having done so they find that the problems have just begun.

NOTES

A longer version of this essay was published as "African Histories and the Dissolution of World History," in *Africa and the Disciplines: The Contributions of Research in Africa to the Social Sciences and Humanities,* ed. Robert H. Bates, V. Y. Mudimbe, and Jean O'Barr (Chicago and London: University of Chicago Press, 1993), pp. 167–212.

1. The statement about the lack of African history at Berkeley is based on University of California, *Bulletin: General Catalogue, Fall and Spring Semesters, 1955–1956* (Berkeley: University of California–Berkeley, 1955). The statement about the University of Chicago is based on University of Chicago, *Announcements: Graduate Programs in the Divisions, Sessions of 1957–1958* (Chicago: University of Chicago Press, 1956). The statement about Columbia is based on memories of my search for an African historian in 1960, when I was an undergraduate. The statement about Princeton is based on personal communication from Robert Tignor. The survey of department chairs is reported in Dexter Perkins and John Snell, *The Education of Historians in the United States* (New York: McGraw-Hill, 1962), p. 32. It is probable that there were a number of graduate students working on the history of Egypt and of the Maghrib who were not reported at the time as studying African history.

2. Philip D. Curtin, "African History," in *The Past before Us: Contemporary Historical Writing in the United States,* ed. Michael Kammen (Ithaca and London: Cornell University Press, 1980), pp. 113–30.

3. William H. McNeill, *The Rise of the West: A History of the Human Community* (Chicago and London: University of Chicago Press, 1963), p. 11.

4. Ibid., p. 240.

5. Ibid., p. 481.

6. New research on early pastoralism is described by F. Wendorf, A. E. Close, and R. Schild, "Early Domestic Cattle in the Eastern Sahara," in *Palaeoecology of Africa and the Surrounding Islands* 18 (1987):441–48; John Bower, "The Pastoral Neolithic of East Africa," *Journal of World Prehistory* 5, no. 1 (1991):49–82, particularly 56–57. On the origins of agriculture, see Jack R. Harlan, Jan DeWet, and Ann Stemler, *Origins of African Domestication* (The Hague: Mouton, 1976); and J. Desmond Clark and Steven A. Brandt, *From Hunters to Farmers: The Causes and Consequences of Food Production in Africa* (Berkeley: University of California Press, 1984).

7. McNeill, *Rise of the West*, p. 252.

8. Roderick J. McIntosh and Susan Keech McIntosh, "From *Siècles Obscurs* to Revolutionary Centuries on the Middle Niger," in *World Archaeology* 20, no. 1 (1988): 140 65.

9. On the indigenous origins of the kingdoms of the East African lakes, see Peter Schmidt, *Historical Archaeology: A Structural Approach in an African Culture* (Westport, Conn.: Greenwood, 1978); Renee Louise Tantala, "The Early Modern History of Kitara in Western Uganda: Process Models of Religious and Political Change" (Ph.D. diss., University of Wisconsin–Madison, 1989); David Schoenbrun, "Early History in Eastern Africa's Great Lakes Region: Linguistic, Ecological, and Archaeological Approaches, ca. 500 B.C. to ca. A.D. 1000" (Ph.D. diss., UCLA, 1990); Iris Berger, *Religion and Resistance: East African Kingdoms in the Precolonial Period*, Annales, no. 105 (Tervuren: Musée Royal de l'Afrique Centrale, 1981); Samwiri Karugire, *A History of the Kingdom of Nkore in Western Uganda* (Oxford: Clarendon, 1971); and Centre de Civilisation Burundaise, *La Civilisation ancienne des peuples des Grands Lacs* (Paris: Karthala, 1981). T. Reefe, *The Rainbow and the Kings: A History of the Luba Empire to 1891* (Berkeley: University of California Press, 1981), writes on the Luba empire. On the indigenous origins of Zimbabwe, see P. S. Garlake, *Great Zimbabwe* (London: Thames and Hudson, 1973); idem, "Pastoralism and Zimbabwe," *Journal of African History* 19, no. 4 (1978):479–93. Henrika Kuklick, "Contested Monuments: The Politics of Archeology in Southern Africa," in *Colonial Situations: Essays on the Contextualization of Ethnographic Knowledge*, ed. George Stocking (Madison: University of Wisconsin Press, 1991), pp. 135–69, describes the interaction between racial politics and archaeological research that led to earlier interpretations of Zimbabwe as alien to Africa. Martin Hall, *The Changing Past: Farmers, Kings and Traders in Southern Africa, 200–1860* (Cape Town: David Philip, 1987), provides a general synthesis of archaeological knowledge on the relationship between political organization and the economy for the southern African region. Graham Connah, *African Civilizations, Precolonial Cities and States in Tropical Africa: An Archaeological Perspective* (Cambridge: Cambridge University Press, 1987), does the same for the whole of Africa. For a general history, see Philip Curtin, Steven Feierman, Leonard Thompson, and Jan Vansina, *African History* (London: Longman, 1978).

10. Fernand Braudel, *The Mediterranean and the Mediterranean World in*

the Age of Philip II, trans. Siân Reynolds (New York: Harper and Row, 1976), 1:170.

11. See Frederick Cooper, *Plantation Slavery on the East Coast of Africa* (New Haven and London: Yale University Press, 1977); Abdul Sheriff, *Slaves, Spices and Ivory in Zanzibar: Integration of an East African Commercial Empire into the World Economy 1770–1873* (London: James Currey; Athens: Ohio University Press, 1987); Paul E. Lovejoy, "The Characteristics of Plantations in the Nineteenth-Century Sokoto Caliphate (Islamic West Africa)," *American Historical Review* 84, no. 5 (1979):1267–92.

12. Fernand Braudel, *The Perspective of the World*, vol. 3 of *Civilization and Capitalism, 15th–18th Century*, trans. Siân Reynolds (London: Collins, 1984), p. 534; and idem, *The Wheels of Commerce*, vol. 2 of *Civilization and Capitalism, 15th–18th Century*, trans. Siân Reynolds (New York: Harper and Row, 1982), p. 134.

13. Fernand Braudel, *Le Temps du monde*, vol. 3 of *Civilisation matérielle, économie et capitalisme, XVe–XVIIIe Siècle* (Paris: Armand Colin, 1979), p. 16.

14. Braudel, *Perspective of the World*, p. 386.

15. Ibid., p. 430.

16. Ibid., p. 434.

17. The literature on these subjects includes hundreds of books and articles. For a discussion of the African roots of notables in a center of Islamic learning, see Elias Saad, *The Social History of Timbuktu: The Role of Muslim Scholars and Notables, 1400–1900* (Cambridge: Cambridge University Press, 1983). For interesting local case studies, see Richard Roberts, *Warriors, Merchants, and Slaves: The State and Economy in the Middle Niger Valley, 1700–1914* (Stanford: Stanford University Press, 1987); and Abdoulaye Bathily, *Les Portes de l'or: le royaume de Galam (Sénégal) de l'ère musulmane au temps des négriers (VIIIe–XVIIIe siècle)*, (Paris: Editions L'Harmattan, 1989). An interesting regional case study is given by Murray Last, "The Early Kingdoms of the Nigerian Savanna," in *History of West Africa*, ed. J.F.A. Ajayi and Michael Crowder (Harlow, Essex: Longman, 1985), 1:167–224. For a general picture of West African economic history, see A. G. Hopkins, *An Economic History of West Africa* (London: Longman, 1973); for later literature on this subject, see Ralph Austen, *African Economic History: Internal Development and External Dependency* (London: James Currey, 1987). Local economic roots of Islamic forms of action are discussed in John Hanson, "Generational Conflict in the Umarian Movement after the *Jihad*: Perspectives from the Futanke Grain Trade at Medine," *Journal of African History* 31 (1990):199–215.

18. Braudel, *Perspective of the World*, p. 434.

19. 'Umar al-Naqar, *The Pilgrimage Tradition in West Africa* (Khartoum: Khartoum University Press, 1972), p. 27.

20. Mervyn Hiskett, *The Development of Islam in West Africa* (London and New York: Longman, 1984), p. 15; see also pp. 29, 34, 55.

21. Fernand Braudel, *Grammaire des civilisations* (Paris: Arthaud-Flammarion, 1987), p. 152.

22. Fernand Braudel, *Grammaire des civilisations* (originally published in 1963), p. 164.

23. Fernand Braudel, *The Structures of Everyday Life: The Limits of the Possible*, vol. 1 of *Civilization and Capitalism, 15th–18th Century*, trans. Siân Reynolds (New York: Harper and Row, 1981).

24. Bartolomé Bennassar and Pierre Chaunu, eds., *L'Ouverture du monde, xive–xvie siècles*, vol. 1 of *Histoire économique et sociale du monde* (Paris: Armand Colin, 1977), pp. 71–73.

25. McNeill, *Rise of the West*, pp. 65, 32.

26. Braudel, *Structures of Everyday Life*, p. 101.

27. Braudel, *Grammaire des civilisations*, p. 48.

28. Ibid.

29. Braudel, *Le Temps du monde*, p. 16.

30. Braudel, *Structures of Everyday Life*, pp. 56–64, 174–82.

31. Bennassar and Chaunu, *L'Ouverture du monde*, pp. 47–51.

32. Ibid., pp. 56, 49n.

33. On the organization and development of precolonial trade, see David Northrup, *Trade without Rulers: Pre-Colonial Economic Development in South-Eastern Nigeria* (Oxford: Clarendon, 1978); and Ukwu I. Ukwu, "The Development of Trade and Marketing in Iboland," *Journal of the Historical Society of Nigeria* 3 (1967): 647–62. Northrup is also the source of the figure on population density (*Trade without Rulers*, p. 13). For a sophisticated interpretation of precolonial Igbo social organization and culture, see Adiele Afigbo, *Ropes of Sand (Studies in Igbo History and Culture)* (Ibadan: University Press Limited in Association with Oxford University Press, 1981). The figure on palm oil exports is from K. Onwuka Dike, *Trade and Politics in the Niger Delta, 1830–1865* (Oxford: Clarendon, 1956). On early long-distance trade, see Thurstan Shaw, *Igbo-Ukwu*, 2 vols. (London: Faber and Faber, 1970); and idem, "Those Igbo-Ukwu Dates: Facts, Fictions and Probabilities," *Journal of African History* 11 (1975):515–33. The literature on Igboland is enormous; the region is practically a separate subfield of African history. On ethnography, see the works of Victor Uchendu and Simon Ottenberg. For some important twentieth-century events, see Susan Martin, *Palm Oil and Protest: An Economic History of the Ngwa Region, South-Eastern Nigeria, 1800–1980* (Cambridge: Cambridge University Press, 1988).

34. Bennassar and Chaunu, *L'Ouverture du monde*, pp. 85–87.

35. John M. Janzen, *Lemba, 1650–1930: A Drum of Affliction in Africa and the New World* (New York and London: Garland, 1982), pp. 28, 32; Phyllis Martin, *The External Trade of the Loango Coast, 1576–1870* (Oxford: Clarendon, 1972).

36. Janzen, *Lemba, 1650–1930*, p. 4.

37. V. Y. Mudimbe, *The Invention of Africa: Gnosis, Philosophy, and the Order of Knowledge* (Bloomington and Indianapolis: Indiana University Press, 1988), pp. 27, 191–92.

38. Eric R. Wolf, *Europe and the People without History* (Berkeley, Los Angeles, London: University of California Press, 1982).

39. Ibid., p. 100.

40. Ibid., p. 310.

41. Arjun Appadurai, "Introduction: Commodities and the Politics of

Value," in *The Social Life of Things: Commodities in Cultural Perspective*, ed. Arjun Appadurai (Cambridge: Cambridge University Press, 1986), pp. 3–63; Igor Kopytoff, "The Cultural Biography of Things: Commoditization as Process," in *Social Life of Things*, pp. 64–91. See also Patrick Geary, "Sacred Commodities: The Circulation of Medieval Relics," in *Social Life of Things*, pp. 169–91; Lee V. Cassanelli, "Qat: Changes in the Production and Consumption of a Quasilegal Commodity in Northeast Africa," in *Social Life of Things*, pp. 236–57.

42. Sharon Hutchinson, "The Nuer in Crisis: Coping with Money, War, and the State" (Ph.D. diss., University of Chicago, 1988), p. 179.

43. Ibid., p. 152.

44. Ibid., pp. 108, 110, 115–16, 148, 149, 152–62, 176, 179.

45. Quoted in Martin Jay, *Marxism and Totality: The Adventures of a Concept from Lukacs to Habermas* (Berkeley: University of California Press, 1984), p. 521.

46. Robert Young, *White Mythologies: Writing History and the West* (London and New York: Routledge, 1990), p. 13. See Young also on the relationship between the general intellectual crisis and the end of empire. He argues that the French intellectual crisis was precipitated by the loss of Algeria, not by the events of 1968. On the place of the Other, see Johannes Fabian, *Time and the Other: How Anthropology Makes Its Object* (New York: Columbia University Press, 1983); Mudimbe, *Invention of Africa*; and Edward Said, *Orientalism* (New York: Vintage Books, 1979). For some of the discussion on ethnocentrism, history, and intellectual categories, see Claude Lévi-Strauss, *La Pensée Sauvage* (Paris: Plon, 1962), pp. 324–60; Jacques Derrida, *Writing and Difference*, trans. Alan Bass (London and Henley: Routledge and Kegan Paul, 1978), pp. 278–93; idem, *Of Grammatology*, trans. Gayatri Chakravorty Spivak (Baltimore and London: Johns Hopkins University Press, 1974), pp. 244–45. Foucault, of course, found the other within European society, in his study of madness.

47. Edward Said, "Orientalism Reconsidered," in *Europe and Its Others*, ed. Francis Barker, Peter Hulme, Margaret Iversen, and Diana Loxley (Colchester: University of Essex, 1985), 1:17.

48. Fabian, *Time and the Other*.

49. Steven Feierman, *Peasant Intellectuals: Anthropology and History in Tanzania* (Madison: University of Wisconsin Press, 1990), pp. 53–64.

50. For a detailed discussion of these positions, see Feierman, "African Histories and the Dissolution of World History," pp. 190–93.

51. Marcia Wright, "Women in Peril: A Commentary on the Life Stories of Captives in Nineteenth Century East-Central Africa," *African Social Research* 20 (1975):800–819; and *Women in Peril: Life Stories of Four Captives* (Lusaka: Neczam, 1984).

52. Wright, *Women in Peril*, p. 2.

53. Godfrey Wilson, *The Constitution of Ngonde*, The Rhodes-Livingstone Papers, no. 3 (Livingstone, Northern Rhodesia: The Rhodes-Livingstone Institute, 1939), p. 13.

54. Wilson describes the ranked bridewealth payments in ibid., p. 44. On adultery with a chief's wife as an act of war among the Bemba, see Andrew

Roberts, *A History of the Bemba* (Madison: University of Wisconsin Press, 1973), pp. 41–42, 107n, 122, 140, 143, 167, 237, 250, 263.

55. Wilson, *Constitution of Ngonde*, p. 18.

56. Ibid., pp. 12–18.

57. Ibid., p. 18.

58. On the Ngoni of this region, see J. A. Barnes, *Politics in a Changing Society: A Political History of the Fort Jameson Ngoni* (London, Cape Town, New York: Oxford University Press, 1954); Donald Fraser, *Winning a Primitive People* (Westport, Conn.: Negro Universities Press, 1970 [1st ed. 1914]); W. A. Elmslie, *Among the Wild Ngoni* 3d ed. (London: Frank Cass, 1970 [1st ed. 1899]); Thomas T. Spear, "Zwangendaba's Ngoni 1821–1890: A Political and Social History of Migration" (M.A. thesis, University of Wisconsin–Madison, 1969), offers a guide to the sources.

59. Alexis Kagame, *Un Abrégé de l'ethno-histoire du Rwanda*, vol. 2, (Butare: Editions Universitaires du Rwanda, 1975), and "La Documentation du Rwanda sur l'Afrique interlacustre des temps anciens," in *La Civilisation ancienne des peuples des Grands Lacs* (Paris: Editions Karthala, 1981), pp. 300–330; Joseph Rwabukumba and Vincent Mudandagizi, "Les Formes historiques de la dependence personelle dans l'état rwandais," *Cahiers d'Etudes Africaines* 14, no. 1 (1974). See also Jan Vansina, *L'Évolution du royaume rwanda des origines à 1900* (Brussels: ARSOM, 1962); A. Coupez and Th. Kamanzi, *Récits historiques Rwanda*, Sciences humaines, no. 43 (Tervuren: Musée Royal de l'Afrique Centrale, 1962); and Jan Vansina, *Oral Tradition as History* (Madison: University of Wisconsin Press, 1985), pp. 38, 86.

60. Feierman, *Peasant Intellectuals; Catharine Newbury, The Cohesion of Oppression: Clientship and Ethnicity in Rwanda, 1860–1960* (New York: Columbia University Press, 1988).

CHAPTER 3

Haiti, History, and the Gods

JOAN DAYAN

The child of savage Africa,
Sold to fall under the colonist's whip,
Founded independence on the soil of slavery,
And the Hill, in its voice, echoed the language
   of Racine and Fénélon!
     (M. Chauvet, Chant lyrique, *1825)*[1]

"RID US of these gilded Africans, and we shall have nothing more to wish," Napoleon wrote to his brother-in-law General Leclerc in 1802. Though successful in Guadeloupe and Martinique, Napoleon's soldiers, commanded first by Leclerc and then by Rochambeau, failed to reestablish slavery in Saint-Domingue. The only locale in history of a successful slave revolution, Saint-Domingue became the first black republic in 1804. Dessalines tore the white from the French tricolor—"Mouché, chiré blanc là qui lan drapeau-là" (Tear out the white from the flag, Monsieur)[2]—as he would remove the name "Saint-Domingue" from the former colony. He called the new nation "Haiti," from the original Amerindian word (*Ayti*) for the island, which meant "mountainous lands."

Called "Black France" by one nineteenth-century observer (Jules Michelet) or this "France with frizzy hair" by another (Maxine Raybaud) or merely a "tropical dog-kennel and pestiferous jungle" by Thomas Carlyle, Haiti forced imagination high and low: expression moved uneasily between the extremes of idealization and debasement. In the background of this textualized and cursedly mimetic Haiti, however, remained certain legends, blurred but persistent oral traditions that resisted such coercive dichotomies as genteel and brute, master and slave, precious language and common voice. Though Haiti's "Africanness," like its "Frenchness," would be used by writers for differing purposes, the business of *being Haitian* was more complex, and the slippages and uneasy alliances between contradictions more pronounced than most writerly representations of Haiti ever allowed.

ROMANCING THE DARK WORLD

A series of articles on Haiti appeared in the *Petite Presse* in Paris from September 8 to December 31, 1881. Written by a black Martiniquais M. Cochinat, the columns reported on everything from vodou to the military, calling attention to the Haitians' love of artifice, their propensity to exaggerate and mime, and their apparent indifference to the bloody revolutions that followed independence in 1804. Cochinat also turned to vodou and to tales of cannibalism and magic in order to prove to his French audience that Haiti remained unregenerate.[3]

Louis-Joseph Janvier published his alternately strident and elegiac response to Cochinat in Paris in 1883.[4] Janvier, born in Port-au-Prince, was the first in his family to be educated. In 1877, when he was twenty-two, he received a scholarship from the Haitian government to study in France. There he remained, for twenty-eight years, until 1905. His collection of meditations, called *La République d'Haïti et ses visteurs, 1840–1882*, contained long passages from the abolitionist Victor Schoelcher, Oliver Wendell Holmes, and M. Victor Meignan, and a preface packed with quotations from Michelet, Chateaubriand, Hugo, Renan, Danton, Lamartine, and Christophe. Janvier claimed that Haitians were on the road to civilization, arguing that the bloodiest political crimes in his country simply proved that "Haiti always imitates Europe."

> Be indulgent, oh sons of western Europe!
>
> Recall—I am citing at random, unconcerned about chronology—recall the Sicilien Vespers, the *holy* Inquisition . . . the Albegensian massacre, the war of the Two Roses, the massacre of Strelitz, the sacking of ghettos, the religious wars in England, which is to say the papists hanged by the anti-papists, and the anti-papists burned by the papists, Saint-Barthelemy, the days of September 1792, the 10th of August, the red Terror, the 13th Vendemiaire, the 18th Brumaire, the white Terror, the June days of 1848, December 2, 1851; the month of May 1871 . . . be indulgent.

When Janvier wrote his defense of Haiti, about 90 percent of the population were peasants. Romanticized for their pastoral innocence and endurance, those whom foreigners had condemned as remnants of "dark Africa" were transformed by Janvier into French-speaking, God-fearing laborers. The ground upon which he constructed his fable of the Haitian nation—proud, vital, earthy, and black—they served as an appropriate symbol of the new Haiti: a gothic Eden resurrected on the ashes of colonial Saint-Domingue. Whether they inhabited the plains or the hills, the peasants Janvier idealized were fiercely independent, attached to their lands, and devoted to their gods. Yet Janvier's sense of "the Haitian" depended on his refutation of vodou, which he denounced as "primitive." He assured his readers that all Haitians were now Catholic or Protestant, that all traces of barbarism had disappeared, and that most Haitians spoke French. After all, Janvier concluded, "French prose, Haitian coffee, and the philosophical doctrines of the French Revolution are the best stimulants of the Haitian brain."[5]

BLACK SKIN, WHITE HEART

The turning of Saint-Domingue into Haiti, colony into republic, demanded a new history that would be written by people who saw themselves as renewing the work of the French, who had once abolished slavery and declared slaves not only men but citizens. Yet the reactionary conceptual flotsam of the old regime, and the appropriate tags of "civilization," "order," and "dignity," would clash with a "fanaticism" that had no proper language and no right to history. Could the history of the Haitian revolution be told in the language of France? As Haitian historians attempted to gain access to "civilization," someone else's language (and at least part of the history that went with it) was necessary to their entitlement.

If the justification of slavery depended on converting a biological fact into a metaphysical truth—black = savage/white = civilized—the descendant of slaves must not only pay tribute to those who enslaved, but make himself white, while remaining black. The complex working out of personal identity through a duplicity or doubling of color proves crucial to the making of a nation, and shapes the way the first two major Haitian historians, Thomas Madiou and Beaubrun Ardouin, introduced themselves. Though a mulatto who lived in Paris for ten years, Ardouin focused on his African ancestry. He announced himself in his "Introduction" as "Descendant of this African race that has been so long persecuted," and at the end of his eleven-volume history (published in 1853–60), he exclaimed: "Glory to all these children of Africa. . . . Honor to their memory!" Madiou, also mulatto, lived in France from the age of ten until he was twenty-one. Unlike Ardouin, who defended the class of *affranchis*, whether mulatto or black (ignoring their interest, after the decree of May 15, 1791, in preserving slavery), Madiou refused to account for Haitian history according to the "official" mulatto view. He would later be claimed by Haitian ideologues as the *noiriste* historian of Haiti. His fiery assessment of Dessalines as a Haitian Robespierre, "this angel of death," based on interviews in the 1840s with former revolutionaries, departed from the critical disdain of the more moderate and elite *éclairées*. If Dessalines was savage, Madiou countered that he remained the "Principle incarnate of Independence; he was barbaric against colonial barbarism."

For both Madiou and Ardouin the labor of writing history demanded that the historian be seen as human while remaining Haitian. They turned to France and the white world, but claimed blackness and repaired the image of Africa, by making Haiti, purified of superstition, sorcerers, and charms, the instrument of reclamation. Their ability to reclaim and represent their "native land" to a foreign audience depended ultimately on their variously authentic and partly spurious claims of color, but, most important, on the wielding of proper language. Both Madiou and Ardouin concluded their introductions by apologizing not for color but for style. In Ardouin's case, especially, the apology helped him prove his nationality, affirmed by nothing less than his resolutely faltering or broken French. He articulated, perhaps for the first time, what Edouard Glissant much later would name *antillanité*, and what Césaire, speaking about his choice of writing poetry in French not Creole, would qualify as French with the *marque nègre*: "If this work finds some readers in Paris, they will see many infelicities of style, still more faults in the rules of grammar: it will offer them no literary merit. But they should not forget that, in general, Haitians stammer the words of the French language, in order to emphasize in some way their origin in the Antilles."[6] Ardouin no doubt remembered his predecessor's conclusion to his introduction. In *Histoire d'Haïti* Madiou had addressed his readers: "I beseech the reader to show himself indulgent concerning the style of my work, all I did was attempt to be correct, since at 1,800 leagues from the hearth of our language, in a country where nearly the entire population speaks Creole, it is quite impossible that French would not suffer the influence of those idioms I have meanwhile tried to avoid."[7]

BETWEEN CIVILIZATION AND BARBARISM

In Port-au-Prince on April 16, 1848, the very black and illiterate President Faustin Soulouque began the massacre of mulattoes he suspected as conspirators. In Paris a "Prince President," Louis Napoleon, who had just come out on the other side of the barricades and blood of the June 1848 revolution, exclaimed, "Haïti, Haïti, pays de barbares!" The nephew of Napoleon—Marx's "caricature of the old Napoleon"—did not have it easy. When he declared himself emperor a year after the coup d'état of December 2, 1851, he found himself not only described as Marx's caricature and Hugo's "Napoleon le petit," but compared to the

Haitian Soulouque. The trivializing of revolution (in Haiti the 1843 and 1844 rebellions in the south) and the spectacle of reaction brought Haiti and France together in a knot of contamination.

Soulouque declared himself Emperor Faustin I on August 25, 1849. Spenser St. John thought this act typical of a racially particular obsession: "All black chiefs have a hankering after the forms as well as the substance of despotic power."[8] Imitating the genuine Bonaparte, Soulouque crowned himself, then crowned the empress, and created a nobility of four princes, fifty-nine dukes, two marquises, ninety counts, two hundred barons, and thirty chevaliers. About three years later, in France Louis Napoleon became emperor and brought the Second Republic to an end.

In *The Eighteenth Brumaire of Louis Bonaparte* (1851), Marx compared what he called "the best" of Louis Napoleon's "bunch of blokes" to "a noisy, disreputable, rapacious bohème that crawls into gallooned coats with the same grotesque dignity as the high dignitaries of Soulouque."[9] Referring to the hollow Bonaparte, Hugo wrote a poem about "A monkey [who] dressed himself in a tiger's skin" ("Fable or History," *Les Châtiments*, 1853). Though most obviously referring to the dubious royalty and bombast of Louis Napoleon, the horrific slaughters of Hugo's poem could not fail to remind readers of Soulouque's outrages. Hugo's parting shot in "Fable or History" could be taken as a product of racialist ideology: "You are only a monkey!"

Gustave d'Alaux (pen name for Maxine Raybaud, the French consul during part of Soulouque's reign), wrote *L'Empereur Soulouque et son empire*, parts of which appeared as a series of articles in the metropolitan *Revue des deux-mondes* (1850–51) and finally as a book in 1856. He introduced his readers to a place where you could find "civilization and the Congo," and "newspapers and sorcerers."[10] Even American abolitionist Wendell Phillips, rendering homage to Toussaint and the Haitian revolution in Boston and New York in 1861, reminded his listeners how much events in Haiti mattered to the new Napoleon in France: "the present Napoleon . . . when the epigrammatists of Paris christened his wasteful and tasteless expense at Versailles, *Soulouquerie*, from the name of Soulouque, the Black Emperor, he deigned to issue a specific order forbidding the use of the word."[11]

A later Haitian historian, Dantès Bellegarde in *La Nation haïenne* (1938), lamented that the reputation of Soulouque suffered from the illegitimate actions of Louis Napoleon. Soulouque's character was defamed when the French made him the vessel for their disdain of their emperor. His words are crucial to understanding how different history might be if we jostle our ideas of cause and effect.

The crowning of the Emperor, celebrated with unmatched magnificence, resulted in cruel jokes about Soulouque in the liberal French press and thus avenged the coup d'état of December 2, 1851 by the Prince-President Louis Napoleon. And when, by the plebiscite of November 20, 1852, he had himself proclaimed Emperor, they accused him of having aped [singé] Faustin I, and the more one blackened Soulouque, the more odious appeared the imitation of his grotesque act by the old member of the Italian Carbonari. The hatred of Napoleon the little, as the poet of the *Châtiments* referred to him, contributed much to giving the chief of the Haitian State his unfortunate reputation as a ridiculous and blood-thirsty sovereign.[12]

Rereading events in France through the quizzing glass of Haiti is to clarify the reciprocal dependencies, the uncanny resemblances that no ideology of mastery can remove. Who is "aping" whom? The question must have haunted Beaubrun Ardouin when he found himself in Paris, having escaped from the murderous Soulouque, happy to find himself in the "Republic" he praised in a letter to Lamartine, only to see *liberty* turn again into *monarchy*: the country he had turned to as example for his "young Haiti" flipping over, again, into empire.

NO EASY LIBERTY

Ardouin appreciated the business of politics. Friend and partisan of the tough mulatto Major General Jean-Pierre Boyer (an *ancien affranchi*), who governed Haiti from 1820 to 1843, Ardouin as senator had negotiated the financial settlement with France in 1825: 150 million francs indemnity to be paid to the dispossessed French planters of Saint-Domingue in order to obtain French recognition of the independence of its former colony, which was given in a royal ordinance from King Charles X.

Madiou, never one to mince words, imagined what the heroes of the revolution would do if they left their tombs only to see the French flag flying in the cities of the new republic, while Haitians curried favor and became indebted to the descendants of colonial torturers. But it was Boyer's 1826 Code Rural that reduced most Haitians, especially those who did not occupy positions of rank in the military or civil branches of the state, to slave status. A small fraction of Haiti's population could live off the majority, collecting fees—with the help of their lackeys, the rural *chefs de section*—for produce, for the sale, travel, and butchering of animals, and even for the cutting of trees. In *Les Constitutions d'Haïti* (1886), addressed primarily to a Haitian audience, Janvier described

Boyer's code as "slavery without the whip." Jonathan Brown, an American physician from New Hampshire who spent a year in Haiti, recalled his impressions of Boyer's regime in *The History and Present Condition of St. Domingo* (1837): "The existing government of Hayti is a sort of republican monarchy sustained by the bayonet."[13]

In 1843 and 1844 there were two revolutions that Ardouin would later describe as the "tragedy" of his generation: the popular army of Praslin, led by Charles Rivière-Hérard, and the next year, the Piquet rebellion, led by the black southerner and police lieutenant Louis Jean-Acaau "to defend the interests of the poor of all classes." The crises of 1843–44 compelled Ardouin to write his history. The "Proclamation de Praslin," though ostensibly speaking for the people, and condemning Boyer's officials, including Ardouin, as traitors, was really a document contrived by Rivière-Hérard and other mulattoes, disgruntled Boyarists who wanted some of the power. Acaau's *l'armée souffrante*, along with the resistance of members of the black elite like Lysius Salomon, resulted in Rivière-Hérard's overthrow. Salomon's petition to the provisional government of Rivière-Hérard (June 22, 1843) is a marvel of recall and revision: "Citizens! Dessalines and Pétion cry out to you from the bottom of their graves; . . . Save Haiti, our communal mother; don't let her perish . . . save her. . . . The abolitionists rejoice and applaud you."[14]

Recognizing that it would be useless to resist these variously contrived liberation movements, Boyer addressed the senate for the last time on March 13, 1843, before leaving, like subsequent overthrown Haitian presidents, for Jamaica. Then began five years of instability comprising four short-lived presidencies. The phenomenon of Faustin Soulouque and Haiti's crisis of legitimacy resulted from what could be called a comedy of color. The mulatto oligarchs of Haiti reacted to the possibility of yet another revolution by contriving what became known as the *politique de la doublure*. The politics of the understudy allowed the light-skinned elites to remain in power, but under cover of blackness. Mulattoes in the turbulent 1840s were the heart of power, while selecting black skins as masks.

After a trinity of old, black illiterates (Philippe Guerrier, eighty-seven years old, directed by Céligny and Beaubrun Ardouin; Jean-Louis Pierot, eighty-four; and Jean-Baptiste Riché, seventy), Soulouque was chosen by those whom Spenser St. John called "the enlightened Ministers of the late General Riché." Beaubrun Ardouin, as head of the senate, proposed the illiterate, black, and apparently malleable General Soulouque as president of Haiti on March 1, 1847. When, a year later, Soulouque killed Ardouin's brother Céligny, Ardouin, former minister of Haiti to the French government, returned to France where he wrote his *Etudes*. He never lost, even in exile, the capacity to name heroes or to please his patrons. Whether praising the Republic of 1848 or the subsequent empire of Napoleon III, Ardouin held fast to France. But he carefully excluded the slave-owners, those who fought for the colonial system, from those he called "the true French."

Who is the true Haitian? Ardouin's answer to the question gives definition the utility of not defining. Though he claimed himself as "Descendant of Africa" and condemned the injustices of the colonial government against "the men of the black race which is my own," he asserted that the road to being Haitian must progress away from the dark continent toward his present audience, those who represented enlightened France. He remained uncomfortable with "oral and popular traditions," and most of all, with "superstitious practices derived from Africa," summed up as "the barbarism . . . that brutalizes souls." Ardouin emphasized the attributes that made Haiti worthy of the France he esteemed (and identified Haitians who thought like him as most qualified to command): same religion, language, ideals, principles, customs, and he concluded, "a taste preserved for French products." For France "has deposited the germ of its advanced civilization." Now, with Napoleon III, under "the reign of a monarch enlightened and just," Haiti could profit from the "lights [*les lumières*] of its former metropole."

"Sucking from the breasts of France," as Ardouin had once put it in a letter to Lamartine (who, as minister for foreign affairs in the provisional government of 1848, would definitively abolish slavery in the French colonies), Haiti would turn, emptied of its gods and its magic, to both "the revolution of 1789 . . . this torch of French Genius" and to the Napoleonic eagle. On January 15, 1859, General Fabre Nicholas Geffrard overthrew Soulouque. Ardouin returned briefly to Haiti and then departed again for Paris as minister plenipotentiary.[15]

DESSALINES, DESSALINES DEMANBRE

On October 17, 1806, Jean-Jacques Dessalines, "chef suprême des indigènes," the first president and emperor of Haiti, was murdered in an ambush at Pont-Rouge by soldiers from the south on the road from Marchand (now Dessalines) to Port-au-Prince. The assassination order came from a clique of mulattoes and blacks from the west and south, including his friend General Pétion. Christophe knew of the plan. A young officer shot Dessalines. General Yayou stabbed him three times. Vaval filled him with bullets from two pistols. Then he was stripped naked; his fingers were cut off so that the jeweled rings could be removed. Stories vary about the details of the mutilation. Even Ardouin, not given to melodrama, hesitated before recounting what happened to the corpse after Dessalines was assassinated by the men with whom he had fought: "one must pause at this appalling outrage."[16]

By the time the body reached Port-au-Prince, after the two-mile journey, it could not be recognized. The head was shattered, the feet, hands and ears cut off. In some accounts, Dessalines was stoned and hacked to pieces by the crowd, and his remains—variously described as "scraps," "shapeless remains," "remnants," or "relics"—were thrown to the crowd. According to Madiou, American merchants hustled to buy his fingers with gold. "They attached an importance to the relics of the founder of our Independence that Haitians, transported by such horrible fury, did not then feel."[17] That foreign merchants bargained for Dessalines' fleshly remnants tells us something about the role of Dessalines as martyr of liberty. Yet this is only part of the story, for popular vengeance turned Dessalines into matter for resurrection. Dessalines, the most unregenerate of Haitian leaders, was made into a *lwa* (god, image, or spirit) by the Haitian people. The "liberator" with his red silk scarf was the only "Black Jacobin" to become a god. Neither the radical rationality of Toussaint nor the sovereign pomp of Christophe led to apotheosis. Yet Dessalines, so resistant to enlightened heroics, gradually acquired unequaled power in the Haitian imagination.

Dessalines was born on the Cormiers plantation in a parish now known as the Commune of Grande-Rivière du Nord sometime in 1758. In 1794 Dessalines became Toussaint's guide through Grande Rivière du Nord. At the time of the revolution, Toussaint was a literate coachman, and later steward of all the livestock on the Bréda plantation. Christophe (born in Grenada) was a waiter, then a manager, and finally an owner of La Couronne, an inn at Cap François. Dessalines, first owned by a brutal white named Duclos, was then sold to a black master. Whenever Dessalines wanted to justify his hatred of the French, it is said that he liked to display his scar-covered back.[18] We should think for a moment about the problems in speaking about the figure of the hero who was once a slave, a man who would refer to himself as "Duclos" (his name in servitude), recalling for his listeners, even as emperor, his identity as an item of property.

Rejecting things French, unconcerned about social graces, turning away from the customs, language, and principles Ardouin would see as that part of the Haitian inheritance that made his country worthy of recognition by "civilized" Europe, Dessalines made a vexed entry into history. Perhaps more than either Toussaint (who had the habit of asking the women who visited him, in a tender but nasal twang, "Have you taken communion this morning?") or Christophe, Dessalines recognized the temptations of civilization, which for him meant a new, more subtle servitude. He understood how easily rebels or republicans could themselves become masters. Speaking of the *anciens libres*, those freed before Sonthonax's General Emancipation decree of August 1793, which abolished slavery in Saint-Domingue, Dessalines declared, "Beware, negroes and mulattoes! We have fought against the whites. The goods that we have won in spilling our blood belong to everyone. I intend that they be shared fairly."[19] Madiou emphasized Dessalines' preference for steering clear of the established cities, "so that European corruption could not reach him," choosing to establish himself at Marchand, situated in the plain of the Artibonite at the foot of the Cahos hills.[20]

Spenser St. John recognized "the only quality" of Dessalines as "a kind of brute courage. . . . he was nothing but an African savage."[21] It is said that when Leclerc, who had earlier praised Dessalines as "butcher of the blacks" in a letter to Napoleon in September 1802, learned of his defection from the French a month later, he cried out, "How could I have been so deceived by a *barbare!*" The two most important twentieth-century poets of Martinique, Aimé Césaire and Edouard Glissant, do not write about Dessalines. Perhaps they had difficulty (in spite of their rhetoric or their desire) acknowledging the chief who called his people to arms with the command, "Koupe tèt, boule kay" (Cut off their heads, burn their houses). Glissant wrote the play *Monsieur Toussaint* (1961). Césaire turned to Toussaint in his *Révolution française et le problème colonial* (1981), as well as writing *La Tragédie du Roi Christophe* (1963).

Haitians especially have had a difficult time writing about the general whose uncompromising ferocity had become legendary. More embarrassing still were stories of the surfeit and abandon of his reign. Surrounded by cunning ministers, Dessalines recognized too late the need to curb their excesses. Madiou and others recount Dessalines' passion for dancing and women, especially Couloute, his favorite mistress. The emperor's ardor inspired a celebrated and much popularized *carabinier* (a wilder, more energetic and undulating kind of *méringue*): "The Emperor comes to see Couloute dance."[22] At one particularly luxurious ball, when a dancing Dessalines leapt into the air and landed on his knee before Couloute, Christophe is reported to have remarked (loud enough for Dessalines to hear him): "See His Majesty! Aren't you ashamed to have such a *sauteur* [meaning both "jumper" and "temporizer" or "chameleon"] as our leader!"

Hyperbolized by Madiou as a "thunderbolt of arbitrariness," Dessalines fought at different times against the French and the African-born former slaves *nèg bosal*, *nèg ginen*, or *nèg kongo* who never collaborated with the French. These *maroons*, such as Ti-Noel, Sans Souci, Macaya, Cacapoule, and other unnamed insurgents of the hills who formed armed bands of nearly a thousand men, refused to surrender to Leclerc as did Christophe and Dessalines after the loss of the battle of Crête-à-Pierrot and the removal of Toussaint in 1802.[23] According to historian Henock Trouillot, writing about Dessalines in the Haitian newspaper, *Le Nouvelliste*, "His name alone, in spite of the contradictions of his attitude, became a symbol among blacks."[24] In December 1802 his authority was so great that the mulatto general Pétion knew he had no choice but to fight under the black who had, only two years before, under Toussaint's orders, bathed the south of Haiti in the blood of mulattos.

A number of oral traditions haunt the written remains of Dessalines, who would become general in chief of the Army of Independence. In a story reported by both Trouillot and Mentor Laurent, African bands called *takos*, including a rebel named Jean Zombi and "other types full of fire," surrounded Dessalines in Plaisance, refusing to listen to him and saying, "We do not deal with whites." According to Trouillot, Dessalines replied: "Look at my face. Am I white? Don't you recognize the soldier of Crête-à-Pierrot? Was I white at the Petite-Rivière of the Artibonite when the expedition arrived? Ask these hills covered with French bones. They will nominate Dessalines as the hero of these trophies."[25]

Historians even disagree about the languages Dessalines could speak. Some say he spoke in "Congo," a general attribution for the specific African "nations" or "tribes" in Saint-Domingue (Arada, Nago, Congo, Fon, Ibo, Bambara) that came to designate "African" or the "secret" or "magic" language of initiates in vodou. In *Les Limites du Créole dans notre enseignement*, Trouillot cites from Antoine Metral's *Histoire de l'expédition français au St. Domingue* words that suggest that even though he did not speak their language, Dessalines could gesturally, figurally become African: "His savage eloquence was more in certain expressive signs than in words." Trouillot concluded: "By fantastic gestures Dessalines managed more than once to make himself understood by Africans, so it seemed, when he did not speak the dialect."[26] We are dealing, therefore, with a Creole who could take on the role of an African as easily as he could serve the French.

Dessalines controlled his own passage between apparent extremes and thrived on the composite histories of his locale. According to Madiou, Dessalines called the populations subject to his authority "Incas or children of the sun," memorializing the 1780 Inca uprising in Peru. According to Haitian Marxist historian Etienne Charlier, when Dessalines called the new black republic "Haiti," retrieving its original Amerindian name, he "transcend[ed] his race and present[ed] himself as the avenger of the Indians."[27] Dessalines, also believed to have been a vodou adept (and in some stories, sorcerer), was known to have massacred cult leaders and their devotees. Yet Gustave d'Alaux in *L'Empereur*

Soulouque et son empire explained that while Toussaint and Christophe, obsessed with the trappings of culture, pitilessly suppressed vodou practitioners, "Dessalines, in spite of his either sincere or pretended infatuation with African savagery, was himself mixed up with the papas (conjure-men)." D'Alaux reported that once, before going into battle, Dessalines covered himself with magic talismans in order to become invulnerable. But wounded in the first discharge of fire, Dessalines beat up the "sorcerer" and took back the money he had paid for the consultation.[28]

Two of the concerns that account for the admiration and disdain summoned by Dessalines' name are race and land. In the constitution of 1805, he declared that no white, whatever his nation, could set foot on the territory of Haiti as master or owner of property (Art. 12). Who could be Haitian? For Dessalines, certain whites could be naturalized as Haitians: for example, white women who had conceived or would bear Haitian children and those Germans and Poles who deserted Leclerc's army during 1802–3 to fight with the *indigènes* (Art. 13). Further, Haitians, whatever their color, would be known as *blacks*, referred to "only by the generic word *black*" (Art. 14).[29] Since the most problematic division in the new Haiti was that between anciens libres (mostly *gens de couleur*, mulattoes, and their offspring) and *nouveaux libres* (the newly free, who were mostly black), Dessalines attempted by linguistic means and by law to defuse the color issue.

If Dessalines promised a reconciliation of persons of differing grades of color, it was nevertheless a conversion that depended, at least verbally, on the blackening so feared by both colonists and the mulatto elite. "In a word, one could say that a colored population, left to itself is fatally destined to become black again at the end of a very few generations." The lapse Pierre de Vassière described in *Saint-Domingue: la société et la vie Créoles sous l'ancien régime (1629–1789)*, the mixture that can transform white into mulatto and then mulatto "to the most absolute black," was for the colonist the feared and fatal "law of regression" or "reversion."[30]

Consider what remained of colonial divisions in Saint-Domingue in 1804:

Color	"Native Land"	Status
whites	France	free
people of color	Saint-Domingue	freed
blacks	Africa	slaves

Though blacks were also *libres* (free) and not all whites were masters, this tripartite organization of white masters at the top, servile blacks at the bottom, and freed *gens de couleur* (people of color) in between operated as the crucial ideological structure in colonial Saint-Domingue. How else could the "mentality" of servitude be sustained, except through an accentuation of the color distinction? Dessalines took the "lowest" rung and made it a synecdoche for the whole.[31]

In his *Description topographique, physique, civile, politique et historique de la partie française de l'isle Saint-Domingue* (written between 1776 and 1789, published in 1797), Moreau de Saint-Méry distinguished 128 parts of "blood" that variously combined resulted in the possible nuances of skin color among free coloreds.[32] The combinatorial fiction, surely one of the more remarkable legalistic fantasies of the New World, reminded the mulatto, especially, that no matter how white the skin, the tainted blood haunts the body. Dessalines' answer to the hair-splitting subtleties of Moreau de Saint-Méry was to get rid of the distinctions, but some would argue that he created a categorization even more coercive than Moreau de Saint-Méry's fable of color. For Dessalines tried to accomplish nothing less than an epistemological conversion: a curse would be removed, and then reproduced as salvation. To be called black on the soil of Haiti would be proof of Haitian identity.

But it was Dessalines' attempt to redefine the ownership of land that cost him his life. In 1804 he rescinded all transfers of property made after October 1802, thus removing mulatto claims to valuable plantations. In 1805 he decided that all land titles would have to be verified. Tradition has it that Dessalines would check for the authenticity of land titles by smelling them to discover those that had been smoked to make them look old: "ça pas bon, ça senti fumée" (it's no good, it smells smoked). According to many this was a direct attack on the anciens affranchis, those who had taken, or had been given land formerly owned by their white planter fathers.

In his constitution Dessalines had given equal rights to both legitimate children and those recognized by their fathers but born out of wedlock, thus accepting the prevalence of *plaçage* or consensual union, not wishing to coerce his people, those he called "natives of Haiti," to follow the marital rituals of the whites. According to Madiou, Dessalines said it would be unjust to establish unequal rights in inheritance between men who had come out of servitude and degradation: "the *indigènes* had all been . . . legitimized by the revolution." However, for Dessalines there could be no kinship with a white colonist. No mulatto could claim that he was entitled to his father's land. Ardouin, a descendant of the disenfranchised anciens affranchis, argued that land reform was "an attack on the sacred right of property." But for Janvier, and other later Haitian historians, Dessalines "wanted to make the genuine independence of the peasant possible by making him an owner of land."[33]

When we ask what made possible the second coming of Dessalines as hero and god, we must attend to his vision of the *true* Haitian. He gave property to those slaves who had, only recently, been considered property. The division of land, his attempt to destroy "false" property titles, and the violence with which he tried to carry out what has been called "an impossible reform of the mentality of the ruling classes, and perhaps his own mentality,"[34] would make him the favorite of left-leaning, twentieth-century novelists like René Depestre and Jacques-Stéphen Alexis. As the sociologist and anthropologist Anténor Firmin put it in *De L'Égalité des races humaines*, his 1885 response to Gobineau's *De L'Inégalité des races humaines*: "For us, sons of those who suffered the humiliations and martyrdom of slavery, we could see there [in Dessalines' actions] the first manifestation of the sentiment of racial equality, a sentiment which Dessalines still personifies in Haiti."[35]

Between Dessalines' death in 1806 and Lysius Salomon's (the finance minister during la politique de doublure) speech in memory of the "emperor-martyr" in 1845, the transition from oblivion to glory had taken place. Speaking at the parish church in Cayes, October 17, 1845, Salomon proclaimed: "Avenger of the black race, liberator of Haiti, founder of national independence, Emperor Dessalines! Today is your glory, the sun today burns for you as radiantly as it did in 1804." Before Salomon's scandalous speech, which blamed "the aristocracy of color" for Dessalines' death (and earned Salomon, who was later called "the eater of mulattoes," their lasting fury), previous governments had ignored or condemned "The Liberator."

One exception was the cunning political move by the mulatto Charles Rivière-Hérard in January 1844, during the forty-first anniversary of the founding of the state of Haiti. As Madiou put it: "He made a speech where, for the first time since the death of Dessalines in October 1806, these words came out of the mouth of a President of the Republic: 'It is to the glorious Dessalines, it is to his immortal comrades that the Country owes the new era into which she enters.' " Madiou reminded his readers that Rivière-Hérard was part of the class that despised Dessalines, the large landowners of Cayes, who had most to lose when Dessalines began his call for property reform. He "belonged to a class of citizens who saw in Dessalines nothing but a barbaric despot that they had sacrificed; but since they planned a *coup d'état*, they had to draw on the sympathies of the people by glorifying the founder of independence."[36] Yet, Madiou concluded, the people were not dupes of these "empty words," for they had heard that Dessalines' remains—unworthy of a mausoleum—still lay in a deserted grave, marked only by a brick tomb with the inscription in Creole: "Ce-git Dessalines, / Mort à 48 ans" (Here lies Dessalines, / Dead at 48 years-old).[37]

Some fifty years after Rivière-Hérard used the figure of Dessalines for his political designs, President Florvil Hyppolite built in France a modest monument in memory of Dessalines. Later, for the centenary cele-

bration of the Haitian nation, which actually marked the beginning of
the state cult of Dessalines, Justin Lhérison composed the national an-
them, the "Dessalinienne." Sung for the first time on January 1, 1904,
the song begins:

> For our Country
> For our Ancestors
> Let us march together
> No traitors in our ranks
> Let us be the only masters of the land.

But the monumentality that turned October 17 from a day that her-
alded liberation from a dictator to a day of mourning for his death was
devised by literate Haitians in the cities. Repressive governments, such
as that of Louis Borno under the U.S. occupation (1915–34), found the
erection of a mausoleum for the Liberator easier than affording their
subjects liberation from internal oppression and foreign control.

Called by the literate elite "The Great One," "The Savior," "The
Lover of Justice," and "The Liberator," the Dessalines remembered by
vodou initiates is far less comforting or instrumental. They know how
unheroic the hero turned god could be. The image of Dessalines in the
cult of the people remains equivocal and corruptible: a trace of what is
absorbed by the mind and animated in the gut. How inevitable are the
alternations back and forth from hero to detritus, from power to vulner-
ability, from awe to ridicule: a convertibility that vodou would keep
working, viable, and necessary.

Not simply master or tyrant, but slave or supplicant, Dessalines and
the religious rituals associated with him keep the ambiguities of power
intact. Unlike the spectacles of sanctification endorsed by the urban literati and the politicians, the history reconstructed by the gods and their
devotees is not always one of revolt and triumph. "Do you have the
heart to march in blood all the way to Cayes?" Dessalines asked the soldiers of his third brigade before his assassination in October 1806. Gods
held in the mind and embodied in ceremony reenact what historians
often forget: the compulsion to serve, the potency and virtue of atrocity.
The very suppressions, inarticulatenesses, and ruptures in ritual might
say something about the ambivalences of *the* revolution: it was not so
liberating as mythologizers or ideologues make it, and the dispossessed
who continue to suffer and remember know this.

DISMEMBERMENT, NAMING, AND DIVINITY

Vodou enters written history as a weird set-piece: the ceremony of Bois-
Caïman. The story is retold by nearly every historian, especially those

outsiders who enjoyed linking the first successful slave revolt to a gothic scene of blood-drinking and abandon. Though David Geggus has written in *Slavery, War, and Revolution: The British Occupation of Saint-Domingue, 1793–98*, that "the earliest mention of the famous Bois Caiman ceremony seems to be in Dalmas's *Histoire* of 1814," what matters is how necessary this story or myth remains to Haitians who continue to construct their identity by turning not only to the revolution of 1791, but by seeking its origins in a service quite possibly imagined by those who disdain it.[38]

On the stormy, lightning-filled night of August 14, 1791, in the middle of the Caiman woods, Boukman, an oungan (priest), and a manbo (priestess) conducted the ceremony that began the fight for independence. Madiou, though given to much melodramatic detail, did not include the ceremony in his history. But vodou, once displaced, reared its head a few pages following his descriptions of the uprising in the north. Madiou described Biassou, who with Jean-François led the revolt, surrounded by "sorcerers" and "magicians." His tent was filled with multicolored cats, snakes, bones of the dead, and other objects of what Madiou calls "African superstitions."[39] Ardouin described the ceremony of Bois-Caïman, but told his readers that he was "transcribing here an extract from the unedited works of Céligny Ardouin" that included information he received from an old soldier who resided in Saint-Domingue, in service of the king of Spain.[40]

Both Madiou and Ardouin recounted how blacks—"phantasiés," as Madiou put it, by sorcerers—threw themselves at cannons, believing the balls dust. When blown to pieces, they knew they would be reborn in Africa. The naturalist Descourtilz (his life was saved during the massacre of whites by Dessalines' wife, Claire Heureuse, who hid him under her bed) remembered how "the Congo Negroes and other Guineans were so superstitiously affected by the utterances of Dessalines that they even let him persuade them that to die fighting the French was only a blessing since it meant that they were immediately conveyed to Guinea, where, once again, they saw Papa Toussaint who was waiting for them to complete the army with which he proposed to reconquer Saint-Domingue."[41]

To reconstruct a history of the spirits in Haiti is no easy matter. How does thought about a glorified, if ambiguous past become palpable? How do we get from now to then, to a history beyond the reach of written history? Until the American occupation—and one could argue, the publication of Jean Price-Mars' *Ainsi parla l'oncle* (1928)—the Haitian elite looked upon vodou as an embarrassment.[42] Even Duverneau Trouillot, who published his "esquisse ethnographique" (ethnographic sketch), *Le Vaudoun: aperçu historique et évolutions* in 1885, while listing (for the first time, as far as I know, the individual spirits), felt that vodou in Haiti demonstrated the inevitable degradation of ancestral practices, reduced to "a tissue of rather ridiculous superstitions." Trouillot prophesied that Christian civilization would soon absorb these atavistic "remnants" or "debris."[43]

Born in Haiti, Dessalines is called a *lwa Krèyol* (Creole god). As "Ogou Desalin," he walks with the African Ogou, the gods of war and politics that remain in Haiti in their multiple aspects. Trouillot warned that after the revolution, African beliefs and rituals would continue to degenerate. But the old traditions and gods remained powerful, embracing the new events and leaders like Dessalines. With independence, the underground opposition to the now defeated white oppressor did not disappear, for the spirits, and the people's need for them, was not contingent on being suppressed. On the contrary, vodou came, to some extent, out into the open to thrive. But haltingly so, as though the people were keeping some of the old secrets hidden, ready to serve in other repressive situations that did not fail to occur.

In transcribing a popular song addressed to Dessalines, a student of oral history faces nearly insurmountable problems of translation and retrieval. Both Alfred Métraux in *Voodoo in Haiti* and Odette Mennesson-Rigaud and Lorimer Denis (Duvalier's comrade in folkloric exploration in the 1940s) in "Cérémonie en l'honneur de Marinette" record the following song, which I heard during a four-day genealogy of the gods in Bel Air, Haiti, in 1970: "Pito m'mouri passé m'couri / Pito m'mouri passé m'couri / Dessalines, Dessalines démembré / Vive la liberté" (Better to die than to run away / Better to die than to run away / Dessalines, Dessalines démembré / Long live liberty).[44] According to Mennesson-Rigaud this song was sung by Haitian soldiers during the revolution and is preserved in the militant Petwo ceremonies.[45] Both Métraux and Mennesson-Rigaud translate *démembré/demanbre* as "powerful." Yet in Creole the word means "dismembered," "beaten," or "battered." How did these two ethnographers come up with power out of accounts of Dessalines shot, kicked, and dismembered?

If we take both words as possible—indeed, as necessary records of the human capacities for knowledge, courage, and composure—then we have a Dessalines who is battered and powerful, dead and living. Talking with practitioners in Port-au-Prince in 1986, I heard another form of the word, which might be transcribed as *denambre*. Could denambre be a form of *dénombrer* or *dénommer*, to count or to name? Both activities—numbering and naming—carry great power for those who believe in the magic of numbers or the secret of naming; hence, such an appellation is powerful. Further, in Haiti *nam* means spirit, soul, gist, or sacred power. So, Dessalines denambre either has his spirit taken away; or, feared as sorcerer, he has the power to de-soul, to steal someone's spirit.

The history told by vodou defies our notions of identity and contradiction. A person or thing can be two or more things simultaneously. A word can be double, two-sided, and duplicitous. In spite of this instability, or what some argue to be the capriciousness of spirits and terminologies, something incontrovertible remains. In parts of contemporary Haiti the demanbre is fundamental to vodou. The piece of family land where the spirits reside, the demanbre, marks the spiritual heritage of the group.[46] Also defined as "the basic unit of peasant religion," "the common family yard," and "the center of the veneration of the dead," this sacred, ancestral land cannot be divided, sold, or given away.[47] Haiti was conceived as earth blooded with the purifying spirit of liberation. Dessalines, who thought of himself as father of all Haitians, the family henceforth to be known as "blacks," died for his attempt to give land to the disinherited. Serving Dessalines reinspirits what many believe to have been his legacy: the indivisible land of Haiti, consecrated by the revolution. Having lost his personal identity, he becomes the place. The dismembered hero is resurrected as sacred locale.

To serve Dessalines is sometimes less a sign of good fortune than the record of a cruel and demanding intimacy. The song about Dessalines demanbre joins the hero to a powerful "she-devil" or "sorceress," known as *kita-demanbre*. The feared Marinette-Bwa-Chèche (Marinette-dry-bones, dry-wood, or brittle arms), said to "mange moun" (eat people), is also called Marinette-Limen-dife (light-the-fire). Served with kerosene, pimento, and fire, she is the lwa who put the fire to the cannons used by Dessalines against the French. The other Petwo gods that bear the names of revolt, the traces of torture and revenge, like Brisé Pimba, Baron Ravage, Général Brisé, and Jean Zombi, recall the strange promiscuity between masters and slaves; white, black, and mulatto; old world and new. These rituals of memory could be seen as deposits of history. Shreds of bodies come back, remembered in ritual and seeking vengeance—whether blacks fed to the dogs by Rochambeau or whites massacred by Dessalines.

The lwa most often invoked by today's vodou practitioners do not go back to Africa; rather, they were born during the revolution. A historical streak in these spirits, entirely this side of metaphysics, reconstitutes the shadowy and powerful magical gods of Africa as everyday responses to the white master's arbitrary power. Driven underground, they survived and constituted a counterworld to white suppression. It is hardly surprising that when black deeds and national heroic action contested this mastery something new would be added to the older traditions.

The dispossession accomplished by slavery became the model for possession in vodou, for making a man not into a thing but into a spirit. In 1804, during Dessalines' massacre of the French, Jean Zombi, a mulatto of Port-au-Prince, earned a reputation for brutality. Known to be one of the fiercest slaughterers, Madiou described his "vile face," "red hair," and "wild eyes." He would leave his house, wild with fury, stop a white, then strip him naked. In Madiou's words, he "led him then to the steps of the government palace and thrust a dagger in his chest. This gesture horrified all the spectators, including Dessalines."[48] Jean Zombi was also mentioned by Hénock Trouillot as one of the takos who had earlier threatened Dessalines in Plaisance. Variously reconstituted and adaptable to varying events, Zombi crystallizes the crossing not only of spirit and man in vodou practices, but the intertwining of black and mulatto, African and Creole in the struggle for independence.

The ambiguities of traditions redefined by changing hopes, fears, and rememberings is exemplified by the brief mention of Jean Zombi in the 1950s by Milo Rigaud in *La Tradition voudoo et le voudoo haitien.* "Jean Zombi is one of the most curious prototypes of vodoun tradition. He was one of those, who on Dessalines' order, massacred the most whites during the liberation of Haiti from the French yoke. Jean Zombi is actually one of the most influential mysteries of the vodoun pantheon: as lwa, he belongs to the Petwo rite."[49] According to anthropologist Melville Herskovits, in Dahomean legend the zombi were beings without souls, "whose death was not real but resulted from the machinations of sorcerers who made them appear as dead, and then, when buried, removed them from their grave and sold them into servitude in some faraway land."[50]

Moreau de Saint-Méry, who presents for the first time in writing the night world of ghosts (*revenans*), spirits, *loup garoux* (vampires), and *zombi*, defines zombi as a "Creole word that means spirit, revenant."[51] The name zombi, once attached to the body of Jean, who killed off whites and avenged those formerly enslaved, revealed the effects of the new dispensation. Names, gods, and heroes from an oppressive past remained to infuse ordinary citizens and devotees with a stubborn sense of necessity, independence, and survival. The dead-alive zombi, recalled in the name Jean Zombi, thus became a terrible composite power: slave turned rebel ancestor turned lwa, an incongruous demonic spirit recognized through dreams, divination, or possession.

In contemporary Haiti, however, the zombi calls up the most macabre figure in folk belief. No fate is more feared. The zombi, understood either as an evil spirit or the zombi in "flesh and bones," is the most powerful emblem of apathy, anonymity, and loss. This incarnation of negation or vacancy—what Jamaican novelist Erna Brodber has defined as "flesh that takes directions from someone"—is as much a part of history as the man Jean Zombi. Zombification in its contemporary manifestations grew out of a twentieth-century history of forced labor, victimization, and denigration that became particularly acute during the

American occupation of Haiti. As Haitians were forced to build roads, and thousands of peasants were brutalized and massacred, tales of zombies proliferated in the United States. The film *White Zombie* (1932) and books like William Seabrook's *The Magic Island* (1929) or John Huston Craige's *Black Bagdad* (1933) helped justify the "civilizing" presence of the marines in barbaric Haiti. This reimagined zombi has now been absorbed into the texture of previous oral traditions, structurally reproducing the idea of slavery in a new context. As lwa, then, Jean Zombi embodies dead whites and blacks, staging again for those who serve him the sacrificial scene: the ritual of consecration that makes him god.

Let us return to Dessalines' constitution of 1805, and to the logic of the remnant turned god. "The law does not permit one dominant religion" (Art. 50). "The freedom of cults is tolerated" (Art. 51). Not again in the many constitutions of Haiti, until 1987, would freedom of religion be allowed. Both Toussaint and Christophe had recognized only Catholicism ("la religion Catholique, apostolique et romaine") as the religion of the state. Dessalines remained close to the practices of the Haitian majority. But according to Milo Rigaud, who does not give sources for his unique details of Dessalines possessed and punished, Dessalines suffered the vengeance of the spirits for ignoring their warnings not to go to Pont-Rouge.[52] Nor did the gods forget the general's attack on their servitors when he followed Toussaint's orders in 1802. But what Ardouin called the "misfortunes" of popular vengeance on Dessalines could be a record of something less verifiable and more disturbing.

General Yayou, when he saw the body of Dessalines, proclaimed: "Who would have said that this little wretch, only twenty minutes ago, made all of Haiti tremble!" When an initiate is possessed by the "emperor," the audience witnesses a double play of loss and gain. The "horse" (in the idiom of possession the god mounts his horse) remains him/herself even when ridden, but stripped bare, as was Dessalines, of habitual characteristics, the lineaments of the everyday. The essential residue, the nam remains. What emerges after the first moments of disequilibrium and convulsive movements is the ferocity commonly associated with Dessalines. It is as if the self is not so much annihilated as rendered piecemeal. Out of these remnants comes the god or mystery who overtakes what remains.

DÉFILÉE

In the last year of the revolution, Dessalines led an army whose spirit and courage were recorded in numerous accounts by the French military. A song from the days when Dessalines and his columns of men (figures

vary from 16,000 men in four columns to 27,000) marched toward victory at Butte de la Charier and Vertières was sung to a generation of
students at the Ecole de Médecine in Port-au-Prince by an old man
named Brother Hossé or José. Timoléon Brutus, one of the students
who heard it around 1901, records it in his homage to Dessalines as the
battle song celebrating the march of Dessalines to the north, where he
would assault Cap François and force the surrender of General Donatien
Marie Joseph de Vimeur Rochambeau:

> Dessalines sorti lan Nord
> Vini compter ça li porté (bis)
>   Ça li porté.
> Li porté fusils, li porté boulets, (bis)
>   Ouanga nouveau (bis)

(Dessalines is coming to the north. / Come note what he is bringing /
What he is bringing. / He is bringing muskets, he is bringing bullets, /
New magic)[53]

A woman marched with Dessalines' troops, peddling provisions to the
soldiers. Known as Défilée, she was born to slave parents near Cap-
François. When she was about eighteen years old, Défilée was violated
by a colonist, her master.[54] During the revolution, she must have escaped, though nothing is known about her until she became sutler to
Dessalines' troops. But with Dessalines' death, Défilée became the embodiment of the Haitian nation—crazed and lost, but then redeemed
after desecrating the body of their savior. A woman's lamentation, as
some Haitians use it, converts a sudden gruesome act into a long history
of penitential devotion. Historian and dramatist Henock Trouillot in
Dessalines ou le sang du Pont-Rouge (1967) gives Défilée the task of
condemning her people: "What the French could not accomplish, have
they really done it, these monsters? . . . Haiti has dared what Saint-
Domingue tried in vain."[55]

The fall of Dessalines and the excesses committed on his corpse are
overshadowed by this final, bizarre drama that writers as diverse as
Madiou and Ardouin record. As the people defiled the remains of their
"supreme chief," Défilée the madwoman entered the scene. Madiou recounted how numerous children, joyously shouting, threw rocks at Dessalines' remains. A wandering Défilée asked these "innocent beings who
abandon themselves to good as to evil," who *was* this bundle of something. They answered, Dessalines, and her wild eyes became calm: "a
glimmer of reason shone on her features." She found a sack, loaded it with
his bloody remnants, and carried them to the city cemetery. General
Pétion then sent soldiers who, for a modest sum, buried Dessalines.[56]

Ardouin, who would have been ten years old in 1806, claimed to have been an eyewitness to the popular vengeance in Port-au-Prince. Refuting Madiou's version, Ardouin explains that he knew Défilée, and she could not have carried Dessalines. "Perhaps Madiou did not recall that Dessalines was hefty, weighing perhaps 70 to 80 kilos: how could a weak Défilée carry such a weight?" According to Ardouin, she followed the officers, and for a long time returned to the site, where she threw flowers over the grave.[57] Though a well-known madman named Dauphin helped Défilée carry the sack, most accounts choose to ignore what is possible in favor of the miraculous: Défilée's lone journey with the hero's remains.

Poet and dramatist Massillon Coicou wrote a drama in two acts, *L'Empereur Dessalines*, performed on the centenary of Dessalines' death in Port-au-Prince on October 7, 1906. In his preface to the published version, Coicou, who was assassinated by President Nord Alexis in 1908, reminded his readers that "Dessalines, beaten, massacred, abandoned to execration, regained his prestige."[58] In this version, Défilée took Dessalines' members, clotted with mud and blood, scorned by everyone, bathed them in tears, and carried them in the folds of her dress. Coicou asks, "Isn't she the most beautiful incarnation of our national consciousness, this madwoman who moved amidst those who were mad but believed themselves sane?"[59]

Other writers described the encounter between the emperor turned fleshly remnant and the madwoman turned sane as a ritual of reciprocal salvation. Windsor Bellegard asks all Haitians to remember "*Défilée-La-Folle* who, on the sad day of October 17, 1806 . . . saw the Founder of Independence fall under Haitian bullets, and when the people of Port-au-Prince seemed suddenly to go mad, she gave to everyone an eloquent lesson of reason, wisdom, and patriotic piety."[60] Others described the encounter as exorcism: the naming of Dessalines, whom Défilée called "this martyr" in the Frenchman Edgar La Selve's account, momentarily chases the demons from her mind.[61]

Oral tradition, while remembering Défilée, does not try to rationalize the terrors of vengeance. Unlike the written accounts, the following song does not depend upon schematic reversal: the exchange between sentiment and enlightenment, or more specifically, the possession of the woman in love by the dismembered hero that makes him whole and her reasonable.

> Parole-a té palé déjà
> Dessalines gangan . . .
> Défilée ouè;
> Défilée pé! . . .
> Général Dessalines Ö! gadez misè moin,
> Gadez tracas pays-là
> Pays-là chaviré[62]

(The word has already been spoken / Dessalines the vodou priest / . . .
Défilée yes; / Défilée is frightened! . . . / General Dessalines Oh! look at
my misery, / Look at the troubled country / The capsized country)

Here, the drama depends upon Défilée's attachment to the vicissitudes
of secular, political life, not to a fantasy of conversion.

It is not possible to verify when the Haitian people began to sing this
song of regret for the death of their "Papa." I suspect that some time
before the literate elite decided it would be wise to resurrect Dessalines
as hero, those who suffered under the rule of Christophe and Boyer
began to recall Dessalines and their own momentary "madness" in re-
joicing over his death. At their moment of greatest failure, still crushed
by confounding, persistent oppression, the poor deified Dessalines. This
deification, unlike the cult of resurrection adopted by the state, does not
promise a new order of things.

In her "Bibliographie féminine, epoque coloniale et XIX siècle,"
Ertha Pascal-Trouillot, one of Haiti's numerous acting presidents since
the 1986 departure of "Baby Doc" Duvalier, gives a reality to the legendary Défilée. Her name was Dédée Bazile. She had spent part of her
youth in Port-au-Prince at Fort Saint-Clair, where she followed Dessalines as a *vivandière* (sutler) for the indigenous army. According to Pascal-Trouillot, "she had a wild passion for Dessalines that exacerbated the
mental troubles caused by the slaughter of her parents by French soldiers."[63] She was not simply a marketwoman or meat vendor, who followed the Haitian revolutionary army as it marched (hence her name
Défilée), but unstrung by the loss of her parents and her love for Dessalines, she supplied the soldiers with sex.

Another story was recalled by the hundred-year-old Joseph Jérémie,
who told it to Jean Fouchard in about 1950. According to him, one
night Défilée's two sons and three of her brothers, enlisted in the army,
did not return from a party in the Cahos mountains, where the "slaves"
secretly assembled. About six hundred "slaves" were surprised and "pitilessly massacred by the sbirri [sergeants or officers] of the bloodthirsty
General Donatien Rochambeau." The news unhinged Dédée's mind,
but she continued to follow Dessalines' army as sutler, "with the same
spirit, the same faith in final victory." Joseph Jérémie describes how she
got the name Défilée. "As soon as the soldiers stopped somewhere to
rest, Défilée also stopped. Abruptly, the madwoman raised the long stick
[used for a crutch] held in her hand, and bravely cried out: defile, defile
(*défilez, défilez*). They obeyed her." Whereas Pascal-Trouillot empha-
sizes Dédée's unrequited love for Dessalines, Jérémie recounts how
Dessalines loved her like a father.[64]

Dessalines, turned into pieces of meat, gets reassembled by the
woman who used to sell meat to him and his soldiers. She alone touches

the befouled remains, doing justice to the emperor. Beyond identification with the Virgin Mary or Mary Magdalene and "the other Mary,"
who presided over the life, death, and resurrection of Christ, Défilée, or
rather, Dédée Bazile fleshes out the sacred. Here, promiscuity and
power, sex and sacrament intermingle. To Dédée Bazile is attributed the
only song of farewell to Jean-Jacques Dessalines, which Joseph Jérémie
says she sang while kneeling before his unmarked tomb and after kissing
it three times:

> Jacquot tol lô cotoc
> Tignan
> Yo touyé Dessalinn
> Dessalinn papa moin
> Tignan
> Moin pap jam'm blié-ou
> Tignan[65]

(Jack *tol lô cotoc* / Ti-Jean / You killed Dessalines / Ti-Jean / Dessalines
my papa / Ti-Jean / I will never forget you / Ti-Jean).[66]

One of Haiti's oldest songs, still repeated as the most moving elegy to
Dessalines, was composed by Défilée to "her jacquot that she had loved,
admired and so faithfully served, braving bullets, in the suite of the
Army."[67]

What does the conjunction of hero and madwoman tell us about Haitian history? The trope of long-suffering or mad *négresse* and powerful
noir became a routine coupling in contemporary Haitian texts. The parallels between literary and historical writing raise questions about the
myth of the Haitian nation and the kinds of symbols required to make
a "national" literature. Haitian history has been written by men,
whether colonizers who distort or negate the past, or the colonized who
reclaim what has been lost or denied. What is the name of the manbo
who assisted the priest Boukman in the legendary ceremony of Bois
Caïman? "As history tells it she made the conspirators drink the blood of
the animal she had slaughtered, while persuading them that therein lie
the proof of their future invincibility in battle."[68] Arlette Gautier has
argued in *Les Soeurs de solitude* that, as opposed to the men of the revolution, women left no records. "They have remained nameless except for
Sanite Belair, Marie-Jeanne Lamartinière for Saint-Domingue and the
mulatta Solitude in Guadeloupe."[69]

Both Madiou and Ardouin mention women during the revolution.
Not only the fierce Sanite Belaire who refused to be blindfolded during
her execution and Marie-Jeanne who led the indigènes in the extraordinary battle of Crête-à-Pierrot, but also Claire Heureuse, the wife of Dessalines, who saved many of the French he had ordered massacred. Yet we

need to consider how these women are mentioned, how their appearances work within the historical narrative. Their stories are something of an interlude in the business of *making history*. Bracketed off from the descriptions of significant loss or triumph, the *blanches* raped and butchered or the *noires* ardent and fearless became symbols for *la bonté, la férocité*, or *la faiblesse*.

What happens to the unnamed black women during the repeated revolutions in Haiti when mythologized by men, metaphorized out of life into legend? The legend of *Sor Rose* or Sister Rose is a story of origins that depends for its force on rape. The Haitian nation began in the flanks of a black woman. I know of only two written references to this ancestress, both from the 1940s, complementary to the noiriste revolution of 1946: Timoléon Brutus' *L'Homme d'airain* (1946), his biography of Dessalines, and Dominique Hippolyte's play about Dessalines and the last years of the revolution (1802–3), *Le Torrent* (1940). In *La Tradition voudoo* (1953), Milo Rigaud noted that the mulatto André Rigaud, ultimately Toussaint's enemy, issued from the coupling of a Frenchman and "a pure negresse of the Arada or Rada race [in Dahomey]: Rose. On his habitation *Laborde*, he 'served' the rada mysteries [spirits] from whom his mother had recovered the cult."[70]

Where did the lived experiences of women figure in the demands for black enlightenment? How did they respond to the call for black and mulatto equality? The legend of Rose, like the land Haiti, begins with a woman "brutally fertilized," as Brutus puts it, "by a slave in heat or a drunken White, a criminal escaped from Cayenne [the French colonial prison]; or a degenerate from feudal nobility in quest of riches on the continent." Summoning this myth of violation, Brutus argues that it is senseless to put mulatto over black or vice versa, since "the origin of everyone is common." No superiority can be extricated from the color and class chaos that began Haitian society. Yet in this locale of blacks, whites, mulattoes, criminals, slaves, and aristocrats, the "black woman" is singular. In an amalgam of neutralized distinctions, she stands out as victim and martyr. In the legend of Sor Rose, *to give oneself to a man*, voluntarily or not, is *to give Haiti a history*.

But what kind of history? And who gets to claim it? In *La Femme* Michelet, who had praised Madiou's *Histoire*, greeted Haiti: "Receive my best wishes, young State! And let us protect you, in expiation of the past!" Yet, while extolling the spirit of this "great race, so cruelly slandered," he turned to Haiti's "charming women, so good and so intelligent."[71] A few pages earlier, he had tried to show that those races believed to be inferior, simply "need love." Tenderness toward women, as colonial historians had argued in their justifications of slavery, was the attribute of civilized men alone. But Michelet extended the possibility of enlightenment to black women who want white men: "The river thirsts for the clouds, the desert thirsts for the river, the black woman for the white man. She is in every way, the most amorous and the most gener ous." Her beneficent desire entitles her, in Michelet's mind, to a partic ular kind of monumentalizing. Not only is she identified as icon of lov ing surrender, but she becomes land: generalized as an Africa named, tamed, and dedicated to serving Europe. "Africa," Michelet concluded, "is a woman."[72]

Michelet's words recall descriptions of the *femme de couleur* in colo nial Saint Domingue—most pronounced in Moreau de St. Méry and Pierre de Vassière, but found in "natural histories" throughout the Ca ribbean. Not only sensual, but beings who lived for love, they embodied the forced intimacies and luxuriant concubinage of the colonial past. In Haiti, Michelet's Black Venus becomes Sor Rose, beautiful but violated. Yet, it remained for a Haitian, Janvier in his *La République d'Haïti et ses visiteurs*, to be explicit about the marvels of a history understood as courtship with one aim: possession.

> The history of Haiti is such: difficult, arduous, thorny, but charming, filled with interpenetrating, simultaneous deeds, subtle, delicate, and entangled.
>
> She is a virgin who must be violated, after long courtship; but how ex quisite when you possess her! . . . She is astonishing and admirable.[73]

The recuperation of emblems for heroism or love in written histories of Haiti often appear as if caricatures or simulations of French "civiliza tion." In this recycling of images, as in the case of Louis Napoleon and Soulouque, we are caught in a mimetic bind. The heterogeneity of vodou syncretism, however, offers an alternative to such blockage. Vodou does not oppose what we might construct as "Western" or "Christian," but absorbs apparently hostile materials, taking in as much as it resists.

On May 18, 1803, at the Congress of Arcahaie, General-in-Chief Dessalines ripped the white out of the French tricolor that covered the table. Trampling it under his feet, he commanded that the red and blue—symbolizing the union of black and mulatto—be sewn together as the new flag and that "*Liberté ou la Mort*" (Liberty or Death) replace the old inscription, "*R.F.*" (*République Française*). In Léogane in the 1970s I heard people recount how Dessalines, possessed by Ogou, cut out the white strip of the French flag. Yet Brutus in *L'Homme d'airain* presents a more compelling version. He tells a story "of undying memory," heard and passed on by Justin Lhérison in his history class at the Lycée Pétion in Port-au-Prince in the 1930s. No spirit of African origins possessed Dessalines, but "the Saint Virgin, protectress of the Blacks." Then, Des salines cursed in "Congo *langage*" [the sacred language for direct communication with the spirits], and "then in French against the Whites who dared believe that the Independents wanted to remain French." Brutus concludes, "He was in a mystic trance, possessed by the spirit when he said: *'Monsieur, tear out the white from that flag.'*"

But who is this spirit? What is the Virgin Mary doing speaking in Congo and in French? Dessalines possessed speaks the language of the spirit who has entered his head. This Black Virgin speaks both French and the general term for African languages, or more specifically, the tongue of initiates. The inherently unreformable quality of this myth goes beyond sanctioned histories, and most important, deidealizes a "pure" type such as the Virgin. We can begin to understand what happens to the idea of virginity or violation when hooked into the system of local spirituality. If priests violated local women while teaching chastity, if they produced impurity, *the mixed blood*, while calling for purity, how was this violation absorbed into the birth of new gods?

One of the rebel Acaau's lieutenants named Frère Joseph was also a vodou practitioner who had great influence in Port-au-Prince during Soulouque's reign. According to Father P. A. Cabon in *Notes sur l'histoire religieuse d'Haïti de la Révolution au Concordat (1789–1860)*, Joseph walked, candle in hand, amid Acaau's bands, edifying them with novenas to the Virgin, but believed by them because of his involvement with the vodou gods.[74] Madiou, writing about the struggle in 1845 between the two "superstitious"or "pagan" sects called *guyons* and *saints*, revealed how confused spirituality in Haiti had become after independence: bags with fetishes, human bones, and snakes were mixed up with Catholic rituals.[75] Duverneau Trouillot had argued that after independence, vodou ceremonies had become so "frenchified" that the old cult would disappear under the weight of Christian civilization. The "advantages of liberty" could not help but contribute to the disintegration of these increasingly disordered and noncodified beliefs and gods.[76]

But what Trouillot praised as the benefits of liberation were never available to the Haitian majority. For them, the gods, saints, and devils of French dogma had to be remade on Haitian soil. Endowed with new qualities, they lost their missionary or conquest functions. Remnants of texts and theologies, once reinterpreted by local tradition, articulated a new history. The Virgin who possessed the militant Dessalines or Frère Joseph would also haunt Haitians as the *djablès*—the feared ghostly woman condemned to walk the earth for the sin of dying a virgin. In the Creole songs of Défilée, virgin and whore, purity and defilement became mutually adaptable.

To serve the spirits is to disrupt and complicate the sexual symbolism of the church and state. In answer to Janvier's correlation between the virgin, long desired and finally violated, and Haiti's history, intractable but ultimately apprehended, the most feared spirits, like the most beloved Virgin, were formed out of the odd facts that made up the discourse of mastery permeated by the thought of subordination. A *vodou history* might be composed from these materials: oral accounts of Dessalines possessed and his emergence as lwa, god, or spirit, as well as equally ambivalent accounts of figures like Erzili, Jean Zombi, Défilée, Virgin or djablès. Sinkholes of excess, these crystallizations of unwritten history force us to acknowledge inventions of mind and memory that destroy the illusions of mastery, circumventing and confounding *any* master narrative.

NOTES

A preliminary version of this essay was presented at the Davis Center for Historical Studies, February 15, 1991. My thanks to Natalie Davis, William Jordan, François Hoffmann, Gananath Obeyeskere, Richard Rathbone, and Drexel Woodson for their comments and criticisms.

1. M. Chauvet, *Chant lyrique* (Paris: Chez Delaforest, Libraire, 1825), p. 9. All French and Creole texts are my translations except where otherwise indicated.

2. Quoted in Timoléon Brutus, *L'Homme d'airain* (Port-au-Prince: Imp N. A. Theodore, 1946), 1:264.

3. In his *Description topographique, physique, civile, politique et historique de patrie française de l'isle Saint-Domingue*, Moreau de Saint-Méry depicts in detail, for the first time, the rites and religious practices of the slaves in colonial Saint-Domingue. He explains that "Vaudoux means an all-powerful and supernatural being upon whom depends all of the events that come to pass on earth." In Moreau's texts "vaudoux" also denotes a dance and/or practitioners of the "cult." I use the term "vodou" to describe the belief system of the Haitian majority, though devotees, when asked about their traditional practices, simply say: "I serve the gods." See my "Vodoun, or the Voice of the Gods," *Raritan* (Winter 1991): 32–57.

4. Janvier published his first responses to Cochinat in the Port-au-Prince journal *L'Oeil*. Other articles appeared in Haiti in the journal *Perseverant*. The 636-page *La Republique d'Haiti et ses visiteurs, 1840–1882* (Paris: Marpon et Flammarion, 1883), was reprinted in Haiti in 1979 with the added title, *Un Peuple noir devant les peuples blancs (étude de politique et de sociologie comparées)*.

5. Janvier, *La Republique d'Haïti*, pp. 319, 420.

6. Ardouin, *Etudes sur l'histoire d'Haïti, suivies de la vie du Général J.-M. Borgella* (Port-au-Prince: Chez l'éditeur, 1958), 1:4.

7. Madiou, *Histoire d'Haïti* [1847–48] (Port-au-Prince: Editions Henri Deschamps, 1989), p. xiii. The first three volumes of Madiou, published in Port-au-Prince with l'Imprimerie Joseph Courtois (1847–48), began with the arrival of Columbus and ended with the struggles between Christophe and Pétion in a

divided Haiti. In 1904, on the one hundredth anniversary of independence, Madiou's descendants published a fourth volume dealing with the events of 1843–46. In 1988 Maison Henri Deschamps undertook the publication of Madiou's complete works.

8. Spenser St. John, *Hayti or the Black Republic* [1884] (London: Frank Cass, 1971), pp. 95–96.

9. Marx, *The 18th Brumaire of Louis Bonaparte* (New York: International Publishers, 1972), p. 134.

10. Gustave d'Alaux, *L'Empereur Soulouque et son empire* (Paris: Michel Lévy Frères, Librairies-Editeurs, 1856), p. 1.

11. Wendell Phillips, *Speeches, Lectures, and Letters* (Boston: Lee and Shepard, 1892), p. 482.

12. Bellegarde, *La Nation haïtienne* (Paris: J. DeGirord, éditeur, 1938), p. 119.

13. Brown, *The History and Present Condition of St. Domingo* [1837] (London: Frank Cass, 1971), p. 259.

14. Salomon's speech is reprinted in the appendix of Leslie Manigat's *L'Avènement à la présidence d'Haïti du Général Salomon: essai d'application d'un point de théorie d'histoïre* (Port-au-Prince: Imprimerie de l'Etat, 1957), pp. 73–78.

15. For a superb analysis of Ardouin's work, see Hénock Trouillot, *Beaubrun Ardouin: homme politique et l'historien* (Port-au-Prince: Instituto Pan Americano de Geografia e Historia, 1950).

16. Ardouin, *Etudes*, 6:74.

17. Madiou, *Histoire*, 3:405.

18. The gruesome details of Dessalines' life in servitude are described in Timoléon Brutus' *L'Homme d'airain*, 2 vols. (Port-au-Prince: Imprimerie de l'état, 1947).

19. Ardouin, *Etudes*, 6:45–46.

20. Madiou, *Histoire*, 3:156.

21. Spenser St. John, *Hayti*, p. 79.

22. See Jean Fouchard, *La Méringue: danse nationale d'Haïti* (Ottawa: Editions Leméac, 1974), pp. 68–72, for his account of Couloute, Dessalines, and the *carabinier*.

23. In *Aperçu sur la formation historique de la nation haïtienne* (Port-au-Prince: Les Presses Libres, 1954), Etienne Charlier, secretary-general of the Haitian Communist party in 1954, condemns historians who concentrate on the actions of "a few great men" and ignore those he calls "the only great midwives" (p. 284). Carolyn E. Fick, in *The Making of Haiti: The Saint Domingue Revolution from Below* (Knoxville: University of Tennessee Press, 1990), demonstrates how *marronage*, fugitive slave resistance by those individuals history has obscured, was crucial to the course of the revolution in Saint-Domingue. The most critical essay on "silences" in the making of "the world of 1804" is Michel-Rolph Trouillot, "The Three Faces of Sans Souci: Glory and Silences in the Haitian Revolution," unpublished ms., 1992.

24. Hénock Trouillot, *Le Nouvelliste*, August 13, 1971, p. 5.

25. Ibid.

26. Trouillot, *Les Limites du Créole dans notre enseignement* (Port-au-Prince: Imprimerie des Antilles, 1980), p. 67.

27. Charlier, *Aperçu sur la formation historique de la nation haïtienne*, p. 307.

28. D'Alaux, *L'Empereur Soulouque*, pp. 239–40.

29. Janvier, *Les Constitutions d'Haïti (1801–1885)* (Paris: Marpon et Flammarion, 1886), pp. 31–32.

30. Pierre de Vassière, *Saint-Domingue: la société et la vie Créoles sous l'ancien régime, 1629–1789* (Paris: Perrin, 1909), p. 219.

31. I am grateful to Drexel Woodson for prodding me to elaborate Dessalines' redefinition of Haitian identity. For the most acute analysis of Haitian representations of race to date, see Woodson, *Tout mounn sé mounn, men tout mounn pa menm: Microlevel Sociocultural Aspects of Land Tenure in a Northern Haitian Locality* (Ph.D. diss. University of Chicago, 3 vols., 1990).

32. Moreau de Saint-Méry, *Description topographique, physique, civile, politique et historique de patrie française de l'isle Saint-Domingue* Philadelphia: Chez l'auteur, 1797–98. Rpt. Maurel and Taillemite (Paris: Société d'Histoire des Colonies Françaises, 1959), 1:71–87.

33. Janvier, *Les Constitutions d'Haïti*, 1:43.

34. Catts Pressoir, Ernst Trouillot, and Hénock Trouillot, *Historiographie d'Haïti*, Publicacion numero 168 (Mexico: Instituto Panamericano de Geografia e Historia, 1953), p. 190.

35. Anténor Firmin, *De L'Égalité des races humaines (anthropologie positive)* (Paris: F. Pichon, 1885), p. 544.

36. Madiou, *Histoire*, 8:77.

37. See *L'Homme d'airain: étude monographique sur Jean-Jacques Dessalines fondateur de la nation haïtienne* (Port-au-Prince: Imprimerie de l'Etat, 1946), 2:246–65, for details about the succession of monuments to Dessalines.

38. David P. Geggus, *Slavery, War, and Revolution: The British Occupation of Saint Domingue, 1793–98* (Oxford: Clarendon, 1982), p. 40. See also François Hoffmann's "Histoire, mythe et idéologie: La cérémonie du Bois-Caïman," *Études Créoles: culture, langue, société* 13, no. 1 (1990): 9–34, for his analysis of what he believes are the French sources of the legend, and of the stylized Haitian renditions of the story, which were then reabsorbed into oral tradition as national myth. Most recently, Geggus has responded to Hoffmann and deconstructed the "exaggerated" mythologizing of "the insurrection of August" in "La cérémonie du Bois-Caïman," *Chemins critiques* 2, no. 3 (May 1992): 59–78.

39. Madiou, *Histoire*, 1:96.

40. Ardouin, *Etudes*, 1:50–51.

41. Michel Etienne Descourtilz, *Voyages d'un naturaliste* (Paris: Dufart Père, 1809), cited in Alfred Métraux, *Voodoo in Haiti* (1959; repr. New York: Schocken Books, 1972), pp. 48–50.

42. Price-Mars, *Ainsi parla l'oncle* (Compigne: Imprimerie de Compiègne, 1928).

43. Duverneau Trouillot, *Le Vaudoun: aperçu historique et évolutions* (Port-au-Prince: Imprimerie R. Ethéaart, 1885), pp. 26, 30–31, 37.

44. See Odette Mennesson-Rigaud and Lorimer Denis, "Cérémonie en l'honneur de Marinette," in *Bulletin du Bureau d'Ethnologie*, no. 3 (Port-au-Prince: Imprimerie de l'Etat, 1947), p. 21. Métraux, *Voodoo in Haiti*, gives the following transcription of the song: "Pito muri pasé m'kuri/Désalin Désalin démânbré / Viv la libèté" (p. 49). Haitian Creole orthography is varied, and the phonetic variants numerous. When quoting from a text I have not changed the spelling of the Creole words, so there is some inconsistency throughout my essay. Though some Haitian writers still use a French transliteration of vodou terms, I have decided generally to follow the most accessible phonemic orthography, which closely approximates that now in official use in Haiti since 1979: Albert Valdman et al., *Haitian Creole-English-French Dictionary*, 2 vols. (Bloomington: Creole Institute, University of Indiana, 1981).

45. The belligerent Petwo nation of lwa (as distinct from the benevolent Rada family (*lwa ginen daomen* or guinea spirits of Dahomey) was born out of the coercions of slavery and the furor of revolution. In practice, however, the division between Petwo and Rada does not always hold.

46. Serge Larose, "The Meaning of Africa in Haitian Vodu," in *Symbols and Sentiments: Cross-Cultural Studies in Symbolism*, ed. I. M. Lewis (London: Academic, 1977), p. 97.

47. See Serge Larose, "The Haitian Lakou, Land, Family, and Ritual," in *Family and Kinship in Middle America and the Caribbean*, ed. Arnaud F. Marks and René A. Röiner (Curaçao, Netherlands Antilles: Institute of Higher Studies, 1978); pp. 482–511, and Jean Maxius Bernard, " 'Démanbré' et croyances populaires," *Bulletin du Bureau National d'Ethnologie* 2 (1984):35–42.

48. Madiou, *Histoire* 3:168–69.

49. Rigaud, *La Tradition voudoo et le voudoo haïtien* (Paris: Editions Niclaus, 1953), p. 67.

50. Melville J. Herskovits, *Dahomey, An Ancient West African Kingdom* (New York, 1938), p. 243.

51. Moreau de Saint-Méry, *Description*, 1:70.

52. Rigaud, *La Tradition voudoo et le voudoo haïtien*, p. 41.

53. Brutus, *L'Homme d'airain*, 1:288–89.

54. The most complete story about Défilée is that preserved by Jean Fouchard in *La Méringue: danse nationale d'Haïti* (Québec: Editions Leméac, 1973), pp. 77–80, where he recounts the stories of Didi Condol, a survivor of Défilée's family in 1916, and Joseph Jéremie, who died at nearly one hundred years old in 1950.

55. Henock Trouillot, *Dessalines ou le sang du Pont-Rouge* (Port-au-Prince: Imprimerie des Antilles, 1967), Act 5, Scene 8, p. 121. I thank Drexel Woodson for making this text available to me.

56. Madiou, *Histoire*, 3:406.

57. Ardouin, *Etudes*, 6:74 n.1.

58. Coicou, *L'Empereur Dessalines: drame en deux actes, en vers* (Port-au-Prince: Imp. Edmond Chenet, 1906), p. iv. The unpublished second act, which contains the murder and apotheosis of Dessalines through the medium of Défilée, is now lost, though writers including Duraciné Vaval, *Histoire de la litterature haïtienne ou "L'Ame Noire,"* Ghislain Gouraige, *Histoire de la littera-*

ture haïtienne (de l'indépendance à nos jours) (Port-au-Prince: Editions de l'Action Sociale, 1982), and Dessalines' biographer, Brutus, *L'Homme d'airain*, vol. 2, focus on the drama of Défilée's devotion.

59. Coicou, *L'Empereur Dessalines*, p. v.

60. Windsor Bellegarde, "Les Héroines de notre histoire," in Dantès Bellegarde, *Ecrivains haïtiens: notices biographiques et pages choisis* (Port-au-Prince: Société d'Editions et de Librairie, 1947), pp. 218–19.

61. Edgar La Selve, *Le Pays de nègres* (Paris: Librairie Hachette, 1881), p. 166.

62. Quoted in Rigaud, *La Tradition voudoo*, p. 63; and cited in Fouchard, *La Méringue*, pp. 77–78.

63. Ertha Pascal-Trouillot, *Retrospectives . . . Horizons* (Port-au-Prince: Imprimerie des Antilles, 1980), p. 392.

64. Cited by Fouchard, *La Méringue*, pp. 79–80.

65. Ibid., p. 80.

66. Although I have translated "Tignan" as "Ti Jean," the word "Tignan," according to Drexel Woodson, is a phrase used when marketing, meaning "a little more." For example, the marketwoman is asked to add extra grain, filling the can above its rim. He adds that when a man asks for "Tignan," he means something like "a piece of ass."

67. Fouchard, *La Méringue*, p. 78.

68. J. B. Romain, *Quelques moeurs et coutumes des paysans haïtiens* (Port-au-Prince: Imprimerie de l'Etat, 1959), p. 59.

69. Gautier, *Les Soeurs de solitude: la condition féminine dans l'esclavage aux Antilles du XVII au XIX siècle* (Paris: Editions Caribéenes, 1985), p. 221.

70. Rigaud, *La Tradition voudoo*, p. 66.

71. Michelet, *La Femme* [1859] (Paris: Flammarion, 1981), p. 184.

72. Ibid., pp. 180–81.

73. Janvier, *La République d'Haïti*, 1:248.

74. Cabon, *Notes sur l'histoire religieuse d'Haïti de la Révolution au Concordat (1789–1860)* (Port-au-Prince: Petit Seminaire Collège Saint-Martial, 1933), p. 391. For other accounts of Frère Joseph as "vodou prophet," see Gustave d'Alaux, *L'Empereur Soulouque*, pp. 71–72; Dante's Bellegarde, *Histoire du Peuple Haïtien (1492–1952)* (Port-au-Prince: Collection du Tricinquantenaire de l'Indépendance d'Haïti, 1953), p. 150.

75. Madiou, *Histoire*, 8:318–19.

76. Trouillot, *Le Vaudoun*, pp. 31–32.

CHAPTER 4

Why Not Tourist Art?
Significant Silences in Native American Museum Representations

RUTH B. PHILLIPS

IN 1989 the largest collection of American Indian objects in the world, held by the Museum of the American Indian in New York, was transferred to the Smithsonian Institution and refounded as the National Museum of the American Indian (NMAI). For Native Americans, this event marks a highly significant moment of visible fracture between colonial and postcolonial museum practice.[1] The core of the old museum was formed as the private collection of a wealthy businessman, George Heye, who continued to control its activities until his death in 1957.[2]

In stark contrast, the new NMAI is directed and managed by Native American professionals. According to its published policy it will ultimately dismantle the great colonial accumulation of objects it has inherited, returning important parts of the collections to their originating communities.[3] The NMAI's director, W. Richard West Jr., has called for a "living museum" that will privilege contemporary life rather than "one frozen chapter of an often romanticized historical past," and one that will introduce, in the service of this goal, "live bodies—not static dioramas."[4] Due to be completed sometime around the year 2000, the new NMAI project has a millenarian resonance. It will occupy the last available museum space on the Mall in Washington, bringing the appearance of closure to the set of named disciplinary and ethnic components that make up the national museum of the United States.[5] For five hundred years the first peoples of the Americas have been last, but the last shall now be first.

The changes in the representation of Native American peoples proposed by West closely parallel a number of radical innovations in museum practice summarized by Eilean Hooper-Greenhill in her incisive Foucaultian study of the museum. She suggests that these developments, by revealing contradictions inherent in modernism, signal the approaching end of the regime of the modern *episteme* that Foucault has himself predicted.[6] As West's remarks indicate, the first task of his institution will be the deconstruction of a dialectic central to the colonialist discourse contained within modernism. This dialectic constructs the primitive as premodern, static, and dead in opposition to the Western as modern, dynamic, and living.

The raw materials with which the NMAI will work in constructing these new representations remain, however, the collections amassed under George Heye's direction, and his tastes and prejudices will thus inevitably have to be factored into the NMAI's new representations. Museum collections such as Heye's are historical formations of the colonial era. Although we have become relatively adept at reading exhibitions as texts, less attention has been paid to the anatomy of collections as historically contingent object records that permit or exclude certain representational possibilities.[7]

There is also today a general recognition that colonial museums are situated within two particular paradigms of knowledge, 'natural history' and 'rare art collecting,' which dominated the "Museum Age" that lasted from about 1840 to 1930.[8] My object in this essay is to demonstrate that collections such as Heye's are historical deposits produced by complex, diachronic processes of textual negotiation. In order to understand the implications of these formations for the postcolonial era it is important to recognize that colonial museum representations are intertextual products not just of two, but of at least four distinct collecting projects. In addition to the roles played by the professional ethnologist and the rare art collector, two other important actors intervened: the Native American collector-agent and the tourist-collector. Although the roles played by science and art in museum formation are widely acknowledged, those played by the ordinary consumer and the 'Other' are not.

I will approach this large subject through the examination of collecting practices in northeastern North America, the area of my own research over the past decade. I began this research with the full quota of standard prejudices inscribed by my disciplinary training as an art historian during the 1960s and 1970s. I sought out the rare and the old, the 'authentic' and the unacculturated for presentation in teaching, exhibitions, and written texts. Working in collections, however, I was regularly sidetracked by the pull of other objects—more numerous, highly colored, richly textured, sometimes bizarre—which lay alongside them on museum storage shelves. The beaded tea cosies, the pincushions inscribed "Toronto Exhibition 1905," the glove boxes of birchbark and porcupine quills, or the Hiawatha and Minnehaha dolls in fringed buckskin seemed to recall the roadside stands of childhood, to illuminate briefly the private lives of unknown strangers, to witness innumerable small meetings across cultural boundaries. These objects were walled off, untouchable according to orthodox curatorial and discursive practices. Rarely exhibited or published, excluded from the canon, they have been shrouded in silence.

The interrogation of this silence provides the title of this essay because I have increasingly come to see the exclusion of tourist art objects as highly significant. One source of this significance lies in the nature of its attraction, which entices us through familiarity into otherness. The central economic importance of tourist art is equally significant; along with other trade wares tourist art made up the major category of commodity production for many northeastern aboriginal communities from the mid-nineteenth to the mid-twentieth centuries, a period that coincides almost exactly with the "Museum Age." I will argue that objects that displayed the traces of aboriginal peoples' negotiation of Western artistic and economic systems had to be excluded from formal programs of collecting and exhibiting in order to support the standard museum representation of Native Americans as other, as marginalized and as premodern. Their exclusion served two sets of mutually contradictory interests: those of the romantic primitivists seeking an escape from industrial modernity, and those of the economic developers seeking hegemony over Indian lands and resources. The same elaborate set of fictions, constructed within the colonial discourse of the museum, served the interests of both groups.

COLONIAL DISPLAYS

This discourse is not yet history. The Ghibertian bronze doors of George Heye's neoclassical museum building on upper Broadway remained open even as the new NMAI developed on the drawing board. Its displays—last reinstalled in the 1960s—were almost indistinguishable in design and conceptualization from those of many museums that remain open across North America and Europe. These displays continue actively to transmit colonial messages about the aboriginal peoples of the Americas; they need to be read, not only into the historical record, but also as a spur to further change in the present.

The visitor to Heye's museum found to the left of the main doorway and centrally placed in the large section devoted to the Indians of the Woodlands a large case entitled "Iroquois Women." The main case label read: "The Iroquois Woman Tilled the Fields, Owned her Home and Chose the Chiefs." In secondary relation to this text, placed beneath it and lettered in smaller print, we read, "Using Quills, Beads and Ribbons Skillfully, She Decorated her Leggings and Moccasins." Placed next to these texts was an unusual group of female 'False Face' masks and craft objects categorized according to medium—bark, basketry, or beadwork.

Despite the assertion of the role of an Iroquois woman as a major economic producer, 'home owner,' and political power-broker, she was thus effectively represented in standard Western patriarchal terms as a craft producer.[9] The partial nature of the Heye display was also the product of the Western stress on objects, on 'seeing' and on 'art' that, as Alpers has pointed out, is fundamental to the museum.[10] In ethnographic exhibits the emphasis on the object has promoted a focus on technologies of making over nonmaterial aspects of culture, such as kinship or political activities, which are far more difficult to narrate through objects.

What *is* offered as a representation of the Iroquois woman is a linear historical account of her production of beadwork:

> In early times, Iroquois women use[d] dyed porcupine quills for decoration, and when White traders introduced glass beads, the traditional quillwork designs were used in a similar technique. In the mid-1700s, foreign influences, particularly learned in French Canadian convents, brought new and bold floral designs into fashion.
>
> But continued White contact resulted in the abandonment of traditional Iroquois art concepts. New patterns, which expressed contemporary tourist tastes, were adopted. The complete degeneration of an ancient art from the beautifully designed pouches into the strictly commercial articles made for sale at Niagara Falls around 1900 is all too evident in this exhibit.

The narrative presented here is standard and familiar. It inscribes colonial concepts of race and purity through its insistence on the detrimental effects of "foreign influences" and "White contact." Contact is tightly linked to an inevitable cultural decline leading toward a vanishing point "around 1900." After this portentous date a silence falls, the stillness of death signifying the disappearance of the Indian that has been foretold in the text by the unremitting use of the past tense.

The spatial arrangement of the objects in the case expresses this declining trajectory visually. The eye is led downward from the 'old' objects of quillwork placed in the top center to a lower row of works in beadwork on cloth and then farther down to the despised Niagara Falls "whimsies" located close to the visual vanishing point at the bottom right hand edge of the side wall of the case. Specifically, the plastic realization of the display articulates the theory of degenerationism, an application of cultural evolutionism to the study of material culture that became popular in American anthropological studies around 1900.[11]

The particular fiction presented here is easily deconstructed by art-historical analysis. The two small quilled pouches that act both as the benchmark of authenticity and the starting point of the alleged decline do not, in fact, exemplify precontact object types, but are themselves acculturated objects. They adopt the forms of eighteenth- and early nineteenth-century Euro-American pocketbooks and were very possibly made for trade. The beaded objects, so rigidly arranged in descending chronological sequence, were, furthermore, all produced during the same period and represent contemporaneous styles of workmanship employed by different Iroquoian-speaking peoples in New York State and Canada.[12] Although these objects were not well documented when they entered museum collections for reasons that will be discussed below, the comparative lack of subsequent research is striking evidence of the way in which the doctrines of cultural evolutionism have controlled and channeled empirical investigation.

WHY TOURIST ART?

The dismissive phrase "strictly commercial" in the Heye case label is also significant. I have discussed elsewhere the ways in which twentieth-century ethnologists have participated in the 'fine art' mystique of their time, subscribing to the standard dichotomy between the sacred and the secular and to the hierarchy of fine and applied arts.[13] The comment also constitutes a willful refusal to represent hard economic realities. The widespread reliance on craft production in the Northeast was the direct result of a gradual but inexorable process of economic marginalization that began in early contact times. It sped up in the nineteenth century with increased expropriations of Native land, the confinement of aboriginal people to reservations, and official policies of directed assimilation. The Annual Report of the Canadian Department of Indian Affairs for 1882, for example, complained about the Indians' unwillingness to emulate their white neighbors' farming methods:

> And consequently basket-making, axe-handle manufacturing, bead work, moccasin-making and other Indian handicraft, have to be resorted to, in order to supply the deficit. And to dispose of these articles the Indians have to visit numerous places, and thus their old, and to them, congenial habit of wandering about the country is fostered, which is attended with evil results to them, morally and materially. [14]

Both assimilationist policy and the aboriginal resistance that caused its ultimate failure can be read between the lines of this passage. Despite the determination of both the Canadian and American governments to transform aboriginal people from nomadic hunters into settled agriculturalists, Native Americans persisted in patterns of production and seasonal trading that were continuous with their earlier lifestyles.[15]

Craft production, furthermore, could support a surprisingly good life. In 1883 the agent at the Mohawk reserve of Kahnawake (Caughnawaga) noted that "the trade in bead-work is progressing favorably and gives large profits to many families. One may see in different parts of the village neat and pretty new houses." Similarly, the agent at Lorette, Quebec, wrote in 1885 that the Huron there "engage more in manufacturing snow shoes, moccasins, lacrosse sticks, bead work, and other Indian wares than in hunting or agriculture. They manage to secure a sufficiency for their families and some of them are quite well off."[16] Market conditions varied in response to such factors as changing fashions or the vagaries of customs controls on the U.S.-Canadian border, and the importance of trade ware production was greatest in communities with easy access to cities and tourist sites. But the overall economic importance of tourist art production is undeniable.[17]

A remarkable petition written during the 1890s by a group of Quebec Abenaki attests to aboriginal peoples' awareness of their conditions of economic production and colonial domination. The petition asks the proprietors of resort hotels in the White Mountains of New Hampshire "not to let any but Indians or those married to Indian women" sell on their premises, "the ladies and gentlemen, American Tourists, being similarly earnestly prayed to patronize the Indians only, in their own and proper Basket Trade." The Abenaki plead their case on the basis of a historical argument that succinctly recapitulates the pattern of development common throughout the Northeast:

> That the primitive occupation of the Indians, for the support of their families, "Hunting and Fishing," has now gone by, because the French Canadians, owing to their number and having themselves taken that occupation, have got such a control in it that the poor Indians have had to GIVE IT UP and look for some other means for their livelihood;
>
> That the next way the Indians had to get their living, which was the "Tanning and making of Moccasins," has also gone by, again because the French Canadians STOLE the trade. . . .
>
> That the only means they now have to honestly earn their livelihood is the "Making of Baskets," but this trade, as the former ones pertaining to Indians, is now being STOLEN AGAIN by the French Canadians, who have already GRABBED it through the carelessness of some Indians who have taught them for the sake of a little pay.

If this continues, the Abenaki warn:

> 'Indian Goods' . . . will unavoidably lose their GENUINENESS; and the ladies and gentlemen in buying those French Canadian INFERIOR QUALITY baskets—counterfeit goods—will be thereby deceived; and all will be for the harm of the Indians, the aboriginals of the country.[18]

The Abenakis employ a language of authenticity ("GENUINENESS") and appropriation ("STOLEN AGAIN") that is instantly recognizable in the debates of the present day. They also equate cultural identity with a specific form of material production ("their own and proper Basket Trade") in terms that would have been familiar to an ethnologist of the day. This should not be surprising; aboriginal people had been learning to speak this language—like English or French—with its encoded concepts of copyright, cultural ownership, and commerce since the earliest days of contact.[19]

The Abenaki petitioners understood that they could appeal to the hotel owners' understanding of the location of value in authenticity—in the 'genuineness' of the objects sold on their premises. But the document also evinces the Abenakis' awareness of a further subtext to which they could appeal, the approval with which the white population of the day regarded Indian handicraft production as direct evidence of 'industrial' competency and progress toward assimilation.[20] In this context a quite different significance was often assigned to objects like those in the Heye Iroquois beadwork display. One of the 'lowliest' and most despised examples in the case, a large pincushion lavishly beaded with a flower-basket motif, is, for example, typologically very similar to beadwork singled out for special praise in a founding work of cultural evolutionist discourse, Lewis Henry Morgan's *The League of the Ho-De'-No-Sau-Nee Iroquois* of 1851.

Morgan's work had helped establish the tradition by which the signs of cultural identity, progress, and decay could be discerned in the study of material objects. Although Morgan lamented the passing of older forms of Iroquois clothing and material production, the stronger voice in his text praised the successful absorption of Euro-North American technologies, styles, and iconographic motifs by Iroquois women as admirable evidence of the civilizability of the whole tribe—a promise of their successful modernization and assimilation: "In the fabrics of the modern Iroquois there is much to inspire confidence in their teachableness in the useful arts. When their minds are unfolded by education, and their attention is attracted by habit to agricultural pursuits . . . this gifted race will be reclaimed, and raised, eventually, to citizenship among ourselves."[21]

As an early museum collector, Morgan had acquired examples of the 'modern' acculturated styles together with older pieces in order to document, not the decline, but the progress of the Iroquois. The Heye museum's Iroquois beadwork case, though inscribing a variant of cultural evolutionism, thus assigns meanings to the objects directly opposed to those of later nineteenth- and early twentieth-century liberal reformers—who were also confirmed cultural evolutionists. Cultural evolutionism was neither a fixed nor a homogeneous discourse. A series of diachronic shifts within the discourse resulted in contradictory readings of the significance of material objects. What had been regarded as crude and pagan became celebrated as authentic and admirable; what had been read as progressive became identified as degenerative. This development is directly related to the formalization of primitivist discourse in the early twentieth century primarily among avant-garde artists, social reformers, and many anthropologists. Their championship of the primitive as a locus of value lost in the course of Western industrialization and urbanization is permeated with a tragic irony, for it threatened the futures of the peoples whose pasts it celebrated.

ETHNOLOGICAL COLLECTORS, OR HOW I SPENT MY SUMMER VACATION

The tension around tourist art can be illuminated by examining in greater detail the collecting practices of major museums. These practices are well documented in the correspondence files of museum archives.[22] From these files I single out several texts that illustrate the activities and attitudes of the four different kinds of collectors I have identified: the professional ethnologist, the rare art collector, the Native agent, and the tourist. These collectors speak from different social, economic, and political positions, although their planes of activity regularly intersect. The texts to be discussed have a broad relevance because the process of collection formation in the large North American museums followed a remarkably standardized pattern—and resulted, in consequence, in similar collection profiles in the major museums.

Professional ethnologists and their graduate students played the dominant role in collecting, providing the large conceptual framework into which objects were inserted. An efficient old boys' network directed the work they carried out; by means of this network the major metropolitan and university museums organized themselves into informal consortia that commissioned summer collecting trips 'to the field' (the season being determined both by climate and by the academic year). The field workers departed with 'shopping lists' of the desired object types and on their return the summer's haul was often divied up according to the 'needs' of several museums.

The museum collectors spread out over the continent in ever-widening circles. As their letters show, their goal was to fill in the boxes of a kind of imagined chart of object types—a cross between a map and a periodic table—in which all functional categories would be represented for all tribal groups. These charts sorted the objects into representational domains of inclusion and exclusion; they universalized Western categories, such as "Transportation," "Hunting," "Toys and Games," "Religion," and "Art," which were not, of course, necessarily recognized by the peoples being studied. The exclusions were as significant as the inclusions; "History" was normally a separate division within the museum dedicated to Euro-American objects, and there was no slot for "Industrial Production."

The project of ethnological collecting rested on the assumption that ethnicity and material culture were isomorphically related, a belief in the perfect coincidence of art and cultural style that was also held by the art historians of the day.[23] Material objects have had undeniable pride of place in ethnological museum displays even though these institutions also carried out serious research in other areas, such as language, oral tradition, and music. The primary goal of all this activity was the physical installation of the object chart in the public halls of the museum. As Edward Sapir put it in 1912, describing the projected ethnological displays of the National Museum of Canada, the aim was to assemble, "as representative collections as we can make of all the tribes of the Dominion."[24] The problem, of course, was that collections that excluded the interchangeable, mass-produced commodities that by 1912 were being used by *all* North Americans could represent only imagined, not actual, lifestyles.

Frank Speck, the most active of the ethnologist-collectors working in the Northeast during the first half of this century, was one of the ethnologists employed by Sapir to accomplish this end. A letter written by Speck to Sapir in 1912 from northern Quebec captures the spirit of the era:

> Now as to Ethnology (material culture). The Lake St. John supplementary collection was shipped & reported on before we sailed I hope it arrived safely, & that you will like it. There are still some gaps that need filling. On the coast here I have secured representative lots from 2 slightly different posts, Seven Island & Moisie river, the latter sort of mixed Naskapi & Montagnais band.[25]

The passage is well stocked with all the key signifiers. The parenthetical insertion of "(material culture)" after "Ethnology" indicates the equation of object types and ethnicity, while the stress on the "representative" nature of what has been collected from different communities carries the related implication that separate bands (economic and political forms of organization) can be expected to produce visually distinct objects. The phrase "filling gaps" is a constant refrain in the documents, pointing clearly to the idealized taxonomic chart of culture that lay behind the ethnologist-collectors' project, with available slots waiting for the insertion of imagined objects—objects which, if they did not exist 'in the field' would have to be (re)invented.

Speck's borrowing of the term "lots" from the language of commerce in referring to his collections is equally significant. In economic terms, the acquisition of objects from Native communities by museums—as well as by private collectors—was a transformative process. The things made by Indians became commodities to be exchanged in a market, and the ethnologist became a buyer—one who had to negotiate with competing buyers as well as with sellers. Most of the archival documentation, in fact, concerns negotiations over price, revealing the role played by the museum as a brokerage house. As Speck noted with reference to a collection from Abenaki Indians in the Adirondacks of New York, "I may say that all of these Indians, through contact with tourists, sports etc. have an exaggerated idea of the basic value of their heirlooms and hold to them for fancy prices which I had to pay."[26]

NATIVE AGENTS AS COLLECTORS: INSCRIPTION AND RESISTANCE

The processes of "filling gaps" and of commoditization are described in some of the most fascinating documents in the museum archives. These detail the process by which the Western notions of commodity and money exchange were communicated to aboriginal people. Professional museum collectors made regular use of well-placed or knowledgeable Native people as independent agents to collect for museums, as well as to make or commission models where original materials were not available.[27] Indeed, we are only now recognizing how large a percentage of the extant ethnological material was collected directly by Native people rather than by the ethnologists who are usually credited.[28] Exchanges of letters between these aboriginal agents and museum administrators show us ethnologists tutoring their Native associates in Western systems of object valuation. Speck's accounts of his collaboration with a Penobscot chief, Gabe Paul, show him busily inscribing the concepts of 'collecting,' the 'type,' and the 'complete' in the Native consciousness:

> [Gabe] Paul has been my right hand man and I think will make a good collector and helper for Eastern Algonkian work. He is now amassing a Penobscot collection which it is his intention to make complete right through, including bark wigwams, full size, of several types. I have encouraged and instructed him as much as possible hoping that it will benefit the work.[29]

The documents provide striking statements of the difference between Native and non-Native object/value systems articulated by Native people in the course of their negotiations with non-Native buyers. Under colonial regimes these conflicts were nearly always resolved in favor of Western systems of value. The acts of articulation constitute a form of resistance that needs to be acknowledged, however, for they lead to the highly effective reassertion of aboriginal concepts of cultural property and replication made in recent years.

An exchange of letters during 1912 between Edward Sapir and another Chief Paul—James Paul, a Malecite from New Brunswick—is particularly revealing of these problems. It begins with the commissioning of a birch bark canoe for the ethnographic museum in St. Petersburg. In each of his letters to Chief Paul, Sapir repeated the same instructions, hammering home the fundamental equation of age/premodernity/authenticity/value: "there are to be no nails or other white man's materials used in the canoe, but . . . it is to be made exactly of the style that the Indians used long ago before they knew anything about white man's ways."[30] When we consider that the Malecite first encountered the French in the seventeenth century and had, by 1911, been in regular contact with white people for over two hundred years, the full burden of Sapir's instructions becomes clear. What he was really asking of Chief Paul was his collusion in the creation of one of the fictions of premodernity typical of the Museum Age—the reinvention of an object that both of them could only imagine.[31]

Soon after he had carried out this commission, Chief Paul wrote to ask about a possible "gap" in the collection. "Have you any Indian carved paddles in your Museum?" he asked. Sapir cautiously asked in reply, "Are such Indian carved paddles as you speak of old fashioned Indian work or have they been made only in late days in order to sell to white people?" Chief Paul's answer evidences so fully the negotiations of value and the process of commoditization that it is worth citing in full:

> I am sending you two paddles. I don't think you have the Maliseet paddles and those I am sending, one of them is very old, but the other is not so old. You will take notice on one, there is some carving on it, that was done by some old Indian that had died long while ago. The oldest looking one is probably a hundred years old. I got them from a friend from Fredericton. He had them in his house for some time and never was used. I had to go to work and make him two new ones in place of the old ones that I got. On account I wanted them because they were so old. New paddles are worth $3.00 a pair. I am charg[ing] the half of what the new ones are worth so there will be no hard feelings between you and I. I think they are worth that to you on account they are so old but carved paddles it would be far much nicer what I make myself then what you see on that old one. I know you wouldn't feel like paying $10.00 a pair, but if you see them after all fixed up, you would say that they couldn't be bought for $25.00.[32]

Chief Paul uses the word "old" no less than eight times in these lines to reassure the ethnologist in Ottawa that his message had been received. A Native system of aesthetics, use, and value, however, is also articulated in the text, resisting the white man's insistence on the old and obsolete. Chief Paul asserts the value of the new and of the replica by assigning a money value that his white correspondent will understand as extravagant. He also urges the proposition that a new paddle could be *more* beautiful than an old one, although his words remain at the level of suggestion, overwhelmed by the dominant culture's obsession with the old.

THE RARE ART COLLECTOR: RARITY VERSUS COMMODITY

The value for age as the criterion of authenticity extended, of course, well beyond the ethnographic museum into many areas of museum practice. There were subtle but important distinctions between the ethnologist's and the private collector's location of value in the old of which the players in the early twentieth-century museum game were keenly aware. George Heye, for example, fitted perfectly the mold of Alsop's rare art collector: the composition of his collections reflects his privileging of rarity and age and his rigid association of the authentically Indian with the premodern.

Heye exercised autocratic control over his museum, and although he commissioned and funded important research and collecting expeditions, he bought from his hired ethnographers only the objects that fitted his tastes. "Heye is particularly mercenary these days," commented Speck in 1912, "desiring only the 'oldest,' 'used,' and 'rare,' specimens, & 'not a cent for ethnology. . . .' I myself have a little bunch of stuff rejected by Heye, including some good things which I was disappointed he did not want."[33] Speck here seems almost to articulate an oppositionality between his project and Heye's—"& not a cent for ethnology"— despite the clear coincidence of their agendas on most occasions. The point of difference is clarified by a further remark. "The mentioned articles are not all *old* and *antique* like Heye wants," he wrote, "but they are all typical of today."[34] Uninterested in representations of the twentieth-century life of aboriginal peoples, Heye wanted only that which came from a 'purer' past.

Though equally committed to the representation of the premodern, the ethnologist was also guided by his desire to complete his representative sets—including examples of the mundane and contemporary where they fitted slots in the taxonomy. He was not interested in uniqueness per se, and actively sought out multiples in order to illustrate typologies of objects. He regularly commissioned replicas where used items were not available, or models when full-sized objects could not be transported or stored. His main interest in market value was in keeping it down so that his acquisition budget would stretch as far as possible.

To the private collector, by contrast, rarity and uniqueness were desiderata that could be separated from criteria of age and use, although the three were closely interconnected. A vivid example of the operation of these aspects of value in the acquisition of Native American objects is contained in a narrative written by the nineteenth-century Canadian author and journalist John Richardson. Richardson describes a pleasure trip he took in the eastern Great Lakes during the autumn of 1848 in the company of several other men to witness the annual distribution of treaty gifts at Sarnia and Walpole Island, Ontario. The men, avid collectors all, purchased several 'rare,' 'old,' and 'authentic' items from the assembled Indians, one prize being a war club covered with a rich patina of use. At the end of the trip one of the group, disappointed at not having acquired a club of his own, persuaded the party to stop at the house of a prosperous Walpole Island Native trader named George Rapp to inquire if he had any war clubs on hand:

> He said he had, and brought two to the large blazing log fire. Both of these, (of different shapes,) he said, he had some trouble in fashioning; but they were clumsy, awkward looking things, and had an air of newness, which did not at all meet our ideas, *cognoscenti* as we had suddenly become in the particular article of war clubs. Indeed, compared with that purchased by Captain Rooke, from the old Pottowattamie, they were as a Norman dray horse to an English blood. Mr. West, who had a desire to obtain one, was discouraged by the comparison; but as Captain Eberts still remained a candidate for one of those "crackers of human skulls," Rapp was told to bring it to the steamer in the morning, at day light. In this he did not fail, when our friend was legitimately installed in the possession of a club. . . . May he live a thousand years to enjoy it as a reminiscence of the very pleasant trip.[35]

This incident parallels Chief Paul's offer of the paddle to Edward Sapir, but it is narrated from the rare art collector's point of view rather than the Native producer's. He sees the contemporary club as plebian while the old club forms part of an elite class of thoroughbred objects because of its very irreplaceability. The privileging of past over present meant that the Indian could never really win, even if he followed the government's script and engaged in commodity production. Only when the old and authentic were completely unavailable did the rare art collector accept the newer replica, but by this very act he merged with the touristic collector. Richardson's heavy irony signaled his discomfort with his companion's compromise; his narrative denied to the new club essential meaning by naming it a mere "reminiscence"—a *souvenir*—of what once was.[36]

THE TOURIST: COLLECTING AS CONSUMPTION

Multiple replication of the object—supply—is the essential precondition for a successful commodity trade, but this same condition empties the object of value for the rare art collector. In this sense his interest runs counter not only to that of the aboriginal producer, but also to that of the tourist-collector. Mohawk women at Kahnawake today remember with pleasure and pride the great quantities of beaded objects that had to be prepared for a successful stint selling souvenirs at Saratoga, or at the annual summer agricultural fairs in Ontario and Quebec. They are keenly aware, as they continue the traditional production of beaded horseshoes and pincushions to sell at the summer powwow recently founded at Kahnawake—arts that have continued to be produced throughout this century—that a plentiful stock is an indispensable prerequisite for attracting buyers.[37]

As a number of writers on tourism have theorized, the tourist was essentially a consumer, a collector of touristic experiences for which souvenirs were essential as 'markers.'[38] From early contact times until the present, Indian souvenirs have been disproportionately popular with visitors to North American tourist sites, a vogue that reached a high point during the late nineteenth century. The full explanation of this popularity is a subject too large to explore fully here, but it is important to note the central connection of the consumption of Indian imagery to emerging nationalisms in the United States and Canada.[39] Both the Niagara Falls buyer of beaded pincushions and the Anglo-Canadian gentleman in search of war clubs were motivated by a common need. Their purchases were displayed as trophies of imperial possession in the gentleman's den and as signs of a sentimental brush with an exotic and noble past in the 'cozy corner' of a lady's parlor.[40] Viewed within the domestic spaces of the home, these trophies represented, in microcosm, the same drama of the displacement of the primitive by the modern as the more schematic and comprehensive public displays of the museum. Both public and private exhibits constituted ritual acts of consumption and display that naturalized immigrants and the descendants of immigrants as Native North Americans.

As museum accession books show, the large majority of the beaded pincushions and souvenir clubs that are now in public collections came neither from the ethnologist-collector nor from the rare art collector, but were donated by a host of ordinary private individuals.[41] Earlier in this century some of the more 'serious' museums refused such donations and even deaccessioned examples of tourist art. But with the passage of time many of these common domestic objects, having acquired their own patina of age, found their way onto museum storage shelves—but, because of their lack of histories of 'authentic' Indian use, not into public exhibitions.

The internal structure of the museum system, its subdivision into separate museums or discrete departments dealing with ethnology, history, folk art, fine art, and so on has prevented other kinds of authenticity inscribed in these objects from being recognized. Tourist art did come with histories of use, although not ones that fitted conventional museum subject categories. The inattention to the testimony these objects offer is, in its way, as significant a silence as the rejection of the objects themselves. Many pieces of tourist art bear inscriptions that note the occasions on which they were acquired—a honeymoon trip to Niagara Falls or a Christmas gift to Aunt Sarah in Yorkshire from her niece in Winnipeg—which are hallmarks of 'authentic' social history. They illuminate histories of interaction between Native and non-Native, an intercultural story that the ethnologist's paradigm of race and exclusive ethnicity could not easily narrate, and in which the fine art curator, imbued with a disdain for popular art, was uninterested.

POSTCARDS FROM THE FIELD:
THE ETHNOLOGIST AS TOURIST

The four kinds of collectors that have been described are ideal types. On many occasions, as we have seen, the different players exchanged roles, swapped lines, or sang in chorus. Even the museum ethnologist, like the rare art collector, merged with the tourist-collector at times, straying across the professional lines that he himself had drawn. Speck carefully instructs the National Museum of Canada staff to forward his wife Florence's purchases of baskets and dolls, packed in with the ethnological specimens, to their summer home in Massachusetts. Chief Paul writes to Sapir asking his shoe size so that he can send him a pair of beaded moccasins as a Christmas present. And all the ethnologists collected Indian postcards while in the field.

The postcard is a quintessentially touristic consumable, interchangeable as a marker of touristic experience with a beaded souvenir. Many of the images on postcards sold in Native communities were also perfect analogues for the ethnologists' reconstructed representations of the past, showing Native Americans dressed in 'traditional' dress, archetypally posed in canoes or looking out across an empty landscape. The numerous examples of the ethnologists' use of these postcards as reasonable facsimiles of the historical past is even more striking evidence of the coincident gazes of scientist and tourist. In at least one case Speck used a postcard to illustrate a major ethnographic publication.[12] If the condition of tourism is an integral aspect of modernity, then the ethnologist was a fully modern man.

So, too, of course, was his subject, the Indian. The successful commoditization of Indian arts and crafts and its capturing of intercultural motifs and forms accomplished a transition from the sophisticated systems of specialized craft production and exchange that had existed well before the arrival of Europeans to the new economic realities of the industrial age. This transition required versatility above all else. The full range of activities in which Native collectors typically engaged is clearly stated on the letterhead used by P. J. Atkins, a Six Nations Iroquois collector-agent, in his correspondence with the National Museum of Canada: "Dealer in Groceries and Provisions, Cured Meats; Contracts taken for Supplying Indians for Camps, Factories and all lines of work. Also for Concerts, Entertainment, Fall Fairs., etc., etc."[43] The mention of "Entertainment" and "Fall Fairs" is a clear indicator of involvement in the souvenir trade, for tourist art was always sold to spectators and visitors on these occasions. Similarly, Speck's own hand-picked Penobscot collecting agent, Chief Gabe Paul, was a seller of tourist art. While on a month's visit to Speck in Philadelphia in 1912, Speck reported to Sapir that Paul "is in great confusion now clearing out his moccasin and basket stock to return home. He has been here three weeks pushing his business to pay expenses, souvenir goods."[44]

One final text is not a postcard but a letter from the field, written to Speck in 1942 by a student reporting on her reconnaissance trip to the Akwesasne (St. Regis) Mohawk reserve. The text is a paradigmatic statement of the salvage anthropology of the day—and it also provides the ethnologist's gloss of the text panels in the Heye museum's "Iroquois Women" case with which we began:

> The four days I was there were just about enough to show me what a job it would be to work the place over right. (by the way, am I mistaken in thinking that the Mohawks as a whole and the St. Regis band in particular haven't been very throroughly covered ethnographically? . . .) Yet, from another point of view, they are so thoroughly acculturated—even prosperously so—that one would have to scratch under the surface pretty deep in some cases to get anything.

This letter shows once again the ethnologist's commitment to freezing the representational moment in the past, for the notion that a community could be 'covered' implicitly denies any interest in diachronic representation or any interest in 'acculturation' itself.[45] The specific implications of this approach for the museum object are made clear in a subsequent paragraph:

> You wanted to know about basketry. Some of the women still make baskets, although not nearly so many as before this war plant boom. Their materials are supplied to them by a trading company, which takes the finished baskets and sells them to the tourist trade on the reservation and outside. . . . So I didn't get you a basket because none of the old plain splint ones are obtainable. These commercial ones are highly colored and made in the usual varied styles of present-day baskets in stores everywhere.[46]

The student takes for granted that the 'impure' incorporation of imported materials, the commoditized (the 'commercial'), the touristic, and the "highly colored" do not belong in the museum.

The lack of a slot for tourist art in the grand museum schema is intimately connected to the intercultural nature of the objects themselves. The problem with Indian tourist art was that it looked too white. The same features that accounted for the appeal of the objects to consumers and their successful entry into the commodity system of Victorian North America prevented them from fitting comfortably into the categories of otherness. Tourist wares were threatening because they blurred the boundaries, they rendered the other unrecognizable. In symbolic terms we can interpret colonial museum representations as simple narratives of geographical displacement of the other by European colonization. If museums had assigned positive value to intercultural objects—as evidence of the ability of aboriginal people to adapt, to survive, and even to thrive without assimilating—they would have subverted the text of colonialism in two critical ways: they would have disrupted the rarity value produced by the evolutionist credo of the disappearing Indian, and they would have denied the escapist fantasy of refuge from industrialism that was structured by the dialectics of primitivist discourse.

DENIAL AND DESIRE IN THE MUSEUM

Such explanations do not completely satisfy, however, in the face of the sheer strength of the avoidance exhibited by many ethnologists of the modernity that was everywhere as they went about their work in Native communities. Igor Kopytoff's analysis of the process of commoditization is helpful in understanding the definitiveness of this rejection. He sets up a model of commoditization as a process that occurs along a spectrum with the singularized (rare) object at one end and its opposite, the replicatable commodity, at the other. In complex societies, he writes: "Publicly recognized commoditization operates side by side with innumerable schemes of valuation and singularization devised by individuals, social categories, and groups, and these schemes stand in unresolvable conflict with public commoditization as well as with one another."[47] The "yearning for singularization" that Kopytoff sees as characteristic of complex societies is immediately recognizable as the driving force behind the rare art collector and the ethnologist-collector. The rare art collector's desire for singularization is connected to aristocratic traditions of collecting, however, while the museum ethnologist values singularity as a cognitive tool. These contrasting motivations for valuing singularization are also related to the competing concepts of elitist "Kultur" and democratized Boasian "culture," both of which, as Dominguez has argued, are Western impositions on the conceptual schemes of many non-Western peoples.[48]

The museum system empowered the rare art collector as patron and the professional ethnologist as gatekeeper. As a result, the singularized was privileged over the commodity in museum representation. The contrasting logic of "publicly recognized commoditization" is identifiable in the collecting activities of the Native agent-producer and the tourist consumer. These other kinds of collectors have also influenced the current shape of the museum collection, subverting its ideal purity through their donations of popular art and their offerings of the replica and the new.

Stewart and Vaessen have further analyzed the sources of the "yearning for singularization"—which Stewart terms "longing"—as products of the same processes of industrialized modernity that fostered extreme forms of commoditization.[49] The individual's alienation from her personal past creates, according to Stewart, needs that the souvenir and habits of private collecting attempt to satisfy. Vaessen, analogously, identifies the loss of ties to communal pasts produced by the dislocations of the industrial age as an important causal factor in the development of nineteenth-century museums. These institutions, he argues, compensated for loss on a public scale through their reconstructions of continuous, linear, and integrated historical narratives. Both of these theories suggest the nature of the desire that lay behind the emphasis on the premodern in museum displays about Indians. The flight of the rare art collector and the ethnologist from the commoditization and dislocation occurring in Western societies led them to make of the museum a shrine to the premodern. The pleasure produced by these acts of museological representation in non-Native viewers was in inverse proportion to the pain of denial they engendered in Native viewers. The avoidance of the commoditized is a sign of the silence about Native peoples' contemporary existences, of the lifestyles that had been imposed on them by force and then ingeniously negotiated under unavoidable conditions of colonial domination.

Tourist art is the product of a careful, anthropological study of the material culture and aesthetics of the Western other by Native artists and craftspeople. As in all such studies, the prototypes tended to rub off on the students; there is abundant evidence for the regular use of the same kinds of beadwork and basketry that were made for sale *within* Native communities. In many ways these souvenir and trade wares seem to be the most authentic representations of the courageous, innovative, and creative adaptation that Woodlands aboriginal peoples made during one of the darkest periods in their history.

In denying this modernity through their exhibitions, museums also operated in apparent contradiction of official government assimilationist policies toward Native Americans. The arbitrary boundaries of time and space that museums established sliced through the unity of everyone's lived experience, Native and non-Native. The silence surrounding tourist art is thus the expression of a tension between nostalgic primitivist desires deeply inscribed in the popular imagination and the official acts of the state.[50] Under colonial regimes this tension was unresolvable. Such a view of the museum helps explain why it has been a major site of political confrontation as we emerge into the postcolonial era. This explanation also suggests that ethnographic museums have acted as arenas for complex negotiations of social constructions rather than—as has been argued—relatively straightforward instruments for the policing and education of the general public.[51]

DEATH AND LIFE IN THE NATIVE AMERICAN MUSEUM

Metaphors of death are frequently used by Native Americans to describe museums and the things they contain. In 1977 the Mohawk of Kahnawake decided to establish a cultural center instead of a museum because they perceived the museum's exclusive focus on the past to be antithetical to their mandate of fostering future cultural development and the revitalization of tradition. According to the gloss of the center's program director, museums contain "things from the past that are dead"— they put under glass "things that no longer exist."[52] In 1988, at the height of the controversy surrounding "The Spirit Sings," the largest exhibition of aboriginal art ever mounted in Canada, the contemporary Cree artist Joane Cardinal Schubert used related imagery in her painting "And Then Comes the Smiling Mortician."[53] She depicted a curator in the guise of a Nazi death camp officer interring an Ojibwa drum, the source of the show's logo, in a coffin-shaped glass display case.[54]

Both the language and the practice of museums—derived from the dominant scientific paradigm of the nineteenth century, natural history—justify, to some extent, these critiques. Ethnologists collect 'specimens' and arrange them in 'taxonomies,' and conservators then 'stabilize' the objects and their environments. The stated goal is to make change in the objects impossible. A relentless logic is contained in this terminology. Growth, change, and reproduction define biological life. The 'specimen' is therefore dead by definition, and fixed taxonomies are produced by taxidermy—the removal of vital organs. In fact, many of the ethnological specimens collected during the Museum Age were vital organs of social process in aboriginal life. Medicine bundles animate rituals and wampum belts keep alive historical memory; their wholesale removal to the museum causes atrophy and decay. Reduced to the terms in which many Native Americans have come to see it, the conventional museum is like the vast chilled room in the movie *Coma*, where bodies lay suspended in a state of irreversible dormancy, waiting to be cannibalized by technicians of science for the benefit of rich transplant patients.

The signs that the colonial era of the museum is drawing to a close reach far beyond the establishment of the National Museum of the American Indian. In the closing days of "The Spirit Sings" the Assembly of First Nations and the Canadian Museums Association established a task force to develop new guidelines for effective partnerships between the two communities. Its report, published in February 1992, recommends among other things, that every future museum representation of First Peoples be the product of an equal collaboration between aboriginal and nonaboriginal peoples.[55]

This process of partnership is already underway. The projects carried out collaboratively, and the increasingly active Native museums, are sites of revisionist history, representing and often privileging the experience of modernity and the contemporary overrepresentations of a more remote past. Iroquois curator Rick Hill prominently featured such tourist-associated objects as a Haida argilite model totem pole and a late nineteenth-century Iroquois beaded Glengarry cap in the historical displays that introduce the installation of contemporary Native American art at the new Institute of American Indian Arts Museum in Santa Fe. In discussing the adoption by earlier Native artists of 'inauthentic' Euro-American styles of floral decoration in their beadwork, he notes: "Even if there were a cross-cultural influence, the Great Lakes Indians believed that this style best represented their world view at that time."[56]

One of the most active Iroquois museums, the Woodlands Indian Museum on the Six Nations Reserve in Brantford, Ontario, has presented, among others, exhibitions about Iroquois high steel workers, quiltmakers, and traditions of aboriginal music. The last of these featured country and western music along with traditional drumming. One of its most successful exhibitions, "Fluffs and Feathers," examined images of Indians in popular culture and included tourist art of all kinds, Native and non-Native.[57] Such shows are beginning to remove the object from its artificial confinement inside spatial, temporal, and cultural boxes, and to loosen its exclusive hold on museum representation.

The ending of the silence about tourist art in both Native and non-Native museums is an augury of the end of the colonial discourse of the museum. As the silence that has surrounded tourist art ends, a new silence has been falling over another class of objects. In another case in George Heye's museum today there are now vacant spaces where Plains medicine bundles used to be displayed. A printed card nearby reads:

> Sacred/Sensitive Objects. The museum is contacting tribal elders and traditional leaders to discover what are the appropriate and sensitive methods for storing, handling, displaying and interpreting objects in its collections. The effects of these discussions . . . will be evidenced by new labelling, display techniques and in some cases the actual removal of objects from display. . . . We hope that our efforts to "relearn" the methods used to display the museum's collections will provide truer insights into the cultures and traditions represented in our exhibit.

This sign is a sign of life, not death. It heralds not only the return of some objects to aboriginal communities—communities that have survived despite the script that was written for them and that the colonial museum helped inscribe—but also the process of 'relearning' that has begun.

NOTES

1. The degree of Native Americans' power over the NMAI project is unprecedented within the Smithsonian system. It is the only one among the museums dedicated to a particular minority group within the United States to be controlled (through a Native American director and a majority Native American board and upper management) by the people who are being represented. Two major legislative acts, the Native American Indian Graves and Repatriation Act of 1989 and the Indian Arts and Crafts Act of 1990, provide further evidence of this change; the first legislates disclosure of museum holdings and the repatriation of skeletal remains and important archaeological materials to Native Ameri-

cans, while the second attempts, however imperfectly, to establish criteria for authenticity in the sale and display of arts and crafts.

2. Heye turned his private collection into a public museum in part to gain tax advantages. The museum became part of the Heye Foundation, a larger entity that funded ethnographic research, collecting, and publication during the first half of this century. See Kevin Wallace, "A Reporter at Large: Slim Shins' Monument," *The New Yorker* (November 19, 1960), for a profile of George Heye and his collecting activities.

3. The policy statement of NMAI was published in *Museum Anthropology* 15, no. 2 (1991): 25–28. See also the debate over this policy between William C. Sturtevant, "New National Museum of the American Indian Collections Policy Statement: A Critical Analysis," in *Museum Anthropology* 15, no. 2 (1991): 29–30, and W. Richard West Jr., "The National Museum of the American Indian Repatriation Policy: Reply to William C. Sturtevant," *Museum Anthropology* 15, no. 3 (1991): 13–14.

4. West, "National Museum," 13. A New York satellite to NMAI is located in the Old U.S. Customs House in lower Manhattan. These remarks are based on the plans and planning process discussed by George C. Horse Capture in a talk delivered to the Native American Art Studies Association in Sioux Falls, South Dakota, in October 1991, and on further statements by W. Richard West Jr. He has stated: "What I want to see are life experiences, all those aspects that constitute Indian culture. That may involve the arts of dance, drama, and literature as well as painting and sculpture. Second, this 'living museum' must reflect the full chronology of Indian culture, not settle on one frozen chapter of an often romanticized historical past. We have to bring our exhibitions forward in time to see what they mean in the context of contemporary life. And to do that, we need live bodies—not static dioramas" (quoted by Donald Garfield, "Cultural Chronology," *Museum News* 70, no. 1 [1991]: 55). See also James Clifford, "Four Northwest Coast Museums: Travel Reflections," in *Exhibiting Cultures: The Poetics and Politics of Museum Display*, ed. Ivan Karp and Steven D. Lavine (Washington, D.C., 1991), for an analysis of the alternative representations that have already been constructed by Native Americans in two Northwest Coast museums.

5. These developments can also be seen as a further stage in the progressive deconstruction of the universalist concepts that underlay the Smithsonian and other nineteenth-century museums. Human and natural history, initially combined within a single institution, are now represented by separate museums that address specific aspects of science, ethnology, technology, fine art, and history—the latter two categories divided along ethnic lines. Like the recently constructed Museum of African Art, the NMAI will present as art many of the same kinds of objects presented as ethnological specimens in the Smithsonian's Museum of Human History (housed together with and formerly part of the Museum of Natural History).

6. Eilean Hooper-Greenhill, *Museums and the Shaping of Knowledge* (New York, 1992), 215.

7. For important recent studies of museum representation, see Ivan Karp and

Steven D. Lavine, eds., *Exhibiting Cultures: The Poetics and Politics of Museum Display* (Washington, D.C., 1991); Ivan Karp, Christine Mullen Kreamer, and Steven D. Lavine, eds., *Museums and Communities: The Politics of Public Culture* (Washington, D.C., 1992); Michael M. Ames, *Cannibal Tours and Glass Boxes: The Anthropology of Museums* (Vancouver, 1992); and Peter Vergo, ed., *The New Museology* (London, 1989). The relationship of past collecting practices to representation has been explored by Spencer R. Crew and James E. Sims with regard to museums of American history in their article "Locating Authenticity: Fragments of a Dialogue." As research in social history developed, they note, museum professionals discovered that "the holdings within their institutions created major stumbling blocks. Many times their collections did not contain the objects they needed" (in Karp and Lavine, *Exhibiting Cultures*, 164–65). Although, as Hooper-Greenhill eloquently argues, "the radical potential of material culture, of concrete objects, of real things, of primary sources, is the endless possibility of rereading," it is important to acknowledge that patterns of exclusion also shape the potential for new representations in museums (*Museums and the Shaping of Knowledge*, 215).

8. For the relationship of museum building to anthropological constructions of knowledge, see William C. Sturtevant, "Does Anthropology Need Museums?" *Proceedings of the Biological Society* 82 (1969): 619–50; and George W. Stocking Jr., ed., *Objects and Others: Essays on Museums and Material Culture* (Madison, Wis., 1985). On rare art collecting, see Joseph Alsop, *The Rare Art Traditions: The History of Art Collecting and Its Linked Phenomena* (New York, 1982). For discussions of 'natural history' as a dominant paradigm of late nineteenth-century knowledges, see Carlo Ginzburg, "Morelli, Freud and Sherlock Holmes: Clues and the Scientific Method," *The History Workshop* 9 (1980): 5–36; and Ludmila Jordanova, "Objects of Knowledge: A Historical Perspective on Museums," in Vergo, *New Museology*.

9. As Jonaitis has shown in "Representations of Women in Native American Museum Exhibitions: A Kwakiutl Example," *European Review of Native American Studies* 5, no. 2 (1991), in Boas' early twentieth-century representation of Northwest Coast women the plastic arrangement of a museum display can convey messages that directly contradict the written anthropological texts of its own author. At the American Museum of Natural History, as at the Heye Foundation, a Western story of patriarchy and gender roles is narrated through representations of the 'other.' See James Clifford's framing discussion of this feature of representation in "On Ethnographic Allegory," in *Writing Culture: The Politics and Poetics of Ethnography*, ed. James Clifford and George E. Marcus (Berkeley, 1986). Although there were important female ethnologists such as Frances Densmore working among Woodlands peoples, patriarchal discourse dominated ethnological museum representation in the early twentieth century. Because most ethnological collectors were men, I use the male in referring to members of the group.

10. Svetlana Alpers, "The Museum as a Way of Seeing," in Karp and Lavine, *Exhibiting Cultures*, 25–32.

11. For an example of degenerationist writing about Native American material culture, see W. H. Holmes, "On the Evolution of Ornament—An American

Lesson," *American Anthropologist* 3 (1890). For historical accounts of cultural evolutionist theories about material culture, see Robert Goldwater, *Primitivism and Modern Art* (New York, 1967), 20–21; and Curtis M. Hinsley Jr., *Savages and Scientists: The Smithsonian Institution and the Development of American Anthropology: 1846–1910* (Washington, D.C., 1981), 103–4.

12. I have discussed this development in "Moccasins into Slippers: Woodlands Indian Hats, Bags and Shoes in Tradition and Transformation," *Northeast Indian Quarterly* 7, no. 4 (1990): 26–36.

13. See Ruth B. Phillips, "What Is Huron Art? Native American Art and the New Art History," *The Canadian Journal of Native Studies* 9, no. 2 (1989); and "Glimpses of Eden: Iconographic Themes in Huron Pictorial Tourist Art," *European Review of Native American Studies* 5, no. 2 (1991): 20.

14. Canada, *Sessional Papers*, no. 6 (1883): xlvi.

15. For discussions of assimilationist policies and Native responses in the United States, see Frederick E. Hoxie, *A Final Promise: The Campaign to Assimilate the Indians, 1880–1920* (Cambridge, 1989); and in Canada, J. R. Miller, *Skyscrapers Hide the Heavens: A History of Indian-White Relations in Canada* (Toronto, 1989), 189–207.

16. Canada, *Sessional Papers*, no. 1 (1886): xxiv-xxvii, John A. MacDonald, superintendent general of Indian Affairs to the governor general of Canada.

17. At Kahnawake a number of people now in their middle years grew up in families that had been entirely supported by single mothers who made and organized the production of beadwork by other women (field notes, Trudy Nicks and Ruth Phillips, January 1992).

18. A copy of the printed petition is found in the Frank Speck papers at the American Philosophical Society, Philadelphia. (Capitalization of words and phrases replicates that in the original.) It is dated "at the INDIAN CAMPS, INTERVALE, County of Carroll, N.H., 189__," and signed with the printed names of members of the Abenaki community. The possibility that a sympathetic non-Native helped draft it and suggested the language that is used does not diminish, but rather reinforces, its value as evidence in support of this argument.

19. Aboriginal peoples had also, of course, been engaged in highly specialized forms of commodity production and long-distance trade in precontact times. These are well documented in such early European accounts as the *Jesuit Relations* and in the archaeological record.

20. The special flavor of this document is owed to an irony of which neither the Abenaki nor the white ethnologists of the period were aware. As Brasser and others have convincingly demonstrated, splint basketry was not an indigenous craft but was learned from colonial settlers, probably Scandinavian or German, in the early contact period (see Ted Brasser, *A Basketful of Indian Culture Change*, National Museum of Man, Mercury Series, Canadian Ethnology Service Paper 22 [Ottawa, 1975]). The thoroughness with which aboriginal groups in the Northeast mastered the craft together with their economic need led to their establishing a near monopoly over basket making in the Northeast. Unaware at the time that splint baskets belonged to the despised realm of the acculturated, ethnologists enthusiastically collected and displayed them in museums.

21. Reprinted as *League of the Iroquois* (Secaucus, N.J., 1962), 32.

22. Douglas Cole's 1985 landmark study of the collecting of Northwest Coast objects (*Captured Heritage: The Scramble for Northwest Coast Artifacts* [Seattle, 1985]), Aldona Jonaitis' study of the collections of the American Museum of Natural History (*From the Land of the Totem Poles* [New York, 1988]), David Penney's careful documentation of the collecting of Chandler and Pohrt (*Art of the American Indian Frontier* [Seattle, 1992]), and Diana Fane's study of Stewart Culin's collections for the Brooklyn Museum (*Objects of Myth and Memory* [New York, 1991]), are important recent exceptions to this neglect.

23. See Hans Belting, *The End of the History of Art?* (Chicago, 1987), 19, for a reflexive discussion of early twentieth-century art historical concepts of style; and my article, "Fielding Culture: Dialogues between Anthropology and Art History," *Museum Anthropology* 18, no. 1 (1994), for further discussion of this issue in relation to anthropological discourse.

24. Letter from Edward Sapir to Mrs. James H. Peck, president of the Canadian Guild of Handicrafts, Ottawa September 11, 1911, in Correspondence of Edward Sapir, Archives of the Canadian Ethnology Service, Canadian Museum of Civilization (referred to below as CANES Archives, CMC).

25. Dated "Seven Islands, St. Lawrence, June 26, 1912," Sapir Correspondence, CANES Archives, CMC.

26. Letter to Edward Sapir, n.d. 1912, Sapir Correspondence, CANES Archives, CMC.

27. Proximity to Native communities, ease and availability of competent Native helpers, academic teaching loads, and liking for the comforts of home are all probable reasons for the shorter and more frequent visits to the field that North American ethnologists made than their colleagues working in other parts of the world. An unexamined consequence of this pattern is, however, their more superficial immersion in community life and a less rigorous use of methods of participant observation—as well as reliance on Native collector-agents.

28. A number of recent projects have begun to raise the consciousness of contemporary museum audiences about the roles played by Native collector-agents. See the review of two recent exhibitions in New York City, "Chiefly Feasts" at the American Museum of Natural History and "Objects of Myth and Memory" at the Brooklyn Museum of Art by Janet Catherine Berlo and Ruth B. Phillips, "'Vitalizing the Things of the Past': Museum Representations of Native North American Art in the 1990s," *Museum Anthropology* 16, no. 1 (1992).

29. Letter from Frank Speck to Edward Sapir from Annisquam, Gloucester, Mass., n.d., 1912, Sapir Correspondence, CANES Archives, CMC.

30. Letter of November 31, 1911, Sapir Correspondence, CANES Archives, CMC

31. Examples of this kind of commissioning abound. Among the most extraordinary were Speck's commissioned 'replicas' of archaic fire drills and tobacco containers, now in the American Museum of Natural History in New York, acquired from the Huron at Lorette, Quebec, during his trip in 1908. This community had lived outside Quebec city since the late seventeenth century, in material conditions that were, by the twentieth century, indistinguishable from those of their French Canadian neighbors. The objects bear no resemblance to any documented Huron artifacts.

32. Headed St. Mary's Reservation, December 26, 1911, Sapir Correspondence, CANES Archives, CMC.

33. Letter from Speck to Sapir, dated Philadelphia, January 15, 1912, Sapir Correspondence, CANES Archives, CMC.

34. Letter from Speck to Sapir, Philadelphia, February 14, 1912, CANES Archives, CMC. He was referring to Penobscot, Abenaki, and Huron objects.

35. John Richardson, "A Journey from Walpole Island to Port Sarnia," *Literary Garland* 7, no. 1 (1849): 25.

36. See the "Introduction," by Nelson H. H. Graburn to his edited volume *Ethnic and Tourist Arts: Cultural Expressions from the Fourth World* (Berkeley, 1976); and his article "The Evolution of Tourist Arts," *Annals of Tourism Research* 11, no. 3 (1984): 393–419, for important theoretical models of the categories of tourist art.

37. Personal communications, Presida Stacey and Penny LeClaire, Kahnawake, Quebec, January 28, 1992.

38. The term is Dean MacCannell's; see his *The Tourist: A New Theory of the Leisure Class* (New York, 1976); and also John F. Sears' provocative historical study, *Sacred Places: American Tourist Attractions in the Nineteenth Century* (New York, 1989).

39. I have explored this problem in an unpublished paper, "Consuming Identities: Curiosity, Souvenir and Images of Indianness in Nineteenth-Century Canada," delivered at Carleton University as the Davidson Dunton Research Lecture in November 1991.

40. See Beverly Gordon, *American Indian Art: The Collecting Experience* (Madison, Wis., 1988), 6–7; and Molly Lee, "Appropriating the Primitive: Turn-of-the-Century Collection and Display of Native Alaskan Art," *Arctic Anthropology* 28, no. 1 (1991): 6–15, for the discussions of specific ways that Indian tourist art was displayed in the home around 1900 and the connection of the vogue for Indian art to the American Arts and Crafts Movement.

41. The largest single private collection of northeastern tourist art, assembled by June Bedford over the past few decades, was recently bought by the Royal Ontario Museum. Bedford bought nearly all the pieces in the collection inexpensively at flea markets and antique shops. See *Mohawk Micmac Maliseet . . . and other Indian Souvenir Art from Victorian Canada* (London: Canada House Cultural Centre Gallery, 1985).

42. The postcard is an illustration for his *Penobscot Man*. It bears the printed caption "John Snow, Penobscot Tribe, Old Town," together with Speck's handwritten suggestions about handling the copyright problem and the figure caption for the book, "Penobscot man with moose skin coat." Speck Papers, American Philosophical Society, Philadelphia.

43. Frederick Waugh correspondence, CANES Archives, CMC.

44. Letter from Frank Speck to Edward Sapir headed Philadelphia, December 16, 1912, Sapir Correspondence, CANES Archives, CMC.

45. For concepts of time in anthropological discourse, see Johannes Fabian, *Time and the Other: How Anthropology Makes Its Object* (New York, 1983). A strong interest in acculturation in American anthropology was even at this moment developing, which manifested itself in a host of studies in the 1950s. Inter-

estingly, this work was largely dissociated from museum collecting; the object record remained fixed by the earlier generation's efforts.

46. Letter to Speck, dated September 14, 1942, signed "Mary," Speck Papers, American Philosophical Society, Philadelphia.

47. Igor Kopytoff, "The Cultural Biography of Things: Commoditization as Process," in *The Social Life of Things: Commodities in Cultural Perspective*, ed. Arjun Appadurai (Cambridge, 1986), 79–80.

48. Virginia Dominguez, "Invoking Culture: The Messy Side of 'Cultural Politics,' " *The South Atlantic Quarterly* 91, no. 1 (1992).

49. Susan Stewart, *On Longing: Narratives of the Miniature, the Gigantic, the Souvenir, the Collection* (Baltimore, 1984); Jan Vaessen, "Opening and Closing: On the Dialectics of the Museum," in *Generators of Culture: The Museum as a Stage*, ed. Rob van Zoest/d'Arts (Amsterdam, 1989).

50. On primitivism and modernity, see Sally Price, *Primitive Art in Civilized Places* (Chicago, 1989); Marianna Torgovnik, *Gone Primitive: Savage Intellects, Modern Lives* (Chicago, 1990); and *The Myth of Primitivism: Perspectives on Art*, ed. Susan Hiller (London, 1991).

51. This argument is made by Tony Bennett in "The Political Rationality of the Museum," *Continuum: An Australian Journal of the Media* 4, no. 1 (1990).

52. Kanatakta, personal communication, Kahnawake, Quebec, January 30, 1992. The cultural center movement developed in Canada in the 1970s as the result of pressure from aboriginal communities on the Department of Indian and Northern Affairs to fund institutions that would foster cultural preservation. They have focused most strongly on aboriginal languages and on education, but also engage in a broad range of other activities including, in some communities, running community museums.

53. "The Spirit Sings: Artistic Traditions of Canada's First Peoples" was organized by the Glenbow Museum as part of the cultural program of the Calgary Winter Olympics in 1988. It became the subject of a boycott organized by the Lubicon band of Cree in support of a land claim that had been shamefully ignored by provincial and federal governments for forty years. Although the immediate cause of the boycott was the corporate sponsorship of the exhibition by Shell Oil, one of the companies drilling on the land claimed by the Lubicon, the protest quickly broadened to include the lack of representation of contemporary conditions of aboriginal life in the exhibition, which focused on the early contact period. I acted as curator of the Northern Woodlands for the exhibition. The experience of the project and its politics changed my approaches to the art-historical study of Native art and to museological representation—as well as those of many other academics and museum professionals in Canada.

54. Cardinal-Schubert's painting is reproduced in Ruth B. Phillips, "The Public Relations Wrap: What We Can Learn from 'The Spirit Sings,' " *Inuit Art Quarterly* 5, no. 2 (1990).

55. The task force report, *Turning the Page: Forging New Partnerships between Museums and First Peoples*, was ratified by the Canadian Museums Association and the Assembly of First Nations in 1992. It makes recommendations on issues of repatriation, access and interpretation, and implementation. It is avail-

able from the Canadian Museum Association, 280 Metcalfe Street, Suite 400, Ottawa, Ontario, K2P 1R7, Canada.

56. Rick Hill, *Creativity Is Our Tradition: Three Decades of Contemporary Indian Art at the Institute of American Indian Arts,* (Santa Fe, N.M., 1992), 23.

57. See Deborah Doxtator, *Fluffs and Feathers: An Exhibit on the Symbols of Indianness, A Resource Guide* (Brantford, Ontario, 1988). The exhibition was remounted and prepared for a North American tour in 1992–93 by the Woodlands Indian Museum in collaboration with the Royal Ontario Museum.

Part Two

COLONIALISM AND CULTURAL DIFFERENCE

CHAPTER 5

The Effacement of Difference:
Colonialism and the Origins of
Nationalism in Diderot and Herder

ANTHONY PAGDEN

Nous seuls en ces climats nous sommes les barbares
(Voltaire, Alzire, ou les Américains, 1:1)

In 1770 there appeared anonymously and with an Amsterdam im-
print—thus signaling its possible radicalism—a six-volume work entitled
*Histoire philosophique et politique des établissemens et du commerce des
Europens dans les deux Indes.* Its author was the abbé Guillaume Thomas
Raynal, a renegade Jesuit and former editor of the *Mercure de France.*
Raynal himself was a moderate reformer, a man who, in the words of
Frederic Grimm, held views that were "more in accordance with established politics than with justice,"[1] and had close, if little known, ties with
the group around the duc de Choiseul who, after the defeat of the Seven
Years War and the loss of Canada, had hoped to reaffirm the French
presence in the Caribbean. Later, in 1785 he also wrote an *Essai sur
l'administration de St. Dominique,* which although it proposed reform,
advocated neither the emancipation of the slaves nor even the abolish-
ment of the slave trade.[2] He was not, therefore, the most likely author
of what was to become not only the most outspoken condemnation of
European colonization, but also one of the most powerful critiques of
the ancien regime itself,[3] a work which, claimed one of its fiercest critics,
had aroused in all its readers a new brand of fanaticism: "the fanaticism
of liberty."[4]

The *Histoire* became an immediate best-seller. More than thirty editions were printed between 1770 and 1787.[5] Napoleon later declared
himself to be a "zele disciple de Raynal" and, significantly in view of
what he did there, took a copy of the book with him to Egypt.[6] The title
of the work alone was sufficiently striking to guarantee it a readership.
The first part, the claim to be both a philosophical and a political history, made it, as Raynal went to some lengths to explain in the preface

to Book I, unique. "I have," he assured his readers, "interrogated the living and the dead. I have weighed their authority. I have contrasted their testimonies. I have clarified the facts." From text to text Raynal had traveled the world with the "august image of truth" always before him as a guide.[7] The second part of his title was equally striking. Here, it claimed, was a history that brought together the two halves of the planet, the East and the West, and the two hitherto unrelated spheres of European colonial activity into one work. It was as if the gaze of the European, "raised above all concerns," so that he could "glide above the atmosphere," could indeed unite "the whole world beneath one."[8] It is not, however, only the "gaze de haut en bas" that has the power to unite such disparate peoples as the "Hindoos" and the Iroquois; it is also that other great eighteenth-century instrument both of acquisition and of understanding: commerce. The *Histoire* is, as Grimm noted, very largely a history of commerce and, more crucially, a defense of commerce against colonization. Grimm, in common with many eighteenth-century social theorists, including Raynal in some of his many moods, regarded commerce, not as a necessary component of colonialism, but as its antithesis. Commerce was the exchange of goods, and much else besides, between free and equal individuals. It was Montesquieu's celebrated *doux commerce*, which alone of human activities had the power to "make men gentle." Colonization, by contrast, was a brutalizing activity that involved the exploitation of one group in the sole interests of another.

In subsequent editions the *Histoire* was reworked probably by a number of the lesser and greater philosophes: Pechmeja, Deleyre, Dubreuil, Valadier, Saint-Lambert, Lagrange, and Diderot's future biographer Naigeon, among others. The original text provided little more than a narrative structure for a series of striking juxtapositions which, by the time of the final edition in 1780, had transformed the work into a kind of mini-*Encyclopédie* on the political, intellectual, and social implications for Europe of colonization. The most original and sustained of these contributions was by Diderot. They were also far more uncompromising in their anticolonialism than the more moderate and reconciliatory tones of Raynal's original text.[9] If, in the words of Diderot's own riposte to Grimm, Raynal's work finally became "the book which I love and which the kings and their courtiers hate, the book which will give birth to Brutus,"[10] this is almost entirely because of his own presence in the text.

Like Bougainville's *Voyage autour du monde* (1771), which had provided the setting and many of the contrapuntal themes for Diderot's other great denunciation of European colonialism, the *Supplément au voyage de Bougainville* (1773), Raynal's *Histoire* offered Diderot a literary and historical context within which to construct his own savage indictment of the European colonizing venture.

The Diderot who is the interpolator of the *Histoire des deux Indes*, takes up the theme of Diderot, the supplementer of Bougainville's *Voyage*. Like his fictional Tahitians, and in common with most eighteenth-century social theorists, Diderot held that it was possible to identify in all human behavior a common core. We are all Hobbesian to the extent that we all share the same basic needs. We are all capable of identifying our interests, and we all ratiocinate in much the same way. Yet, although we all may be rational agents, none of us, in the real worlds in which we live, ever make fully independent rational choices. For we actually live in societies that limit and determine the range of choices that are open to us. Or, in the terms Diderot uses again and again in his political writings, all humankind is governed by three codes: the natural, the civil, and the religious.[11] Only when these are in harmony with one another is a life of virtue possible. For Diderot, conflict among his three codes amounts to a disharmony within the constitution of the person.[12] But the inescapable human communities are constructed by customs (*moeurs*) and custom is the unreflective obedience ("un soumission générale et un conduite consequente")[13] to the second and third of these laws, frequently in violation of the first. The brief history of nearly all our customs, says the figure called "B" in the dialogue that occupies much of the *Supplément au voyage de Bougainville*, can be reduced to one exemplary tale: "there is a natural man, and on top of this natural man an artificial one has been placed. And a civil war has broken out in the cave which will last all his life."[14]

For Diderot, the various arenas for these struggles are aggregates of moeurs, each of which constitutes a "national character" (*esprit national*). Each one of these, he believed, is composed of two elements, "the moral" is variable and allows for variations over time; "the physical" is fixed and dependent upon climate.[15] Like Montesquieu, Diderot had some difficulty with the determinism of climatic ascriptions. He was prepared to believe that no matter how a people's social world might change, they remained in some sense what their environment had willed them to be. Look, he said in the *Histoire*, at the Indians of "Indostan," a people who have suffered for centuries at the hands of a tyranny by comparison with which even the Spaniards might seem benign, yet they still remain "douce, humaine, timide," incapable of revolt, their only vice being their timidity.[16] But like Montesquieu, Diderot saw in the environment only a limiting condition. It is the Indians' gentle nature that they owe to their "climate," not their present social and cultural state. The complete collapse of a culture that had once rivaled that of the

Egyptians and to which the Greeks had gone to learn their science "in the days before Pythagoras," is entirely to be attributed to the barbarism of India's Mughul rulers.[17] The same was true of the African slaves in the Caribbean. If they seemed, even to such sympathetic eyes as those of the marquis de Chastellux—author of that small best-seller *De la félicité publique* (1772)—to be "slavish by nature," this was the inescapable consequence of their being slaves.[18]

Given a wider, more general definition, however, "climate" could be made to include the land, and a love of the land, that "vibrant and powerful emotion" that was "the primal core of society," and which might plausibly be identified as the principal force behind love of "patrie."[19] Yet for Diderot, climate, even in this extended sense, operated only at the level of the needs and desires we all share. It may make men gentle, as it had with the Indians, or, as with the Tartars, make them fierce, or, again, like the American Indians, disinclined to hard labor. But the full force of the "national character" is "moral"—it belongs, that is, to *mores*, to the civil and religious law, the habits and customs, the *habitudines* that constituted, in Pascal's celebrated phrase, "a second nature which destroys the first."[20]

It follows that if each character, each culture, is the product of a distinct environment and is built up from a complex pattern of norms, no two will ever be alike. There may exist conglomerates of cultures united by a common cultural ancestry. Like most eighteenth-century social theorists Diderot acknowledged the existence of a cosmopolitan environment that reached from Russia to Greece and that might be called "Europe." As a Frenchman he had a civil and religious existence that was sufficiently like that of a Englishman or an Italian for him to have no difficulty in understanding these peoples. But he recognized that faced by a Huron or a Tahitian he could have no discernible access to the mental worlds of those men, nor would they have any access to his. If, therefore, no "patrie" is commensurable with any other, contact between cultures—the long and hard sea-journeys that are the beginnings of all acts of colonization—becomes merely the fruitless expression of a potentially destructive human restlessness. Yet it is perhaps only the "savage" who, as the perfect "inward man," to use Augustine's phrase,[21] fully understands this. "Happy is the Tahitian," exclaims B, in the *Supplément au voyage de Bougainville*, who, unmoved by "fantasies from across boundless oceans," is content to "stay where he is."[22] Civil man has for centuries allowed his restlessness, his inability, in Pascal's' famous image, to remain still in a room, to drive him continually overseas. This is, of course, an ancient topos, one that belongs to a tradition that locates the source of all moral life within the civil or political community, the Ciceronian *civitas*, beyond which, in Aristotle's metaphor, only beasts and gods can flourish. All men who leave their native homes, other than pilgrims, are in some sense leaving behind, not merely a habitat, but what it is to be themselves. And pilgrims, of course, put themselves, in Michel de Certeau's words, to "the test of travel," only in order that they may return home purified. Their objective is the return itself, not the journey.

Because of this, said Diderot, all travelers are suspect, but there is "no state more immoral than that of the continual traveler (*voyageur par état*)." He who travels constantly, he wrote in the *Histoire*, "resembles a man who owns a huge house and who, instead of remaining by the side of his family, wanders constantly from room to room." What he carries with him from room to room is a catalogue of human vices: "tyranny, crime, ambition, misery, curiosity, I know not what restlessness of spirit, the desire to know and the desire to see, boredom, the dislike of familiar pleasures—these things men from all ages have carried abroad (*expatrié*) with them, and will continue to do so."[23]

In part Diderot's attack on errancy belongs to a common eighteenth-century concern with population growth, for travelers, or so Diderot claimed, leave no progeny.[24] But it is only partly that, for Diderot's "voyageur par état" is a particular being; one who not only wanders from room to room but, like Bougainville himself, must possess each in turn. Like Bougainville, that is, he is also, potentially, a colonist.

Such men are generally to be found among those who seek to fulfill ambitions for which their native land offers no scope. They are, that is, the products (or the victims) of what no civilization can avoid: the inescapable gap between ever-increasing human needs and the society's capacity to meet them. Happiness for the children of Prometheus, as Helvetius had pointed out, was a "machine which has constantly to be rebuilt."[25] Just as the savage who never experiences any desire to leave his patrie is always content with his lot precisely because it *is* his lot, so these travelers are forever discontented with theirs because they are theirs. Such men, Diderot believed, carry with them "in the bottom of their hearts the germs of depredation" that under another sky and far from the public gaze grows "with inconceivable fury."[26]

Even those who may have gone to Africa or India or America or the Pacific for more benign reasons than those of the habitual colonist inevitably suffer the fate that befalls all immigrants. For the metropolis is where that self-defining, self-creating "esprit national" is generated. In abandoning it, the traveler is compelled to become another kind of being. "I will accept that there are very few exceptions," wrote Diderot. "The greater the distance from the capital, the further the mask of the traveller's identity slips from his face. On the frontier it falls away altogether" ("Il tombe sur la frontière"). "From one hemisphere to another," he continued, "what has he, the traveller, become? Nothing. Once past the equator a man is neither English, nor Dutch, nor French, nor Spanish nor Portuguese. All that he preserves of his homeland are the principles and prejudices which authorize or excuse his conduct."[27] "Les expeditions de long cours" have thus "reared a new generation of savage nomads . . . Those men who visit so many countries that they end by belonging to none . . . These amphibians who live on the surface of the waters."[28]

The faceless European traveler has, in a sense, reversed the journey that his ancestors once made from the state of nature to civil society. By traveling through space, he has gone backwards in time; by going from Europe to America or India or the Pacific, he has also gone from civility to savagery. But the person he has thus become is not the *bon sauvage*, the natural man, whom (in Diderot's fictional account) Bougainville had met on Tahiti and who had lectured him on the virtues of a natural life. For all great revolutions, as Diderot said elsewhere, change irradicably the human and social landscapes over which they move. The principles and prejudices that the mask of civility inevitably leaves behind clutters the mind of the new savage quite as much as it did that of the old civil man. For what lies hidden beneath civil man is no longer natural man. Time and the civilizing process have changed the whole person. This decomposed civil being is what Diderot nicely calls the "domestic tiger who has returned to the jungle."[29]

The only possible exception to this dismal rule was the English. For uniquely the English had been driven overseas not by greed, the "soif d'or" that inevitably brings with it the thirst for blood.[30] They had not even gone with the desire to impose their beliefs upon others. They had gone, instead, in pursuit of liberty. Whereas the rest of Europe had exported its worst, the English had driven out the best. Whereas the Spanish, Portuguese, and French Creoles in America had now become "more or less degenerate,"[31] the English-Americans had sustained and developed their concern for liberty. It was even possible for Diderot to ignore the Indian massacres and the expropriation of Indian lands which, as others less friendly to the Thirteen Colonies could point out, were every bit as bad as those committed by other Europeans in other parts of America. The new United States was clearly not Utopia. But then Diderot had little time for utopias, and if it was not the ideal society, it was, at least, an attainable optimal society.

All other Europeans, however, "have . . . shown themselves, indistinguishable, throughout all the countries of the New World."[32] They had, in effect, become not savages, but what Diderot had defined elsewhere as "barbarians," those who have been cursed by "that sombre disposition which makes man inaccessible to the delights of nature or art and the sweetness of society."[33] "Savages" exist only in a particular cultural milieu, but "barbarians" are with us always, no matter how civilized we may appear to have become. These new barbarians have destroyed, or have attempted to destroy, as do all barbarians, the cultures of the peoples among whom they settled. But the "Féroces Européens" in America have added to this crime one that has, possibly, been still more tragic in its consequences: slavery.

If the *Histoire* is at one level a history of commerce, since only commerce, "the new arm of the moral world,"[34] as Diderot called it, can offer some hope of redemption for the European colonizing venture, at another it is among the most powerful contributions to the antislavery literature of the late eighteenth century.[35]

For Diderot, as indeed for Raynal, slavery is an obvious evil because it denies man his one inalienable right, his "propriete de soi." This, which is more than the free capacity for agency, constitutes, after reason itself, "the distinctive character of man." For, as one prominent abolitionist later argued before the *Convention nationale*, slavery not only "made of the human race a merchandise"; it also valued men precisely for that thing, physical strength, which was the least intrinsic to the human identity, and was thus "the greatest affront to our nature."[36] Freedom even to choose one's own modes of human indebtedness—which distinguishes the slave from the European day-laborer with whom his condition was frequently compared—is a mode, as Diderot phrased it, of "enjoyment in one's own mind" (*esprit*). The slave denied this feature of what it is to be a man is thus reduced to a level lower even than that of the dogs that the Spaniards had brought to America, for the dog is only an automaton, whereas the slave still retains some grasp on what, in the end, nothing can deprive him of: his consciousness.[37] The possession of a fully human consciousness meant, also, that, unlike the free man who may be similarly restricted as far as his real capacity for individual choice is concerned ("la plupart des nations," as Diderot observed, "sont dans les fers"), the slave can have no cause for hope, no expectation of "those happy times, those centuries of Enlightenment and of prosperity" that might allow even the most miserable laborer to preserve his humanity.[38] As Condorcet pointed out in his *Réflexions sur l'esclavage des nègres* in 1781, slavery, since it was governed by the laws of property, constituted a purely private relationship. Even the indentured servant who had in some sense sold himself into slavery had, in fact, only sold the right to the use of his labor and in his relationship to his masters was bound by public not private law. The slave, by contrast, was merely a legal thing (a *res*), precisely as he had been under Roman law, and thus wholly dependent upon "the caprice of his master."[39]

Slavery as it was practiced in the Americas, however, involved not merely servitude, but, more far-reaching in its destructive effects on human society in general, mass migration. For Diderot, it is above all the slave trade that is the true evil. He in no way attempts to diminish, as many apologists for slavery did, the condition of the slaves once they had reached America, and he shared Condorcet's view that those who argued for a more rigid code of conduct to protect the slaves, in place of full emancipation merely "added hypocrisy to barbarism."[40] But the traffic that was responsible for the annihilation, literally or culturally, of entire races was ultimately more devastating in its moral consequences than the actual condition of the slaves themselves. Many, far less radical in their views than Diderot, were prepared to agree that the slave trade was a new and special kind of evil. Even the frequently virulent pro-colonist lawyer, Michel René Hilliard d'Auberteuil, was willing to concede that whereas the condition of most slaves in the French Caribbean was "better than a European day labourer," to contemplate the trade was to experience "a moment of horror which freezes all the faculties." Enjoying the fruits of the slave's labor, claimed Hilliard d' Auberteuil, was a lamentable but necessary condition of survival for a colonial society based very largely on the production of sugar in climates that white laborers were commonly believed to be unable to endure. But the acquisition of slaves was a morally corrupting business, and in "this enlightened century" was best left in the hands of the English and others of "our political enemies," who were, in any case, better at it.[41]

Diderot shared Hilliard d'Auberteuil's "moment of horror," but the reasons he gave for doing so were linked back to the moral objections he had raised against the entire colonial project. The ancient world, as Diderot knew full well, could not have existed without the institution of slavery, and it was, in the last instance, slavery that made the ancient republics impossible models for any kind of modern liberty. As even Turgot, who as a minister of the Crown was sometimes forced to take a more pragmatic view of the practice, admitted, with one eye on the nascent United States, "slavery is incompatible with a good constitution."[42] This is why, Diderot argued, after the destruction of the European slave-states, "the people were a hundred times more happy, even under the most despotic empires, then they had been under the most well-ordered democracies."

But if the Ancients could not be excused from depriving their fellow creatures of their power of self-determination, they could, at least be excused from trading in them. In the brief history of slavery that Diderot provides at the beginning of chapter 24 to Book XI of the *Histoire*, modern slavery comes about not, as its ancient counterpart had done, in response to internal domestic need and from the unfortunate but natural human tendency for the strong to exploit the weak. It comes about solely as a consequence of colonization. For Diderot, modern slavery is possibly the worst of the deleterious consequences of modern travel.

Slavery in Europe had died in the late Middle Ages as the unintended consequence of the wars between the new European monarchies and their feudal nobilities, which had led to such "ruses" by the monarchs as "the protection of slaves against the tyranny of their masters" in order "to sap the power of the nobles by diminishing the number of their subjects." This "happy policy" may have been the consequence of the operation of personal interests rather than—as the modern opposition to slavery was—the defense of the "principles of humanity and benevolence," but the objective had been the same, and, unlike the modern opposition, it had been successful.[43] By the early fifteenth century slavery in Europe had almost ceased to exist. What began with the colonization of America, and the realization that for political and social reasons the Native Americans could not successfully be enslaved was, therefore, like the discovery itself, a new and odious departure in European history. For the first time instead of taking slaves in so-called just wars, instead of, as the Roman law of slavery had insisted, "saving" (one of the etymologies given for the term *servus*) a captive from the death his captor was entitled to inflict on him,[44] men began to buy slaves who were innocent of any act of aggression toward their captors, and having bought them to transport them from one side of the world to another.

The argument, which had long underpinned the Portuguese jurists' defense of the legitimacy of their trading activities—that the Africans had been seized in a just war "at home"—was, for all abolitionists, entirely specious, since no state can sell what it cannot own. But for both Diderot and Condorcet this particular argument conjured up the still more horrific image of African wars fought solely to provide the white men with their labor. Europe, claimed Condorcet, "is guilty not only of the crime of making slaves of men, but, on top of that, of all the slaughter committed in Africa in order to prepare for that crime."[45] The disorders and conflicts within African society that had allowed the slavers to present a widely accepted, if logically incoherent, legal argument, were themselves, therefore, the creations of Europe's colonial empires. Furthermore, unlike ancient slavery which, however evil, was a function of the kind of society that it sustained, modern slavery, said Diderot, "is a trade which is based upon injustice and has only luxury as its object"— the twin evils that menaced the well-ordered society of Diderot's imagination.[46] Paradoxically, it is this traffic that yokes together the two main themes of the *Histoire*: travel or migration and commerce. For with the discovery of America, slavery, which had hitherto been a product of warfare became instead a species of commerce.[47] The final outcome of this new and deadly combination had been to generate a form of mass involuntary migration. "In order to people one part of the world which you have devastated," Diderot accused the "Féroces Européens," "you have corrupted and depopulated another."[48] Depopulation, the specter that haunted much eighteenth-century social theory, threatened for Diderot, and many of his contemporaries, to make a wasteland not only of America but also of Africa. Because Africa was being emptied of its native populations to meet the "insatiable greed" of the European settlers in America; because the once populous Native Americans, now decimated by disease and conquest had proved unwilling and unable to bring their population levels up to anything like their preconquest numbers[49]; because the degenerate colonists in America were seemingly unable to breed, and the African slaves would rather destroy their offspring than see them born into slavery,[50] Diderot believed that humanity was faced with the prospect of a rapidly emptying world. "Free the slaves," as the Louis, chevalier de Jaucourt, author of the article on the "Traité des Nègres" in the *Encyclopédie* demanded, and "within a few generations this vast and fertile land will be filled with inhabitants."[51]

Freeing the slaves in America, would also, Diderot argued, be economically advantageous. "Give them a homeland, a shared set of interests, lands to work, and a form of production in accordance with their tastes, and your colonies will not lack arms. Freed of their chains, they will be both more active and more robust."[52]

In the end, as he had always insisted, modern slavery was not only a violation of all human rights, an insult to human decency; it was also "prejudicial to the interests" of the "cruel oppressors" themselves.[53]

The moral impact of slavery, however, could not be confined to the colonies. Like Montesquieu, Diderot knew that one of the consequences of modern colonization and the new trade routes that it had helped create was that the metropolis could never be fully insulated from the consequences of the processes of overseas expansion that it had itself initiated. Colonies in the ancient world had been, to use Turgot's metaphor, "like fruit,"[54] which had clung to the tree only until mature. But modern colonies, created not to ease population pressure, but for the purposes of trade, remain attached to their mother countries long after they have reached their maturity.[55] What took place in Miletus or Ephesus could have had no significant moral effect on what happened in Athens. But the behavior of the American colonists, and in particular the laws that had been made in the metropolis, had a constant and frequently devastating impact on what took place in Europe. The vision of a safe, sanitized haven for the potentially destructive forces within European society ignored the fact that, remote though the "Two Indies" were, the European colonies there were still socially, culturally, and politically linked to Europe. The European overseas empires had not merely spawned a new breed of criminals; because of their dependence on their mother countries, they had also hugely multiplied the possibilities for corruption. The same routes that had carried the colonist out would also allow his vices, his "tyrannies and his cruelties," to seep back into the motherland. You cannot, as Montesquieu had observed, practice tyranny abroad while remaining free at home; of this, as he had demonstrated, the Spanish Empire in America was the paradigmatic example.[56] Neither can you hope to lead a civilized or enlightened life in a world in which slavery still flourishes. Even Hilliard d'Auberteuil was prepared to concede that if the slave trade was not "dangerous and contrary to public well being," it was certainly a threat "to custom" and a potential moral danger to the metropolitan French.[57] Just as the republics of the ancient world, for all their apparent virtue, had been corrupted beyond recall by their reliance upon slavery so, as Condorcet claimed, a society such as his own, which tolerated slavery anywhere in the world over which it had some authority, "would not be a society of men but a band of brigands."[58]

For a century now, claimed Diderot, Europe had endorsed the "most sane, the most sublime moral maxims," in which innumerable errors had been "courageously unmasked." The fraternity of all humankind has been "established in the most moving manner in a number of immortal writings." In the silence of the study, or in the theater, every conceivable human misery was capable of reducing every educated European man and woman to tears. Except one. In the end, Diderot said, it seems that "it is only the fatal destiny of the unhappy negroes which is of no interest to us."[59]

It was, however, less the fact of their subjugation that had made both the plight of the African invisible to even the enlightened European, and his subjection possible, than it was the claim to racial inferiority. As Morreau de Saint-Méry pointed out, in "l'état actuel des choses" the difference between the color of their skins was a greater barrier between the slave and his master than the fact of servitude itself.[60] Discrimination by color had, Diderot argued, as with so many of the other ills that afflicted Europe, been a creation of the church. "Theology," he explained, "which has attempted to make everything seem marvellous and mysterious so as to reserve the right of explanation to itself" had invented this "atrocious extravaganza" which is the story of the descendant of Cain.[61] Only Christianity was capable of constructing a genealogy for man that divided the human family into two distinct groups and distinguished between those two groups by the mere color of their skins.

Modern slavery, which was entirely a product of the commercial features of modern colonization, had appropriated a primitive Judaic myth to create a race of subhumans whose moral identity had been crudely assimilated to the color of their skin so that even so sophisticated and enlightened a man as the marquis de Mirabeau could speak of the Africans as "a race of men apart distinct and separated from our species."[62] But for Diderot, the relative ease with which most Europeans had thus accepted, if only tacitly, these racist arguments, or the arguments from utility—neatly summed up in Barnave's claims that "each time that one thinks one is doing something for philosophy, you do infinitely more against peace and tranquility"[63]—or even the yet more specious, and in Diderot's view, malign argument that slavery had introduced the African to the true religion, was the inescapable outcome of the steady loss of identity that colonization had inflicted not merely on the colonists themselves, but also on the metropolitan culture. For Raynal himself it may have been the case that "the discovery of a new world alone could provide food for our curiosity,"[64] but for Diderot the very reverse was true. Navigation and long sea voyages may have had the effect of familiarizing people who once believed that their cultures were the only possible measure of all things, with a diversity of human types of which they had no previous experience. But the outcome of this had not been tolerance or the erosion of superstition, but rather a decrease in the capacity for imaginative response. "The difference of cults and of nations," wrote Diderot, "has familiarized even the grossest minds with a spirit of indifference for the objects which would once have startled their imagination."[65] Diderot was prepared to accept that because of the oceanic discoveries European customs had, to some degree at least, become deregulated and religious hatreds had cooled. But accompanying these unquestionable goods was another kind of loss. "The variety and multiplicity of objects which our industry has presented to our minds and senses," he wrote, "have diminished the affections of man and have weakened the energy of all our sentiments."

Travel, prolonged sea-voyages, had thus left all Europeans morally and imaginatively the poorer. It had also, and more damaging still, increased their tolerance of the sufferings of others, the sufferings of which the enslaved African was the enduring symbol. For the understanding of suffering requires not only the recognition of the humanity that the observer shares with the sufferer; it requires also a leap of the imagination. The intrusion of other worlds into the Europeans' imaginative and cognitive space had made this leap possible now only for those enlightened few who could still keep the existence of a universal benevolence firmly within their imaginative grasp. For the majority, however, the discovery of "new" worlds had not only created the condition of their own human destruction; it had also provided the means to a useful moral indifference. For this reason, claimed Diderot, we had in the end no alternative but to "curse the moment of their discovery."[66] For this reason, too, he came finally to believe, only a revolution led by a new "Black Spartacus" could hope to open the eyes of the European colonial world to the iniquities it had created. Later Diderot's highly impassioned tribute to this figure came to seem like an prophetic evocation of Toussaint-Louverture.[67] But Diderot's new Spartacus is not only an avenger, or even the necessary instrument of political liberation; he is also—as Bartolome de las Casas, the sixteenth-century "Apostle to the Indians," had been before him—the means of redemption for the European.

The writer who came closest to sharing these views is Kant's pupil, Johann Gottfried Herder (1744–1803). It might seem odd to link Diderot, the cosmopolitan, to Herder, the supposed father of German nationalism. Diderot's attack on colonialism in the name of the inevitable incommensurability and the necessary integrity of all cultures stops well short of any kind of exclusivism. It is also the case that Herder's ultimate appeal to religion as a form of knowledge that could unite all peoples would have sounded very odd indeed to Diderot.[68]

There is, however, a sense in which Herder, who never mentions the *Histoire des deux Indes* although he had clearly read it,[69] carries Diderot's arguments to the point at which they become, in effect, a rejection of the whole argument, which Diderot had no wish to challenge, for the unity of the human race.

For Herder, as for Diderot, colonialism is an evil because it reduces, or threatens to reduce through human and thus artificial means, the number of cultural variants that exist in the world. That is an evil because plurality is part of the way the world is constituted. For Herder, as for Diderot, travel is a source of moral corruption because it violates nature's intentions, which, for Herder, are always to preserve things in their original state. "Nature," he wrote, in what is perhaps his best-known work, the *Ideen zur Philosophie der Geschichte der Menscheit* (Outlines of a philosophy of the history of man), "has not established her borders between remote lands in vain." But whereas for Diderot the "voyageur par état," the savage nomad, is a menace to those he encounters, for Herder, such an assault upon nature can only result in the mental and physical collapse of the assailant. "The history of conquest," he observed,

> as well as of commercial companies and especially that of missions afford a melancholy and in some respects a laughable picture. . . . We shudder with abhorrence when we read the accounts of many European nations, who, sunk in the most dissolute voluptuousness and insensible pride have degenerated both in body and mind and no longer possess any capacity for enjoyment or compassion. They are full-blown bladders in human shape, lost to every noble and active pleasure, and in whose veins lurks avenging death.[70]

This last assertion was meant to be taken literally. Europeans in America, he claimed, quoting the Swedish botanist Peter Kalm's *Natural and Political History of Pennsylvania* (1768), mature more rapidly and die younger than they do in Europe. This phenomenon has nothing to do with the environment since the same source confirmed that the Native Americans, whose rate of maturation was thought to be notoriously slow, sometimes lived to be very old indeed.[71] Exactly what the mechanism is by which nature produces such effects Kalm does not say. But it clearly follows from its very existence that not only can no people hope to transport its own culture intact to another world; it cannot mate with an autochthonous one to produce a new hybrid culture. The only possible mode of transplantation, is for the traveler himself to go native. "But how few," Herder lamented, "such people are there." All those who fail to assimilate in this way find themselves, sooner or later, the victims of a superior nature. "And does not Nature revenge every insult offered her?" he asked.

> Where are the conquests, the factories, the invasions of former times, when distant foreign lands were visited by a different race, for the sake of devastation and plunder! The still breath of climate has dissipated and consumed them, and it was not difficult for the natives to give the finishing strokes to the rotten tree.[72]

The extravagance of this claim, in the aftermath of the creation of the United States and on the eve of the independence wars in the Caribbean and South America (the *Ideen* was written between 1784 and 1791), may now seem absurd. But Herder's image of the degenerate colonist finally succumbing to the influence of nature is a function less of any observation about the real world than it is of his belief in the utter impenetrability of all cultural forms. "The idea of every indigenous culture," he claimed, "is confined to its own region," so confined, that the possibility of communicating just what it is becomes seemingly impossible. "For the European has no idea of the boiling passions and imagination which glow in the negro's breast; and the Hindu has no conception of the restless desires that chase the European from one end of the world to the other."[73]

We are all, Herder believed, in the same position as the "king of Siam" who, on being told about ice and snow, declared them to be nonexistent. The Siamese, who had no possible access to extremes of cold, could only dismiss such things as the ravings of foreign travelers. Literally nothing that does not come within the range of our own cultural experience—and hence within the range of our own language—can have any meaningful existence for us.

Herder's claim for both incommensurability and incomprehensibility went far further than any previous argument in favor of cultural integrity. Such extensive claims had also to be grounded in an entirely new vision of social development. Diderot operated well within the limits of the traditional Hobbesian, Grotian model of sociability. According to this model all societies have their beginnings in the general recognition of the desirability of an escape from the state of nature. They grow and develop in order to satisfy human needs, which in turn increase "as the patterns of our lives have increased and become more perfect."[74] This process, despite innumerable local variations, is universal and universally recognizable. Although Herder accepted that all communities began in this way as "savage," and although he speaks of savagery as a single uniform state, and ascribes to all human beings common methods of understanding, he rejects the claim, to which most seventeenth- and eighteenth-century social theorists (including Rousseau) subscribed, that social evolution was ultimately the outcome of the rational calculation of interests. Such a theory, since it made all men the agents of mere rationality, was, Herder believed, inherently implausible. "I find myself unable to comprehend," he wrote in *Auch eine Philosophie der Geschichte zur Bildung der Menscheit* (Yet another philosophy of history) (1774), "how reason can be presented so universally as the single summit and purpose of all human culture. Is the whole body just one big eye?"[75]

Herder's attack on what, in effect, amounts to the whole basis of the eighteenth-century "Science of Man" begins where much of his argument for cultural singularity, and many previous claims for cultural homogeneity, begins: with language. Perhaps Herder's best-known work, beside the *Ideen*, is his early *Ueber den Ursprung der Sprache* (Treatise upon the origin of language) (1770). In this he set out to refute the theory that languages are created and develop as a function of, and in response to, the user's increasing social needs. What the proponents of this belief had never been able to explain, argued Herder, was *how* the first men had progressed from sounds to words, and from words to phrases, phrases to sentences, and so on.[76] And they had failed to do this because these changes were simply inexplicable as the consequence of some purely social, and hence observable, mechanism.

For Herder, therefore, there could be only one explanation for the seemingly inevitable developments in human speech and human modes of association: they are, in some sense, innate.[77] When applied to language this claim was hardly startling. The critiques that Smith, Ferguson, Millar, Filangieri, Grimaldi, and Linguet had all directed against Rousseau's theory of language, for instance, were based on similar observations. But Herder also claimed that just as we inherit our language-knowledge from our forebears, so, too, do we inherit our social and cultural understanding from them. The imagination which, like Diderot, he believed to be "the least explained of all the powers of the mind," rather than reason, was the instrument of social and cognitive change. And the imagination, the "knot that tied body and mind together, the bud, as it were, of the whole sensual organization,"[78] has to be, to some degree, innate.

This move effectively reduced the power of all human agents to shape successfully their own social and cultural ends. No matter what we do, we are all isolated as cultural groups within a given "mind-set," what Herder called, variously, "opinions," "fancies," and "mythologies." These can and do change over time, but each changes in its own, untransferable way. The impulses for modification, the imaginative grasp of contingency, are transmitted from parent to child, along with the expressive tools, the language, in which these changes can be made intelligible.

Having thus detached the process of change from any direct causal link with the temporal, Herder was now free to attach it to the spatial. The imaginative grasp—and it is that which determines cultural form— inevitably varies from region to region, as indeed it must from one mode of production to another. "The shepherd," as he phrased it, "beholds nature with different eyes from those of the fisherman or hunter."[79] Language, too, must vary from culture to culture. "A new language," he claimed, "must arise in each new world, a national language in each new nation." The diversities of human cultural types can be accounted for, and determined over time, by the diversities of environments. Since men are unique among animals in being globally distributed, it would be unnatural to suppose that an Eskimo *could* have any cultural features in common with an African, particularly if cultural traits have now to be thought of as, in some sense, genetically transmitted. [80]

The way is now open for a vision of a deterministically pluralist universe, which has turned the entire Enlightenment image of relative incommensurability around. Underpinning Herder's social theory is the persistent image of nature as a harmonious whole with which we tamper only at our peril. And if our cultural habits are genetically transmitted, not only must they be in harmony with the particular environment to which nature has assigned us; they must, in a quite specific sense, be a *part* of that environment. The natural world that has shaped men's culturally diverse forms was clearly in place before "the artificial ends of great societies" came into being. "How wonderfully," Herder exclaimed,

> [has nature] separated nations, not only by woods and mountains, seas and deserts, rivers and climates, but most particularly by languages, inclinations and characters, that the work of subjugating despotism might be rendered more difficult, that all the four quarters of the globe might not be crammed into the belly of a wooden horse.[81]

The Trojan Horses that seek to subvert this naturally plural world are, of course, the European empires. "Nothing," Herder wrote, "appears so directly opposite to the ends of government as the unnatural enlarge-ment of states, the wild mixture of various races and various nations under one sceptre." The use of force and economic interest may tempo-rarily have "glued together" the world's empires into "fragile machines of state," but underneath this apparatus, they are all "destitute of inter-nal unification and sympathy of parts."[82] Sooner or later they will all collapse into their natural constituent parts, as had the Athenian, the Persian, the Mughal, the Roman, and the empire of Charles V. Whatever colonies these leave behind struggle on to preserve lifestyles long since abandoned in the metropolis until, as we have seen, they are finally sub-sumed by whatever cultural form nature had originally designated for that particular environment.

As Isaiah Berlin has pointed out, this is not, as has so often been claimed, a form of relativism.[83] Cultures for Herder remain absolute within their own compounds. Any attempt to understand one in terms, relative or otherwise, of another is to misunderstood the fundamental and insurmountable incommensurability that they all share. This is what, for Herder, makes "ethnocentrism" of any kind so absurd. The European claim to have invented the arts and sciences, he wrote, is as ludicrous as the belief of the "madman of Piraeus" that all the inventions of the world must be Greek simply because he lived at "a confluence of these inventions and traditions." "Steer thy frigate to Otaheite," Herder contemptuously told Bougainville. "Bid thy cannon roar along the shore of the New Hebrides, still you are not superior in skill to the in-habitant of the South-Sea islands who guides with art the boat he has constructed with his own hands."[84]

On this account, there can be no common cultures, no common be-liefs or certainties that we can all claim to share by virtue of our common humanity. There cannot even be a common set of descriptive terms upon which we could all agree. Herder accepted that at some deep level, there might be such a thing as "human nature," which would allow us instinctively to recognize the "other" as one of "us"; but this did noth-ing to help us understand human beings as they are currently consti-tuted, and nothing at all to make the particular life-ways of the other commensurable with our own. Herder was one of the earliest, and re-mains perhaps the fiercest, opponent of the comforting argument that in order to understand "others" we have to accredit them with not only the beliefs and desires but also the *values* that we all, as human beings, supposedly share.

Herder pushed the notion of incommensurability to the point where the very concept of a single human genus became, if not impossible to conceive, at least culturally meaningless. If all peoples are in effect bound by the horizons of their own particular local understanding, if the only possible response to difference is not wonder but bewilderment, then the idea of "human nature" itself becomes redundant. Herder's man might come to the aid of another from another culture because he could distinguish him from, say, a giraffe; but there was nothing in Herder's account to imply that he would have any *moral* obligation to do so. If we are to take Herder seriously (and, as Kant recognized, it is not always easy to do so) then one might as well argue that just as the "negro" can find happiness in his own way, so, too, can he go to hell in his own way.

This was just the conclusion that Diderot and all those (including Kant) who had argued for a universalism, a brotherhood of all humankind, had most feared. If anything could be saved from the European empires in the New World, it could only be a greater, rather than a lesser, awareness of the presence of others. This would not merely enable "us" to help "them," though that, too, was part of the project; it would also help unravel some of the deleterious effects of our own murderous parochialism. On Diderot's account, the traveler and the colonist had effaced difference, and so had made Europeans insensitive to the suffering of others. But, in Diderot's view, this condition might still lead, now that the butchery was done and the older colonies were beginning to break away, to something altogether more subtle and more humane than Herder's "nationalism."

For Diderot was not always so pessimistic as the voices he had created. In the *Histoire* he constantly holds up the possibility that, at some time in the future, the colonizers and the colonized might combine to form a new society for which we might all have greater hopes than we can at present have of any existing community "civilized" or "savage." In both the *Supplément au voyage de Bougainville* and in the *Histoire*, as in much of Diderot's other writings, sex, released from the ill-conceived limitations and interpretations imposed upon it by the religious "code," is offered as a form of liberation. Not only is sex a mode of understanding; perhaps in the absence of a common language, it is the only mode of understanding that can pass between distant and incommensurable cultures. It is also the only means to bring into being the new society that alone can resolve the conflicts that those misconceived empires have created. Young men and women, he fantasized, should now be sent to the Americas, and "through consanguinity the foreigners and the natives of the place would have made a single and common family." There, he said wistfully, there would "have been no weapons, no soldiers, only large numbers of many young women for the men, and many young men for the women."[85]

In his sexually liberated, miscegenated world, neither European nor Indian, but fully "American" men would be uniquely placed to benefit from civilization without being corrupted by it. They would also be able to see the evident superiority of European technology to which the "imperious and imposing tone" of the "masters and usurpers" had blinded the Native Americans. Such a society would thus have achieved what all eighteenth-century dreams of commercial harmony had aimed at: a union "between men with reciprocal needs."[86] Yet this, like the community Diderot had once hoped to establish on the remote Mediterranean island of Lampedusa, where "a small band of happy men" would create that "mid-way point" between civility and savagery where the "happiness of the species resides,"[87] must also in the world we all actually inhabit remain an illusion. Even in those parts of the world, such as Tahiti, where the Europeans still had the opportunity to create such societies, Diderot fully recognized they would never have the vision or the will to put them into action. In the end even the miscegenated society could only ever be yet another device by which to measure the failures of European civilization.

Diderot and Herder were the first to articulate the two interpretations of the colonizing process with which, *mutatis mutandis*, we are still struggling. Both lead inexorably away from any kind of colonial dependence. Both begin with the premise that it would have been better for the world if the Europeans had remained quietly at home. But whereas Diderot had the creation of new communities as his final objective, Herder rejected any claim that "nationhood" could be anything other than the outcome of centuries of accumulated cultural habits. On this account the United States or Haiti is only new in the sense of being transplanted. Although it is clear that with time they must become entirely sui generis, it is also clear that transformation will not be the outcome of a cultural encounter. The impact of European domination on such new nations will be, if anything at all, merely pernicious. The postcolonial world is still divided between these two contrasting visions. But if Diderot might be able to see in the modern republics of Latin America something of his miscegenated state, and Herder in much of modern Africa and India confirmation of belief that no human can for long resist "nature's revenge," I doubt that either would find the spectacle a very reassuring one.

NOTES

I would like to thank the members of the Davis Center seminar, and in particular Natalie Zemon Davis and Anthony Grafton, for their comments on an earlier draft of this essay.
1. *Histoire philosophique et politique des etablissemens et du commerce des Européens dans les deux Indes* (Geneva, 1781), 9:487–88. On Raynal's associa-

tion with Choiseul and the *Bureau des colonies*, see Michele Duchet, *Anthropologie et histoire au siècle des lumières* (Paris, 1971), p. 126; and Yves Benot, "Diderot, Pehcmeja, Raynal et l'anticolonialisme," *Europe* 41 (1963): 139.

2. He did, however, like so many others, express moral outrage at slavery, which he described as "le droit terrible du plus fort," but claimed that its abolition would be politically unacceptable (*Essai sur l'administration de St. Dominique* [N.D. 1785], p. 13). The text is, however, primarily concerned with the free-trade question and like most of Raynal's writings was a composite work, much of which was probably written by Pierre Victor Malouet, governor of Guyana between 1776 and 1778. See Anatole Feugère, *Un Précurseur de la Révolution. L'abbé Raynal (1713–1796)* (Paris, 1922), p. 364.

3. On this aspect of the *Histoire*, see Reinhard Koselleck, *Critique and Crisis: Enlightenment and the Pathogenesis of Modern Society* (trans. of *Kritik und Krise. Eine Studie zur Pathogenese der burgerlichen Welt*) (Oxford, New York, Hamburg, 1988), pp. 178–82.

4. F. Bernard, *Analyse de l'histoire philosophique et politique* (Leiden, 1775), p. 39.

5. For the printing history, see Anatole Feugère, *Bibliographie critique de l'abbé Raynal* (Angoulême, 1922), pp. 15–48.

6. Quoted in Hans Wolpe, *Raynal et sa machine de guerre. L'*Histoire de Deux Indes *et ses perfectionnements* (Paris, 1956), p. 8.

7. *Histoire*, 1: 3. (I, Introduction).

8. Ibid. This section, however, was in fact written by Diderot.

9. I have followed the now definitive reconstruction of Diderot's contributions in Gianluigi Goggi, *Denis Diderot. Pensées detachées. Contributions à l'*Histoire des Deux Indes, 2 vols. (Siena, 1976–77); and Michele Duchet, *Diderot et l'*Histoire de Deux Indes *ou l'écriture fragmentaire* (Paris, 1978). And see Yves Benot, who in what is still the only sustained examination of this aspect of Diderot's work, concludes that, in this context, the *Histoire*, "couronne toute son oeuvre de penseur politique," as the "Neveu de Rameau achève et synthétise toute sa creation littéraire" (*Diderot de l'athéisme à l'anticolonialisme* [Paris, 1970], p. 259).

10. "Lettre apologétique de l'abbé Raynal à M. Grimm," in Diderot, *Oeuvres philosophiques*, ed. Paul Vernière (Paris, 1956), p. 640. According to Malouet, Diderot's more obvious and forcefully radical contributions were not altogether to Raynal's liking. Raynal frequently spoke "en opposition avec son livre ou plutôt avec les intercalations de Diderot," and claimed that he had only turned to Diderot "por la correction de son style," but that Diderot had taken over and "l'abus qui celui-ci fit de sa confiance, la condition tyrannique qu'il y mit: *tout ou rien*, l'ont exposé à des justes reproches; tandis que ce qu'il y a d'instructif et d'important dans son ouvrage est véritablement la partie qui lui est propre." (Pierre Victor Malouet, *Mémoires de Malouet publiés par son petit-fils le baron Malouet* [Paris, 1868], I, 81).

11. *Histoire*, 10, 285 (XIX, 14). For the significance of the fact that these are codes, see Donald Kelley, *The Human Measure: Social Thought in the Western Legal Tradition* (Cambridge, Mass., and London, 1990), p. 223.

12. *Histoire*, 10, 285 (XIX, 14).

13. Diderot, *Supplément au voyage de Bougainville*, ed. Herbert Dieckmann (Geneva-Lille, 1955), p. 52.

14. Ibid., pp. 59–60.

15. *Histoire*, 5, 1–2 (IX, 1).

16. Diderot, however, was not the first to employ this analogy. See Victor Riqueti, marquis de Mirabeau, who refers to the Spaniard as the "vrai Mongul de l'Amérique" (*L'Ami des hommes, ou traité de la population* [The Hague, 1758], 3:21).

17. *Histoire*, I, 41 (I, 7).

18. Ibid., 6, 130 (XI, 24). *Voyages de M. le Marquis de Chastellux dans l'Amérique septentrional, dans les années 1780, 1781 et 1782* (Paris, 1786), 2:146.

19. *Histoire*, 8, 210–11 (XVII, 3).

20. See Kelley, *Human Measure*, p. 90.

21. "In interiore homine habita veritas," *De vera religione*, 39:72.

22. Diderot, *Supplément au voyage de Bougainville*, p. 51.

23. *Histoire*, 5, 16 (IX, 5).

24. Ibid., 10, 296 (XIX, 15).

25. "Réfutation suivie d'ouvrage de Helvétius intitulé L'Homme," in Diderot, *Oeuvres complètes*, ed. Jules Assevat and Maurice Tourneaux (Paris, 1875–77), 2:431.

26. *Histoire*, 5, 138 (X, 1).

27. Ibid., 5, 3 (IX, 1).

28. Ibid., 10, 297 (XIX, 1).

29. Ibid., 5, 2 (IX, 1). Cf. Voltaire's description of pirates—another group who, because of their nomadism, travel down the chain of civility—as "des tigres qui auraient un peu de raison" (*Essai sur les moeurs et l'esprit des nations*, ed. René Pomeau [Paris, 1963] 2: 376). On the place of piracy in the *Histoire de deux Indes*, see Girolamo Imbruglia, "Diderot e le immagini della pirateria nel '700,'" *Belfagor* 45 (1990):493–511.

30. See "Sur les cruautés exercées par les espagnols en Amérique," in *Oeuvres complètes*, 6:451–52.

31. *Histoire*, 10, 107–9 (XIX, 3).

32. Ibid., 5, 2 (IX, 1).

33. In the *Discours preliminaire* to his translation of Shaftesbury's *An Inquiry concerning Virtue or Merit* (1745), in *Oeuvres complètes*, 1:9.

34. *Histoire*, 10, 152 (XIX, 6).

35. Carminella Biondi has called it the "testo chiave degli anni Settanta" (*Ces esclaves sont des hommes. Lotta abolizionista e letteratura negrofila nella Francia del Settecento* [Pisa, 1979], p. 239).

36. Benjamin Frossard, "Observations sur l'abolition de la traité des nègres presentées a la Convention nationale" (1793). Frossard was also the author of "La cause des esclaves nègres et des habitans de la Guinée portée au tribunal de la justice, de la religion et de la politique" (Paris, 1788).

37. *Histoire*, 6, 126 (XI, 24).

38. Ibid., 6, 133 (XI, 24).

39. Condorcet, *Réflexions sur l'esclavage des nègres* (Neufchatel, 1781), pp. 6–7 (hereafter cited as *Réflexions*). The work was published under the pseudonym, M. Schwartz. The legal status of French slaves under the so-called Code Noir of 1685 was, in fact, more complex than Condorcet allows. The code, however, as it was almost entirely based on Roman law, observed the principle of *partus ventrem sequitur*, which made the offspring of female slaves the property of their masters, and thus implied that slaves were "moveable goods." See Yvan Debtasch, *Couleur et liberté. le jeu du critère ethnique dans une ordre juridique esclavagiste* (Paris, 1967), 1:30–33.

40. *Réflexions*, p. 56; *Histoire*, 6, 117 (XI, 24).

41. "Du commerce des colonies, ses principes et ses loix" (n.p., 1785). On Hilliard d'Auberteuil and his role in the free-trade debates of 1785, see Jean Tarrade, *Le commerce colonial de la France a la fin de l'ancien régime: l'evolution du régime de "l'Exclusif"* (Paris, 1972), 2:563 n. 112.

42. In his famous letter to Dr. Richard Price, "sur les constitutions américains," March 22, 1778, in *Oeuvres de Turgot et documents le concernant*, ed. Gustav Schelle (Paris, 1913–23), 5:538. However, in his "Memoires sur la manière dont la France et l'Espagne devraient envisager les suites de la querelle entre la Grande-Bretagne et ses colonies" of April 6, 1776 (Paris, 1791), p. 31, Turgot urged the Crown to give up its American possessions.

43. *Histoire*, 6, 124–25 (XI, 24).

44. Cf. the comments of Montesquieu (*De l'esprit des lois*, XV, 2), on this aspect of the Roman law of slavery, which he dismisses as "senseless," since it supposes "qu'il soit permis de tuer dans la guerre autrement que dans le cas de nécessité."

45. *Réflexions*, p. 9; *Histoire*, 6, 130–32 (XI, 24).

46. *Histoire*, 6, 135 (XI, 24).

47. As Carminella Biondi has pointed out, there are passages in the *Histoire* (none of them, however, by Diderot or Raynal himself) which slip uncomfortably into discussing the African as a piece of merchandise (*Ces esclaves sont des hommes*, p. 247). See especially *Histoire*, 6, 245 (XII, 21).

48. *Histoire*, 4, 215–16 (VIII, 22).

49. Ibid., 6, 235 (VIII, 32). Raynal also repeated the old claim that the number of priests had contributed significantly to the supposed population decline of the criollo society, among whom "le célibat devint la passion dominante dans un pays desert" (Ibid., 4, 229 [VIII, 25]).

50. Abortion was common in the slave communities. See Père Nicolson, who described the practice as "une espèce de compassion se joint au plaisir de la vengeance, pour outrager la nature," and lays the blame with the Colons, "plus barbares que ces mères homicides" (*Essai sur l'histoire naturelle de l'île Saint Dominique* [Paris, 1776], p. 55). Mirabeau took much the same gloomy view of the inability of any of the three groups in America to reproduce themselves with sufficient speed to prevent subsequent depopulation (*L'Ami des hommes*, 3:255).

51. *Encylopédie, ou dictionnaire raisonné des sciences des arts et des métiers* (Neufchatel, 1772), 16:533. There is, however, a marked difference in tone

between this article, Jaucourt's article on "Esclavage"—which is a paraphrase of Book XV of the *Esprit des lois*—and the essay on "Nègre" by Boucher d'Assis which, in discussing slavery, limits itself to a commentary on the Code Noir.

52. *Histoire*, 6, 136–37 (XI, 24).

53. Ibid., 6, 117 (XI, 24).

54. "Tableau philosophique des progrès successifs de l'esprit humain," in *Oeuvres*, 1:222.

55. This distinction was made by many eighteenth-century writers. See, in particular, the author of the article on "Colonie" in the *Encylopédie*, who underscores the novelty of the American colonies in that they uniquely had "commerce et culture tout à la fois pour objet de leur etablissment," a condition that demanded conquest, as the ancient colonies had not, and that they exist wholly for the benefit of the mother country (*Encylopédie*, 3: 649–50).

56. See Anthony Pagden, *Spanish Imperialism and the Political Imagination* (New Haven and London, 1990), pp. 7–8.

57. *Du commerce des colonies*, p. 51.

58. *Réflexiones*, p. 14.

59. *Histoire*, 6, 105 (XI, 22).

60. *Observations d'un habitant des colonies* (Paris, 1789), p. 20; and see the observations of Mirabeau, *L'Ami des hommes*, p. 254.

61. *Histoire*, 6, 40–41 (XI, 10).

62. *L'Ami des hommes*, 3:254.

63. "Rapport de M. Barnave sur les colonies, et décrets rendú sur cette affaire par l'Assemblé constituante, le 28 Septembre 1791" (Paris, 1791), p. 26. Although Barnave, in common with most of the revolutionaries, held slavery to be a moral iniquity he claimed that any attempt to secure the immediate release of the slaves would lead to the loss of the colonies, which amounted to placing the well-being of six hundred thousand men before the "intérêt national" of the entire French people.

64. *Histoire*, 3, 209 (VI, 2).

65. Ibid., 10, 10–11 (XIX, 1).

66. Ibid., 5, 140 (X, 1).

67. Ibid., 6, 127–28 (XI, 24). This has been described as a "rewriting" of a passage in Louis-Sébastien Mercier's *L'An deux mille quatre cent quarante* of 1770. But neither Diderot nor Mercier was alone in predicting an eventual slave revolt of massive proportions. See Biondi, *Ces esclaves sont des hommes*, pp. 250–52.

68. It is, however, overly crude to describe Herder as a "nationalist" since his concept of a "people" (*Volk*) makes no more claims to the political entitlement that a "nation," in the modern sense of the term, must surely possess, than does Diderot's *patrie*.

69. See Max Rouché, *La Philosophie de l'histoire de Herder*, Publication de la Faculté des Lettres de l'Université de Strasbourg 93 (Strasbourg, 1940), p. 84.

70. *Outlines of a Philosophy of the History of Man [Ideen zur Philosophie der Geschichte der Menschheit]*, trans. T. Churchill (London, 1800), p. 185.

71. Ibid., p. 186.

72. Ibid., p. 189.

73. Ibid., p. 221.

74. Article on "Société (Morale)" from the *Encyclopédie*, in *Oeuvres complètes*, 17:144.

75. *Yet Another Philosophy of History [Auch eine Philosophie der Geschichte zur Bildung der Menscheit]*, in *Herder on Social and Political Culture*, trans. and ed. F. M. Barnard (Cambridge, 1969), p. 199.

76. *Treatise upon the origin of Language [Abhandlung uber den Ursprung der Sprache]* (London, 1827), pp. 12–15.

77. Ibid., p. 101.

78. *Outlines of a Philosophy of the History of Man*, pp. 200–202.

79. Ibid., p. 199.

80. A not dissimilar claim for the genetic transmittability of the instruments of material culture is to be found in Clifford Geertz, "The Growth of Culture and the Evolution of Mind," in *The Interpretation of Cultures* (London, 1975), pp. 55–83.

81. *Outlines of a Philosophy of the History of Man*, p. 224; and cf. p. 250, where the same image is used again.

82. Ibid., p. 249.

83. See "Alleged Relativism in Eighteenth-Century Thought," in *The Crooked Timber of Humanity: Chapters in the History of Ideas*, ed. Henry Hardy (London, 1990), pp. 70–90.

84. *Outlines of a Philosophy of the History of Man*, p. 241.

85. *Histoire*, 5, 4–5 (IX, 2).

86. Ibid., 5, 3 (IX, 1).

87. *Entretiens sur le fils naturel* (1757), in *Oeuvres esthétiques*, ed. Paul Vernière (Paris, 1968), pp. 105–6.

CHAPTER 6

Retribution and Remorse: The Interaction between the Administration and the Protestant Mission in Early Colonial Formosa

LEONARD BLUSSÉ

> On Few matters in life is the gap so great as
> between a dry, antiseptic statement of policy
> by a well-spoken man in a quiet office and what
> happens to people when it is put into practice.
> (*J. K. Galbraith*)

IN 1650 II. Jessei, "a Servant of JESUS CHRIST," published a tract with the curious title *Of the* CONVERSION *of five thousand nine hundred* EAST INDIANS *in the* ISLE FORMOSA *neere* CHINA, *To the Profession of the true* GOD, *in* JESUS CHRIST, *By meanes of M. Ro: Junius, a Minister lately in* DELPH *in* HOLLAND.[1] In the introductory notice "to his Christian Friends, in England, New-England, or elsewhere, that pray for the *Comming in of the fullnesse of the* GENTILES *that so all* ISRAEL *may be saved*," Jessei explains what prompted him to translate and publish this account. A certain M. Edward Cresset, who had spent some time in Holland, had reported about the triumphant homecoming of the Dutch missionary Robertus Junius to the city of Delft in 1643. In Formosa this Protestant cleric was said to have converted "some thousands of Indians by means of conversing amongst them!"

Because Jessei wished to hear more about this successful preacher, he had asked Cresset to send a letter on his behalf to Junius. In reply he received a Latin treatise, written by a confrere of Junius, Reverend Caspar Sibellius, which he now published for the first time in English. In a nutshell, the contents dealt with the missionary's "INGRESSE, or entrance into that holy vocation . . . for opening the eyes of the blinde, and turning them from Darkness to Light . . . ; then secondly, his PROGRESSE in the same . . . And so great and laudable PROGRESSE both of men and women, young and old, chiefe ones, middle sort, and meane ones made therin . . . and thirdly and lastly, his EGRESSE from the same

. . . FIRST, He was moved with a great desire of seeing his aged and most deare Mother . . . SECONDLY, of seeing againe his own deare Countrie . . . And THIRDLY, that he might promote and further . . . the Conversion of the Lords VINEYARD, that is alreadie Planted and Watered in the Formosan Iland."[2]

Why had Junius been successful in spreading the gospel while his Protestant brothers-in-faith were failing to do so elsewhere? Sibellius offered a twofold explanation: After having been nominated by the Dutch East India Company "for the Conversion of Easterne-Indians," the aspiring missionary not only had devoted himself to mastering the language—"he happily learned the barbarous Language and rude Idiome of those Heathen"—but had also settled down and made his home among the natives for more than ten years.

Today such a strategy would seem to be an utterly sensible course for a missionary to steer—if not the only one. But it should be remembered that, in the seventeenth century, the missionary agenda still had to be worked out in Protestant circles. Members of the Roman Catholic orders had already devoted themselves to spreading the gospel among "Pagan Indians" for more than one hundred years and had gained great experience in doing so. This kind of "participant-preaching" abroad so typical of Franciscans or Jesuits, however, was a relatively new phenomenon for the Protestant denominations, who had had to apply all their energies to safeguarding their own religious survival at home during that same period.

Upon his return to Delft Junius first accepted the ministry of a local church and later on, in 1653, was called to Amsterdam. The heroic features of Junius's missionary work "among the blinde Heathen" enormously appealed to the Dutch public. His portrait was even painted on Delft ware and sold in porcelain shops. In Holland Junius continued to promote the Formosan mission by having cathechisms and schoolbooks printed in the Sinkan language and giving linguistic instruction to prospective missionaries.[3]

In 1662, when the Dutch East India Company lost its colonial possession of Formosa to the Chinese warlord and Ming loyalist Cheng Ch'eng-kung, the memory of the seemingly miraculous deeds of Junius soon faded and was replaced by another quite different image. The Formosan mission lived on in the memory of the Dutch public in the lurid tales of the tortures to which Dutch missionaries had been subjected by the invading Chinese troops. Popular prints vividly depicting the crucifixion of these missionaries by cruel Chinese were sold in the streets of Dutch towns. Thus even the Dutch Reformed Church had its share of martyrs.[4]

Some 250 years were to pass before a Scottish clergyman, Reverend William Campbell, wrested the tales of early missionary success from oblivion. Campbell, who worked for the Presbyterian Mission in Taiwan in the 1880s, was so impressed by the work of his Dutch predecessors that he published a volume full of translations of Dutch seventeenth-century sources on the Formosan mission, *Formosa under the Dutch*.[5] Campbell assessed Dutch missionary efforts on Formosa as the first example of a concentrated Calvinist effort of simultaneously proselytizing and ruling a heathen people.

The central theme of this essay is essentially of a revisionist nature. The Protestant mission in Formosa will be studied on the basis of new interpretations and of thus far unused source materials in the holdings of the Dutch East India Company archives, but against the background of the sources and images outlined above.[6] Focusing on the first ten years between 1626 and 1636—the incubation period of the conquest and the colonization of Formosa—I shall analyze the genesis of a peculiar relationship between the clerics and the administration, which was to structure and influence all further administrative efforts on the island. Because the number of principal actors is quite small, it is possible to analyze their contribution on an individual basis and thus reach a degree of detail and concreteness uncommon in this kind of research, which often suffers from an excess of abstraction and ideological interpretation.

Why did the Dutch East India Company (VOC) send missionaries to such a remote trading post as Formosa in the early seventeenth century, while it was so lax in promoting the gospel elsewhere? Did Junius perceive himself as being as successful as he was portrayed to have been? As even Campbell points out, Junius's methods of proselytizing were challenged by some of his fellow missionaries in the field.[7] Moreover, the relationship of the Dutch clerics with the colonial administration of Formosa was not as smooth and unproblematical as the Dutch public may have thought. Apparently returning a happy, fulfilled man, Junius came home to tell the directorate of the East India Company a terrible story that lay heavily on his conscience. This narrative, buried in the holdings of the East India Company archives at The Hague, shows an inner incompatibility between colonial conquest and the idea of Christian conversion.

THE CHURCH AND THE COLONIAL STATE

The organic relationship between the mission and colonial administration in the historical process of European expansion overseas and its encounter with non-Western cultures has been singled out as a very controversial one in the Christian church. The relationship is an old one indeed. After Pope Alexander VI had officially sanctioned colonialism in

1494 at Tordesillas by dividing the world into two missionary acres to be plowed by his champions, the kings of Portugal and Spain, religious and temporal interests crossed the oceans for centuries hand in hand.

The religious sphere in the early-modern Dutch expansion overseas is less apparent than in the Iberian one. References to the curiously subdued character of the Dutch in their religious and, for that matter, missionary activities in Asia permeate colonial literature. Is it justified to suggest that the "phlegmatic Dutch" displayed less religious fervor than their "ardent" Iberian rivals? This would scarcely seem to have been the case, since the population of the Low Countries was involved in a fierce and protracted struggle for independence against the Spanish king on no other grounds than that they claimed freedom to practice the Protestant religion—*religionis libertas ergo*. The explanation should be sought along other lines.

Charles Boxer has convincingly shown that there were particular institutional and organizational features in the Dutch process of overseas expansion that helped "Mammon ruling over God."[8] Within the trade-oriented organization of the *Verenigde Oostindische Compagnie* (VOC), religious duties came second to the worldly occupations of business enterprise. Clergymen were not sent by their own church organization in the same way that Roman Catholic priests were dispatched for the overseas mission, but they were hired by the company and made directly responsible to the administration of the company rather than to the classis in Holland that had selected them.

The directors of the VOC, the "Gentlemen Seventeen," soon realized that they could not deny the religious sphere in their overseas trading enterprise completely. They had to make special provisions for the spiritual needs of their personnel, who often remained abroad for many years. They also had to reckon with the Christians in the Spice Islands who had been converted to Roman Catholicism by the Portuguese. In order to win these "native Christians" over to the Dutch side, their religious needs had to be catered to: only by officiating at their marriages and by baptizing their children, could they herd these people progressively into the Dutch camp.

With the exception of the power strategy oriented proselytizing work among the Christian Ambonese, and the Christian Tamils in Ceylon, it may be said that during the two-hundred-year history of the Dutch East India Company (1602–1798) almost no concerted efforts were made to convert the indigenous populations. Almost is the operative word, for it is against this background of a lack of missionary zeal that the early successes of the Dutch Protestant evangelical work in Taiwan become the stunning phenomenon they are.[9] The Taiwanese example would seem to have constituted a special case and thus begs for further study and, if possible, explanation.[10] Before we do so, let us first briefly survey the curious institutional arrangements that were worked out between the Dutch East India Company and the Dutch Reformed Church in Asia.

When the VOC was established in 1601 with sole rights to navigation, trade, and warfare, no reference to religion was made in the first charter issued by the States General of the Dutch Republic. During the first ten years of the VOC's existence there was only one legally appointed clergyman to serve the whole of Asia.

Reverend Adriaan Jacobsz. Hulsebos, stationed at Jacatra (later Batavia), set the cat among the pigeons in an epistle dated March 29, 1618. He warned his fellow clergymen in Holland of two practical problems in the colony that demanded immediate action: Were merchants and lay readers allowed to baptize? How should children of company servants born out of wedlock be dealt with?

At the 19th Session of the Synod of Dordt (1619) it was decided that no baptisms should occur until the prospective church members had received adequate instruction. This meant that children could only be baptized after the *beleidenis* (confession of faith) of both parents. As later history has shown, this directive fell on deaf ears and throughout the seventeenth and eighteenth centuries similar exhortations continued to be issued to little avail. A more remarkable offspring of the discussions that were held during the synod was the declaration that the gospel should be propagated among the heathen in the overseas territories.[11] A *Deputatio ad res Indicas*, a Commission on Indian Affairs, consisting of six members from Dutch towns and two from the countryside was established to deal with the overseas mission.

While these issues were under discussion, Reverend Sebastiaan Danckaerts returned from the Spice Islands on furlough and published a treatise on the *Historical and profound narrative of the Condition of Christianity at Ambon*, in which he explained how missionary efforts should be organized in the future.[12] During his three years in Holland (1621–23) he actually saw his proposals to establish a training college for prospective missionaries implemented.

In the second charter of the VOC (December 22, 1622) the conservation of public religion was added to the duties of the company; and one year later, in 1623, the *Collegium Indicum* (Missionary college) was established in Leyden under the direction of Reverend Anthonius Walaeus. During the ten years of its existence—the VOC stopped its operations in 1633 because the running of a missionary college was deemed too expensive—Walaeus prepared a total of ten clergymen for the mission field.[13] As we shall see, two of his graduates were to play a crucial role in the propagation of the faith in the colony of Formosa, the first extensive territorial possession that the Dutch acquired in Asia.

EARLY FORMOSAN EXPERIENCES

In the late summer of 1624 Dutch troops occupied a spit of land commanding the bay of Taiwan on the west coast of Formosa with the intention of building a fortified trading factory. At the time the board of the Dutch East India Company harbored no ambitions to subjugate the native peoples of the western plains of the island. The prime motive for the construction of a stronghold was to fortify and protect a trading beach where Chinese and Japanese merchants used to engage in secret trade. Thus the Dutch presence in Formosa was not geared to interaction with the aborigines, but was directed toward the development of trade with the Chinese mainland across the Straits of Formosa.[14]

In a letter of February 3, 1626, to the Gentlemen Seventeen, only one year after the Dutch started to construct Castle Zeelandia, Governor-General de Carpentier wrote: "With the inhabitants of the country [Formosa] do our people maintain good intercourse and friendship, not so much on account of the profits that may be expected, but in order to keep them from becoming too antagonistic towards us."[15] Despite de Carpentier's propagation of a policy of noninterference on Formosa, matters took a different turn. Only ten years later, on January 4, 1636, one of his successors in office, Governor-General Hendrick Brouwer, expected the island "within a very short time to become as magnificent a colony as the Portuguese have ever possessed in India, a possession to which (even) Ceylon cannot bear comparison."[16] This change of strategy was confirmed by the actions of the local administration in Formosa. From 1634 on the Journals of Zeelandia Castle testify to a sudden wave of territorial expansion marked by a sharp increase in baptisms among the natives. This was by no means a mere coincidence, but a logical development of a process of interaction between the administration and the clerics on the island. As I shall point out, Dutch Protestant ministers in Formosa actually provoked the colonial administration into extending its jurisdiction over heathen villages so that their missionary field might be expanded.

GETTING TO KNOW EACH OTHER

In 1613 Hendrick Brouwer, who was at the time active as chief of the Hirado trade factory in Japan, was already pointing out the strategic position of the island of Formosa along the sea lane between the South and East China seas.[17] Neither Japan, China, nor the Iberian rivals to the company had yet laid a territorial claim to this political "no man's land."

Initially Brouwer's proposals went unheeded, but after several attempts to gain a foothold on the Chinese coast had failed, the Dutch decided in 1624 to settle in Formosa in order to establish an entrepôt for the China-Japan trade. Commerce, not the colonization of the island, was their main objective. Of course, this does not mean that they had never inquired into the potential of the island and into the local conditions.

In the autumn of 1622 the VOC ship, the *Gouden Leeuw*, anchored close to the small island of Lamey, today Hsiao Liu Chiu, off the southwestern coast of Formosa. The *Gouden Leeuw* was known as a happy ship that had made the long voyage from Holland to the Archipelago in the unprecedentedly short time of 127 days, without the loss of a single crew member.[18] The lucky spell was now running out, however. The captain of the ship sent some crew members ashore to fetch fresh water, but nothing more was heard from the men after they disappeared into the lush vegetation. A squall forced the *Gouden Leeuw* to leave before a search party could be sent; it was not until many years later that it was established that all the sailors had been murdered by the fierce islanders shortly after they had gone ashore.

On a second visit to Formosa—this time the island proper—the Dutch met with a friendlier reception. In 1623 two Dutch merchants, Jacob Constant and Barent Pessaert, paid a visit to the village of Soulangh on the west coast of Formosa and received a pleasant welcome from the village elders according to their succinct report.[19]

The two merchants first enter a coastal creek on a small sampan. A riverbank covered with a crust of dried sea salt immediately fuels an interesting discussion between the Dutchmen and their guide, *Kapitein China*, the Chinese headman of the sojourning Chinese community.[20] When Pessaert asks Captain China why the Chinese import salt from mainland China and sell it to the local Formosan inhabitants when it would be much more convenient to instruct the latter how to make it locally, their Chinese companion answers with a shrug:

> that the Chinese were perfectly aware of this, and skilled enough to extract it (the salt) from this natural abundance. But, if they had shown the inhabitants how to do this, then their profitable trade would have collapsed, as it is an art, a skill that can be learned only by observing; therefore they were keeping them (the natives) at their rustic pastime and simpleness.[21]

Via a well-beaten track along which there are frequent shady arbors for resting, the traveling company then rather unexpectedly comes upon the "township" of Soulangh, a settlement of three thousand inhabitants, which from the outside remains hidden from the eye by a fence of bamboo and extends over an area estimated to be "as big as Leiden" within the walls (at the time the second largest city of Holland).

Constant and Pessaert first give a detailed description of the houses, their decoration and interiors. Then they give an account of the outdoor life and the work that is carried out in the gardens by women. Their remarks about social intercourse, marital customs (men live in men's houses and only stealthily visit their wives, who stay with their own kin at night), education, outward appearance, language, and so forth have the freshness of open-minded, curious observation. Other passages about religious customs, warfare, government ("there are no chiefs"), and funeral ceremonies are a mixture of personal observation as well as interpretation of the information provided by their Chinese interpreter.

The Dutch are amazed at the reception they enjoy at the house of the wife of one of the village-elders. The husband first sends a young man to his wife's parental home, and asks to be admitted. As she invites him to come, the party enters the house and is heartily entertained. The husband withdraws into a corner with his wife where they briefly make love. The lovemaking completed, she is offered to the two Dutchmen, a proposal which, "To their great surprise was met with our refusal as we deemed it unchristian."

POOR POLITICS

When the Dutch established themselves on the sandbank of Tayouan directly in front of the island of Formosa in August 1624, they consequently had some knowledge of the customs of the local inhabitants. A small plot of land across the bay, belonging to the villagers of Sinkan, was leased as a place where goods could be bartered by the Dutch for deerhides, which were in great demand in Japan. Initially this trade with the Formosans was of little value, however, and the only criterion by which the Dutch factory on Tayouan was judged was its strategic position for the trade with China and Japan.

Soon after the construction of Zeelandia Castle had been started, friction developed between the Dutch invaders and the crews of visiting Japanese junks. Japanese merchants had already traded for decades at Tayouan with both sojourning Chinese merchants and the Formosans. Quite understandably they showed little regard for the Dutch demand that from now on all Japanese or Chinese shipping were to pay an anchorage fee to the Dutch garrison, "which protected them from possible incursions by Chinese pirates." The Dutch relationship with Chinese traders also deteriorated when the Dutch found out that their trade with China was not formally acknowledged by the provincial authorities of Fukien but had to be carried out by stealth with pirates.

In 1627 a young and unexperienced councillor of the Indies, Pieter Nuyts, was sent from Batavia to Formosa to deal with these two issues in the capacity of governor of Formosa. It was in the suite of this new governor that the first Protestant clergyman, Georgius Candidius, arrived at Zeelandia Castle in June 1627.

Nuyts had also been entrusted with an extraordinary embassy to the court of the shogun in Edo to solve the problems with the Japanese merchants. As a result he proceeded on July 24, 1627, after a month's sojourn on Formosa, to Japan. For a variety of reasons, this diplomatic mission was a complete failure. Upon having been refused admittance to the court of the shogun, Nuyts returned in December to Formosa in a despondent mood. Yet he took heart at the thought that at long last he could take the reins of government in hand and devote his attention to the promotion of the all important trade with China.

Many surprises awaited the new governor at his arrival, one of them being that Dominee Candidius, who was supposed to have been delivering sermons to the local garrison during his absence, had moved out of Zeelandia Castle across the bay and pitched his tent in the village of Sinkan. It took Nuyts some time to find out why the reverend gentleman had taken this unusual step.

CANDIDIUS CULTIVATES HIS OWN GARDEN

Georgius Candidius, a native of Küchardt in the Pfalz, born in 1597, was in many ways representative of the new breed of missionary. Fleeing from the horrors of the Thirty Years' War, he settled in Holland and studied theology at Leiden between 1621 and 1623, where he was strongly influenced by Reverend Sebastiaan Danckaerts.[22] As we have seen, Danckaerts' call to arms had led to the establishment of the *Collegium Indicum* under the able leadership of Anthonius Walaeus. Although technically speaking Candidius did not graduate from the Collegium—he was already too advanced in his studies to join the courses offered by new school—he was nonetheless a personal student of Walaeus.

Two months after his admission to the ministry by the classis of Amsterdam (November 1623), Candidius joined Danckaerts and two other confreres on the Indian fleet, and arrived at his first mission post in the Moluccas in October 1625. Problems were bound to follow when the youthful and idealistic missionary undauntedly started to criticize the behavior of the Dutch company servants, which in his eyes was uncouth. From the pulpit he even called the local governor, Jacques Lefebre, to account for his concubinage. Lefebre, notorious for his irascible temper, lodged a complaint against the young minister, dismissed him from his office, and sent him to Batavia to be judged. Lefebre's incriminations were found to be baseless, but the church council was still quite embarrassed about deciding where to send this extremely outspoken minister.

The appointment of Candidius to the ministry of Formosa brought relief all round, all the more so because in 1625 Nuyts' predecessor, Martinus Sonck, had already asked for two or three ministers for missionary purposes.[23] Even though Candidius was attached to Nuyts' retinue to take care of the church services in Zeelandia Castle, Governor-General de Carpentier foresaw that this minister would also feel an inner drive to devote himself to the propagation of the gospel among the Formosan heathen. Therefore, in the political instructions to Pieter Nuyts he emphasized that the governor should ensure that any missionary activities be carried out with great circumspection.[24]

As soon as Nuyts had left for Japan, Candidius crossed over to Sinkan, where he built himself a bamboo cabin and started to study the language. He made abundantly clear where his priorities lay in the letters he wrote to Holland. He signed them with the concluding phrase: *Verbi divini inter gentes praeco*, "I preach the Holy Gospel among the heathens."

How could this Dutch missionary establish himself in a Formosan village without meeting any local protest or resistance? Perhaps the question should be reversed. Did the Sinkan people have a particular goal in mind when they welcomed the clergyman in their midst and, if so, was this goal of a religious nature? It is very doubtful that the latter was the case. The real reason lay elsewhere. From the point of view of the Sinkan village elders it was a sensible political move to admit Candidius to their village. By accepting a few Dutch residents in their midst, the *Tackasagach* or village council of Sinkan sought to protect the settlement from incursions by neighboring hostile tribes.

The general opinion among the villagers was that in times of danger the Dutch would certainly come to the aid of their countrymen residing in Sinkan. At no particular cost to themselves or loss of identity, the village council thus placed the settlement under the protective umbrella of Dutch arms. Little could the villagers foresee that in the seemingly innocent person of Candidius, a cuckoo's egg was being placed in the nest. The missionary wasted no time in putting his hand to the plow and soon he was able to collect a sizable following of young and avid students of the Holy Writ around himself.

Candidius's expectations that his missionary efforts would take root in Sinkan society proved somewhat premature. When Governor Nuyts imprisoned sixteen Sinkandians who had conspired with Japanese merchants against Dutch authority, Candidius's position in the village was imperiled. As long as their fellowmen remained behind bars, the villagers were no longer willing to listen to him. Quite understandably nobody in the village wished to have anything to do with one of those treacherous Dutchmen infiltrated into their midst. When one month later the Sinkandians were released, the freed men made a triumphant entry into their native village:

> having now regained their liberty, these Sinkandians proceeded with a great number of Japanese who accompanied them to the village of Sinkan. There they celebrated their return and were very merry, praising and lauding the Japanese . . . whereas they painted the Dutch in ugly colours. . . . In this way the hearts and minds of the inhabitants have been turned away, and filled with bitterness against us. Thus, the bad feeling that they entertain . . . is an impediment which has been standing in my way ever since last April, and which is still alive.[25]

Somehow Candidius, quarrels notwithstanding, managed to hang on to his cabin, but he was faced with an uphill task. Among the obstacles that blocked his path, the religious conflicts he had with the priestesses in the village were perhaps the most difficult to overcome. Candidius complained: "these priestesses, called *Inibs* by the people, are old crones who teach the very contrary of what I teach. They will not suffer that the least tiny bit of their superstitious idolatry and malpractices should be altered or disparaged."

The crucial thing about Candidius's letters from this period is not so much what he remarks about Sinkan customs or his own problems, but the picture he sketches of the astute behavior of the Sinkandians themselves. They challenged Candidius to demonstrate his powers, "asking me to perform miracles, to give or withold rain or wind, to foretell future events, or to reveal what is actually occurring elsewhere; and because I cannot do so, they despise me and say that their priestesses can do all these things."[26] The villagers even poked fun at the missionary by proposing that he should first confine his Christian instruction to one house only, and that all its inmates should abandon their native manners and customs and adopt Dutch customs promising that "If their gods still continue to bless that house by giving it an abundance of rice and other things during the next two or three years, they, too, would willingly adopt our religion." How impractical this suggestion was may be adduced from Candidius's lamentation that "If those who are inclined to listen to me meet others who are not, the latter take apart and destroy more in one hour than I can build up in ten."[27]

Because there was no central authority within Sinkan society to support his efforts, Candidius looked in the direction of Zeelandia Castle for some help, even though Governor Nuyts had failed to provide him with the support he needed. Candidius deemed it absolutely necessary that formal protection should be offered to Sinkan against the attacks by other villages, and that the Inibs be banished from the village. Finally he proposed a school system that would enable him to educate the whole community.

Candidius believed that only if Nuyts was willing to support him would his missionary work be crowned with success. Because the governor seemed primarily interested in the trade with China, the missionary grew disheartened and addressed himself secretly to Governor-General Coen, thus bypassing Nuyts. How despondent he was becomes clear from the concluding words of this letter: "I can only say that if the means I have now proposed succeed, I would be full of courage; but if not, it would be better to discontinue the work as soon as possible, so that no more time may be wasted. *Verbi divini inter gentes praeco.*"

LONG- AND SHORT-TERM PERSPECTIVES

The impatient Candidius was mistaken about Nuyts' intentions. That same autumn the governor personally visited Sinkan, wined and dined the elders, and bestowed thirty *cangans* (textiles) upon them, adding, not altogether truthfully, that they were a personal gift from Candidius. All parties seemed mollified by Nuyts' unexpected magnanimity. The Sinkandians felt relieved that the governor bore them no further grudge and judged him good company as a carouser; Candidius for once was prepared to look the other way and was happy with the attention shown to his missionary labors.

On Nuyts' commission Candidius now composed his *Discourse and Short Narrative of the Island of Formosa.*[28] This detailed ethnographical treatise on Formosan southwestern plains society will only be mentioned here insofar as it is instrumental for the understanding of the further interaction between the Dutch and the Sinkandians.

The villagers of Formosa's western plain had no formal kings or headmen but were ruled by councils of elders. They lived in a perpetual state of belligerence with their neighbors. Prestige among men was largely based on the martial prowess shown during headhunting expeditions. The two most important means of subsistence, riziculture and fishing, were both taken care of by the women. Men either hunted or practiced the martial arts in preparation for the occasional headhunting expeditions. Candidius provides a few examples of the progress of such expeditions, which were singularly treacherous and cunning in their execution.

The structure of government or rather the presumed absence of it on the village level was explained by Candidius as follows. The council of village elders was renewed every two years and consisted of men of the same age group who were no longer active in hunting. Important decisions were not taken by this council alone, but discussed in the people's assembly. Candidius was amazed at the eloquence displayed at such meetings: "Yes, I believe Demosthenes would not have been richer and more fluent in words."

Rules of abstinence were paid special attention in the Dutch minister's report, as they were the manifestation of the religious practices in the village. Candidius mentioned the objectionable role played in Formosan society by the priestesses or Inibs "who have daily conversation with the spirit world and know what is right and teach the Sinkandians accordingly." Candidius concluded that in many respects these women dominated Sinkan life: all sorties outside the settlement either for hunting or headhunting purposes were controlled by the divination of the Inibs. Women were not allowed to bear children before the age of thirty-five and were aborted by these Inibs as many as sixteen or seventeen times!

Delighted with the survey, Governor Nuyts inevitably asked Candidius what expectations he had of this society as a missionary field. Candidius foresaw a garden of Eden that he wished to cultivate himself. The missionary turned a feature of Sinkan society to his advantage: because it was an acephalous society, no treaties had to be concluded with local rulers before conversion could be started. Precisely because of the fact there was no central temporal power, Candidius wanted the governor of Zeelandia Castle to extend his powers to the Formosan coast and enforce his administration directly upon the villagers. The implication is clear: according to Candidius mission work could only be carried out with administrative backing.

If Nuyts seemed favorably impressed by Candidius's missionary work, he supported it, as it soon transpired, purely for political motives. For him Candidius was a pawn in his almost personal struggle against Japanese interests in Formosa. In January 1629 the governor suddenly invaded Sinkan while Candidius was absent in order to take his revenge on the sixteen villagers whom he had freed recently. When he could not find these men, he issued an ultimatum. He would return in a few days and if by that time the men had not been extradited, he would reduce the village to ashes. When his threat fell on deaf ears, he toned down his initial harshness and demanded thirty pigs and ten bundles of rice from each household as a punishment. This time the actions of the governor really undid all Candidius's efforts.

Upon his return to Sinkan on January 26, Candidius was confronted with a complete change in attitude. He was no longer trusted. The Sinkandians saw him as the governor's creature. Under these circumstances further missionary work became almost impossible. As a result of this fiasco, Candidius again sent a secret letter to Governor-General Coen in Batavia complaining about the beastly treatment he was receiving. With his missionary endeavors in tatters the clergyman asked to be released from his mission post.[29]

Understandably Governor Nuyts, in his correspondence to Governor-General Coen, did not refer to his raids into Sinkan, and how these had undermined any future work that Candidius might undertake.

> Candidius still remains in Sinkan, but presents us with so many problems that we despair of his work. His principal demand, which he deems necessary for further progress, is that the natives should be coerced to listen to him through laws and punishments imposed by us. We cannot introduce punishments however, without bringing our existence here into grave danger. These people must and should be taught through good example (and not by way of punishments).[30]

How limited Nuyts' power actually was, we learn from a letter written three years later, in which his successor states that during Nuyts' governorship several hundreds of *cangangs* had been presented to the large villages in the vicinity of Zeelandia two or three times a year: "What else has this been but a subservience by means of which our people have clearly professed themselves to be tenants and not the owners of the land."[31] Nuyts adhered to a policy of noninterference and was only interested in playing off people against each other. In his eyes the Formosans and Candidius himself were, as I have already said, little more more than pawns in a constantly changing powerplay.

Candidius was not the only one to lodge complaints against Nuyts' intemperate behavior. As a result the governor-general and council in Batavia decided to recall Nuyts and replace him with Hans Putmans, who had distinguished himself during the Javanese siege of Batavia in 1628. Only eight days before the latter's arrival in the Tayouan roads, Nuyts made one last false step that was to determine all Dutch political moves on Formosa for the next few years and put a mighty weapon in the hands of the missionaries, even if they did not realize this at the time.

On July 13, 1629, the governor personally commanded a force of handpicked Dutch musketeers on an expedition to the northern village of Mattauw in order to capture some Chinese pirates. On the way back to Zeelandia, while crossing a river, all sixty soldiers except for the governor, who had returned earlier, were ambushed and massacred by Mattauw warriors and their allies. Elated by this easy success the warriors then proceeded to overrun Sinkan and destroy all Dutch possessions in the island.

At this point we should pause to survey the balance of Dutch-Formosan relations during the first five years of the Dutch presence. The Dutch had met a bellicose population on the island of Lamey, but on Formosa proper they were welcomed. As a result Candidius could settle down in Sinkan and learn the local language, thus becoming quite familiar with the customs of the inhabitants. The colonial administration had chosen to keep itself aloof but, whenever it did choose to interfere, it made some terrible mistakes, totally disregarding the advice of Candidius, the man on the spot. By 1630 the colonial administration was painfully aware of the fact that it would have to cooperate closely with the clergy-men in the field and involve them in its policy-making if it expected to regain the lost ground.

The missionaries, for their part, were facing the formidable task of how to challenge and enter into the mental world of the Formosans. In the minds of the latter the outside world, the world outside the village perimeter, was of a chaotic nature—a hostile world into which one would only venture after consultation with the Inips. It was fully under-stood that it was only in this chaotic cosmos that prestige could be acquired: in a fast foray outside one's own safe territory, either head-hunting or deerhunting. These were both feats of great daring. Conse-quently intervillage violence was not so much a political, but rather an inescapable socioreligious phenomenon, a central feature of village life.

In Formosan plains society men and women trod two different paths. The men invaded hostile territory, struck down the enemy, cut off his head—the seat of the vital powers—and brought it back to the home village. This was the path of men. The path of women led to the super-natural world, where they could safeguard the expeditions through prayers and offerings. This was the spiritual path monopolized by women. Small wonder that Candidius, a man, who consequently had no access to the traditional supernatural domain, begged permission to marry a local girl so that through her he could reach the female part of Sinkan society, which was most familiar with religious affairs.[32]

THE WATERSHED

One of the first things Governor Hans Putmans did upon arriving in Formosa in the summer of 1629 was to consult Candidius to determine "namely by which means the violent sentiment of the local inhabitants could be soothed, and how the propagation of the Christian religion

could be promoted." Note that at this point the temporal authorities
had finally called in the assistance of the clerics. Governor-General Coen
had even advised Putmans in so many words that he was to comply with
the advice given by Candidius.[33] Candidius, who had been reinforced in
the meantime by the arrival of another minister, Robert Junius of Delft,
advised that the cannibals of the island of Lamey who had massacred the
crew members of the *Gouden Leeuw* in a cowardly way should be punished and that the conspirators from Mattau, Soolangh, and other villages that had joined in the looting of Sinkan should likewise be called
to account.

The ringleaders in the plunder should be executed, their possessions
burned! Only by the meting out of retributive punishment would Candidius be able to return to Sinkan, where he now had become a total
outcast. All this was easily said but not so easily done. Putmans understood that, from the military point of view, he could not follow up this
advice. Not only were the number of troops at his disposal after the Mattau massacre too small, but even more important, the Dutch were not
familiar with the terrain, an advantage enjoyed by their Formosan opponents.

For the time being Putmans did not dare to attack Mattau, but on
November 17, 1629, he felt strong enough to send a punitive expedition to the small village of Bacloangh, which had collaborated with Mattau. He included warriors from Sinkan in this expedition, promising
them a share in the spoils. As far as the Sincandians were concerned, the
expedition was a great success: a few captured heads restored their in-
jured pride. Although the real ringleaders from Mattau remained out of
range, the Sinkandians were once again brought into the Dutch camp as
allies. Therefore, on February 2, 1630, Candidius could return to "his"
village. This time, conditions were favorable to his missionary work.
Starvation was imminent due to a bad harvest. Twenty-one families,
consisting of 122 persons, accepted the Christian creed; many others
were won over as Candidius started to distribute rice and cloth to the
needy.[34]

Now Candidius seized the initiative, exploiting the attention that he
received from Putmans; he personally vowed to the villagers that the
attack by Mattau would be revenged one day. He thereupon transmitted
this promise to Putmans, who in turn felt forced to mount such an expedition. On December 19, 1630, troops were sent against Mattau by sea
via the coastal stronghold of Wankan, as Putmans still deemed it unwise
to cross overland through unknown territory and risk ambushes. Due to
the northerly winds Wankan was never reached, but in order to comfort
the large contingent of Sinkan fighters on board it was decided to turn
around, head southward, and attack the coastal village of Tamsuy,

where the villagers still had an old dispute to settle. It was nothing less than a headhunting expedition under the auspices of the company. Although only one head was taken, the expedition proved a success.

The enthusiastic people's assembly of Sinkan expressed its willingness to adopt the Christian creed en masse and solemnly offered the company a plot of land where a brick house could be constructed for the clergymen. At the end of 1631 Candidius decided that the time had finally come to baptize the first fifty persons. This was the crowning glory to his work. A few months later he left on furlough for Batavia. If Candidius was a diligent and pious worker, his successor Robert Junius proved to be much more a man of action.

ONWARD, CHRISTIAN SOLDIERS!

Robertus Junius was a "new style" missionary who had graduated from the *Seminarium Indicum* in Leiden. He was only twenty-three years old when he arrived in the retinue of Governor Putmans in the summer of 1629. Max Weber has pointed out that "religious specialists" function either as protagonists of social change or as preservers of tradition.[35] The "modern" missionary, through the foundation of schools and the introduction of improved technology and agricultural methods, is instrumental in bringing about socioeconomic change to the non-Western countryside. In his role as a protagonist of social change, Junius was indeed a modern missionary.

First of all Junius rationalized Christian religious ideas for his prospective Formosan followers. It is in this context that Junius's frequent confrontations with the Formosan priestesses, the Inibs, should be seen. Because these women formed the key to the supernatural world of the Sinkandians, he first tried to win them over. When he failed to do so, the missionary petitioned Governor Putmans to have them deported inland. Far away from the Christian villages he deemed them harmless.[36] In Calvinistic fashion he tried to liberate the cosmos from angry ghosts, pernicious influences, and the like, and he wanted to substitute the notion of the One True God, who offers all-embracing protection, for these animistic beliefs. His catechisms are a model of simplicity and common sense. In later days Junius was criticized by his successors for having oversimplified the gospel, and for having adapted it too much to local needs—a recurring colonial predicament indeed.[37]

On horseback Junius commanded expeditions of allied Formosan troops against hostile villages. In doing so he swept aside the Inibs, on whose divinations success traditionally depended in war. He personally represented the avenging God, "petitioning the Lord of Battles Who must teach our hands to fight, so that Israel, God's own brethren, may emerge, while Amalek succumbs."[38]

At this point in time it should have dawned upon the missionaries that the successful dissemination of the gospel required gross perversion indeed. War has been described as a type of collective policy involving the use of force or violence, and a type of political situation that may obtain between units as a result of the employment of such politics.[39] In the case of the intervillage violence in Formosan plains society, one wonders whether such a definition really suffices. However, once the Dutch began to interfere in this process and started to pacify the countryside, institutionalized violence indeed turned into war. Through Christian-inspired punitive expeditions, colonial war was introduced to the Formosan countryside. Bearing these general remarks in mind, let us now focus on the period 1633–36, and analyze how church and state carried out the conquest of southwest Formosa.

In the autumn of 1633 a trade agreement was finally achieved between Governor Putmans and the Chinese authorities. Because Putmans' main worries about the resumption of trade had been removed, he could at last turn his attention to the pacification of the western plains of Formosa.

In the spring of that same year he had mapped out a plan in conjunction with the Indian government in Batavia. It had been decided that, as a matter of principle, the perpetrators of the massacres at Mattau and Lamey should be punished. To teach all Formosans a lesson both villages had to be razed and their inhabitants deported and relocated. In other words, retribution had to be executed.

Governor Putmans decided to postpone any warlike excursions against Mattau for the time being, because this large village was located inland at a two days' march from Zeelandia Castle through unexplored territory, and he still lacked enough troops and native allies to confront these redoubtable warriors. He therefore opted for a punitive expedition against Lamey, which could be reached by ship from Zeelandia within one day. It was generally understood that this small volcanic island, measuring five by two kilometers, could easily be conquered by a relatively small task force. One of the main attractions of the expedition was that prospective allies of the company could also be given the opportunity to seek revenge for the raids they had suffered at the hands of the Lamey people in the past. The Dutch force, 140 soldiers, 60 sailors in excess of the normal crew, and some 250 Formosan warriors left on November 9, 1633, under the command of Claes Bruyn.

The expedition was a total failure. The troops went ashore, met with little resistance, burned the village of Lamey on top of the hill, but were not able to catch a single islander. The people had gone into hiding in caves that seemed to honeycomb the whole island. However, during the search the flotsam and jetsam of the yacht *Beverwijck* were discovered and soon afterwards utensils and garments of its crew were found on land. Thus it was established that this ship, which had been reported missing in 1631, had also been shipwrecked on the island and that its crew had met the same fate as the unfortunate party of sailors from the *Gouden Leeuw*.[40] This discovery could only strengthen the indignation of the Dutch and intensify the clamor for retribution.

Set back by the lack of success in getting hold of the refractory Lamey islanders, Governor Putmans decided to wait for sizable reinforcements from Batavia before trying a second time. Junius and Candidius (who had come back from Batavia to continue his missionary labors) made sure that the governor did not forget about the necessity of retribution and punishment. They did so in a remarkably crafty manner. A number of examples will demonstrate how Junius, as vanguard in the field, carried out orders from, but simultaneously manipulated, the governor of Zeelandia Castle, and even maneuvered him into faits accomplis by drawing attention to his own perilous position whenever it suited him to do so.

As stated before, the first expedition to Mattau, which never fully materialized, was a forced move provoked by Candidius's warnings against further hostile action by the Formosans. Junius exploited this strategy even further. He repeatedly warned that the population of Sinkan was becoming increasingly restive, and even threatened to apostatize as long as the company did not take some tough action. Junius's letters to Putmans abound with evidence of this kind. On one occasion women threatened the missionary that they would take up "dancing on the trough" again, an intoxicating dance for the traditional gods.[41] When Junius wanted to retrieve his hunting-dog entrusted to the care of a Formosan, he met with rebuke: "If you take the greyhound back, I shall become heathen again and take leave of the God of Heaven."[42] When he tried to reconcile a man with his estranged wife and did not grant him permission to divorce, the irate husband threatened to murder any Dutchman who attempted to reunite him with his wife.[43] Junius believed that the governor's indecision in the punishment of Mattau ridiculed the Dutch: if Sinkandians took revenge for the theft of one pig, as they frequently did, how could the Dutch leave the murder of seventy of their compatriots unavenged? "Our nation is subject to ridicule. In Mattau the skulls of the victims are displayed on the stage for abuse and play. During their banquets they amuse themselves by mimicking the cries of agony of the victims in the river; our nation has become a byword, and object of mockery, a laughing stock."[44] All these expressions of disdain convinced Putmans of the necessity to take action. While the governor requested an expeditionary force in his letters to Batavia, Junius sent scouts everywhere to reconnoiter the local conditions and set out possible routes.

The religious specialist also made himself indispensable in other respects. Under Junius's supervision, a number of Chinese were set to work cultivating rice and sugar-cane in the immediate vicinity of Sinkan. He advanced money for the necessary investments and even sent a Chinese to Fukien to purchase a millstone for the sugar production. When this indispensable tool was delivered Junius borrowed two water-buffaloes from the castle to turn the mill, and thus set the refining process in motion. When Chinese pirates attacked Zeelandia Castle and isolated it from Formosa for weeks, Junius managed to keep the population of Sinkan in check, even employing them to search for the enemy.

The wide range of activities of the two clergymen and their staff is singularly striking. Apart from spreading the true gospel, they acted as agricultural developers and tax officials (an initial tax on deerhunting was imposed and collected by Candidius and Junius). They wrote ABC primers in the Siraya language,[45] prepared expeditions with the aim of conquest, and thought out a formula for colonial administration.

PUNISHMENT FROM HEAVEN

Junius's "finest hour" came in the summer of 1635, when a large campaign against Mattau and other hostile villages was at last geared into action. Full of high spirits he led the way in the van of native troops, shoulder to shoulder with the Dutch expeditionary force that had arrived from Batavia in the meantime. Twenty-six villagers were killed in the fracas and all houses were set on fire with the exception of the houses of a few people who had provided the Dutch with information. It was like Joshua ordering all of Jericho be "devoted to the Lord for destruction; only Rahab the harlot and all who are with her in her house shall live, because she hid the messengers that we sent."

Fortunately the sacking of Mattau was a less messy affair than the battle of Jericho. On December 18, 1635, the vanquished formally submitted and, contrary to the instructions received from Batavia, were even allowed by Putmans to rebuild their village on the same location. Now the pacification campaign of the Formosan plains society was really set in motion. All further skirmishes were of the same character: they were largely fought by proxy. After the Dutch musketeers had opened fire and sent the enemy running, the Formosan allies set off in pursuit and took the heads. Leading the troops of their Formosan allies under the banner of the Ever-Victorious Christian God, the Dutch clerics easily toppled the existing dynamic pattern of Formosan intervillage violence and succeeded in establishing a thus far unheard of peace among the formerly warring tribes by imposing a policy of divide and rule.

How did Junius arrange the submission and transfer of sovereignty of the Formosan villages? The attempts by "allied villages" to draw the Dutch into wars by attacking their own hereditary enemies actually pushed the latter into the arms of the Dutch. The mere proposal of transfer of their soil and the acceptance of Dutch sovereignty safe-guarded the erstwhile enemy from further depredations by Dutch allies. Because there were no headmen or chiefs in the villages, the problem of representation in their relations with the VOC posed itself.

To solve this issue, Junius now proposed that the company delegate three or four prominent persons who could represent the village with the colonial administration after the transfer of sovereignty and act as "native chiefs." As tokens of authority these dignitaries were to be pro-vided with a hat, a red cape, and a baton with a silver grip. Authority within the village, once flexible and loosely stretched, was thus institu-tionalized in the hands of a few leaders imposed by an outside ruler, the inevitable result of the colonial interference. As token of this transfer of sovereignty, the Formosans had to hand over fruits of the soil like coco-nut and areca nut trees at Zeelandia Castle. The Dutch authorities tried to ensure that the Formosans actually understood what the transfer of sovereignty implied: "You [Junius] should clearly explain to them its meaning so that they do know what our intention is, and do not think that the affair is settled by the mere gift of some small trees."[46] By the end of 1636 fifty-seven villages had already either submitted or shown their willingness to do so. With the notable exception of the island of Lamey, to which we shall presently turn, this rapid expansion of the Dutch territorial perimeter occurred without much bloodshed or loss of life on either side. Junius and Candidius had every reason to be content with themselves—but not for long.

APOCALYPSE

On the repeated orders of Governor-General Hendrick Brouwer that the island of Lamey should be swept clean of the murderers of the Dutch crews, preparations were now made to subjugate the island. As the is-land has been described in detail by Commander Claes Bruyn, who went ashore in 1633 and was the first Dutchman to return alive, let us briefly look at the gist of his report:

The island is about three miles in circumference, and difficult to approach because of reefs. . . . A large mountain which rises from the valley, forms the centre of the island. . . . On the way to the top of this mountain one reaches the village—two rows of small houses adjoining a pathway. . . . Behind the village is the entrance to a large cave where the population, 1100 people or so, can go into hiding when the enemy approaches. . . . The inhabitants are very savage—the whole world is their enemy! They occasionally make headhunting forays to Formosa and rob and kill the people residing near the coast.[47]

As evident from de Bruyn's writings, the Lamey people were not much different than the other tribes on Formosa. Intervillage violence was a socioreligious phenomenon, a central feature of Formosan society. What set the Lamey people apart was that they were living on an island of their own and were quite difficult to approach.

On April 16, 1636, the army captain Jan Jurriaensz van Linga departed with one hundred Dutch musketeers and a considerable following of Formosan allies. The captain's instruction stated that he should starve the people into submission if they were not willing to leave their island and to gas them out of their hidden caves "with sulphur, tar, and other nauseating malodours" if necessary.[48] The first assault misfired as a result of the rainy weather, but on April 26 the troops landed again and after a great deal of searching managed to seal off most entrances to the cave and started to smoke out those inside.

As most of the able-bodied men had withdrawn into the hills, making unexpected sallies from their hideouts, it was clear from the outset that only invalids, women, and children were hiding in the cave. After three days the first forty-two people came creeping out of the cave. We read that the heartrending crying by women and children could be overheard during one full week. When on May 4 no further sound was heard from below the troops descended into the cave and, by the light of their torches, witnessed an appalling sight: scattered throughout the passages lay corpses of asphyxiated men, women, and children. Initially the number of dead islanders found inside the cave was estimated at about 200 to 300 "as we could not count well as a result of the great stench." Of the people trapped in the cave some 293 people—23 men, 125 women, and 145 children—survived the ordeal. This ratio speaks for itself: very few warriors had hidden themselves in the main cave. The grisly details of Captain Van Lingga's report of the massacre drew the following sheepish comment from Governor Putmans at Zeelandia: "From the letter received I understand the misery of these people, who due to their stubborn character have refused to surrender, has been a deplorable sight." And as if to share the responsibility for this with the Lord he added, "It seems it has pleased the Almighty to conduct this affair in this way while meting out to them the deserved punishment for the crimes they have committed against our people and others, crimes which run counter to the natural and reasonable character of the human race."[49]

In subsequent days many of the Lamey warriors, who had been demoralized after what had happened to their kin, were caught and deported. Without going into too much detail we can establish that, by the time Jan Jurriaens departed with the bulk of his troops—he left 20 men behind in a stockade—some 134 men, 192 children, and 157 women of the island population followed as captives. As another 500 had been killed, more than 300 by asphyxiation, it was estimated that 100 people still remained hiding in the hills. Putmans, upon whom it had started to dawn what had been perpetrated in the name of the company, became almost apologetic when on June 2, 1636, he entered in the Zeelandia Journal that, according to information recently received, the island had been so overpopulated prior to the assault that one day the inhabitants would have inevitably turned violently against each other in the struggle over sparse resources.[50] One can only conclude ironically that under the new conditions created by the mass deportations that possibility had become very remote indeed.

What happened to those unfortunate people who survived the "black hole" but were deported to Taiwan? Some 130 men were put in the chain gangs and used for forced labor on construction works in Formosa as well as in Batavia. In the resolution of Batavia of January 16, 1637, we see that these chain-gang slaves died at such an appalling rate, that the few who survived were divided among the burghers of the town.[51] All women and children were distributed among the population of Sinkan while awaiting further orders from Batavia.[52] At Zeelandia twenty-five boys and girls from Lamey were selected to be educated according to the Christian religion. The others were divided among the Sinkan population as potential servants.

Reverend Robertus Junius, a personal friend of Putmans and his main counselor on native affairs, witnessed all this happening on the doorstep of his church in Sinkan and raised the matter in his correspondence with the governor. On June 13 he wrote that there were daily complaints about the Lamey women: "They scream for their husbands and ask to be permitted to return to their island, some scream for their children." Two months later he continued:

> It is pitiful to see how these people muddle along. Their crying would move a heart of stone. I cannot even write down their names as they run from one Sinkan household to another hoping to arrive at a better household than before, but they are actually reduced to even worse conditions. Little compassion is shown with them by the Sinkandians.[53]

He urgently pressed Putmans to let the survivors return to their ancestral island and even proposed to accompany them there and live in their midst, so that nobody would have to worry about them in the future. It is clear that Junius did not want to stand idly by any longer and was willing to share the burden. A few days later a junk carrying another ninety-nine captured Lamey people, among them thirty-five men, returned from the island to the roadstead of Zeelandia Castle. This time governor and council decided to send them on to Batavia.[54]

In the resolutions of Zeelandia we read that governor and council were wondering whether the twenty-one men and women and seven children who were still on the island should also be deported. It was decided to postpone further action until new instructions came from Batavia. Governor Putmans of Formosa, who was on the brink of transferring his office and leaving for Batavia, had by now become thoroughly embarrassed about what to do with the remaining islanders. He no doubt hoped to persuade Governor-General Van Diemen that further deportations were unnecessary.

From letters written by Sergeant Barentz, who had remained behind with a few soldiers, we know that when the latter tried to convince them "to leave for their friends in Batavia who were well off over there, they looked at him with gloomy faces, and burst out in tears, answering that they would have to go, if it was the desire of the Governor-General in Batavia, but that they hoped they could remain behind."[55]

This turned out to be a vain hope. On June 13, 1640, Governor-General Anthonie van Diemen wrote once more to the governor of Formosa that he did not understand why the continued presence of some forty islanders was still tolerated on Lamey. "They provide no service to the Company, on the contrary, by multiplying they will cause further trouble," he remarked.[56] The governor-general ordered them to be deported forthwith.

After one more admonition from the governor-general and council in Batavia it was decided to round up the survivors. More soldiers were sent. Once more people who had taken flight were killed; once more a few escaped. Finally, in January 1645, the Chinese merchant Samsjack, who was leasing the once prosperous island for the miserly sum of sixty reals a year, managed to catch and bring in thirteen of the remaining fifteen people and was rewarded with one hundred reals. One month later the final two were caught. Lamey was now totally stripped of its population. The Batavian administration could set its mind at rest. At long last the "savages" had been taught a lesson.

Yet the gruesome story reached the Netherlands. After Junius had returned to Delft in 1644 and the enthusiastic welcome celebrations were over, he went to see his fellow townsman Hans Putmans, the former governor of Formosa, who had returned seven years earlier. Discussing the "good old days," they decided that there was a story to be told to the Gentlemen Seventeen. In 1647 the directorate of the company met on several occasions with both Junius and Putmans.[57] They were so aghast about what they heard that they sent a report of the conversations to Governor-General van der Lijn in Batavia asking him to discuss the contents with his director general, Francois Caron, who from 1644 to 1646 had been governor of Formosa. They also informed the governor-general that from now on one should deal less harshly with Formosa's refractory tribes. After all this kind of punishment inevitably meant "the shedding of much blood of simpletons . . . simpletons, who should not be imposed upon too much at the same time, as they cannot understand what it is that one desires from them."[58]

The outcome of this discussion was that the then president of Zeelandia Castle, Over 't Water, was ordered to collect all materials he could find concerning the deportation of the Lamey people in the archives of the castle.

In due course Over 't Water sent the collected papers to Batavia where they were provided with an accompanying comment by Governor-General van der Lijn.[59] He drew the balance sheet: during the assault 405 people had been killed; 191 men and women had been sent to Batavia; 482 had been shared out among the people of Sinkan; 24 children had been brought up in Dutch families. He was wise enough not to mention that a large number of these 697 people had died shortly after their deportation. At the time of his writing (January 1649) van der Lijn believed that the exiles in Sinkan had by now been assimilated into the local population. He proudly noted that as recently as 1646 one more group of 14 Lamey children had been selected to be educated in Dutch families in Batavia. "It is to be hoped," he concluded, "that many of the Lamey people may rejoice in the fortune which has befallen these children, for the daughters who have married Dutchmen have shown to be good housewives, as proven by the earlier mentioned 24 children, many of whom are now well established burgher wives."[60]

Judging by their comment one year later on the report, the Gentlemen Seventeen were not at all satisfied with van der Lijn's answer. Without doubt they could have remarked that there were very few Lamey people left to rejoice in anything, but more generally speaking they realized that punishing indigenous people for putative crimes in order to set examples hardly reaped the desired result: "It is a natural shortcoming of the people of our nation to be either too gentle or too severe in their actions when governing the areas that are under their rule; this is amply proven by those living in the East and West Indies."[61]

CONCLUSION

Protestant missionaries played a decisive role in the territorial expansion of the Dutch East India Company on Formosa. They put their stamp on this process in various ways: they manipulated the policy-making of the governor and skillfully exploited the dynamics of intervillage violence while introducing the concept of centralized power to native Formosan society. The establishment of colonial rule had indeed been brought about by the synergy of church and state with judicious timing of when to strike while the iron was hot.

Yet ironically the two main protagonists in pacifying the Formosans, Governor Putmans and *Dominee* Junius, became themselves appalled by the dreadful effects of the reprisals that they had to mete out against the population of Lamey. They actually felt remorse for having carried out the orders of Batavia and appealed to the Gentlemen Seventeen that, in the future, these harsh retributive actions should be avoided. It was their intention to expose the utter futility of calling native peoples to account for putative "crimes" committed when these people had no conception of why they were being punished in such a massive and brutal fashion. In this respect not even the Old Testament could offer consolation to Junius. If on earlier occasions he had proudly likened his exploits to the battle with the Amalekites, now this servant of God may have felt like the apprentice in whose hands the "rod" of the Lord had spun out of control. The Lamey expedition had no missionary objectives. It had been nothing but an act of revenge for the deaths of Dutch sailors at the hands of local headhunters—headhunters who most probably had seen the shipwrecked sailors washed ashore as a plentiful bounty offered to them by the sea.

Junius realized he had flaunted Christian precepts when he assisted the colonial authorities in the meting out of "retributive justice" to headhunting fellow human beings. In the Name of God and the East India Company he was supposed to convert and win over savages, but for some of these ultimately no mercy was in store. Trapped in this colonial paradox Junius failed to draw the ultimate conclusion that empire and Christian mission were incompatible.

NOTES

This essay is an elaboration of earlier research on the activities of Dutch missionaries in Formosa. See L. Blussé, "Dutch Protestant Missionaries as Protagonists of the Territorial Expansion of the VOC on Formosa," in *Conversion, Competition and Conflict*, ed. D. Kooiman (Amsterdam, 1984), pp. 155–84.

1. H. Jessei, *Of the Conversion of five thousand nine hundred* EAST INDI-ANS *In the Isle Formosa neere China, To the Profession of the true* GOD, *in* JESUS CHRIST *By Meanes of M. Ro: Junius, a Minister lately in* DELPH *in* HOLLAND. *Related by his good friend M.C. Sibellius, Pastor in* DAVENTRIE *there, in a* LATINE *Letter. Translated to further the Faith and Joy of many here, by H. Jessei, A Servant of* JESUS CHRIST. (London, 1650).

2. This letter, written on July 25, 1646, was prefixed to Sibellius's book *Antidotum Ambitionis* (Amsterdam, 1646). Caspar Sibellius was a clergyman of the town of Deventer, who had met Junius for the first time at the Provincial Synod of North Holland in Haarlem in 1645.

3. William Campbell, *An Account of Missionary Success in the Island of Formosa* (London, 1889), p. 23. The adventurous preacher had not quite rid his spirit of adventure, for during the First Anglo-Dutch war he signed up for personal participation in the struggle and served from August to November 1653 as a naval chaplain in the Dutch fleet. He died of smallpox at the relatively young age of forty-nine on August 28, 1655.

4. C.E.S., the author of this book, most probably was the last governor of Formosa, Frederic Coyett (*Coyett et Socii*). *'t Verwaerloosde Formosa of Waerachtig Verhael, Hoedanigh door verwaerloosinge der Nederlanders in* OOST-INDIEN, *het Eylant* FORMOSA, *van den Chinesen* MANDORIJN, *ende Zeerover* COX-INJA, *overrompelt, vermeestert, ende ontweldight is geworden* (Amsterdam, 1675). Recently a reprint with the same title has been edited by G. C. Molewijk in the *Werken uitgegeven door de Linschoten-vereeniging*, vol. 90 (Zutphen, 1991).

As noted below the book has been partly translated by William Campbell. For possible political reasons he did not insert the appendix on "Some Considerable Facts Touching the True Cause of the Chinese Cruelties and Tyranny Committed upon the Pastors, Schoolmasters, and the Netherlanders there." The English translation of this appendix by A. Blussé van Oud-Alblas has been added to the unexpurgated edition published by Incz de Beauclair, *Neglected Formosa, a Translation from the Dutch of Frederic Coyett's 't Verwaerloosde Formosa* (San Francisco, 1975), pp. 89–103.

5. William Campbell, ed., *Formosa under the Dutch: Descriptions from Contemporary Records* (London, 1903). The text is a compilation of translations made from three contemporary Dutch sources: F. Valentijn, *Van Oud- en Nieuw Oostindië* (Dordrecht, 1724–26); J. A. Grothe, *Archief voor de Geschiedenis der oude Hollandsche Zending* (Utrecht, 1884–91); and C.E.S., *'t Verwaerloosde Formosa*.

6. The best historical survey of the Dutch mission on Formosa so far has been given in the doctoral thesis by Willy Abraham Ginsel, *De Gereformeerde Kerk op Formosa of de lotgevallen eener handelskerk onder de Oost-Indische-Compagnie, 1627–1662* (Leiden, 1931).

7. The converts "pronounce sentences without understanding them, and like magpies, merely trying to utter such sounds as have been repeated to them" (statement made by Governor and Council of Taiwan, cited in Campbell, *Formosa under the Dutch*, p. 211). See also Ginsel, *De Gereformeerde Kerk*, pp. 95–103.

8. C. R. Boxer, *The Dutch Seaborne Empire 1600–1800* (Harmondsworth, 1973), pp. 148–72.

9. It has been postulated that never again after 1620–40 was there such a lively interest in the overseas mission. "The churches were, however, so much frustrated by the Company that largely for this reason this first love soon faded and languished on account of the impediments encountered" (C.W.T. Van Boetzelaer van Dubbeldam, *De Gereformeerde Kerken in Nederland en de Zending in Oost-Indië in de dagen der Oost-Indische Compagnie* [Utrecht, 1906], pp. 174–75).

10. Laurence M. Hauptman and Ronald G. Knapp have compared in a very interesting study Dutch expansion in Taiwan and North America (Hauptman and Knapp, "Dutch-Aboriginal Interaction in New Netherland and Formosa: An Historical Geography of Empire," *Proceedings of the American Philosophical Society* 121, no. 2 [1977]: 166–82). Although these authors state that Dutch policies toward nonwhite people were neither uniform nor consistent over time, they do agree that both in Formosa and New Netherland the commercial motive was most significant (p. 181).

11. Van Boetzelaer, *De Gereformeerde Kerken*, p. 46.

12. Sebastiaen Danckaerts, *Historisch ende grondich verhael van den Standt des Christendoms in 't quartier van Amboina, mitsgaders van den hoope ende apparentie eenigher Reformatie ende beternisse van dien gestelt* ('s Gravenhage, 1621).

13. J. A. Grothe, "Het Seminarie van Walaeus," *Berigten van de Utrechtsche Zendingsvereeniging voor het jaar 1882* (Utrecht, 1882), 23:17–57.

14. Hauptman and Knapp, "Dutch-Aboriginal Interaction," pp. 166–82.

15. W.Ph. Coolhaas, *Generale Missiven* ('s-Gravenhage, 1960), 1:126.

16. Ibid., p. 518.

17. A.R.A., VOC 1056, fol. 32. H. Brouwer to Governor-General Both, January 1, 1613.

18. See J. R. Bruijn et al. *Dutch-Asiatic Shipping in the 17th and 18th Centuries* (The Hague, 1979), 2:48–49.

19. L. Blussé and M.P.M. Roessingh, "A Visit to the Past: Soulang, A Formosan Village anno 1623," *Archipel* 27 (1984): 63–80.

20. This person is Li Tan, the chief of the Chinese residents in Hirado, Japan, who happened to arrive in the roadstead of Taiwan from Japan on his junk on April 22, 1623. See Iwao Seiichi, "Li Tan, Chief of the Chinese Residents at Hirado, Japan in the Last Days of the Ming Dynasty," *Memoirs of the Research Department of the Toyo Bunko* 17 (1958): 51.

21. Blussé and Roessingh, "Visit to the Past," p. 72.

22. Sebastiaan Danckaerts, *Historisch en grondich verhaal van de standt des Christendoms in 't quartier van Amboina* ('s-Gravenhage, 1621).

23. Ginsel, *De Gereformeerde Kerk*, p. 11.

24. François Valentijn, *Oud en Nieuw Oost-Indië* (Dordrecht, 1724), 4:8.

25. Ibid., p. 94.

26. Ibid., p. 95.

27. Ibid., p. 96.

28. Campbell, *Formosa under the Dutch*, pp. 9–25.

29. Letter of February 1, 1629, in Campbell, *Formosa*, pp. 97–102.

30. Letter from P. Nuyts to G.G. J. P. Coen, February 4, 1629, in Ginsel, *De Gereformeerde Kerk*, p. 85.

31. Letter from H. Putman to G.G. Specx, October 10, 1631, in ibid., p. 26. This account does not square with the oft-cited statement that in 1625 "fifteen *cangans* were traded with the aborigines for a tract of land on the site of the present city of Tainan" (Hauptman and Knapp, "Dutch-Aboriginal Interaction," p. 178; Campbell, *Formosa under the Dutch*, p. 37). The land was leased, not purchased.

32. Ginsel, *De Gereformeerde Kerk*, p. 24.

33. H. T. Colenbrander ed., *Jan Pietersz. Coen, Bescheiden omtrent zijn bedrijf in Indië* ('s-Gravenhage, 1923), 5:497.

34. Ginsel, *De Gereformeerde Kerk*, p. 25.

35. The *Sociology of Religion*, cited in the entry on "Religious Specialists" by Victor W. Turner in *International Encyclopedia of the Social Sciences* (New York, 1968), 13:438.

36. Ginsel mentions that Governor-General van Diemen deemed this measure inadequate and ordered the women to be sent to Batavia: "This order was executed, but Junius strongly disapproved of this measure which he found much too severe" (*De gereformeerde Kerk op Formosa*, p. 50).

37. Junius's method of teaching and the criticisms by his detractors are discussed by Ginsel, *De Gereformeerde Kerk*, pp. 87–95.

38. A.R.A., First Division, *Teding van Berkhout Collection*, letter from Junius to Putmans, November 8, 1633.

39. P. B. Huber, "Defending the Cosmos, Violence and Social Order among the Anggor of New Guinea," in *War, Its Causes and Correlates*, ed. M. A. Nettleship, et al. (The Hague, 1975), p. 619. Huber states that "any examination of intergroup violence in non-Western societies under the rubric of war entails a very serious risk of begging the question."

40. VOC 5051, "Verhael van de tocht gedaan uut Tayouan onder 't beleyt ende Commande van den Edele Commandeur Claes Bruijn, op 't Lamey ofte Goudeleeuws eilant 1633."

41. Letter from Junius to Putmans, November 25, 1633, in *Teding van Berkhout Collection*.

42. Letter from Junius to Putmans, November 25, 1633, in ibid.

43. Ibid.

44. Letter from Candidus to Putmans, November 25, 1633, in ibid.

45. Letter of May 15, 1636, in ibid.

46. Letter from Putmans to Junius, March 25, 1636, in *Teding van Berkhout*.

47. *ARA* VOC 5051, "Corte beschrijvinge van de gelegenheijt ende cituatie van 't Goude Leeuws eylant."

48. "Instructie voor de Luitenant Johan Jurriaensz ende vordere Raetspersonen waer naer hun in 't aentasten van het Goude Leeuws eylandt ende (soo het Godt belieft te segenen) bij veroveringe desselfs sullen hebben te reguleren," April, 19, 1636, VOC 1170, fol. 628.

49. *Dagregisters van het Kasteel Zeelandia*, May 7, 1636, p. 247.

50. Ibid., pp. 255–56.

51. VOC 1122, fol. 360.

52. Letter from Putmans to Junius, June 2, 1636, in *Teding van Berkhout Collection*.

53. Letter of September 8, 1636, in ibid.

54. Letter from Putmans to Junius, September 17, 1636.

55. VOC 1170, "Extract uyt de resolutieboecken," May 23, 1639, fol. 594.

56. "Missive aen President Paulus Traudenius," VOC 864, fol. 250.

57. Letter from the Gentlemen Seventeen to G.G. and Council in Batavia, October 4, 1647, VOC 317, fol. 78. The minutes of the several talks with Junius and Putmans have unfortunately been lost. The existence of a report is mentioned in the Resolutions of the Gentlemen Seventeen of September 14, 1647, VOC 102, fol. 58.

58. Letter from the Gentlemen Seventeen, March 28, 1648, in VOC 317, fol. 102.

59. The report sent by Over 't Water on November 2, 1648, may be found in VOC 1170, fols. 581–627, "Extract uyt de resolutieboecken des casteels Zeelandia raeckende 't eylant sedert 2-6-1636 tot 27-2-1645," and fols. 628–37, "Copie van verscheyde instructien raeckende het eylant Lamey."

60. Letter of January 18, 1649, in Coolhaas, *Generale Missiven*, 2:353.

61. Letter from the Gentlemen Seventeen to G.G. and Council in Batavia, October 14, 1651, in *ARA*, VOC 317, fol. 240.

CHAPTER 7

Coping with (Civil) Death:
The Christian Convert's Rights of
Passage in Colonial India

GAURI VISWANATHAN

IMPASSES OF IDENTITY

While colonial Indians were relatively complacent about the effects of missionary activities (the numbers of Christian conversions never coming close to the efforts and labors expended by missionaries), the event that triggered widespread panic about mass conversions had less to do with missionaries than with the publication, in 1845, of the draft of the new "law of the land," the Lex Loci Act, which would be enacted in 1850 as the Caste Disabilities Removal Act.[1] Among other things, this act (referred to in the British records as the "Emancipation Act"[2]) sought to revive an inactive clause in the 1832 Bengal Code aimed at protecting the inheritance rights of converts from what British administrators considered some of the most punitive features of Hindu and Muslim personal law, including the forfeiture of rights to ancestral property by individuals who declared allegiance to another religion. The logical justification for depriving converts of their rights to property rested on what legal scholars today term a "legal fiction," that is, the fiction of civil death—the construction of the convert as deracinated and, as an outcaste, no longer recognizable by scriptural law as a functioning member of his or her former community. Given the explanatory appeal of caste as a category of analysis in official British discourse, it is not surprising that British legislation showed more than unusual interest in interpreting changes of religion in terms of the loss of caste by converts and the pronouncement of civil death by Hindu law. On the question of conjugal rights, the resulting uncertainty in the status of converts married earlier under a different personal law exercised no less fascination for the British. For instance, how binding was the marriage of a Christian convert if the unconverted husband or wife testified, as a free agent, that he or she did not wish to live with his or her spouse upon the latter's loss of caste? Could the declaration of civil death be sufficient to dissolution of a Hindu marriage, as it seemed to be regarding forfeiture of property under Hindu law?

The British response to these legal challenges was complex and contradictory. A paradoxical but persistent pattern of rulings emerges from a random survey of cases filed in civil courts by converts petitioning for restitution of those rights that were revoked by Hindu or Muslim personal law. While seeming to protect the rights of converts, British judicial decisions, responding to the fiction of civil death as the central problem in applying liberal principles on English lines, dissociated Christian converts from a broad-based community of Christians to which converts may have believed they had gained admittance and recast their religious identity in the form of the religion they had renounced, the rationale for this move being the judgment that customs and usages (often deferred to in civil suits as a last resort) were slower to change than beliefs. The way out of the impasse created by the offending clause in the Lex Loci Act was to declare that converts to Christianity, however divergent their doctrinal inclinations from the original faith, could still remain Hindus for purposes of law, especially if their habits and manners remained essentially undifferentiated from so-called Hindu customs. The rationale for this discursive move is fairly obvious. If Christian converts were really Hindus, they could not be treated as civilly dead and their civil rights could not justifiably be revoked under Hindu law.

But while this tactic may have served the immediate end of ensuring that converts were not discriminated against by Hindu or Muslim personal law, in the long run the British legislation of religious identity that rewrote conversion from a spiritual to a material act complicated the self-definitions of converts and reduced existing heterogeneous and fluid populations of India to two fixed categories—Hindu and Muslim. In the name of protecting the civil rights of Christian converts, British legislation characteristically endorsed a homogeneous, essentially Hindu, social identity, rejecting both the assertions of converts about real differences in the content of their past and present religious convictions and a parallel move by communities to enforce those differences on the grounds that loss of caste was irreversible. Legislation that was ostensibly designed to protect converts' inheritance rights often led to an even greater infringement of rights, especially in the case of female converts who, seeking redress against the trammels of either Hindu or Muslim personal law, found their pleas unheeded, with the British government, in a gesture of placid indifference, washing its hands of involvement in the internal workings of indigenous caste society. What was at stake for British administrators was not amelioration of the socially alienating features of conversion, or of the exilic condition of civil death to which converts were doomed, but an abstract concept of inalienable rights vested in such things as inheritance and succession to private property (but, significantly, not extending to marriage and divorce). The defense of that concept was so impassioned that it created the illusion that its true subject was the personal and historical experience of exclusion suffered by those who had exchanged one religion for another. But rulings that confirmed Christian converts as Hindus (or Muslims, as the case might be) for purposes of law were by and large indifferent to the conditions of liminal existence that converts were forced to cope with, and "Native Christians" were left floating in a nebulous space, neither Hindus nor Christians in their social existence.

For Christian converts, the experience of colonial history is thus one of contradictory and disingenuous moves. While native converts were treated as dead by their former religious community, the lease of life they were given by civil courts was founded on an equally unreal fiction, a perverse denial of their adopted religious identity. Though British officials could claim that they took legal measures to protect the rights of converts, the fact that they chose to do so by reaffiliating them to the religion they had repudiated further alienated native converts from both the old and the adopted religion. Moreover, the increasing numbers of cases that involved converts or their families as plaintiffs[3] reveal that changes of religion of any kind (which, under other circumstances, might be taken as positive signs of a society's fluid, adaptable nature) posed insuperable problems for British rulers, who were more inclined to deal with stable, fixed categories. Rulings in favor of an undifferentiated social identity, conflating Hindu and Christian, Christian and Muslim, were conservative and fearful reactions to change, inasmuch as they were also defenses, at the same time, of what the British categorically adjudged to be certain inalienable rights.

The court decisions reveal with astonishing clarity how not only Hindus and Muslims but also the British regarded conversion as a disruptive act, complicating the smooth functioning of compartmentalized laws in Indian society—laws that were historically differentiated to reflect the customs and practices particularly of its two major communities, Hindus and Muslims. The prerogative of the courts to determine the laws by which a convert was to be governed brought conversion—which theologians and historians of religion might view as an act of religious conscience and will—squarely within the province of the British legislative and judicial system.

The political concerns extended to a devaluation of the status of belief and religious conviction itself. Virtually marginalized in judicial rulings was how converts perceived and experienced their new religion—the degree of their commitment to and investment in it, the strength of their faith in its doctrines and teachings. Indeed, the devaluation of belief followed from a cynical assessment of conversion as no more than ample testimony to the efficacy of Christian ideology. Often anticlerical in bias and deeply suspicious of evangelical fervor, the British judges characteristically dismissed the converts' repeated assertions of Christian sentiments as having less to do with belief or conviction than with the power and forcefulness of missionary instruction; therefore, if a convert chose to embrace Christianity or any other religion, such a choice could not be taken as proof of personal commitment to the beliefs embodied in that religion, but more likely represented the successful realization of proselytizing intentions for which missionary institutions were set up in the first place.

In short, this essay is concerned with tracing the calculated mediation of religious conversion, through the instrumentality of the British law courts, from its potential aspect as catalyst of social and cultural change to a more conservative function as preserver of the status quo, regardless of the changes in the content of religious beliefs experienced by converts. That is to say, this essay seeks to document the privileging of a *legislated* religious (translated as *social*) identity over private or subjective religious experience.

Needless to say, terms like "religious identity" or "subjective experience" are no less open to critical scrutiny for their suggestions of a fixed referential meaning than the split between public and private realms of experience that they come to signify. The hierarchic reordering of religious identifications with community and caste is achieved in at least two closely related ways: first, the positing of the unstable and indefinable category of "private religious experience" as a separable, essentialized, and even inconsequential reality falling outside historical affiliations of caste or community; and second, the isolation of belief as wholly extraneous, indeed even irrelevant, to determining an individual's membership in community. In proportion to the marginalization of religious conversion as an active agent of cultural change, religious identity is fixed both conceptually and historically as a construct of the institutional discourses of law, among other social systems. If belief is a disengagable aspect of community or caste affiliation and made separate and antithetical to socially determined identities, the erasure of the convert's subjectivity is the logical outcome of this process, for even as liberal discourse upholds a notion of individual subjectivity as the emergence of the free, private self under bourgeois capitalism, the colonial context denies that such a notion can be accommodated by the logic of institutionalized social practices. Indeed, the suppression of converts' self-definitions in the official British records runs parallel to the relegation of religious experience to the realm of religious ideology—to the self-delusions of errant individuals presuming a naive transcendence of the inclusive hold of community.

But a new form of agency and subjectivity emerges from the denial of the individual, private self, which transcends the simple polarity of legislative will and free, autonomous selfhood. It is true that in suppressing converts' self-definitions, colonial discourse may have trivialized spiritual experience as inconsequential to how communities were to be defined, but it merely succeeded in banishing religious experience to the realm of uncolonized space from where new forms of resistance could be asserted. In other words, agency in religious experience, specifically in the colonial situation, is defined in terms outside those provided by liberal humanism, which describes the emergence of the bourgeois idea of the private self as autonomous from the coercive machinery of legislative definitions. In the colonial situation, on the other hand, resistance to the law takes the form of a spiritual struggle for converts—a struggle that remains outside doctrinal content. The emergence of spiritual agency as a form of resistance to legal definitions suggests an alternative form of conversion, subjectivity, and will that produces another knowledge of the liberal norms of conversion understood as subjective transformation—a form of conversion that unsettles colonial discourse even as it is produced precisely at the moment when colonial rule establishes itself over its subjects in specifiable ways. While liberal discourse may have had its own trajectory within the confines of English intellectual history, the emergence of the colonial context irrevocably displaces and disturbs its prevailing categories, and seriously qualifies the liberal notion of individual subjectivity. Though colonial discourse contains the ambivalence produced by the disavowal of the free, private self by invoking legislative reason, the need for order, and the like, it could not but render problematic the notion of conversion as a private, subjective experience.

BELIEF, MEANING, AND COMMUNITY

In the conflicting messages that converts received about their religious identity—how were they to reconcile themselves to their legal status as "Hindus" or "Muslims" when they had adopted Christianity?—native Christians had little recourse to anything like a language of religious experience, a language of subjectivity that would offer them the means to express their relation either to doctrine or community. Indeed, with rules of law establishing the terms for self-definition, to the point that it could be said that the identity of Christian converts was legislated rather than self-determined or self-determining, the very concept of "a language of religious experience" is necessarily reduced to an abstraction. Among other things, such a concept presupposes an unencumbered self metonymically standing in for (but not displacing) community. In the humanist script that traditional conversion narratives follow, the lines between self and community, consciousness and culture, vanish in the ideological figuration of religious experience as an experience of change *that is not change,* which signals at the same time the teleological fulfillment of a culture's innate aspirations for itself.

The ideology of self-sufficiency and self-transcendence promoted by such a tradition of thought is fundamentally incompatible with the historical elision of converts' self-definitions, especially wherever there exists a structure of laws invested with final determining power over what forms of religious experience constitute the basis of a particular religious identity. The pressure of such social and political constraints upon the presumed autonomy of religious experience is precisely what is absent in a work like William James' *Varieties of Religious Experience,* but I make this observation not to dismiss James' extraordinarily powerful and moving argument, but to situate it historically in relation to narratives of conversion that are dispersed through a multitude of texts ranging from the biographical-literary to the juridical and official, but all framed by situations of discrepant social transactions. If the conversion narrative is associated more familiarly with the confessional, experiential mode of spiritual autobiography, the governing tropes by which the "spiritual" becomes a self-constituting category of experience remove the debilitating consequences of restrictive social contexts and legal structures on the construction of religious identity. Religious experience is thus understood and described, as it is by William James, as one of the potentially great turning points in cultural development, whose main stabilizing features lie in the recovery of authenticity, integrity, unity, and selfhood.

This is, of course, far from saying that the conversion narrative is inherently constituted in a purely spiritual domain, or that political and social contexts are always removed from the confessional mode of presenting religious experience. Indeed, an important question raised by the colonial negotiation of the conversion experience is the degree to which the idea of personalized religious experience even within the Christian tradition has always required the authorization of institutions such as law. Augustine's *On Christian Doctrine* dispels the myth of autonomous religious experience as readily as do the British legal judgments that I cite later in this essay; this work also suggests perhaps more clearly than does the *Confessions* the connotations of political strife in spiritual transformation. What interests me is the fictionalization of religious experience as self-engendered and separable from the authority of law and other institutions. My discussion of William James is framed by this interest, and is not intended to polarize Western religious experience from other cultural or historical traditions, or same-religion conversion experiences from those involving conversion to a different religion.[4]

In William James' work the use of "turning" as a literary trope of transformation from lower to higher mental states—from dullness to vibrancy, from division to wholeness, from delusion to enlightenment, and, perhaps the most celebratory of all movements, from imprisonment to freedom—dispenses with the need to engage with history, more specifically, with the contradictory aims of societal norms. Whether the crisis of conversion is caused by a real, verifiable event or is merely based on a suggestive fiction is of less consequence to James than the very real movement it initiates into a new phase of creative self-reconstruction. Conversion is thus presented as more than a change in the state of one's belief: it is for the Jamesian individual what archaeological tools are for the historian, a literary instrument for plotting out life-stories and resituating oneself in relation to forgotten signposts of individual identity covered over by the dust of neglect, indifference, repression, and mental enslavement, be it coerced or self-induced. Conceptualized as a democratic, emancipatory critique of the self, the conversion narrative for James is interchangeable with cultural narratives of progressive modernization, of which the story of American democracy is its most exemplary instance. The emancipated selfhood that emerges from the conversion experience ensures some measure of congruence and continuity between the American religious experience and the secular goals of American democracy. The trope of "turning" embedded in conversion turns on metaphors of enslavement to posit conditions of political freedom as the end point of religious awakening.

By casting the leap into freedom in the language of Platonism, the full measure of which is brought out in idealist notions of "selfhood," "authenticity," "wholeness," and "unity," James provides some clues as to why conversion narratives, spiritual autobiographies, and religious confessions have held such an unyielding, privileged place in Western cultural history, overshadowing narratives of conversion that are produced in situations of discrepancy among civil society, religion, and political authority. In the Jamesian scenario the unshackling of bonds by the regenerated individual is never compromised by a state of intolerable alienation to which he or she might well be subject, as one who has detached himself or herself from some larger group. On the contrary, the state of division in which the unregenerate spend their lives is what James regarded as especially alienating and illusive, a thwarting of any effective attempt at community as it might be conceived in an ideal political society. The moment of spiritual regeneration, of receiving grace, is the moment of achieved community for the transformed self, now triumphantly freed from the illusion that it is a bounded entity wholly encompassed by social laws, which need the fiction of boundaries to exert their true force.[5] The appeal of the conversion topos rests on the fact that it makes the experience of conversion the central, self-authenticating moment in cultural development, which competes with, but never actually challenges, the power of law and other social and political institutions to confer their own brand of legitimacy on individual identity and legislate the forms in which that identity is socially serviceable and politically meaningful. For James, the ever-present possibilities for self-regeneration and transformation offered by religious experience are resources peculiarly available to a homogenized culture, which allow it some degree of autonomy from the authority of state machinery to set itself up as supreme legislator of individual identity. The "self-appropriation of interiority"[6] by which theologians and psychologists of religion explain the heightened self-differentiation produced by the conversion experience is not a purely inward or subject-centered process, but an activity of objectification aligning the subjective state with structures of thought, laws, and beliefs that remain at a latent level of consciousness until they are activated by a transformed subjectivity. To suggest that the advance of culture influences (and is influenced by) an ever-differentiated consciousness is to say that the culture in which the conversion experience occurs lends its own structural features to the content of the new religious consciousness, which in turn activates an elaboration of the full range of meanings of cultural forms and institutions to which the developing religious sensibility now gains unmediated access.

The socially alienating quality of conversion is thus diminished in proportion to the self-differentiation that ensues, by which culture, including its various realms of meaning, becomes available as an object of appropriation to the convert, duly transformed. If the relation between culture and conversion is not construed as oppositional in James' narrative of religious experience, it has a great deal to do with the terms in which the religious experience itself translates into social understanding and enters social practice. As willed consciousness of religion, conversion, in the Jamesian meaning of "sudden turning" to a religious faith that had been abandoned, forgotten, or unknown, draws much of its force from a unitary theory of civil society. James' confidence in the transformative power of religious experience stems from his conviction that however worldly certain Western secular institutions such as law might be, no institution that is part of Christian culture can remain untouched by its pervasive influence. If both law and religion (as understood in Christian society) are said to be joined in a common purpose to achieve an undivided community of regenerate persons, it is easy to see why the recovery of an authentic self becomes a necessary fiction for sustaining the symmetry between civil society and Christian religious experience.

The underlying tension between the transgressive and the assimilative aspects of conversion erupts most obviously and dramatically in situations of asymmetry between civil society and religion, where the adopted identity of the convert is at variance with the cultural meanings sanctioned by that society. The radical displacements of meaning brought about by religious change are unquestionably major political disruptions and treated as such in the discourse of the dominant community. By vitally affecting the numerical strength of one group or the other and rendering the relation between "majority" and "minority," "dominant" and "subordinate" groups forever uncertain, unstable, and unpredictable, the material impact of conversion on patterns of demography undermines—and renders illusory—what the dominant community would like to regard as the self-perpetuating strength of its cultural norms.

The colonial context exacerbates these tensions, not least because of competing claims to the status of "dominant community" based on numerical as well as political criteria. It might be expected that every act of transgression against the native community(ies) is an act of assimilation into another—an act that is encouraged and indeed even promoted by colonial authorities. But where the cultural and religious identity of a colonized civil society is itself at stake, to regard individual acts of conversion as incontrovertible evidence of transgression for the sake of separation from a predominant religious culture ignores the structure of civil laws operative in that society, rendering problematic the simple movement between religious communities. It may be true that, politically, British colonial power in nineteenth-century India represented an ultimate point of authoritative and legal reference, but when indigenous elite groups, occupying positions of power and privilege in that society, still continued to function according to their own laws, customs, and usages in civil matters, as was the case in colonial India,[7] assimilation into the colonizer's religion often meant legal excommunication from Hinduism or Islam for converts from either religion. The power of these laws to enforce complete forfeiture of rights on converts (often confirmed by the British courts, despite legislation supposedly to the contrary) casts dubious light on the extent to which conversion-as-assimilation was truly desired by the colonizer himself. Indeed, when placed in the context of the structure of laws enacted under British colonialism, Christian conversion is less identifiable with an assimilative practice, designed to induce colonial subjects into a community affiliated with the governing class, than with permanent dislocation and exile from a sense of community at large.

Under these constraints, religious change is severely strained and qualified. Because of civil laws governing such things as inheritance rights, conjugal rights, succession to property, and so forth, religious conversion in the political context of British colonialism is reduced to being an expression of the individual's shifting allegiance to community. The laws that regulate the daily activities of individuals from birth to death are not easily shed with a change of religion: these laws track converts into their new identity, their new selfhood, to mock their self-willed renunciation of the old faith and the adoption of the new. Jamesian formulations of the recapturing of authenticity, the shattering of metaphysical illusions that the great conversionary moment is expected to bring about—formulations that indeed have long been the mainstay of missionary ideology—vanish in the constructed identity legislated by the colonial law courts, which wipes out in an instant the epiphany of transcendence putatively marking the inner experience of conversion. Indeed, it is more true to say that the private, subjective changes that occur in colonial societies are progressively regulated by the laws that manage and define self, even when that self moves away from a natal community and religion.

It should be apparent, therefore, that my use of William James is not intended to set up opposing models of conversion in the post-Enlightenment West on the one hand and in colonial societies on the other, with Western culture offering a paradigmatic liberal model whose normativity is perverted in colonial transactions. On the contrary, the colonial context does not so much distort the norms of liberal discourse as expose its insufficiencies and interrogate its founding categories. The inability of liberal discourse to address the colonial context explicitly—or, when it does, that it can do so only by privileging legislated identity over individual and private self—suggests that the colonial situation has a more active role than mere historical background for the evolution of liberal doctrine, for it sets in motion a contingent disavowal of the liberal notion of individual subjectivity as belonging to the privatized realm of meaning.

Furthermore, the colonial disturbance of the categories of liberal humanism exposes a deeper split in English social and intellectual history. The cultural ideology within which narratives of conversion in British colonialism can be interpreted is obviously not limited to the discourse of civil law, though it is within the secular structures of civil legislation that the social rewriting of conversion takes place most regularly. The liberal spirit of tolerance that entered English public life by the mid-nineteenth century may have enfranchised Dissenters, Roman Catholics, and Jews, whose incorporation into the structures of political governance showed an England moving toward a more open pluralism in which a multiplicity of beliefs was seemingly acknowledged—what Robert Pattison in his work on John Henry Newman calls the "deregulated market of religious belief."[8] And certainly the ascendancy of courts of appeal—with the state's refusal to pronounce judgment on the rightness or wrongness of dissenting opinion—appeared to rob the church of its spiritual authority. The Gorham judgment of 1850 marked the irrevocable break between church and state in England, when the determination of doctrinal meaning was declared outside the function of a secular body like the Judicial Committee of the Privy Council, which incidentally was originally intended primarily to hear appeals from the colonies, even though later as a secular body it came to exercise jurisdiction as a court of final appeal in ecclesiastical cases.

The state's relegation of doctrine to private interpretation followed from its insistence on preserving the so-called heretic's legal rights to whatever position he or she held prior to the heresy. As long as a dissenter's beliefs were basically compatible with the doctrines laid down in the Church's Articles, the question of heresy did not arise: what might have been an opinion contrary to accepted doctrinal meanings was declared nonheretical by the Privy Council by the standards of compatibility. Accentuated by the spirit of secularization, the new tolerance may have been the first step toward separating religious belief from social identity. The abolition of tests of religious belief in Parliament, the relaxation of the laws of blasphemy, and the removal of divorce from the ecclesiastical realm all combined, as Anton Lentin notes, to "shift religion to the ceremonial margins of state affairs."[9]

The form of tolerance that secularization represents reinstitutes a homogeneous national identity mediated by law in which differences of belief are effaced: while individual rights are protected—and the rectitude of law is upheld—the self-definitions of individuals or the beliefs they hold are rendered irrelevant in the national incorporation of hitherto marginalized dissenting groups. In not only rendering self-perceptions of religious identity a mere formal subset of social classification but also leaving no place for private faith altogether, the usurpation of spiritual authority by the mid-nineteenth century English state highlighted the failure of Anglicanism and the failure of a national church to provide such authority.

One of the effects of this progressive split between religion and state is the separation of national identity from religious affiliations of any kind. As long as allegiance to the articles of faith was a prerequisite to such things as a seat in Parliament and education at Oxford or Cambridge, an Englishman was defined as a member of the Anglican Church. The new tolerance toward dissenting groups, Catholics, and Jews now dispensed with the concept of "heretic" as defining what an Englishman was *not*. With criteria of doctrinal allegiance no longer determining Englishness, national identity increasingly required a differentiation between political and civil society, the latter emerging as the privatized domain onto which are displaced a variety of religious distinctions that have no place in political society, or in what is now construed as the more transcendent plane of the secular. Secularization not only polarizes national and religious identity; it also privatizes belief and renders it subordinate to the claims of reason, logic, and evidence, all of which are hence identified with the administrative rationality of the state and its institutions.

Juxtaposing the relations among the heretic individual, episcopal authority, and the secular court (the Privy Council) of mid-nineteenth-century England on the one hand and the relations among the convert, Hindu scriptural authority, and English civil law on the other produces a distinctive cultural reading of the changing status of belief. In protecting a heretic's rights to titles and property, the civil courts in England efface not only his or her heresy but paradoxically also the subjectivism of religious belief. Similarly, in protecting the convert's rights to inherit property as if he or she were still a Hindu or a Muslim, English law in colonial India virtually nullified both the fact and the subjective experience of conversion.

RECLAIMING THE RENOUNCER

What is the minimum condition for removing someone permanently from a religious community? For some religions such as Hinduism, neither agnosticism nor blasphemy alone can remove a person from the community in which he or she is born; however, complete adherence to a foreign religion automatically signals excommunication for that individual.[10] A plausible inference is that, in Hinduism at least, community outweighs personal belief: regardless of the extent to which beliefs may undergo transformations, or be subject to individual caprice and variations of mood or disposition, membership in community is not severed even for a blaspheming agnostic. The other, far-reaching inference, following from the first, is that a change of religion is less a change of beliefs than a change of community. The antagonism between the individual and the community inherent in this description would seem to overtake the compulsions of private conviction: precisely this impression is fostered both by British colonial authority and the dominant community from which the apostate Hindu escapes.

Cases brought before British authorities by Hindu parents seeking to reclaim their apostate children provide one of the most readily accessible representations of both the social antagonisms between community and individual and the attendant derogation of private belief. One of the most thoroughly documented conversion cases in the British records is the petition filed in 1844 by the parents of Ananda Row, an eighteen-year-old Brahmin youth of Mangalore who, his family alleged, had been "abducted" by his missionary-teachers and forcibly converted to Protestantism. What brought a "reluctant" British administration into this case was the part played by the local English magistrate who, according to the parents of the boy, had abetted the missionaries by turning a blind eye on their activities. The sole redress that the family sought, they repeatedly asserted in a phrase that would have sounded ominous were it not for the pathetic transparency of the euphemism, was to have the boy returned home so that "he could be brought to reason."[11] The magistrate rebutted in his turn that, as a result of his refusal to intervene, the family had staged an ambush on the mission house to reclaim Ananda Row, and when that failed, (again according to the magistrate's testimony) they had concocted a macabre plot to implicate Christians in the desecration of a nearby mosque, so that in the ensuing melee the family would be able to whisk the boy away, undetected.

The local officials whom Ananda Row's family petitioned for redress refused to get involved in the case, stating firmly that individuals had to be "left to [themselves] with regard to their religious principles" and that British officials had no authority to "enable [Ananda Row's] relations to enforce any control over him in these respects."[12] The local magistrate, having cast the full weight of his support on the side of the missionaries who had sheltered the young convert, justified noninterference on the ground that matters of religious conscience were well beyond the purview of the administrative machinery of government, there being a private area of personal autonomy in native experience that not even a colonial government had the power to regulate. The company's court of directors in London also urged noninterference, but on quite different grounds. It was not the place of government, they argued, to enter into family disputes; if Hindu or Muslim parents wished to reclaim their "apostate" children, it was up to them (the family) to decide on the means to achieve that aim. The court of directors refused to countenance appeals to the "will," "religious conscience," and "conviction" of native youth, deeming these considerations wholly irrelevant to the main concern of secular administration, whose smooth functioning required that the Hindu social structure remain intact.

Such instances of radical disagreement on the extent of desirable involvement in parent-child disputes replay the debates on women's reform in Bengal, particularly the issues of widow burning and widow remarriage. If the British government desisted for a long time from actually outlawing sati, instead setting up distinctions between voluntary and coerced self-immolations as instances of "good" satis (in which case British noninterference was the preferred course) and "bad" satis (justifying British intervention), it was primarily because it sought to leave a space where the British reformist impulse could be accommodated to the strictures of traditional Hindu society.[13] As with the earlier history of sati, in the case of young Hindu converts the government's position was to refrain from giving any appearance of wishing to disturb the upper-caste Hindu family structure: to intervene in disputes between parents and children, as between husband and wife, was to transgress the tacitly accepted demarcation between private and public domains. The government made clear its wish to preserve inviolate indigenous forms of parental authority, no matter how differently these relations were construed in England and no matter how far English law was able to extend itself in England wherever that authority conflicted with the "free will" of youths.

However, as again with sati, the British stated policy of noninterference in cases of voluntary conversions obscured the main issues considerably. At the higher administrative levels, the decision to intervene or not in disputes between parents and children did not emerge from empirical observations of what could clearly be construed as voluntary or involuntary conversions, but was based on redefining will and agency in terms that decided beforehand what constituted a voluntary conversion. For instance, age was a major determinant in assessing whether conversions were voluntary or involuntary, since minors were presumed to be ill-fitted to exercise choice. In Ananda Row's case, it was his young age that predisposed the British government to heed the parents' charge that their son had been mentally coerced to adopt Christianity. But the view from the top was not necessarily shared by the local British officers, whose indifference to the parents' pleas for government intervention was supplemented by their own pious appeals to "will," "conscience," and "conviction." In a case that remained curiously unresolved (at least from the viewpoint of the Hindu parents) because the British refused to intervene, resolution was presented in the form of a London order to transfer the recalcitrant local magistrate who allegedly precipitated the trouble to a remote province of British India.

The internal divergences in British responses are even more glaring in the conflict between missionaries and higher-level administrators. Not surprisingly, many missionaries protested against the antiprogressive, self-serving deference shown by British officials to the authority of Hindu parents. To give one example of the later forms that this protest took, some missionaries made an ambitious but ultimately futile effort to amend the Native Christian Marriage Act of 1864 to lower the legal age at which native converts could marry without their parents' or guardians' consent to age fourteen. In the original act, the legal age for marriage was set at twenty-one. But as one missionary, Reverend Thomas Boaz, pointed out, the act was made to apply generally to all Christians, including Europeans and East Indians, as well as native Christians, whereas native Christians "have until the passing of this Act always been dealt with by the Government of India as Hindus and have been ruled and judged by Hindu law."[14] If, under Hindu law, the legal age for marriage was sixteen years "for all purposes," then the 1864 marriage act placed the legal age for native Christians five years beyond that recognized by Hindu law, and three years beyond that sanctioned by the company's regulations for the inheritance of property. The act put native converts in an anomalous position, for as Boaz pointedly argued, Indians tended to marry earlier in life than Europeans did. To maintain the same age of consent as the one prevailing in England was to work against the cause of conversion, since young Christian converts—who were civilly dead under Hindu law—could not expect to secure their Hindu (or Muslim) parents' consent to their marriage and were essentially discouraged from converting if they wished to marry. In seeking an amendment to the marriage act, Boaz emphasized that "the legal age for marriage ought not to be regulated by the practice of western nations, but from the habits, feelings, and practices of the people of India."[15] The motivation for seeking this differentiation of native Christians from European Christians was, of course, to remove barriers to conversion that were sure to prevail if young Indian converts still had to secure the consent of their parents to marry.

Thus, the missionaries, no less than British administrators, participated in the dissociation of Indian Christians from a larger community of Christians and continued to identify the customs, practices, and usages of native converts with those of Hindus. In this case the government declined to amend the legislation, but the fact that it was unyielding about lowering the legal age for converts to marry threw a pall of gloom over minors, whose parents' authority was undoubtedly strengthened by its provisions. Despite the evidence of maturity, intelligence, conviction, and self-conscious judgment displayed by young converts, acknowledged even by judges in certain cases, chronological age rather than maturity or discretion was used as the basis for determining whether young people were free to exercise their options. The effect of bringing English law to bear on the prevalent customs and practices of Indian Christians was an attempt to standardize the community of "Christians," but it simultaneously worked against a recognition of the individual will and religious conscience of its members.

At a strategic point in the Ananda Row papers, the London office cautioned local British administrators against encouraging any situation that threatened Hindu society with cataclysmic religious change, producing violence and mayhem of the kind that accompanied widespread Islamic proselytism under Tipu Sultan.[16] Placed in a continuum that included Islamic conversion at one end, Christian conversion evoked, for British rulers, a familiar picture of religious fanaticism and violence, a picture so threatening to British rule that it prompted a call to enact legislation to regulate conversion. The paradox, of course, is that the regulation of Christian conversion takes the form of civil legislation to protect converts from the forfeiture of rights to property and life. Rather than banning conversion or treating it as a crime, the solution to the problem of divisions within indigenous communities brought on by incidents of conversion is to treat the convert as still a member of the community in which he or she was born, and therefore entitled to all its rights. While not a ban on conversion, such a discursive move effectively minimizes, and even negates to some extent, the radical force of the will to renounce one religious identity for another. It is indeed telling that nothing was more effective in regulating Christian conversion as an actual change of religious belief than the legislation enacted to protect converts from civil disabilities imposed by Hinduism or Islam. It was so effective that even usually astute scholars could comment, as does J. Duncan Derrett, that "it does not seem practicable to enquire too closely into the genuineness of a conversion, once it is established as a fact."[17]

In the framework of a history of Islamic conversions in India, Christian conversion takes on an unusually charged political significance, reflected in the markedly different and complex ways that converts to the two religions are described. To castigate Islam as a historical agent of violent and ruthless change, British commentators commiserate with Muslim converts from Hinduism for their loss of rights and isolation from their former community, and treat their plight with almost heavy-handed concern.[18] On the other hand, not Christianity but *Christian converts* are blamed by British administrators as the cause of a community's disruption, disorientation in the rules of caste, and reckless challenges to parental authority. Ananda Row may have reached the age of eighteen, "when the law recognizes his right to act for himself"[19] and his family no longer had the right to control his actions, but the fact remains that his rights as an individual to exercise reason and free will are usurped by the absolute primacy accorded to community. The background of Islamic proselytism and the perceived threat of communal violence induced by Hindu resistance to Muslim "fanaticism" partly explains the reactive edge of legislative enactments that appeared determined to protect and preserve Hindu society. In the final analysis, the British government's position is to concur with the Hindu family in deciding that conversion has "ruined the caste of the boy"[20] and produced estrangement of family connections, domestic misery, disturbance of the peace, and dangerous communal tension among Muslims, Christians, and Hindus.

Yet while the British were anxious to preserve intact the main structures of traditional Hindu society—even if that meant ignoring the right to self-determination by Indian youth who were of an age to act for themselves—they were not willing to impose civil disabilities on converts as requested by some Hindu families. Such legislation, it was argued, would be "at variance with a just regard to the rights of civil and personal liberty, with the principles sanctioned by the British Parliament, and with the express precedents of past legislation in India."[21] This statement points to a major irreconcilable contradiction in the British position—to maintain the status quo in the Hindu community, even if that meant denying the self-willed actions of would-be rebels and apostates, while at the same time defending the civil rights of converts to property and life wherever those rights were revoked by Hindu society. The more interesting question to ask at this stage is how the conflict of goals is resolved—in what manner and on what terms. My contention is that the contradiction not only remains unresolved but gets effaced by making the convert the ground, rather than the subject or even object (the British records are neither of or about converts), on which the whole question of rights was worked out.[22] In other words, if the British task was to accommodate the "rights of civil and personal liberty" to the preservation of the Hindu community without diminishing either, the convert's subjectivity—an account of his or her own spiritual and material needs—is necessarily suppressed in the process of upholding the principles of constitutional liberty so valued by English political doctrine. It is of no small significance that the Ananda Row papers, which run over two hundred pages in the board's collections, has not a single account of Ananda's conversion from his point of view, though there are letters and depositions from his parents, wife, neighbors, teachers, community leaders, and so on.[23] (And in other cases, such as the case that follows in my discussion concerning a young female convert called Huchi, testimony given by the convert is constantly challenged by the dramatic structure of interrogation and judicial pronouncement that frame it.)

When the focus falls on converts and their civil rights, it is apparent that the contradictions inherent in the very premises of English liberalism are sustained only by excluding the converts' self-definitions from the British records. Clearly abstract concepts of rights lend themselves more readily to political expression *outside* the self-perceptions of the convert whose rights are presumably being defended, especially when legal protection of those rights requires converts to be considered as members of the community they have renounced, not of the one they have chosen to embrace. For British administrators to heed the self-definitions of converts was invariably to expose the attempted erasure of their self-proclaimed identity through civil legislation. It is, therefore, not surprising that in the British records converts become abstractions for the articulation of a notion of rights based on English liberal doctrine, designed to ensure "civil and personal liberty."[24]

ESCAPE FROM COMMUNITY

The discursive representation of aberrant youth is reinforced in an astonishing case that appears in the 1876 government records concerning Huchi, a young female convert in Mysore who was baptized as Helen Gertrude.[25] The case reveals, as none other does in quite the same way, the startling contradictions in the legal reforms initiated by the British in colonial India. First, it dramatically illustrates how, while British law commissions and judicial deliberations were shot through with a reformist impulse, the objects of reform in actual case rulings often tended to be "errant" youth, especially females, who dared to rebel against Hindu patriarchy. The Huchi case is fascinating in the way the liberal rhetoric of self-determination and free will informing it is constantly qualified by deference to a Hindu scriptural tradition that the British themselves had codified and made the basis for judicial pronouncements. (In this particular case William Grady's *Hindu Law* is the text most consistently drawn upon.)

Second, the case reveals two conflicting definitions of free will and self-determinism, with the ruling British judges increasingly loading the terms in the direction of legalism and constitutionalism, whereas native converts sought to recreate themselves in an area broadly defined as the "spiritual," but not necessarily connoting a predetermined credal belief. This last point is important if we are to see that what emerges from Huchi's court depositions and testimony is a definitional concept of agency and free will that is not specifically tied down to any doctrinal content. The relation between converts' subjectivity and their spiritual needs is better understood, not in the Jamesian sense of the merging of self-consciousness in a determinate religious philosophy, but in terms of the resistance of converts to the legislated identities thrust on them by the law courts—a resistance that, for them, takes on the character of a spiritual struggle. The creation of a space for subjective self-definition, which is how the conversion experience can be described for young converts like Huchi, is constantly contested by the operative categories of a scripturally derived Hindu personal law, adapted by the British in India to new legislative enactments regulating the shape that religious identities were to take.

Huchi's story begins with her education at a missionary school where, by her own account, she was deeply influenced by Christian teachings, as a result of which she requested several times to be baptized by the missionaries. At the time, the missionaries had declined to comply with her request, fearful that baptizing a minor would expose them to the wrath of the Hindu community. Huchi, not only by her own testimony but that of her parents and relatives, had repeatedly declared that she had "joined" the Christians and had become a Christian, even though she had not yet gone through formal baptism. Alarmed by her repeated declarations of renunciation of Hinduism, Huchi's parents withdrew her from school and tried to arrange a marriage for her without further delay. However, the men that they sought to engage as her husband declined to accept Huchi because of her unyielding stance about becoming Christian and severing her ties with Hinduism. Eventually an aunt of Huchi's forcibly took the girl to her home in another village in Mysore, and arranged for the betrothal of her son Appiah to Huchi, who was then thirteen and a half years old. In her court deposition Huchi stated that she had protested fiercely against the marriage, but that arrangements for the marriage ceremony were nonetheless finalized and she was forced to go through the main rituals, even though she had become very ill during the moments immediately preceding the actual ceremony and could no longer maintain a vigorous resistance to the marriage. She claimed that she was forced to live with her husband for about six months, at which time she suddenly departed, taking refuge with one of her former schoolteachers, Louisa Anstey. It was there that she again requested and was finally administered baptismal rites.

The *thali*, or betrothal symbol, was returned to her in-laws as a sign that the marriage with Appiah was dissolved, and a marriage arranged between Huchi and Lutchmiah, another Christian convert. At this point Huchi's former husband Appiah reappeared, claiming that Huchi's first marriage to him was still binding. He insisted on Huchi's returning to him, but warned that once she did so she would have to reconcile herself to living with him not as his wife but as his prostitute, because by having renounced Hinduism she could be treated as nothing but an outcaste by him! With the assistance of the missionaries, Huchi filed a suit to have the marriage with Appiah dissolved, on the grounds that as a Christian she had been married against her will to a non-Christian and that her parents' authoritative action exposed her to the ignominy of excommunication by her husband and the rest of her caste society.

To make a long and complicated story short, the final verdict of the case went in Appiah's favor. Drawing heavily on William Grady's *Hindu Law* for support,[26] the judge declared that dissolution of the marriage was possible only if Appiah had either committed adultery or deserted his wife, but that Huchi's conversion to Christianity by itself could not be taken as sufficient grounds for dissolving the husband's conjugal rights conferred by Hindu law. As far as the courts were concerned, Huchi was married under Hindu law and remained a Hindu, baptism or no baptism. And especially because she had not been baptized at the time of her marriage, she had no choice but to be subject to Hindu law, her self-declarations of Christian belief evidently annulled by the absence of formal rituals attesting to the same fact. For purposes of the law, Huchi could not claim recognition of her Christian identity until her husband consented to dissolve the marriage. Though technically Appiah could have ended the marriage on the ground that Huchi was civilly dead, having forfeited her caste by "joining" the Christians and communing with them, the fact that he did not do so virtually left Huchi in his unchallenged control.[27] The power to decide whether the marriage was to continue or not rested with Appiah, not Huchi, despite the outcaste status that Huchi was consigned to live with by converting to Christianity. British legislation had effectively excluded change of religion as in itself a ground for dissolution of marriage, presumably to thwart abuse of that provision (i.e., of people changing faiths only to get out of bad marriages), yet the evidence shows that such laws consolidated the power of Hindu patriarchies, the right to continue or discontinue a marriage resting exclusively with the unconverted husband.[28]

In thus confirming that the marriage between Appiah and Huchi was legal and still binding, the final court judgment rejected Huchi's claim that in sentiment and in conviction she was a Christian and not an assenting party to the marriage performed according to Hindu rites. It also declared that Huchi's remarriage was not allowable or "practicable" under the Native Converts' Marriage Dissolution Act of 1866, though apostasy from Hinduism caused her to be regarded as civilly dead. Huchi's petition was based on an appeal to invoke the provisions of the Caste Disabilities Removal Act of 1850, which protected converts from forfeiture of their rights upon conversion. This act, however, turned out to be quite irrelevant in this case, since Huchi as a Christian convert wanted to detach herself from her former community, whereas the 1850 act was intended to mitigate the severance of community and restore to converts the civil rights they had *before* conversion. Continuity with community, in short, is what the act hoped to ensure rather than disruption. Contrary to the impression generated by the string of legislative acts in the 1850s and 1860s designed to protect converts' rights, converts were no better off in having their new religious identity acknowledged in law. Indeed, the Caste Disabilities Removal Act was so framed to ensure the rights of converts to inherit property *as if they had not converted at all* and still remained Hindus in terms of the law. Similarly, the Native Converts' Marriage Dissolution Act of 1866 allowed a marriage to be dissolved if the *unconverted* spouse refused to cohabit with his or her partner following conversion; the act was not intended to help converts seek release from a marriage on the grounds of religious incompatibility if their unconverted spouse refused to assent to its termination. The fact is that there was no law to apply to the peculiar circumstances of Huchi's case, where protection of her rights as a convert meant acknowledging her right to sever herself from ties contracted by a community that she had already repudiated through her conversion.[29]

The case was further complicated by a multiplicity of conflicting agendas. About Huchi's objective there was little or no ambiguity: she was singlemindedly determined to have her marriage to Appiah dissolved and her chosen identity as a Christian recognized in law. The missionaries were supportive of Huchi on all points except the crucial one regarding the dissolution of her marriage with Appiah. Indeed, they were far less interested in responding to Huchi's immediate needs, her resistance to her parents' attempted effacement and derogation of her spiritual wants and physical desires, than in disclosing the "appalling bondage" in which women in India were held by recondite Hindu custom. The courts, on the other hand, were more interested in addressing other issues, foremost among them the following: first, whether Huchi had converted to Christianity of her own accord and free will and whether she was "then and now" a free agent, capable of acting and judging for herself; second, whether her marriage was performed against her will and consent; and third, since she was a minor at the time, whether the marriage was valid according to Hindu law, irrespective of her consent (which was really a nonissue since she was a minor).[30]

In the lower court's judgment of 1873, it was ruled that Huchi, not being sixteen, could not be considered in law as a free agent capable of deciding for herself either in religion or in marriage. However, the presiding judge did confess that Huchi during her examination "exhibited sufficient intelligence and discretion to judge for herself; but I regret that the law does not permit her to use that discretion in opposition to the wishes of her parents or her husband."[31] The judge went on to say that Huchi's reluctance to marry was one thing, but such hesitancy could not be taken to imply either total rejection of the marriage or actual coercion by other parties: "The marriage having taken place, the question of discretion is at an end, for the maxim applies that a fact cannot be altered by a hundred texts."[32] One lone judge in the court proceedings voiced a dissenting view that "the discretion of the child, its competency to form a correct judgement and not an arbitrary point of time, is the true criterion. There is no age at which a child may not be said to be of a weak, of a foolish, or of a precocious intellect . . . there is no such age in fact—and there is none in law."[33] But his was a solitary view, and political expediency dictated contrarywise, for "to make discretion rather than age in every case the criterion by which a minor's claim to liberty of conscience and protection of the law shall be tested would probably prove impolitic."[34]

It is clear from the debates even among the British judges that the relation between age and discretion was not easily settled by empirical observation. In trying to establish specific ages at which the capacity for rational choice was manifested, the judges refused to countenance the possibility that free will and self-determinism were not circumscribed by chronological age. Instead, without denying agency or giving up on notions of free will and self-determinism, they reestablished these as appearing at specifiable stages in an individual's development, and as linear, chronological, commensurable, and amenable to legal definition. The redefinition of agency along these linear, legalistic lines provides the dramatic tension in the Huchi proceedings, where Huchi's attempt to present herself as a mature, thoughtful, and self-aware young woman at the age of thirteen is rendered irrelevant in establishing her credentials as an independent agent capable of acting on her own behalf. The brilliance of the British discursive strategy of substituting chronological age for discretion as the basis of agency lay in the fact that the judges at no point could be accused of going against the norms of English liberal rhetoric by claiming that Huchi had no right to act on her own, while at the same time they were able to maintain that her actions would be recognizable in law only if they conformed to the pattern of grading established by "natural" human development (i.e., when she would be in a position to act as a free human being). In placing autonomy within a temporal scheme, the British were successful in accommodating regulation of errant Indian youth to English principles of self-determination.

Free to be neither Christian nor Hindu, Huchi was thus caught in an impossible double bind, the religion that she now declared her own not allowing her to remarry as long as her Hindu husband still claimed her as his wife (or rather his prostitute), and the religion that she had renounced refusing to accept her as a member of that community. On the question of releasing Huchi from this intolerable condition of liminality, the British government maintained a position of outright hostility that

belied its avowed espousal of converts' rights. Where questions of marriage and divorce were concerned, the alacrity with which Hindu law
was deferred to (despite it being, in the words of one British judge, "difficult, if not impossible, to reconcile the principles of that law with the
principles of the law of England, and those whose sentiments are formed
under the one system must naturally disapprove of the results of the
other"[35]) was as startling as the unwavering determination with which
the British opposed the imposition of civil disabilities on converts by the
punitive action of Hindu law. Yet the common feature of both responses
to conversion is the recasting of Christian converts as Hindus, despite
the self-declarations of converts to the contrary.

The derogation of Huchi's Christian belief was further accentuated
by the outside counsel of three London advocates, James Fitzjames
Stephen, Charles Bowen, and Henry Manisty.[36] These three radically altered the emphasis of the case by categorically stating that, in order to
change the personal law by which one was governed, an actual change of
habits of life was necessary, and that a mere change of religious belief,
coupled with a *wish* to change habits of life, especially when such a wish
was frustrated by parental authority, was not sufficient to change the
personal law. The question they proposed for determining religious
identity was not "what are your beliefs" but "how do you live your life,"
not private belief but social behavior and habits. Even though Huchi
provided extensive testimony on how she had deliberately and openly
changed her habits of life so as to accord with her change of religious
belief, the three London advocates refused to be convinced, decrying
what they saw as the obvious plan of a girl of "such tender age" to use
change of religion as a way of putting "an end to her father's right to
have the custody of her, and to dispose of her in marriage by a form of
compulsion not in itself illegal."[37] In a conflation of Hindu patriarchal
and British colonial interests, British legal opinion weighed heavily in
the direction of the authority of Hindu social structure: "Huchi's parents have succeeded in forcing her against her will into a binding marriage; but if the marriage is void, it will follow that changes in the religious opinion of children of tender years have the legal effect of taking
away a right which Hindus value above all others—the right of disposing
of their daughters in marriage."[38]

The Huchi case demonstrates the complex and subtle shifts of blame
for social disruptions that are now placed on youth, especially women,
whose developing religious consciousness is seen as contributing to the
destabilization of Hindu patriarchy. Huchi's resistance to the will of her
Hindu parents and her Hindu husband is translated, in the British records, as the errant action of an excitable and immature girl indulging in
the illusion of a newfound religious sensibility. If Huchi is marginalized

and ostracized by both colonial authority and Hindu patriarchy and her self-consciousness as a woman (not a child) and a Christian convert consistently denied, it would seem, as Gayatri Chakravorty Spivak argues, that there is no space from which the female subject can speak, "the dubious place of the free will of the constituted sexed subject as female"[39] having been successfully effaced by the symmetrical alignment of the legal systems of the colonized and their colonizers.

The exercise of English law in Indian civil cases, where Christian converts were still regarded as Hindus under the law, could not but rewrite conversion as a principle of self-willed change—a crossing over between discrepant social spaces—into a homogenizing agent of cultural continuity, the reduction of disparate belief-systems into an essential sameness of form. I have presented these two cases as exemplary social texts of British colonialism, whose interpretation depends on an analysis of the status, function, and nature of personal conviction in the determination of identity in legal discourse. What is put on trial in both these cases is not so much the family's right to reclaim their child, as in the Ananda Row case, or the husband's right to reclaim his young wife, but the religious sensibility of these children, as is evident in the small sample of questions posed by the British administrators and judges: What should count as evidence of maturity and discretion? How real is the assent of these converts to the new religion? Are their conversions merely a protest against a restrictive caste society? For both these young converts, to prove that their conversions had grown out of a developing sense of selfhood and conviction requires a new form of narration altogether—a narration that bears only minimal resemblance to spiritual autobiography.

NOTES

Research for this paper was made possible by fellowships from the John S. Guggenheim Memorial Fund, the National Endowment for the Humanities, the American Institute of Indian Studies, and the Council for Research in the Humanities and Social Sciences, Columbia University. I wish to thank these foundations for their generous assistance, as well as seminar participants of the Davis Center for Historical Studies, Princeton University for valuable comments and suggestions.

1. Among the most vehement protests was a memorial to Dalhousie by a group of Bengali Hindus, whose combined solidarity against the proposed measures to protect converts' rights to property succeeded in preventing the act from becoming law. For a short while the clause to protect converts' inheritance rights, which had already been introduced in the 1832 Bengal Regulations but remained inactive, became a dead letter again. But in 1850 the act was revived and passed into law. Act XXI of 1850 henceforth became known as the Caste

Disabilities Removal Act. Another memorial was presented to the government to make a plea similar to the earlier one in 1845, but this time it made no dent on the government (India Office Library and Records, Board's Collections, Legislative Department, No. 12 of 1851, draft 875 [F/2436]: Memorial from the Hindoo inhabitants of Bengal praying for the repeal of Act XXI of 1850).

2. Standish G. Grady, *A Treatise on the Hindoo Law of Inheritance, Comprising the Doctrines of the Various Schools with the Decisions of the High Courts of the Several Presidencies of India, and the Judgments of the Privy Council on Appeal* (London: Wildy and Sons, 1868), 26.

3. For example, the British had great difficulty in arriving at a decision to determine the rightful heirs to the property of a Hindu woman converted to Roman Catholicism, who died intestate in Cochin. Two nephews claimed the property, but because it was uncertain whether the property was acquired before the conversion (in which case, according to Hindu law, the nephews were sole heirs) or after (in which case the property could devolve only on those who professed Christianity—being Hindus, the nephews were not then entitled to inherit), the case dragged on for years. Even when, on the advice of the pundits who were employed to interpret Hindu law for British judges, the Sadr Diwani Adalat (or appeals court) decided to rule in favor of the nephews, the government at Madras hesitated to take final action until it could obtain information from the governor-general in Calcutta whether any rule or precedent existed in Bengal that determined the succession to property in cases of conversion from Hinduism (India Office Library and Records, Board's Collections, Legislative Department, November 4, 1843, no. 21 of 1844, para. 43; Tamil Nadu Archives, Madras Judicial Consultations, vol. 472, March 21, 1843, no. 40; vol. 502a, March 10, 1846, no. 41; vol. 515, September 1, 1846, No. 45.

4. This paragraph owes a great deal to my conversations with Kathy Eden and Paula Richman.

5. See Jennifer Nedelsky, "Law, Boundaries, and the Bounded Self," *Representations* 30 (Spring 1990): 162–89, for a compelling discussion of the notion of rights as boundaries, which suggests a link between liberty and the security provided by law and government.

6. See Robert Doran, *Psychic Conversion and Theological Foundations: Towards a Reorientation of the Human Sciences*, American Academy of Religion Studies in Religion 25 (Ann Arbor, Mich.: Scholars Press, 1981), 24.

7. While a uniform criminal code was developed for British India, the personal laws of the two major religious communities, Hindus and Muslims, continued to be administered in British courts where issues of marriage, divorce, inheritance, adoption, and the like, were involved, the assumption being that these were too closely intertwined with Hinduism or Islam to be amenable to a common civil code derived from English law. For all practical purposes, Buddhists, Jains, Parsis, and Sikhs all came under Hindu law. See J. Duncan Derrett, *Religion, Law, and the State in India* (London: Faber and Faber, 1968); A. C. Banerjee, *English Law in India* (Atlantic Highlands, N.J.: Humanities Press, 1984); and Marc Galanter, *Law and Society in Modern India* (Delhi: Oxford University Press, 1989), for useful historical background to the administering of personal laws in British India. Derrett and Galanter are especially informative in

showing how the application of personal laws reflects assumptions about the structure of Indian society that still guide modern Indian law.

8. Robert Pattison, *The Great Dissent: John Henry Newman and the Liberal Heresy* (New York: Oxford University Press, 1991), 6.

9. Antony Lentin, "Anglicanism, Parliament, and the Courts," in *Religion in Victorian Britain: Controversies*, ed. Gerald Parsons (Manchester: Manchester University Press, 1988), 2:32.

10. Galanter, *Law and Society in Modern India*, 120.

11. India Office Library and Records (IOLR), Board's Collections, Judicial Department, July 8, 1844, no. 12 of 1844, draft 866 (F/4/2065); Tamil Nadu Archives, Madras Judicial Consultations, vol. 472, July 2, 1844, nos. 22–30. Henceforth abbreviated as IOLR, Judicial 1844; TNA Madras Judicial 1844. The case was thought important enough to be forwarded to the Court of Directors in London, along with all the relevant minutes, depositions, and petitions, which included an extraordinary letter written by Ananda Row's young wife, in which she pleads that if her husband's conversion were not reversed and he failed to return home, she would henceforth be considered a widow by her community and would have to suffer another version of civil death as alienating and horrifying as the one endured by her young husband.

12. IOLR, Madras Judicial Despatches (F/4/2065), November 27, 1844, 986.

13. Lata Mani, "The Production of an Official Discourse on Sati in Early Nineteenth Century Bengal," *Europe and Its Others* (Colchester: University of Essex, 1985), characterizes the movement toward British abolition of sati as a simultaneous process of accommodation and censure.

14. IOLR, Board's Collections, Legislative Department, no. 10 of 1852, draft 859, 4.

15. Ibid., 5.

16. One measure by Thomas Strange went so far as to seek the "suppression of fanatical outrages" by Mapillas in Malabar through criminal legislation, though British administrators were hesitant about creating a wholly new category of crime under the name of "fanatical outrage" and meting out a heavier punishment than similar outrages caused by other motives. The position finally adopted was that the cure for religious extremism was to *not* make it the object of special punishment (IOLR, Madras Dispatches, Judicial Department, vol. 119 [E/4/979], January 4, 1854, 866).

17. Derrett, *Religion, Law, and the State in India*, 52.

18. IOLR, Judicial 1844, 65.

19. Ibid., 15.

20. Ibid., 52.

21. Section 9, Regulation 7, Bengal Code, 1832; IOLR, Judicial 1844, 148.

22. Lata Mani has brilliantly shown a similar process at work in the British outlawing of sati, where women are constituted as the ground for the redefinition of Hindu tradition as scripturally derived. See Mani, "Contentious Traditions: The Debate on Sati in Colonial India," *Cultural Critique* 7 (Fall 1987): 119–56. Interestingly, in nineteenth-century English novels dealing with the subject of conversion from Hinduism, the plight of the hapless widow receives

extraordinary emphasis, acting as a prelude and background to the visual enactment of sati. Among some of the more extraordinary nineteenth-century novels on this subject are Sydney Owenson's *Luxima the Prophetess* (1819; rev. ed., London: Charles Westerton, 1859) and M. Mainwaring's *The Suttee, or The Hindu Converts* (London: A. K. Newman, 1830).

23. The first attempt to tell Ananda's story of his conversion is presented, ironically, in fictional form in a remarkable novel by Fanny Penney, *The Outcaste*, written in 1901, which is transparently based on the Ananda Row case (even the name of the hero, Ananda, remains the same, as are other details of the case). But the novel, which promises in the beginning to unfold events from Ananda's point of view, shifts in focus to social criticism, and the dominant voices in the latter part of the book are the Englishmen who shelter Ananda and muse abstractly on the legal challenges facing the British in overcoming the civil disabilities of converts like Ananda (but not specifically focusing on Ananda himself). Ananda's conversion is reduced to an aberration, the result of a highly emotional frame of mind following the death of a close friend.

24. Julian Saldanha is surely right to point out that the Caste Disabilities Removal Act only preserved the natural rights of converts and left untouched the question of succession applicable after conversion. Such legislation was intended less to favor converts than to "prejudice the fundamental peculiar social and religious rights of the caste and family from which the apostate is cut off" (Saldanha, *Civil and Ecclesiastical Law in India* [Trichy: Catholic Truth Society, n.d.], 22).

25. National Archives of India, Home Department—Public Proceedings, September 1876, nos. 71–78, 702. Henceforth abbreviated as NAI, Home Department 1876.

26. Grady, *Hindoo Law of Inheritance*, 8. Grady cites Hindu law to the effect that the husband had the option either of separating completely from his wife or replacing her with another woman, the first wife still continuing to be legally bound to him.

27. The Native Converts' Marriage Dissolution Act of 1866 made provisions for such eventualities, where unconverted spouses could file for dissolution of the marriage when their partner's loss of caste threatened them with a similar fate. This act, like so much else in British civil legislation, was designed to enable unconverted persons to retain their membership in caste society. If he so chose, Appiah could have appealed to the provisions of this act, especially since by his own admission he had no intention of taking Huchi back as his wife but only as his prostitute. Huchi's (ultimately misguided) appeal to the Native Converts' Marriage Dissolution Act may have also been motivated in part by the wish that Appiah would invoke it to release her from the marriage. See William Theobald, ed., *Acts of the Legislative Council of India, 1866–1867* (Calcutta: Thacker, Spink, 1867), 8:247.

28. It might well be asked whether a different conclusion can be drawn wherever the situation was reversed, and the convert was the husband rather than the wife; whether the power to end the marriage in such cases shifted from the husband to the unconverted wife; and whether this does not dispute my earlier contention and conclusively prove, to the contrary, that it was not so much patriar-

chal structures that were affirmed but the exclusive right of unconverted spouses to continue or discontinue a marriage. The available records, however, suggest that in the majority of instances in which converts were men, their wives were invariably persuaded to convert along with them, whatever reservations the wives might have had. One of the most moving testimonies of the agonizing decision to convert is by Lakshmibai Tilak, wife of the Christian convert Narayan Viman Tilak, who resisted for a long time and eventually gave in, virtually conceding that hers was Hobson's choice—either to remain unconverted and lose her husband (in which case she would be shunned by Hindu society and treated as a widow, as Ananda Row's wife pointed out) or to convert and thereby renounce the religion with which she had deep emotional and cultural ties. See P. S. Jacob, *The Experiential Response of N. V. Tilak* (Madras: Christian Literature Society, 1979).

29. In a related case in Bengal involving yet another female convert, Ram Kumari, who argued that her civil death dissolved her first marriage, the Calcutta high court ruled that civil death pertained only to civil rights, "but we find no authority in Hindu law for the position that a degraded person or an apostate is absolved from all civil obligations incurred before degradation or apostasy." (*Collection of the Decisions of the High Courts and the Privy Council on the Hindu Law of Marriage and the Effect of Apostasy after Marriage up to March 1891* [Madras: Scottish Press, 1891], 13).

30. NAI, Home Department 1876, 757.

31. Ibid., 759.

32. Ibid., 760.

33. Ibid., 706.

34. Ibid., 705.

35. Ibid., 712.

36. James Fitzjames Stephen's counsel was sought not long after he returned from India in 1872 as legal member of council, where he carried out codification of law in a post-Mutiny setting. In 1873–74, immediately after his return to England, he prepared a bill consolidating acts relating to the government of India, but the bill was never passed into law. His signed response to Huchi's petition is dated July 24, 1875.

37. NAI, Home Department 1876, 712.

38. Ibid., 712.

39. Gayatri Chakravorty Spivak, "Can the Subaltern Speak?" in *Marxism and the Interpretation of Culture*, ed. Cary Nelson and Lawrence Grossberg (Urbana and Chicago: University of Illinois Press, 1988), 302.

CHAPTER 8

Exclusion and Solidarity:
Labor Zionism and Arab Workers
in Palestine, 1897–1929

ZACHARY LOCKMAN

BOTH AS A nationalist ideology and as an organized political movement, Zionism was strongly influenced by, and had much in common with, the other nationalisms of eastern, central, and southern Europe among which it emerged during the last third of the nineteenth century. What most clearly set Zionism as it actually crystallized apart from those other nationalist ideologies and movements, and shaped much of its specific character and trajectory, stemmed from the fact of Jewish dispersion among non-Jewish majority populations. That dispersion made it impossible to contemplate emulating the Italians, Poles, Ukrainians, Hungarians, and so on, by seeking to create a Jewish state in eastern Europe, where the majority of the world's Jews actually lived. Zionism therefore had to be a movement of migration and settlement, a project whose goals were to promote the transfer of large numbers of Jews to, and achieve Jewish sovereignty in, some necessarily extra-European territory.

Had the Zionist movement found some completely uninhabited island, organized the immigration of a substantial number of Jews to it, and there established a Jewish state, it might have been reasonable to categorize Zionism simply as one of many variants of nationalism. But Palestine, the territory that not very surprisingly was actually selected as the site of Zionism's settlement and state-building project, was of course not uninhabited. Moreover, that project was launched by Europeans (albeit marginalized and often victimized ones) in the late nineteenth and early twentieth centuries, the heyday of European colonial expansion and rule. As a result Zionism, and especially the conception of Palestine and its indigenous inhabitants prevalent among its adherents, cannot be fully understood outside the context of contemporary European colonial discourse and practice, including the models provided by other projects of European overseas settlement.[1]

In addition to its character as both a nationalist and a settlement movement, Zionism can also be distinguished in another (and not unrelated) way. For a lengthy historical period—roughly from the early 1930s to the mid-1970s—the Zionist Organization, the *Yishuv* (the Jewish community in Palestine), and from 1948 the State of Israel were to a large extent dominated by the parties and institutions of the left wing of the Zionist movement. In that period the "labor-Zionist" camp was usually able to set policy and exercise effective control over most of the key levers of political and economic power in the Yishuv and later in Israel, and to exert a dominant cultural influence as well, though it often had to work with secular-centrist and religious Zionist parties as junior partners. For a crucial phase of its history, then, especially "on the ground" in Palestine itself, Zionism was a nationalist movement which, while in principle appealing to all Jews across class lines, was largely led by political forces that professed a commitment to social democracy and saw themselves as standing at the helm of a working-class and labor movement whose role it was to act as the vanguard of the broader Zionist movement.

Until relatively recently, the dominant tendency among historians and sociologists studying Zionism, particularly in Israel, was to explain many of that movement's distinctive features, and particularly the leading role that the labor-Zionist camp played within the Zionist movement and the Yishuv, largely in terms of the labor-Zionist leaders' and activists' possession and articulation of that set of values that proved most conducive to successful institution-building. On this view, the immigrants of the Second *Aliya* (the 1903–14 wave of Jewish immigration to Palestine), having become imbued with socialist-Zionist ideals in their countries of origin (mostly within the Tsarist empire), brought those values with them to Palestine and there sought to implement them as they laid the foundations of a new Jewish society.

Underpinning this interpretation is an implicit or explicit representation of the Arab and Jewish communities in Palestine as essentially separate, coherent, and self-evidently cohesive entities that developed along entirely distinct paths as the result of factors largely unique and internal to each community. The matrix of Arab-Jewish relationships and interactions in Palestine, and more broadly the local (largely Arab) environment in which the Yishuv and the Zionist project developed, are thereby defined a priori not as formative but as essentially marginal and limited in impact. From this perspective the Yishuv seems to have developed in a vacuum and Palestinian Arabs, rendered external to its history, are largely excluded from the picture.

I would like here to offer an alternative reading of one aspect of Yishuv history, a reading that also bears on a number of questions addressed in recent work on colonialism. This reading draws on but also extends the critique advanced by members of what might be called the "revisionist" school of Israeli historians and sociologists, and also by a number of Palestinian and foreign scholars. Challenging the premises underpinning the conventional perspective, the revisionist scholars have insisted on the constitutive role that various forms of interaction with its Palestinian Arab environment played in shaping the Zionist project. They have tended to give special emphasis to the structural economic relationships between Arabs and Jews in Palestine, notably the markets for labor and land in which Jewish immigrants found themselves when they arrived in the country before the First World War and during the interwar period.[2]

That emphasis has been salutary as a corrective to the conventional historiography's functionalism, its inability to transcend nationalist mythologies, and its failure to achieve critical distance by putting Zionism in comparative perspective. But it has perhaps also tended to marginalize questions of meaning and may conduce to an economistic reductionism. As I see it, the processes by which Zionism's specific practices and institutions in Palestine were shaped, by which a Jewish working class was formed, and by which labor-Zionist hegemony was constructed should be understood as discursive as well as material, requiring us to address the ways in which labor Zionists (among others) conceived of themselves and others as well as—indeed, in interaction with—a set of economic relationships.

I will try to make this point, and more generally to explore the nationalist, colonial, and working-class/socialist dimensions of the labor-Zionist project as it took shape within a specific historical conjuncture, through an exploration of labor-Zionist discourse and practice with regard to Arab workers in Palestine, from the emergence of socialist Zionism as a distinct tendency within Zionism through the late 1920s, when the foundations of labor-Zionist hegemony were largely in place. I will be suggesting that one cannot make sense of the labor-Zionist project without taking into account not only labor market strategies, on which the revisionist scholars have focused, but also the ways in which "the Arab worker" and the Arab working class in Palestine were represented, and the roles they were made to play, in labor-Zionist discourse. At a crucial stage, it was to a significant extent in relation to those (always contested) representations of Arab workers that labor Zionism articulated its own identity, its sense of mission, and its strategy.

This is not to depict Palestinians as passive and uninvolved in shaping this or any other aspect of their history, or as important merely for the roles in which they were cast in the Zionist imagination. Palestinian agency will surface here, and I have explored it at length elsewhere.[3] My purpose, rather, is to focus on how that agency, and more broadly Arab-Jewish interaction in various forms, provided much of the context within which class formation and state-building in the Yishuv, and especially the labor-Zionist movement's rise to preeminence, unfolded.

SOCIALIST ZIONISM AND PALESTINE

It has often been noted that in early Zionist discourse Palestine was generally represented as an essentially "empty" land, because it was not inhabited or developed by Europeans, and specifically by Jews, whose possession of this land and right to it enjoyed ontological status, notwithstanding the fact that relatively few Jews actually lived there at the turn of the century. This conception was manifested in an early Zionist slogan, "A land without a people for a people without a land." In this sense as in others, Zionism's attitude toward Palestine's indigenous Arab population, on the verge of its own national "awakening," was profoundly influenced by contemporary European colonial discourse.

By and large, this conception was shared by socialist Zionism, which emerged as a distinct tendency very soon after Theodor Herzl's transformation of a diffuse proto-Zionism into an organized international political movement embodied in the Zionist Organization. The first major theoretician of socialist Zionism, Nahman Syrkin (1868–1924), published his essay "The Jewish Question and the Socialist Jewish State" in 1898, only a year after Herzl had convened the First Zionist Congress, to which Syrkin was a delegate.[4] Syrkin sought to synthesize his conception of socialism—ethical and utopian rather than Marxist—and his strong commitment to Zionism, arguing against bourgeois Zionists like Herzl that only the proletarianized Jewish masses could realize Zionism (which therefore had to be socialist in content), and against anti-Zionist Jewish socialists that there could be no solution to the Jewish problem without the creation of a Jewish state. But Syrkin apparently felt no need to justify Zionism's claims to Palestine or its likely impact on the country's indigenous population in terms of socialist principles: none of his pre-First World War theoretical or programmatic works makes any implicit or explicit reference to Arabs or to an "Arab problem."

The work of the other preeminent early socialist-Zionist thinker, Ber Borokhov (1881–1917), who laid the theoretical foundations of the synthesis of Marxism and Zionism espoused by Po'alei Tziyon ("Workers of Zion"), the largest of the socialist-Zionist parties in eastern Europe and Palestine, exhibits a more complex but not essentially dissimilar attitude.[5] Borokhov elaborated a theory of the nation and nationalism rooted in the positivist and mechanistic Marxism characteristic of the ideologists of the Second International in order to demonstrate that the achievement by oppressed nationalities of "normal" "conditions of production"—that is, their own independent nation-state—was a prerequisite for, rather than a hindrance to, the successful waging of the class struggle and, ultimately, socialist revolution. The utility of Borokhov's theoretical work was immediately obvious: it provided a seemingly rigorous Marxist rationale for dissolving the apparent (and, to many eastern European socialist Zionists, deeply troubling) contradiction between socialism and Zionism by making the latter an essential precondition for the realization of the former, a necessary and unavoidable means to an end, rather than an illusory and even reactionary diversion—which was how many Jewish as well as non-Jewish socialists regarded Zionism.

In Borokhov's view, the Jews were unassimilable and persecuted wherever they lived in the Diaspora because of their "abnormal" social structure: they were overwhelmingly concentrated in the interstices and on the margins of national economic life, in petty trade, small-scale service enterprises, moneylending, and the like rather than in agriculture and basic industry. Unable to compete successfully in economies dominated by non-Jews and arousing antisemitism wherever they went, the petty-bourgeois Jewish masses would ultimately—inexorably—be compelled to migrate to Palestine, the only territory in which they could successfully achieve economic "normalcy" by becoming wage workers in industry and agriculture. Here this new "normal" Jewish proletariat would finally be able to wage the class struggle and achieve a Jewish socialist society.

But why Palestine in particular? Borokhov sought to provide a purportedly objective rationale cast in Marxist terms for the choice of Palestine as the site of this project, as opposed to the emotional, religious, or historical justifications advanced by other Zionists. For Borokhov, Palestine was unique in one crucial respect: only there would the Jewish immigrants criss-crossing the globe in search of a permanent haven

> not encounter organized and united resistance and displacement. In all the other lands legal restrictions and prohibitions on entry are an expression of the needs of the local population, which does not want foreign competitors. As a result no democratization of the regime or of international relations in bourgeois society can remove these restrictions. By contrast, prohibitions on the entry of Jews from Russia and Austria to Eretz Yisra'el (the "Land of Israel") are only a manifestation of the [Ottoman] sultan's arbitrariness, without any connection to the real needs of the population of Eretz Yisra'el itself.[6]

Borokhov thus understood that Palestine was not actually unpopulated, but like most early Zionists he was certain that the country's inhabitants presently did not, and for the foreseeable future would not, constitute a coherent or distinct community that might rationally oppose Jewish immigration. Although the ignorant might call Palestine's inhabitants "Arabs" or "Turks," Borokhov insisted, "they in fact have nothing in common with Arabs or Turks, and their attitude toward both of these is cold and even hostile."[7] He went on to argue that

> The natives of Eretz Yisra'el have no independent economic or cultural character; they are divided and disintegrated not only by the structure of the country's territory and by the diversity of its religions, but also by virtue of its character as an "international hostel." The natives of Eretz Yisra'el are not a single nation, nor will they constitute a single nation for a long time. They very easily and quickly adapt themselves to every cultural model higher than theirs brought from abroad; they are unable to unite in an organized act of resistance to external influences; they are unsuited for national competition, and their competition has an individualistic and anarchic character.

Borokhov, who never actually set foot in Palestine, concluded that "it is the Jewish immigrants who will undertake the development of the forces of production of Eretz Yisra'el, and the local population of Eretz Yisra'el will soon assimilate economically and culturally to the Jews."[8]

THE ENCOUNTER IN PALESTINE: THE ARAB WORKER AS COMPETITOR

For a time, Borokhov's comrades and disciples who actually emigrated from eastern Europe to Palestine during the Second Aliya remained loyal to this vision and to the conception of Palestine's indigenous population that it entailed. The first program (1906) of the "Jewish Social-Democratic Workers' Party in Eretz Yisra'el" (i.e., Po'alei Tziyon in Palestine), known as the "Ramle Platform" after the Arab town in which it was drawn up, opened with a Borokhovist paraphrase of *The Communist Manifesto*: "All human history is a history of national and class struggles." The only reference to the indigenous population appeared in the context of a reiteration of Borokhovist orthodoxy: since the capitalism developing in Palestine required "educated, energetic workers, and since the local worker is still in a lowly state (*natun beshefel madrega*), capitalist development in Palestine depends on the immigration of more developed workers from abroad"—that is, Jews. Here the Palestinian Arab worker makes an early appearance, though not explicitly denoted as such and only as a figure whose backwardness requires another more advanced kind of worker, the immigrating Jewish proletarian, to take center-stage.

Yet as the syntheses of Zionism and socialism elaborated by Syrkin, Borokhov, and others in the early years of the twentieth century were put to the test in Palestine itself, the question of "the Arab worker" was to assume larger proportions for socialist Zionists. The Second Aliya included several thousand young men and women, mostly of eastern European middle-class origin, who saw themselves as the vanguard of the Jewish working class in Palestine—a class that as yet hardly existed. Some of these, adherents or sympathizers of Po'alei Tziyon, wanted to implement the Borokhovian synthesis of class struggle and Zionist settlement by transforming themselves into agricultural or industrial wage workers, thereby constituting a Jewish proletariat in Palestine that could then wage its class struggle in the country's developing capitalist economy. Others belonged to or inclined toward Po'alei Tziyon's main rival within the labor-Zionist camp, Hapo'el Hatza'ir ("The Young Worker"), which rejected both Marxism and class struggle and instead, influenced by Tolstoyan principles, expounded a commitment to physical labor, self-sacrifice, and settlement on the land as the means by which Zion would be "redeemed" for the Jewish people.

Those who considered themselves (or wanted to make themselves into) workers placed great emphasis on "productivizing" themselves by means of what they called the "conquest of labor" (*kibbush ha'avoda*): the demand that in Palestine Jews should master the kinds of work (especially heavy physical labor in agriculture) which relatively few performed in the Diaspora. These men and women saw themselves as the vanguard of the social transformation of the Jewish people, discursively transforming themselves into a working class even before they quite managed to actually find jobs as wage workers. As they saw it, only the establishment in Palestine of a large and solidly rooted class of agricultural workers subsisting by the sweat of their brows, and as capitalism developed of industrial workers as well, would allow the Zionist project to succeed and avoid the reproduction in the Yishuv of the Diaspora "abnormalities" denounced by Syrkin, Borokhov, and others.

However, these new arrivals soon encountered obstacles that had not been foreseen by the theoreticians of labor Zionism; indeed, Borokhov's prognosis for capitalist development in Palestine was quickly proven inaccurate. Borokhov had predicted that both Jewish capital and Jewish wage labor would inexorably be channeled into Palestine by what he called (in the fashion of Second International Marxism) "stychic" processes, resulting in the creation of a capitalist economy there that would provide Jewish immigrants with jobs and make class struggle both possible and necessary. It soon became obvious, however, that the process would be neither rapid nor automatic. Neither Jewish nor non-Jewish private capital rushed to invest in Palestine, while "national capital"— the funds collected worldwide by the financial, land-purchasing, and settlement institutions of the new Zionist Organization—did not even begin to suffice for large-scale settlement of new immigrants, at least along the lines followed up to that point in the *moshavot* (sing., *moshava*)—the "colonies" or "settlements" (some of which would eventually become substantial towns) established during the First Aliya (1882–1902) and dominated by Jewish planters. Many of the moshavot had only been saved from bankruptcy in the 1890s by heavy subsidies from the Rothschilds and other European Jewish philanthropists, and most had come to operate on what might be called the Algerian model, with the Jewish farmers employing Arab peasants as agricultural wage laborers.

So not only were land and capital for settlement scarce, but the jobs to which the would-be Jewish proletarians of the Second Aliya aspired— agricultural employment in the moshavot—were monopolized by Arab workers. The Jewish newcomers, who possessed no capital of their own with which to set themselves up as farmers, thus found themselves competing with an abundant supply of cheaper Arab labor, which was naturally preferred even by Jewish employers, especially the citrus plantation owners and those engaged in viniculture. The new Jewish immigrants could not subsist on the wages paid to Arabs, and were in addition unaccustomed to heavy physical labor, resentful of their employers' efforts to discipline and control them, and prone to vociferating loudly about class struggle and socialist revolution, all traits that did not endear them to prospective Jewish employers. They thus found themselves with few prospects either for settlement on land acquired by the Zionist movement or for employment on land owned by private Jewish farmers. In this bleak situation, exacerbated by disease and Arab hostility, many (perhaps most) of the Second Aliya immigrants soon left Palestine, either returning to Europe or (more often) continuing on to a wealthier and more attractive "promised land"—the United States.

THE STRUGGLE FOR "HEBREW LABOR"

It was in this context—the inability of these Second Aliya immigrants to compete effectively in the prevailing market for labor, and the resulting prospect that the Zionist project would founder because neither jobs nor resources for settlement were available to maintain those who had come or to attract others to follow—that the struggle for the "conquest of labor" was transformed from a matter of individual proletarianization into a campaign to replace Arab workers employed in the Jewish sector (especially in the moshavot) with Jewish workers. Hence the doctrine of "Hebrew labor" (*'avoda 'ivrit*), which came in the decade preceding the First World War to occupy a central place in labor-Zionist discourse and practice.[9] The fate of the Zionist project in Palestine came to be seen as dependent on the success of this campaign of "conquest," on the achievement of a maximal proportion of Hebrew labor (that is, Jewish employment) in every enterprise of the Jewish sector of the Palestinian economy—which inevitably meant displacing at least some Arab workers. In the decades to come, the campaign for Hebrew labor would play an important role in shaping relations between Arab and Jewish workers in Palestine.[10]

For adherents of Hapo'el Hatza'ir, adoption of this strategy was relatively easy, given their lack of interest in, if not outright rejection of, the principle of proletarian internationalism and their insistence that priority always be given to the needs of Jews and of Zionism. But members of Po'alei Tziyon, who took their Marxism very seriously, found this a much more difficult and anxiety-provoking issue. The most carefully elaborated and durable rationale for Po'alei Tziyon's embrace of this policy was provided by Yitzhaq Ben-Tzvi (1884–1963). A childhood friend and early disciple of Ber Borokhov, Ben-Tzvi had arrived in Palestine in 1907 with several years of both legal and underground work in the service of Po'alei Tziyon in Russia already behind him. He soon became one of the leaders of the fledgling Jewish labor movement in Palestine.

In a two part article published in 1912 and entitled "National Defense and the Proletarian Perspective," Ben-Tzvi sought to ease his comrades' consciences by arguing that in certain historical circumstances, national interests must take precedence over class solidarity. At the present time, he argued, the organized and class-conscious Jewish workers in Palestine had the right to demand that the cheap and unorganized Arab workers be excluded from jobs in the moshavot and elsewhere in the Jewish sector: this was a question of life or death for the Jewish working class. Only later, when capitalist development had proceeded further and employment opportunities were abundant for all, would a material basis be created for solidarity between Jewish and Arab workers.[11]

Not a few party members were initially dismayed at the prospect of an avowedly socialist party giving priority to depriving fellow workers of their livelihoods simply because they were Arabs rather than Jews; as one of them put it, "instead of the slogan of 'the conquest of labor' by displacing Arab workers, the task of the Jewish worker [should be] to organize the Arab worker and reduce the [Arab landowners'] influence over him."[12] But eventually the desperate need for jobs largely silenced opposition.

The exclusion of Arab workers from employment in the Jewish sector of Palestine's economy was thus conceived as the main means by which a Jewish working class was to be formed, at least in the short term. The practice of exclusion was not, of course, depicted or understood as such by those who engaged in it, or as constituting the kind of discrimination from which many of these Jewish immigrants had themselves suffered in their countries of origin. Nor was the conflict this practice entailed seen as ethnic or national in essence. Rather, the Jewish workers saw themselves (or were encouraged to see themselves) as the innocent victims of a vicious "boycott" of Jewish labor on the part of Jewish employers: they were engaged in a defensive battle to protect the rights and gains of "organized" (that is, Jewish) against the threat of "unorganized" (that is, Arab) labor. David Ben-Gurion, who in the early 1920s would emerge as the preeminent leader of labor Zionism in Palestine, would later go so far as to accuse even Jewish citrus grove owners of "economic antisemitism," depicting the Jewish workers as engaged in a life-or-death struggle for the "right to work."[13]

Ben-Gurion was prepared to admit that the struggle for Hebrew labor might "contradict the *personal* interest" of some Arab workers, by causing them to lose their jobs. But, he insisted, the struggle of Jewish workers to secure jobs and increase their wages in the face of cheap local labor would ultimately improve the economic situation of Palestine as a whole, create new and better jobs in the Arab sector as well, and thereby benefit the Arab workers. Thus, Ben-Gurion argued, the struggle for Hebrew labor "completely conforms to the *class* interest of the Arab worker in Palestine no less than to the class interest of the Jewish worker."[14]

CLASS FORMATION AS JOB CREATION

The Zionist labor movement's efforts to achieve Hebrew labor enjoyed only limited success. In these early years, and even through the interwar period, that movement was generally not strong enough to enforce its demands on private Jewish employers. Moreover, the strategy of replacing Arab with Jewish workers was in and of itself unlikely to resolve Zionism's problems on the ground in Palestine. For it was clear that, given the weakness of the Yishuv's economy and the low level of investment by private capital, even the achievement of a relatively high level of Hebrew labor in the Jewish private sector could not possibly provide enough jobs for the large numbers of immigrants needed to make the Zionist project feasible. Nor was private capital likely to invest in ways that efficiently facilitated the absorption of immigrants or enhanced the infrastructural development and self-sufficiency of the Yishuv.

The struggle for Hebrew labor had therefore to be supplemented by the development of an exclusively Jewish, high-wage enclave within the Palestinian economy through the establishment by the labor-Zionist movement of its own industrial, construction, transport, and service enterprises. This was to be funded in large part by "national capital," raised from among the wealthier nonworker elements that at the time still dominated the Zionist movement and were initially quite hostile to socialist Zionism, and channeled through the institutions of the Zionist Organization.[15]

Before the First World War this sector was still tiny, but after 1920, under the auspices of the new Histadrut (the "General Organization of Hebrew Workers in Eretz Yisra'el," which quickly became the central institution of the labor-Zionist camp), it gradually expanded, though not without failures and setbacks. The Histadrut would eventually become the Yishuv's (and Israel's) largest employer, monopolizing or dominating whole sectors of the economy while providing a broad range of social and cultural services as well. New sources of Histadrut-controlled urban employment were complemented by new forms of agricultural settlement, the collectivist *kibbutz* (the first of which was established shortly before the First World War) and from 1920 the *moshav*, a cooperative smallholders' village. These new types of settlement seemed to allow for more cost-effective absorption of immigrants and more efficient use of their labor than had earlier forms of Jewish agricultural settlement in Palestine. The kibbutzim in particular also proved an efficient means of effecting the spatial extension of the Yishuv and would later play an important military role as well.

The extent to which this new labor-Zionist strategy amounted to an abandonment of orthodox Borokhovism was fully acknowledged only in the 1920s, when the old schema was supplanted by a new doctrine referred to as "constructivism." Since "normal" capitalist development seemed unlikely to create a substantial Jewish working class in Palestine, this task would have to be accomplished by the fledgling labor movement itself, through the construction of a noncapitalist, worker-owned Jewish economy in Palestine. Backed by the resources of the world Zionist movement (and thereby entailing an alliance with the bourgeois forces within that movement), the labor-Zionist movement in Palestine would create employment for itself and for the immigrants to come, both by securing as many existing jobs as possible for Jews and by creating an economic sector under its control that would become the dynamic motor propelling the development of a self-sufficient Yishuv. It was on the basis of this program, which seemed to offer a way out of the problems that the Zionist project had encountered on the ground in Palestine, that the labor-Zionist movement would enhance its economic, political, and cultural power to the point where it could effectively assert its leadership of the Yishuv and the Zionist movement.

Of course, it must be kept in mind that it was in fact a dramatic change in the larger political context that rendered this strategy, and indeed the Zionist project as a whole, even remotely feasible. In November 1917, even as its armed forces were conquering Palestine from the Ottoman Empire, the British government had proclaimed its commitment to the creation in Palestine of a "national home" for the Jewish people (the "Balfour Declaration"). After the war, Britain constituted Palestine as a distinct political entity, established its own rule (in the form of a League of Nations "mandate"), and implemented its wartime pledge by facilitating the Zionist project in a variety of ways.

The British-Zionist alliance was never free of conflict and would break down just before the Second World War as the two parties' interests diverged. It is nonetheless clear that it was British colonial rule over Palestine which, in the face of growing Palestinian Arab nationalist opposition to Zionism and demands for self-determination, opened the way to Jewish immigration, land acquisition, and development of the Yishuv's infrastructure and economy on a scale that would have been unimaginable had Palestine either remained under Ottoman rule or achieved independence under an Arab government. The relative success of labor Zionism's strategy of pursuing Hebrew labor and building up a (relatively) self-sufficient Jewish high-wage sector, and the labor-Zionist camp's attainment of hegemony within the Yishuv and world Zionism, were in this sense inconceivable in the absence of a sympathetic colonial regime that could hold the indigenous majority (still two-thirds of the country's population in 1947) in check until the Yishuv was demographically, economically, militarily, and politically strong enough to stand on its own.

THE HISTADRUT AND THE ARAB WORKING CLASS

The formation and cohesion of a Jewish working class in Palestine were thus to be achieved in large part through the practice of exclusion: the exclusion of Arab workers from employment both in private Jewish enterprises and in the still small but expanding Histadrut-controlled sector of the economy. But this did not exhaust the roles that the Arab worker was to play in labor-Zionist discourse. As the Zionist workers' movement claimed for itself the role of vanguard and struggled to achieve hegemony within the Yishuv, the question of its relationship with Palestine's Arab working class not only persisted but grew more complex, both as a theoretical problem and as a pressing practical problem in "mixed" workplaces (that is, those employing both Arab and Jewish workers). In this context, a new conception of the Arab worker surfaced in the early 1920s, coexisting in uneasy tension with the practice of exclusion and the accompanying portrayal of the Arab worker as a competitor for jobs, a threat to the Jewish worker and to Zionism. This new conception instead portrayed the Arab working class as labor-Zionism's ally and was accompanied by a proposed strategy of Arab-Jewish working-class solidarity.

The issue of Arab-Jewish class solidarity surfaced already at the founding congress of the Histadrut in December 1920. The congress was dominated by Ahdut Ha'avoda ("Unity of Labor"), the successor to the prewar Po'alei Tziyon, and by its junior partner Hapo'el Hatza'ir. (These two labor-Zionist parties would grow closer during the 1920s and would in 1930 merge into MAPAI, the acronym for "Workers' Party of the Land of Israel," which with its successors—including today's Labor Party—would dominate the Yishuv and then Israel into the 1970s.) In keeping with the emerging doctrine of constructivism, these two parties envisioned the new Histadrut not as a trade union federation on the European model, but rather as an instrument to foster the settlement of Jewish workers in Palestine and the construction of a Jewish commonwealth there. The Histadrut would thus embody the labor-Zionist synthesis by being both a workers' organization and a key institution of the Zionist project, and it would therefore also have to be an exclusively Jewish organization.

This majority conception was opposed by a small but vocal contingent from the Socialist Workers' Party (SWP), which though formally Zionist regarded itself as the Jewish affiliate of the new Communist International. (The Comintern would eventually decide otherwise, and out of the splintering of the SWP would emerge both the explicitly anti-Zionist Palestine Communist Party and Po'alei Tziyon Smol ["Workers of Zion—Left"], which occupied the far left end of the Zionist spectrum.) SWP delegates repeatedly raised the question of Arab membership in the new Histadrut, arguing that class solidarity required the Histadrut to admit Arab workers (though in a separate national section). But the dominant parties were unwilling to take up the question, and it was deferred for later consideration. When the congress resolved that the new Histadrut would "unite all the workers and laborers in the country who live by their own labor without exploiting the labor of others, in order to arrange for all the settlement, economic and also cultural affairs of all the workers in the country, so as to build a society of Jewish labor in Eretz Yisra'el," it meant of course Palestine's Jewish workers.[16]

THE QUESTION OF "JOINT ORGANIZATION"

Most immediately, what made it difficult for a reluctant, even uninterested, Histadrut leadership to set this issue aside was the specific situation of the Jewish workers employed by the state-owned (and British-managed) Palestine Railways, and it was among the Arab and Jewish railwaymen that the theoretical and practical questions surrounding the issue of "joint organization" (*irgun meshutaf*) were first put to the test. The Jewish railway workers—a few hundred out of a workforce of several thousand—could not hope, however well-organized their own exclusively Jewish Railway Workers' Association was, to improve their low wages and miserable working conditions without the cooperation of their unorganized Arab fellow workers. At the same time, they and the Histadrut leadership were anxious about the possible consequences of organizing Arab workers and the degree to which those consequences might conflict with the goals of Zionism.

A Histadrut executive committee discussion of the railway workers' situation in December 1920, only a few weeks after the organization was established, illustrates the dilemma that labor Zionism faced in grappling with this issue. Berl Katznelson (1887–1944), one of the leading figures in Ahdut Ha'avoda (and later MAPAI), opened the discussion by stating that he saw no danger in the Arab railway workers organizing themselves and cooperating with their Jewish co-workers. Clearly mindful of the SWP's proposal at the recent Histadrut congress that Arabs be allowed or even encouraged to join hitherto exclusively Jewish trade unions, he also expressed concern that the Arab railway workers might want to join the Jewish union, which would thereby lose its Jewish and Zionist character. Other executive committee members agreed with Katznelson that Jewish and Arab workers should belong to separate organizations.

But some went beyond insistence on maintaining separate organizations to express anxiety about the whole idea of helping Arab workers organize, for fear that organized Arab workers would inevitably turn against Zionism. "From the humanitarian standpoint, it is clear that we must organize them," said Eliezer Shohat of Hapo'el Hatza'ir, "but from the national standpoint, when we organize them we will be arousing them against us. They will receive the good that is in organization and use it against us." Someone else pointed out that the trade unions in Egypt were under the influence of the nationalists. It was also well understood, even in this early discussion, that organizing Arab workers might conflict with the goal of achieving Hebrew labor on the railways: higher pay and better conditions might attract more Jews to railroad work and keep them there, but it might have the same effect on Arabs, thereby making it more difficult for Jews to gain a larger percentage of railroad jobs.[17]

In the end the executive committee decided to procrastinate, affirming the principle of Arab-Jewish workers' solidarity but avoiding any practical decisions pending further clarification of the question. But the issue was to loom larger in the years that followed, as labor-Zionist leaders were compelled to reckon with the emergence in Palestine of a growing class of Arab wage workers outside agriculture. While Palestinian Arab society was still largely rural, a deepening agrarian crisis (manifested in, among other things, a growth in the number of landless peasants) and new employment opportunities in the towns resulted in substantial migration from the countryside to urban areas. These migrants, who often retained links to their home villages and to peasant life, were joined by propertyless urban dwellers as wage laborers in construction, in public works, on the docks, on the railways, in small-scale manufacturing and service enterprises and elsewhere. A stratum of skilled and semiskilled Arab workers also emerged, some of whom began to take an interest in trade unionism.[18]

The issue was posed most acutely in Haifa, a "mixed" Arab-Jewish city that was becoming Palestine's main seaport and industrial center. Here, in the middle of 1921, a group of Arab railway workers approached their Jewish co-workers to discuss cooperation, and some even expressed interest in joining the Histadrut. The question thus became increasingly difficult for the Histadrut leadership to ignore, and in subsequent years it would be the subject of considerable debate both in public and in the more restricted circles of the organization's leadership, dominated by Ahdut Ha'avoda with Hapo'el Hatza'ir as a junior partner. Through that debate Histadrut leaders sought to work out a clear position on joint organization, and more broadly on the whole question of the labor-Zionist movement's policy toward Arab workers—a position that would reconcile labor-Zionism's commitment to the goals of Zionism with its commitment in principle to Arab-Jewish class solidarity. In these discussions the question of Hebrew labor naturally played an important role, and the goal of maximizing Jewish employment was never absent from the calculations of Zionist labor leaders of various stripes as they grappled with the question of joint organization and Arab-Jewish class solidarity.

THE ARAB WORKER AS ZIONISM'S ALLY

It was David Ben-Gurion who, in the summer of 1921, most clearly articulated what would be labor-Zionism's dominant conception of its own role vis-a-vis Arab workers in Palestine until the later 1920s.[19] Ben-

Gurion (1886–1973) had emigrated from Russia to Palestine in 1906 and soon emerged as a leading figure in Po'alei Tziyon and then in its successor, Ahdut Ha'avoda. In 1921 he was elected secretary of the new Histadrut and quickly established himself as the preeminent leader of labor Zionism. Under his guidance the Histadrut became a highly centralized and powerful institution, and the vehicle through which Ben-Gurion's party MAPAI would a decade later achieve a dominant position in the Yishuv and in the world Zionist movement, a triumph signaled by Ben-Gurion's election in 1933 to the executive of the Jewish Agency (the de facto leadership of the Yishuv) and then by his election in 1935 as chair of both that body and the Zionist Executive.

In a proposal to Ahdut Ha'avoda's forthcoming party congress, Ben-Gurion argued that the basis for relations between Jewish and Arab workers must be "joint economic, political and cultural work, which is the necessary prerequisite for our redemption as a free working people and for the emancipation of the Arab working people from enslavement by its oppressors and exploiters, the dominant landowners and property-owners." It was, he insisted, "the conscious and cultured Jewish worker, whose historic mission is the building of a free community of labor in Eretz Yisra'el, who must lead the movement of liberation and rebirth of the peoples of the Near East" and "educate the Arab worker to live an orderly and cooperative life of labor, discipline and mutual responsibility."[20]

It is easy, and not incorrect, to see in this formulation what might be termed a sort of Jewish proletarian *mission civilisatrice* toward Arab workers in Palestine. But this conception of the relationship of the Jewish and Arab working classes in Palestine needs to be unpacked and contextualized in order to elucidate its economic and political dimensions. Ben-Gurion would elaborate on his conception of the economic dimension of the relationship in a January 1922 speech to the Histadrut council:

> Until the last few years the activity of the Jewish worker in the country was almost entirely restricted to a difficult and desperate struggle for the right to work in the few enterprises of the Jewish community, which were closed to the cultured and conscious Jewish worker as a result of the existence of unorganized and easily exploitable cheap labor. Unwillingly and unconsciously, the Arab worker, by virtue of his degraded state, his minimal needs and his primitive culture, was undermining the Jewish worker's possibility of existence even in the only sphere of employment intended for him. In this situation there was hardly any basis for joint action and class influence. Now conditions have changed. The Jewish worker now works together with the Arab worker in government enterprises, that is in country-wide, general enterprises, on equal terms. But the extent of this "equality" is now determined by the worker with lesser culture and fewer needs;

wages and working conditions are determined in accordance with the needs and demands of the Arab worker, a situation which is oppressive to the Jewish worker. Improvement in working conditions in these trades by the Jewish workers cannot be imagined without the active participation of the Arab worker. And the creation of an organized class force of Jewish and Arab workers in order to improve the workers' situation and their working conditions is a necessary condition for the survival of the cultured worker in these occupations.

Ben-Gurion concluded that "the creation of a single common front for all the country's workers to deal with their common affairs is the obligation and right of the pioneers of labor culture in Palestine—it is the mission of the Jewish workers. Not a metaphysical or theological mission, but a mission that derives from and is conditioned by the conditions of our life and work in Palestine."[21]

At the same time, Ben-Gurion and his colleagues in the Histadrut leadership were adamant that joint organization in mixed workplaces take the form of separate Jewish and Arab unions, or at the very least, of separate and autonomous national sections within joint unions. This would allow the Jewish workers in mixed workplaces to improve their circumstances through cooperation with their Arab co-workers while preserving the exclusively Jewish character of the Histadrut and its trade unions, which would thus be free to carry out their "national" (that is, Zionist) tasks, notably the struggle for Hebrew labor. On the same grounds they insisted that Arab workers should not be allowed to join the Histadrut.

CLASS SOLIDARITY AND PALESTINIAN NATIONALISM

Politically, this representation of the relationship between Arab and Jewish workers should be read as a response to the emergence in Palestine of a distinct and vocal Arab nationalist movement demanding the cessation of Jewish immigration and land purchases, and the independence of Palestine as an Arab state. In defending Hebrew labor a decade earlier, Ben-Tzvi had argued that the conflict between Arab and Jewish workers in Palestine was social rather than national, a struggle between organized and unorganized labor. In changed circumstances, Ben-Gurion now developed this social/national opposition somewhat differently by insisting that the real conflict in Palestine was not between the country's Arab majority and the Zionist project of Jewish immigration, settlement, and statehood, as the Palestinian Arab nationalist movement claimed, but rather between the Arab workers and their Arab oppressors.

This was to be labor-Zionism's new formulation, articulated in the language of class struggle and class solidarity, of Zionism's long-standing rejection of the authenticity and legitimacy of Palestinian Arab nationalism, and as such it immediately became a central (though not unchallenged) theme in labor-Zionist discourse. Palestinian nationalism was depicted as lacking any authentic popular base or social content: it was the entirely artificial instrument of the Arab *effendis*, labor Zionism's codeword for what it saw as the reactionary large landowners, greedy moneylenders, and obscurantist clerics who wanted self-government only so that they could more ruthlessly exploit the Arab peasants and workers. To this false nationalism was counterposed a class alliance of Jewish and Arab workers grounded in their shared objective economic interests. By assisting their enslaved and ignorant Arab brothers, the more advanced Jewish workers would not only liberate them from their real enemies, their oppressive compatriots, but would be helping achieve Zionism's goal of Jewish national "redemption." In the process the Arab workers were to be uplifted and transformed into "real" proletarians, and would thereby come to grasp the beneficial and progressive character of the Zionist project. At the same time, organizing Arab workers under the tutelage of the Histadrut would help insulate them from the influence of "outside agitators" (i.e., Palestinian nationalist activists) who might seek to mobilize them beyond, and even against, the Histadrut's influence.

Both the economic and the political meanings built into this conception of the Arab working class and its role were rendered even more explicit in the course of a 1924 debate within Ahdut Ha'avoda. The British Colonial Office and the mandatory government of Palestine had initiated negotiations with the Arab and Jewish leaderships about the establishment of a legislative council with limited powers. This put the Yishuv and the Zionist movement in a complicated and somewhat contradictory position. On the one hand, the Zionist leadership formally endorsed the principles of self-government and representative democracy and very much wanted to play a role in governing Palestine; on the other hand, it could not accept a fully representative form of self-government for Palestine, since the country had an overwhelmingly Arab population and a representative government would inevitably mean a largely Arab (and therefore anti-Zionist) administration. Zionist leaders in Palestine and abroad disagreed over how to respond to various British proposals.

The linkage between a legislative council for Palestine on the one hand, and relations between Arab and Jewish workers on the other came to the fore at the third congress of Ahdut Ha'avoda, held at Ein Harod in May 1924. Shlomo Kaplansky, a prominent veteran of the Second

Aliya who had emerged as leader of the party's left wing, proposed that Ahdut Ha'avoda favor the immediate establishment of a democratically elected parliament with broad powers. Kaplansky acknowledged that this parliament would inevitably have an Arab majority, but he argued that the vital interests of the Yishuv could be safeguarded, and the long-term goals of Zionism achieved, through an agreement with the Palestinian Arab nationalist leadership.

Ben-Gurion, with the support of the majority of the delegates, strongly opposed Kaplansky's proposal. Insisting that Zionism was essentially a state-building project, he demanded that all proposals for representative government, however democratic in the abstract, be judged by the extent to which they advanced that project. Any system of government based on the current demographic and political balance of forces could only damage Zionism's long-term prospects.

In this debate, Ben-Gurion again depicted the Palestinian Arab national movement as an inauthentic tool of the effendis. He told the congress: "We must not be afraid to proclaim openly that between us, the Jewish workers, and the leaders of today's Arab movement, the effendis, there is no common language." "Certainly," Ben-Gurion went on,

> the Arab community in the country has the right of self-determination, of self-rule. It would never occur to us to restrict or minimize that right. The national autonomy which we demand for ourselves we demand for the Arabs as well. But we do not admit their right to rule over the country to the extent that the country is not built up by them and still awaits those who will work it. They do not have any right or claim to prohibit or control the construction of the country, the restoration of its ruins, the productivization of its resources, the expansion of its cultivated area, the development of its culture, the growth of its laboring community.

But then, Ben-Gurion asked rhetorically, with whom could Zionism come to an agreement, if not with the Arab leadership? "We must take the longer and more difficult path—the path toward the Arab worker. There is no common platform between us and the ruling class among the Arab people. But there is a common platform between us and the Arab workers, even if this platform still exists only potentially and not yet in reality." The Arab worker, he continued, is "an inseparable, organic part of the country, just like one of its mountains or valleys." It was the historic mission of the Jewish workers to raise their Arab brothers from poverty and ignorance, not out of charity but out of self-interest.

> The fate of the Jewish worker is linked with the fate of the Arab worker.
> Together we will rise, or together we will fall. The Jewish worker will not

work 8 hours a day if the Arab worker will be forced to work 10–12 hours. The Jewish worker will not get 30 piasters a day if the Arab sells his labor for 15 piasters or less. . . . We must seek agreement and understanding with the Arab people only through the Arab worker, and only an alliance of Jewish and Arab workers will establish and maintain an alliance of the Jewish and Arab peoples in Palestine.[22]

The Arab working class in Palestine was thus assigned an important role in Ben-Gurion's political vision of this period. By representing it as Zionism's potential ally, Ben-Gurion could overcome the apparent contradiction between his unwavering commitment to a Jewish majority and (ultimately) a Jewish state in Palestine, on the one hand, and on the other his formal commitment to democracy and to the right of the Palestinian Arabs to self-determination. Indeed, the Arab working class played the role of a deus ex machina in labor-Zionist discourse at this time: it compensated for the objective weakness of the Jewish labor movement in Palestine and in effect guaranteed the ultimate success of the labor-Zionist project at a time when a Jewish majority and Jewish sovereignty in Palestine seemed a very long way off and the path to their attainment highly uncertain.

In this discourse the Arab workers' elemental authenticity ("just like one of [Palestine's] mountains or valleys") was affirmed, but mainly in order to delegitimize the actually existing Palestinian nationalist movement. Concomitantly, the Arabs' right to self-rule was recognized in principle, only to be immediately subordinated to the rights, needs, and interests in Palestine of the Jews, who were developing the land and therefore had a stronger right to possess and rule it. By definition, Arab objections on *nationalist* grounds to Jewish immigration, and to Zionism more generally, were inauthentic and artificial, the product of manipulation by the effendis.

JOINT ORGANIZATION AMONG THE RAILWAY WORKERS

The Histadrut's formal endorsement of Ben-Gurion's conception of joint organization and of efforts to develop links with Arab workers did not result in much concrete action. The Histadrut leadership only began to pay serious attention to joint organization when confronted with the loss of control of a key union. Toward the end of 1923 members of Po'alei Tziyon Smol, a small but vocal party that had remained loyal to Borokhovist orthodoxy, saw itself as both resolutely Zionist and communist (a stance that both the Comintern and the Palestine Communist Party rejected), and opposed from the left what it saw as the class-collaborationist leadership of the Histadrut, won the leadership of the Jewish railway workers union. The union's new left-wing leadership acceded to the demand long advanced by the Arab railway workers' leaders that any joint Arab-Jewish railway workers' union be unitary in structure, that is, without separate national sections, as the Histadrut had specified. To win over Arab workers already suspicious of the Histadrut's Zionist character, the new union leadership also called on the Histadrut to divest itself of its settlement and cooperative functions and become a territorial trade union organization open to Arabs as well as Jews—much as the SWP had demanded when the Histadrut was founded in 1920. These steps opened the way to the formation of a joint Arab-Jewish railway workers' union toward the end of 1924.

To thwart Po'alei Tziyon Smol's call for radically transforming the Histadrut, a call that found some support elsewhere in the Jewish labor movement, Ben-Gurion proposed that the next Histadrut congress (still some years off) establish an all-Palestine workers' alliance, in essence an umbrella organization that would include both the Histadrut and its as yet nonexistent Arab counterpart; joint Arab-Jewish unions in mixed workplaces would have separate national sections affiliated with their respective national federation. This scheme would provide a framework for Jewish-Arab class cooperation while preserving the Histadrut's independence, and thus its continued ability to engage in Zionist work.[23] At the same time, Ben-Gurion and his colleagues sought to reassert the Histadrut majority's influence over the Jewish railway workers, a group of considerable political and economic importance but historically resistant to outside control.

The joint Arab-Jewish railway workers union was in any case short-lived: most of its Arab members left it early in 1925, mainly because they and their leaders had come to feel that their Jewish colleagues, drawn largely from the ranks of Po'alei Tziyon Smol, were not being straightforward about their Zionist priorities. As one of them put it in an article in *Haifa*, the Palestine Communist Party's Arabic-language organ, "the foundations and principles of this [joint] union were based not on the interests of the worker and the improvement of his condition (*raf' mistawa'hi*) but rather on the implementation among the workers of the goals of Zionism."[24] They grew dissatisfied, for example, with what they perceived to be the evasive or disingenuous responses they received when they queried their Jewish colleagues about the union's continuing affiliation with the Zionist Histadrut.[25]

We know that there were also instances of deliberate deception: for example, at a crucial January 1925 meeting of the joint railway union's council, the first at which Arab delegates participated fully, the Jewish translator who was rendering the proceedings into Arabic for the benefit of the Arab delegates deliberately watered down the Zionist content of a speech by Ben-Gurion so as to make it more palatable to the Arabs.[26] The Arab unionists were in fact correct to suspect that behind the scenes, their Jewish comrades in the railway union leadership were continuing to work with the Histadrut to induce Palestine Railways management, the mandatory administration, and the Colonial Office to get more Jews hired—a source of tremendous resentment among the Arab rank and file.[27] The Arab trade unionists who left the joint union soon formed their own organization, the Palestinian Arab Workers' Society, which until the emergence of a rival communist-led Arab trade union movement in the 1940s would constitute the main Arab labor organization in Palestine, uniting a fluctuating membership drawn from various trades and locales around a more stable core of Haifa railway workers.[28]

REFIGURING THE ARAB WORKER

In other sectors, the Histadrut did in the mid-1920s sponsor efforts to establish links with Arab workers, opening a club in Haifa that helped organize strikes by Arab carpenters and tailors and publishing (with subsidies from the Zionist Organization) an Arabic-language newspaper, *Ittihad al-'Ummal* (*Workers' Unity*). These projects were implemented by a small group of Jewish unionists who were committed to the idea of Arab-Jewish class solidarity, both because they believed that Jewish workers would ultimately benefit if Arab workers organized and raised their wages, thereby reducing the Arabs' competitive edge and increasing employment opportunities for Jews, and because of their internationalist convictions. But the Histadrut leadership was never very enthusiastic about such activities and found it increasingly hard to justify the continued allocation of funds and staff for this purpose, especially during periods of economic crisis and high Jewish unemployment. Moreover, many Zionist labor leaders, especially those from Hapo'el Hatza'ir, explicitly rejected the idea of organizing Arab workers as not only futile but counterproductive.

The most cogent critique was advanced by one of Hapo'el Hatza'ir's preeminent leaders, Hayyim Arlosoroff, in a 1927 essay entitled *On the Question of Joint Organization*.[29] Arlosoroff claimed to be undertaking a strictly realistic and rational economic analysis, unencumbered by the ideological considerations which, he argued, had distorted the thinking of Ahdut Ha'avoda leaders like Ben-Gurion. Arlosoroff accused the latter of trying to theorize out of existence the real, everyday and essentially national conflict between expensive Jewish and inexpensive Arab labor, and rejected the notion that joint organization could significantly raise the general wage level in Palestine and thus facilitate the struggle for Hebrew labor by making Jewish workers more competitive with Arab workers.

To support his argument, Arlosoroff cited the case of South Africa, where as he saw it conditions most closely paralleled those that confronted the Jewish workers in Palestine. In a labor market dominated by cheap African and Indian labor, the white workers there had organized to exclude nonwhites from skilled and supervisory jobs. In effect, Arlosoroff argued that the Jewish workers in Palestine had to do something similar, by continuing the struggle for Hebrew labor and by devoting their resources and energies to developing their own exclusive modern high-wage economic enclave that would coexist with the low-wage Arab economy. Joint organization was thus at best a pipedream and a waste of resources, and at worst it might even intensify Jewish-Arab enmity.

In principle, Ben-Gurion and Ahdut Ha'avoda continued to reject this approach, insisting that the fate of the Jewish working class in Palestine was inextricably linked to the fate of the Arab working class. "It is inconceivable," he told a party congress in the fall of 1926, "that we should succeed in entrenching ourselves in Palestine, in creating a large Jewish working class, in putting masses of Jews to work and in building a lasting Jewish economy if, alongside the Jewish worker and the Jewish economy, there will remain the downtrodden and unorganized Arab worker, who will compete with us and see us as his enemy."[30] But in fact Ben-Gurion and his party were moving toward acceptance of Arlosoroff's position, a shift first signaled by articles in Ahdut Ha'avoda's organ *Kuntres* advocating what might be called a policy of "benign neglect" toward Arab workers.[31]

Soon thereafter the Histadrut launched what would be the first of a new series of large-scale campaigns to compel Jewish citrus farmers in the moshavot to dismiss their Arab workers and hire Jews instead. Most immediately, the Histadrut's rationale for renewing the struggle for Hebrew labor in the moshavot was the urgent need to relieve very high unemployment among urban Jewish workers in a period of economic crisis. The campaign also served to deflect Jewish workers' anger and frustration about their plight onto Arab workers and, by heightening intra-Yishuv tensions, it enhanced the power and authority of the labor-Zionist leadership and the institutions it controlled as against competing sociopolitical forces in the Yishuv.[32]

The shift in Ahdut Ha'avoda's attitude toward the Arab working class was made explicit at the Histadrut's third congress, held in July 1927. Among those greeting the congress was Ahmad Hamdi, present as an observer on behalf of a number of Arab workers who wished to join the

Histadrut—but not on any terms. "When the Arab workers approach the Jewish workers," Hamdi told the congress, "their enemies say, 'You are Zionists!', and others say, 'You are communists!', and the Arab worker is confused." As he saw it, the Jewish workers' movement as such was not Zionist, and that distinction should be made explicit so that there would be no divisions between Arab and Jewish workers.

Hamdi's remarks seem to have aroused Ben-Gurion's ire, and he did not mince words. While welcoming any sign of "awakening" among the Arab workers, he wanted Arab workers and intellectuals to understand that "the Jewish workers in Palestine *are* the Zionists."

> They came to Palestine only thanks to Zionism. Had it not been for Zionism there would not be 30,000 organized workers in Palestine, there wouldn't be this congress, nor the Histadrut nor the movement which will raise the [Arab] worker from his degradation. And I want to tell you, Comrade Hamdi, what the workers' Zionism is. You say that the Arab worker is oppressed and his situation is degraded. But our situation is even worse. If the Arab worker works in difficult conditions, the Jewish masses don't even have the opportunity to work. . . . This is Zionism: the return of the Jewish masses to Eretz Yisra'el and their transformation into a productive work force on which the country's future regime will be based.

That is why, Ben-Gurion argued, the effendis were fighting Zionism: this new force would put an end to their plundering and exploitation. "You, the Arab workers, must not harness yourselves to the cart of the effendis in their war against Zionism," he warned. "We believe that to the extent that our strength in the country grows, so will grow the strength of the working class which Hamdi and his comrades hope will liberate this country."[33]

So the equation had now been reversed. The organization of Palestinian Arab workers and Arab-Jewish working-class solidarity were no longer seen as the guarantors of Zionism's success, as essential elements in the struggle to secure the basis for a large and powerful Jewish working class in Palestine and to defeat the effendis' opposition to Zionism. Instead, it was the strengthening of the Histadrut and the development under its guidance of a growing and increasingly self-sufficient Jewish economic enclave that would enhance the ability of Arab workers to win higher wages, improve their working conditions and living standards, and by organizing themselves become a significant force in their own community. From this perspective, the Jewish working class would still play the leading role in "awakening" the Arab workers, but it would be a much less direct role than initially envisioned, entailing not so much the commitment of significant human and material resources to the organization of Arab workers as the provision of an attractive model of a well-organized and powerful labor movement that Arab workers could emulate, along with the creation of a high-wage sector that would help raise wages throughout the Palestinian economy.

From this point on, Arab workers ceased to play a central role in labor-Zionist discourse; they were in a sense no longer needed, except in certain sectors, and the script was rewritten so as to eliminate their part in the labor-Zionist version of the drama of Jewish redemption in Palestine. In the 1930s and 1940s the Histadrut would sponsor small-scale efforts to organize Arab workers through a Jewish-run auxiliary, and the issue of cooperation would remain important in those sectors where Arabs and Jews worked side by side. But it was now usually a question of relations between separate Arab and Jewish unions, and the Histadrut would have to contend with a small but active Palestinian Arab trade union movement that was unequivocally anti-Zionist. The question of Arab-Jewish class solidarity and joint organization receded in importance, becoming the concern mainly of the smaller left-Zionist parties along with a few dedicated but isolated individuals within MAPAI, which as a party had come to see this whole arena as a minor side-show useful mainly for propaganda purposes.

Even as Arab workers and the Arab working class receded into the background, however, a different figure, that of "the Arabs of Eretz Yisra'el," loomed ever larger in the perception of labor Zionists. Palestine's Arab population, more or less *en bloc*, came to be seen as a force to be reckoned with, mainly because Arab resistance to Zionism grew stronger and more violent in the 1930s and could no longer be ignored or attributed to the machinations of a few schemers. This reorientation was hastened by a country-wide explosion of violence against Jews in August 1929, rooted in growing Arab popular resentment of perceived Zionist encroachment and touched off by an increasingly politicized dispute over rights of access and worship at the Western Wall in Jerusalem's Old City.

This outbreak of violence shocked Ben-Gurion into a reevaluation of Palestinian Arab nationalism. He now began to tell his colleagues that Zionism had to come to some agreement with the Arab national movement, indeed with the very same "effendis" whom he had denounced for much of the previous decade as bloodsucking exploiters with whom the Jewish workers could have nothing in common. This was a marked departure from labor Zionism's steadfast denial of the existence of a distinct Palestinian Arab people and the legitimacy of its national movement, though not (as future events would show) an irreversible one. This shift also implied abandonment of the notion, reiterated by Ben-

Gurion and his colleagues in the 1920s, that the Arab working class was the Zionist project's natural ally, and hence the loss of both a rationale for, and an interest in, organizing those workers under the Histadrut's tutelage.

LABOR ZIONISM AND ITS OTHERS

Much of labor-Zionist discourse in the period I have been discussing echoes themes found in colonial discourse generally: the denial of rational agency to the indigenous population, the definition of that population as lacking the characteristics of a nation and therefore as not entitled to self-determination, the attribution of anticolonial and nationalist sentiment and action to the malign influence of a small minority of self-interested "outside agitators," the conception of the land as empty because not settled or utilized in familiar ways, the sense of European civilizing mission, and so forth. But labor Zionism's deployment of these themes was made distinctive, and perhaps especially complicated, because they were couched in the language of socialism, class struggle, and international working-class solidarity.

As a nationalist project, labor Zionism posited ethnic/national boundaries between the Jewish and Arab working classes in Palestine, and more generally between Jews and Arabs, boundaries that often involved elements drawn from colonial discourse. But because labor Zionism simultaneously conceived of itself as a working-class project, as part of the international socialist and labor movements, it also posited valid boundaries along class lines. It therefore had to find ways of managing the noncoincidence of those sets of boundaries. The discursive contestation within labor Zionism over this issue was bound up with the articulation over a period of several decades of those exclusionary practices that shaped the Yishuv and later Israeli society in crucial ways, practices that were themselves grasped as the basis not only for Jewish working-class formation and solidarity but for the realization of the Zionist project in general. These Jews in Palestine recreated themselves as workers by securing or creating jobs as workers but also by endowing their acts with both working-class and nationalist meaning, a process of self-definition in which, at a certain stage, Arab workers played an important role. Here as elsewhere, working-class formation (indeed, class formation in general) was as much a discursive as a material process.[34]

It was in this sphere of Arab-Jewish interaction, and more generally in the way in which elements of a national project, a colonial-settler project and a socialist or working-class project interpenetrated, that much of Zionism's specificity can be located. Comparison of Zionism with other contemporary cases of European colonization and settlement would, I believe, bear out this claim by showing how very different political, social, and economic outcomes can be traced back to (for example) varying labor market strategies as well as differing discourses with regard to the indigenous population, which in the case of Palestine can in turn be related to the labor-Zionist movement's struggle for hegemony within the broader Zionist project.

It is of course true that the realization of labor Zionism's vision of a "normal" Jewish society could be attained only *after* the establishment of a sovereign Jewish state in Palestine, as civil and interstate warfare led to the displacement of most of the Palestinians who lived in what became that state's territory and a massive influx of poor Jews (mainly from Arab countries) ensued. Yet labor Zionism's relative success in excluding Arab workers from the Jewish sector and constructing as self-sufficient a Jewish enclave as possible in the four decades before 1948—a strategy bound up with the articulation of certain visions of itself and of Arabs—was a key factor in making partition and Jewish statehood in most of Palestine possible. Many of the institutions most characteristic of Israeli society through the 1960s also took shape in the context of these specific practices and representations. After 1967, of course, things would change again, as Palestinians from within Israel but especially from the occupied West Bank and Gaza would come to dominate the lower ranks of Israel's working class, a development that was closely connected with the decline of labor-Zionist hegemony.

The historical evolution of the Yishuv cannot therefore be understood unless it is seen as in large measure shaped by its complex interactions with Palestine's indigenous Arab population. This influence was manifested in such arenas as economic relationships, but also in the meanings with which actual or imagined interactions between Arabs and Jews in Palestine were endowed and which exerted a significant influence on the various (often conflicting) strands of Zionist thought and practice. Thus for labor Zionism during a crucial formative stage, Arab workers, represented in certain ways, could be both the enemy to be mobilized against, for economic as well as political ends, and the ally, the passive junior partner, whose presence could be read as a guarantee of, and a justification for, the Zionist project.

Until quite recently, Zionist historical narratives tended to treat the indigenous Arab population of Palestine as largely marginal, as an external obstacle that Zionism had to overcome. My analysis here suggests, however, that the Palestinians were not only in some sense always present, both materially and discursively, but that they exerted a constitutive influence on Zionism as it developed in Palestine. Whether they seemingly conformed to the roles they were assigned in Zionism's stories about itself or whether their actions intruded upon and altered those stories in unexpected ways, Palestinian agency always registered itself on, and helped shape, the Zionist project. Like other colonized peoples, and like subaltern classes, subordinated minorities (including, of course, Jews in Europe and elsewhere), and women, the Palestinians were often rendered invisible or marginal in the discourses and historical narratives of the powerful. They were nonetheless always "there."

NOTES

For their helpful comments on earlier versions of this essay, I would like to thank the participants in the weekly seminar of Princeton University's Shelby Cullom Davis Center for Historical Studies at which it was first presented, and especially David Abraham (my discussant) and Natalie Zemon Davis, the center's director at the time.

1. Edward Said elaborates on this theme in *The Question of Palestine* (New York, 1980).

2. For specific references and a fuller discussion of the literature, see my "Railway Workers and Relational History: Arabs and Jews in British-Ruled Palestine," *Comparative Studies in Society and History* 35, no. 3 (July 1993): 601–27.

3. See ibid., and also my "'We Opened Up the Arabs' Minds': Labor-Zionist Discourse and the Railway Workers of Palestine, 1919–1929," *Review of Middle East Studies* 5 (1992): 5–32. I will be exploring relations between Arab and Jewish workers, trade unions, and labor movements in Palestine during the mandate period (1920–48) more fully in a forthcoming book.

4. See *Kitvei Nahman Syrkin* (Tel Aviv, 1938–39), 1:1–59.

5. Borokhov's collected works have been published in Hebrew as *Ketavim* (Tel Aviv, 1955).

6. "Our Platform," *Ketavim*, 1:283.

7. "Zionism and Territory," *Ketavim*, 1:148.

8. "Our Platform," *Ketavim*, 1:282–83.

9. Early Zionists, especially left-Zionists, often used the term "Hebrew" (*'ivri*) instead of "Jew" (*yehudi*) to refer to themselves and their project. This was an expression of labor Zionism's denigration and rejection of Diaspora Judaism, which it associated with statelessness, powerlessness, and passivity, as well as a way of identifying themselves with the (suitably mythologized) Hebrews of ancient times, depicted as a "normal" people deeply rooted in, and exercising sovereignty over, their own land.

10. For a study of early debates over this issue, see Yosef Gorny, "Ha'ideologiya shel kibbush ha'avoda," *Keshet* 10, nos. 37–38 (1967–68): 66–79.

11. The articles were published in the Po'alei Tziyon organ *He'ahdut*, nos. 16–17.

12. In Yehuda Slutski, "MPSI beve'idat hayesod shel hahistadrut," *Asufot* 1, no. 14 (December 1970): 135.

13. In *Jewish Labour* (London, n.d.), an English translation of a pamphlet published in Hebrew in 1932, especially pp. 18ff.

14. *Kuntres* 211 (March 27, 1925); emphases in the original. These remarks were made with reference to a strike at the Nesher quarry and cement factory at Ya'jur (Yagur) near Haifa, launched by the Histadrut to compel Nesher's Jewish owner to get rid of his Egyptian quarry workers, employed through a Palestinian contractor, and hire only Jews.

15. Michael Shalev has aptly characterized this as a "practical alliance between a settlement movement without settlers [i.e. the Zionist Organization] and a workers' movement without work." Cited in Gershon Shafir's very important book *Land, Labor and the Origins of the Israeli-Palestinian Conflict, 1882–1914* (Cambridge, U.K., 1989), p. 198.

16. See the protocols of the Histadrut's founding congress published in *Asufot* 1, no. 14 (December 1970).

17. Minutes of the executive committee of the Histadrut, at the Archive of Labor and Pioneering, Lavon Institute for the Study of the Labor Movement, Tel Aviv (hereafter AL), December 30, 1920.

18. On the Palestinian working class and labor movement, see inter alia Musa al-Budayri, *Tatawwur al-haraka al-'ummaliyya al-'arabiyya fi filastin* (Beirut, 1981); Rachelle Taqqu, "Arab Labor in Mandatory Palestine, 1920–1948" (unpublished Ph.D. diss., Columbia University, 1977); Salim al-Junaydi, *al-Haraka al-'ummaliyya al-'arabiyya fi filastin, 1917–1985* (Amman, 1988); and 'Abd al-Qadir Yasin, *Ta'rikh al-tabaqa al-'amila al-filastiniyya, 1918–1948* (Beirut, 1980).

19. Ben-Gurion's formulation drew on an important essay, *The Arab Movement*, published earlier that same year by Ben-Tzvi.

20. These theses were first published in the Ahdut Ha'avoda organ *Kuntres* 91 (August 1921), and later in a collection of Ben-Gurion's articles, essays, and speeches on "the Arab question," *Anahnu veshcheineinu* (*We and Our Neighbors*) (Tel Aviv, 1931), pp. 61–62.

21. *Kuntres* 106 (January 1922).

22. *Have'ida harivi'it shel ahdut ha'avoda*, Ein Harod, May 1924, in Aharon Cohen Archives, Hashomer Hatza'ir Archives, division 90/box 1/file 2. See also *Kuntres* 172.

23. *Kuntres* 166 (March 28, 1924).

24. *Haifa* 15 (April 30, 1925).

25. AL 208/14a, central committee of the Union of Railroad, Postal and Telegraph Workers to the executive committee of the Histadrut, November 30, 1924; and *Haifa* 6 (January 1, 1925): 43–44.

26. Interview with Avraham Khalfon, AL, Center for Oral Documentation, January 29, 1976.

27. See, for example, Bulus Farah, *Min al-'uthmaniyya ila al-dawla al-'ibriyya* (Haifa, 1985), pp. 42–43. Farah was a Palestinian railway worker and later a communist activist.

28. I explore relations between Arab and Jewish railway workers more fully, and discuss the Palestinian side of the relationship more extensively, in "Railway Workers and Relational History" and "'We Opened Up the Arabs' Minds.'"

29. Published in Tel Aviv (in Hebrew).

30. *Anahnu veshchneinu*, pp. 131–33.

31. For example, Yosef Yudelevitch, *Kuntres* nos. 280 and 282 (November 1926).

32. On these Hebrew labor campaigns, see Anita Shapira, *Hama'avak hanikhzav: 'avoda 'ivrit, 1929–1939* (Tel Aviv, 1977).

33. *Anahnu veshchneinu*, pp. 138–39.

34. I make this argument at greater length in "Imagining the Working Class: Culture, Nationalism and Class Formation in Egypt, 1899–1914," *Poetics Today* (forthcoming 1994).

CHAPTER 9

The Postcolonization of the (Latin) American Experience: A Reconsideration of "Colonialism," "Postcolonialism," and "Mestizaje"

J. JORGE KLOR DE ALVA

THE PAST AS PERFECT FOR THE TENSE PRESENT

In the first version of this essay I argued that colonialism and postcolonialism are (Latin) American mirages because, while seeming to name the actual processes that have taken place in the hemisphere, neither term is applicable to the set of policies and practices that defined the historical experience of nonindigenous Latin or Anglo America.[1] Here I want to develop my arguments more fully in order to respond to criticisms provoked by my thesis, to link the thesis more closely to some pertinent issues being raised today in cultural studies and world history, and to underline the ways in which the (Latin) American experience has been "colonized" after the fact.

Although the study of colonialism has enjoyed a long and prolific life in the West, a series of political, intellectual, and demographic transformations in the late twentieth century—including decolonization, poststructuralism, ethnic "resurgence," and the large-scale immigration of non-Europeans into former metropoles—have been accompanied in the United States and Europe, among other places, by an updated academic interest in the nature of colonial practices, the so-called critical study of colonial discourse,[2] and what has come to be labeled "postcoloniality."[3] Numerous progressive scholars, many in search of redemptive agendas to fill the vacuum left by the collapse of Marxist programs, have been busily attempting to discover the cultural integrity and subversive presence of the oppressed in both Western narratives of the "colonial" enterprise and in the indigenous responses or, for those working on topics closer to our time, in the record of the confrontations between "peoples of color" and the dominant "white" communities. In the meantime, even as some nationalist movements continue to grow, at home and abroad, by imposing rigidly defined concepts of ethnoracial identity, many "organic" or "native" intellectuals, swept up by the poststructuralist/postmodern tide, are struggling to promote ethnic unity and pride while paradoxically attempting to make out, in the transnational ethnoscapes of their respective communities, nonessentialized patterns of collective identity.

These conflicting initiatives form part of the contemporary debates among both ethnic fundamentalists (of the Right and Left) and anti-essentialists over the meaning of nationalism (and nation), the morality of separatism (and ethnic cleansing), and the political utility of ethnic resurgence movements.[4] It is precisely in the context of this highly contested terrain of identity politics that I wish to make a case for the importance of reconsidering the meanings and histories of colonialism—the category of experience commonly assumed to have set global hybridization in motion since the early modern period—postcolonialism, and *mestizaje*, the supposed genetic/cutural hybridity itself.

The term "colonialism" has been applied in dissimilar ways at distinct times to a variety of experiences so that today it signifies something different depending on whether the user is referring, for instance, to sixteenth-century Latin America, the eighteenth-century Caribbean, nineteenth-century India, or twentieth-century Africa. However, although the historical circumstances of these areas, and others such as Indonesia and the Philippines, have been quite different, two principal motivations, at least in the twentieth century, seem to have led to the common use of a single term to designate such widely disparate sets of experiences. The first of these is primarily intellectual: the need to understand the exploitation of one corporate group by another, as found in each of these regions, as a form of patterned behavior determined primarily by nonlocal forces. In this case, I question the popular but misleading conflation of imperialist expansion with colonial dependence.

The other motivation for the use of the label is primarily political. The rubric "colonialism," especially in the past century, carries with it much political and moral freight. For many it implies unjust social asymmetries, human abuses, and moral imperatives, which call for acts of resistance, demands for justice, and struggles for liberation. As moral constructs, colonialism, colonized, colonizer, and (today) postcolonial can be applied to an infinite variety of referents in order to characterize these as unjust or righteous, or as worthy of redemption or opprobrium. Not surprisingly, the labels "colonial" and "postcolonial" have been adopted by many subalterns and their supporters, however imprecise the term may be to the formers' historical antecedents and present political circumstances (and interests?). In short, colonial/ism, like any collective label, has a history that points to the ways in which its existence is an effect of its location in the webs of power/knowledge to which Foucault,[5] among others, drew our attention.

Mestizaje/hybridity is an even more complicated notion. Among others, Ann Stoler and Irene Silverblatt[6] describe mestizaje as an internal frontier in a perpetual state of creation and decomposition. The constant flux is the logical result of sexual interactions—between and among the colonizers and the colonized—which continually create peoples whose progressively more ambiguous social identities and unstable political loyalties challenge every attempt to impose rigid cultural boundaries around them. It is also the result both of the need on the part of those in power to fix and order all social sectors, especially those least susceptible to the rulers' self-disciplining practices, and of the need of subalterns either to make ambiguous the circumscribing boundaries in order to escape them or to make them firm in order to promote opposition through a presumed sense of commonality. In either case, the cultural constructions of mestizaje have been and are a critical object of colonialism's attention. Different forms of colonialism, therefore, are likely to create differing senses of mestizaje. Therefore, mestizaje as genetic and cultural hybridity has not only stood for a variety of processes and states at different times and places throughout the world, but even in Latin America the term and its cognates have never had an unequivocal sense. Its meanings have always been politically charged and these have always held a culturally ambiguous place in nation-building projects throughout the American hemisphere. It could not be otherwise.

In most places the original inhabitants, who had logically grouped themselves into separate cultural units (i.e., ethnicities), all but disappeared after contact, wiped out physically by disease and abuse, and, later, genetically and socially by miscegenation, and, lastly, culturally by the religious and political practices of the Europeans and their mixed progeny. Even in the regions where native peoples survived as corporate groups in their own greatly transformed communities, especially in the "core areas" of Mesoamerica and the Andes, within two to three generations they were greatly reduced in number and politically and socially marginalized from the new centers of power. Thus, those who escaped the orbit of native communities but were still the most socially and economically proximate to these dispossessed peoples could be expected to distance themselves from them wherever possible. Along with the *criollos* (initially those of European origin born in the Americas), these transitional/"border" figures, whom we today call "mestizos" following the early usage of Spanish Americans who wished to distinguish mongrels from themselves, denigrated most things considered "Indian" by identifying them with whatever was considered base, deviant, menacing, or powerless. Throughout much of the core of Spanish America, however, a glorified memory of local precontact states, especially in the eighteenth- and early nineteenth-century criollo imaginations, led numerous members of the controlling sector, who nonetheless disparaged the mixed and unmixed descendants of the original natives, to identify themselves as legitimate heirs of the ancient indigenous empires.[7] And in our century, claims to authentic ethnic (and moral) precedence over the conquering Europeans, made by those who identified themselves as *indígenas* (indigenes), transformed Amerindian symbols and cultural practices into critical building blocks for many nation-building narratives defining modern nation-state identities.

Each historian, each period's social thinkers, then, have revealed their relation to the central question of national identity by how they have dealt not just with the "Indians" but especially with the hybrids. Before the twentieth century, with minor exceptions, their often morally ambiguous texts sought to locate either the historical trajectories of the indigenous Americans (prior to contact) or those of the neo-Europeans (the criollos and the Americanized *peninsulares* [the Spanish born]). Until our century they generally left Africans, mulattos, and mestizos as mere furtive, subversive presences at the margins and interstices of either the "civilized" white society or the "barbarian" Indian world. Yet it is the mestizos, mulattos, and their mixtures, coming into their own in this century as political forces, that have brought to the fore in our days the fundamental question of the nature of colonialism and postcolonialism as categories/practices of contestation and as mechanisms critical to the constitution of new collective identities. And it is by attempting a rhetorical and conceptual pruning of the dense thicket of assumptions about how these categories came to be that this essay seeks to contribute to the clarification of this important question. But to begin this task, a word on postcolonialism/postcoloniality is in order.

In place of the impossible task of rigorously assessing here the significance of the currently popular applications to U.S. Latinos and Latin American mestizos/mulattos of the label "postcolonial," my analysis of this phenomenon begins by arguing that the "post" of the would-be Latin American postcolonials is either a misnomer or does not require an antecedent colonial experience as a referent. From a modernist perspective the term is a misnomer because the postcolonial condition, strictly speaking, has yet to occur among those who became colonial subjects of the empire and, later, of the nation-state: the tribute-paying indigenous peoples who remained in corporate "Indian" communities. Likewise, those indigenes, who are descended from peoples not colonized in the past and who remain at the far economic margins of the nation-state (as, say, members of the "Fourth World"), are also not postcolonials in any significant sense. Lastly, and most important, the racially mixed *castas*, or castes, many of whose members identified with (and were part of) the *gente de razón*—the elites who triumphed in the wars of independence—although they were mainly subalterns, were never colonial subjects, as I will attempt to show below. In effect, one of the main points I would like to suggest is that a subaltern condition, rather than a postcolonial one, best describes the nineteenth- and twentieth-century subjectivity of both indigenes who did not reside in indigenous communities and the nonelite racially mixed groups. Subaltern, a term popularized in the 1980s by a community of South Asian scholars, is used here—as it is among them—"as a name for the general attribute of subordination in . . . society whether this is expressed in terms of class, caste, age, gender and office or in any other way. . . . [All the while recognizing] that subordination cannot be understood except as one of the constitutive terms in a binary relationship of which the other is dominance, for 'subaltern groups are always subject to the activity of ruling groups, even when they rebel and rise up.' "[8]

From a postmodern/poststructuralist perspective I agree with Fernando Coronil,[9] among others, that postcoloniality does not need to follow from an "actual" colonial condition. Indeed, as Gianni Vattimo points out in his *The End of Modernity*,[10] "post" here means more than merely one thing after another. The dismissal of the modernist view of history as a linear (teleological) process, the undermining of the foundational assumptions of linear historical narratives, and the rejection of essentialized identities for corporate units lead to a multiplicity of often conflicting and frequently parallel narratives within which postcoloniality can signify not so much subjectivity "after" the colonial experience as a subjectivity of oppositionality to imperializing/colonizing (read: subordinating/subjectivizing) discourses and practices. That is, we can remove postcoloniality from a dependence on an antecedent colonial condition if we tether the term to the poststructuralist stake that marks its appearance. That, I believe, is the way postcoloniality must be understood when applied to U.S. Latinos or Latin American hybrids.

What I propose, then, is that postcoloniality can best be thought of as a form of contestatory/oppositional consciousness, emerging from either preexisting imperial, colonial, or ongoing subaltern conditions, which fosters processes aimed at revising the norms and practices of antecedent or still vital forms of domination. In short, postcoloniality is contained both within colonialism, as a Derridian supplement completing the meaning of this antecedent condition of dependent, asymmetrical relations, *and* outside of it, by its questioning of the very norms that establish the inside/outside, oppressor (colonizer)/oppressed (colonized) binaries that are assumed to characterize the colonial condition. Thus, postcoloniality as a category of social existence is in some real sense an artifact of poststructuralist forms of analysis that emphasize identities as effects of power, rather than fixed entities or "imagined communities" bounded by supposed sets of common traits, sentiments, and practices.[11] This approach to the nature of identity, as nonessential, contingent, and negotiated, is served by taking into consideration the "strategic essentialism" advocated by Gayatri C. Spivak,[12] wherein essentialism is postulated solely as a pragmatic maneuver in the broad field of identity politics. My argument, therefore, is that in strategically assuming a postcolonial "essence," as many indeed have done, subaltern Latin American mestizos, U.S. Latinos, African Americans, and others similarly situated have created common identities that have been used (with mixed results) to advocate collectively for common needs. But these "strategic" identities, however useful they may be among some of the West's subalterns, should not be confused with the ones non-Western postcolonial subjects must develop if they are to overcome the very different legacies of their tragic colonial pasts.[13] With these distinctions in mind, I now turn to my central thesis.

THE CENTRAL THESIS: PART I

As is well known, the original populations of the Americas began to suffer a devastating demographic collapse on contact with the Europeans. With minimal exceptions this population loss, and the accompanying decline in the autonomy of the former city-states and local communities, had the effect, by the late sixteenth century, of restricting to the periphery of the nascent national polities those who continued to identify themselves (or who were identified) as the descendants of the contact-period natives. As a consequence of the subordinate condition attendant on this state of disempowerment, the greater part of the mestizos, whose numbers grew quickly as a result of progressively more widespread European-Indian-African sexual relations, removed themselves wherever possible from the Indian communities of their mothers (the usual case) and migrated to the cities or towns, or the Spanish-dominated countryside, where they replaced or augmented the otherwise decimated indigenous labor force. The identification of superior status with Spanish cultural objects and practices and the proximity of the mestizos in question to the higher-ranking, lighter-skinned Spanish-speakers (many themselves also mestizo) led a large number of them to attempt to fashion their potentially ambiguous ethnic selves primarily (and perhaps at times exclusively) after local versions of European or criollo models of cultural behavior. Together with Euro-Americans—most of whom, by the eighteenth century, were of mixed genes although culturally criollo—and some Europeans (commonly called peninsulares), these substantially Westernized mestizos, in subaltern and elite sectors, made up the bulk of the forces that defeated Spain during the anti-imperialist, nineteenth-century wars of independence.

The newly independent countries, under criollo/mestizo leadership, sought to construct their national identities through three sets of maneuvers. First, they promoted regional Euro-American practices and outlooks (often embellished with indigenous beliefs, foods, words, and technologies), promulgated the use of Spanish (even at the cost of losing the local notarial services provided by speakers of indigenous languages), and supported Christianity and the church, to the extent it did not get in the way of liberal/republican agendas. Second, they sought to weaken local "Indian" identities (and increase the criollo economic base) by disestablishing indigenous corporate communities (and lands), hoping that as a byproduct anticriollo sentiments would disappear with the indigenous villages. Third, they championed, among all social and cultural sectors (excluding the corporate native communities and slaves, wherever these remained), the sense of a new, common ethnicity woven out of a supposed shared experience of mestizaje/criollismo and/or imperial exploitation (depending on the region, the date, and the degree of inclusion sought).

This close identification of the postindependence national cultures with their European templates and the different global circumstances of their immediate postindependence period, make evident that the Americas, in contrast to many Asian and, later, African societies, did not need to undergo an experience of decolonization, although the negative effects of political and economic devastation left most of the new countries in a state of violent turmoil. The above conditions lead me to assert that it is misguided to present the preindependence, *non-Indian* sectors as colonized; it is inconsistent to explain the wars of independence as anticolonial struggles; and it is misleading to characterize the Americas, following the civil wars of separation, as composed of postcolonial states. In short, the Americas, as former parts of empires which, after a series of civil wars, separated themselves politically and economically, but not culturally or socially, from their metropoles, cannot be characterized as either another Asia or Africa; Mexico is not another version of India, Brazil is not one more type of Indonesia, and Latinos in the United States—although tragically opposed by a dominant will that has sought to exclude and disempower them—are neither like Algerians in France, Pakistanis in Britain, or Palestinians in Israel.

In light of our current knowledge of the imperial processes in the Americas, and today's insistence on ethnicity and race over (but not to the exclusion of) economics and class, as critical components of social cohesion and as determinants of socioeconomic experience, and as a result of our recently heightened awareness of the negotiated/constructed nature of ethnoracial identity, "colonialism"—with its taxonomic emphasis on binary relations and its analytical focus on the exploitation of "natives" by nonsettlers—is not a particularly useful concept for making sense of the complex political and cultural processes that engendered postcontact and postindependence American societies. It follows from all of the above that where the use of "colonialism" is not warranted, neither "decolonization" nor "postcolonialism"—as opposed to "postcoloniality"—can be considered germane in any manner other than metaphorically. But given the entrenched use of "colonialism" to define the postcontact American experience, the term and its supposed referents should be problematized and put in question. That is what I now propose to do.

HYBRIDITY/MESTIZAJE AS FOIL AND FETISH

Colonialism, especially among contemporary subaltern peoples in the former metropoles, is a strategic label: identification with the experiences connected with it can serve to mobilize insiders and distinguish them from outsiders. As such, on the metaphoric level any discourse on colonialism today can be interpreted as a manifestation of colonialist history and cannot be divorced from the history of colonialism.[14] On another level—the political—colonialism refers not only to a class of dependent international relations of domination but, as in the case of contemporary Puerto Rico, to a way of speaking about intra/interstate relations in which ethnic differences are asymmetrically ordered. Because the histories of the world's colonialities have been until recently usually articulated as a clash between opposing cultures, yet almost everywhere colonialism has included the presence of hybrids, collaborators, mediators, and—on all sides—multiple holders of political, social, cultural, and moral authority, any attempt to deconstruct colonialism as a binary relation must do the same for ethnicity. Here, I believe, is where mestizaje comes in. As an ideological construct it is as much a strategy in the cultural wars of the past and present as are the ethnic labels, such as "Indian," which peoples have imposed on themselves or have had imposed on them. And, like them, it is itself subject to deconstruction.

The category "Indian" (or indigene, indigenous, or native) has always been problematic. Precontact peoples in the Americas identified themselves primarily by their ethnic ("national") names. "Indian" and similar labels, which erased or hid the cultural pluralism that existed behind the collective nouns, were imposed on the many contact-period groups because ethnic differences among them were considered irrelevant to the settlers' agendas. They were also imposed to simplify imperial administrative procedures and/or to weaken feelings of loyalty toward the corporate non-European communities. In the case of the Nahuas (the so-called Aztecs and their Nahuatl-speaking neighbors), it was not until the nineteenth century that the term *indio* was used by them to refer jointly to the descendants of the precontact Americans.[15] Today the use of "Indian" and its cognates, by me here or anyone elsewhere, is itself a part of current colonial and colonializing discourses. However, the fact that a transformative demographic catastrophe can be attributed to some original inhabitants of the New World, but not to those mestizos who also can claim to be natives, makes "indigenous" sound essentialized when applied to the Americas. It is this quality of seeming essential that has made the term so entrenched in our speech and in our historical constructions in spite of its being an ambiguous misnomer. No place else in the world does the polarization of "indigenous" on one side seem as natural as an ethnic descriptor. In fact, many places in the world, such as Bali or the Caribbean after the sixteenth century, do not have a way to articulate a category that could have any force to it of "indigenous." This fact alone differentiates the so-called colonial discourse of Latin America to those other forms, including, in a peculiar way, to that relevant to British North America where "Indians" could only disappear physically, and not by being transformed into new hybrids.

Unlike Anglo-Americans, then, whose ancestors, although they reproduced with both Native Americans and Africans, bypassed mestizaje as a social category,[16] the non-"Indian" sectors in those areas of Latin America formerly densely settled by precontact peoples came, by the twentieth century, to define themselves culturally, if not always genetically, as mestizo. Although mestizaje had many detractors, especially throughout the nineteenth century, as presently taught in the schools, frequently proclaimed by politicians, and commonly expressed in the popular media, the most important effect of colonialism in Latin America is said to be the genetic and cultural mixing that came to constitute the assumed distinct "ethnicity" of almost every one of the American nations that had a large native population at contact. The core of this mestizo narrative of ethnonational identity, although meant to be unique for each new sovereign state, is repeatedly intoned in similar terms by most Latin American politicians and scholars. For instance, in his comments on the nature of Ibero-American cultural identity, presented at a conference on the topic, Filoteo Samaniego Salazar, representing Ecuador's Ministry of Foreign Relations, concluded his description of the devastation suffered by the natives of the Americas, as follows:

> from the confrontation . . . also resulted felicitous and positive matters: first of all, the coexistence [*convivencia*] of those dominating and the dominated ended in the present racial mestizaje . . . with its impressive mix of America, Europe, and Africa.
>
> First, during the three centuries of the Iberian colonial process, later, as a consequence of the subsequent migrations of the nineteenth and twentieth centuries . . . colonial life [was] a "historical theater" of mestizaje, an instigator of "hybrid cultures or mestizo societies." And the Laws of the Indies ended up being mestizo . . . along with the Baroque Christian arts developed during the colonial period, which counted primarily on a native labor force to produce the temples and ornamentation required by the God of the West, and [mestizo also] the religion itself, "which united the orthodoxy of the Christian principles with the nostalgia of the prohibited myths."
>
> Unifying and diversifying destinies, are those of the race, religion, arts, Christian architecture, cities . . . , and, in conclusion, of the sister languages generalized throughout Iberoamerica which came to the New World . . . and facilitated and embellished the forms of comprehension with the manner of speech of Cervantes and Camoens. . . .
>
> Iberoamerica is . . . a historico-cultural unity, while being a diversity of attitudes and behaviors, which precisely at the same time that they give it contradictions, conflicts, and dramas, [they give it] a unique way of being in the world, impossible to produce in other continents.[17]

In this brief passage we have a catalog of all the critical elements of the official narrative on mestizaje in twentieth-century Latin America: (1) it is the felicitous product of the coming together of the various "races"; (2) drawing from all of these, it became the essence of American reality; and (3) it is the unique expression of a synthesis that (through a revealing contradiction) culminates with Christianity, the Spanish language, and the embrace of the West. This paradoxical final point alludes to the common but problematic application of the concept of mestizaje as both a euphemism for the overwhelming presence of Western influences and as an excuse for eliding/dismissing that which is indigenous. This latter phenomenon is represented by Jorge Salvador Lara who, as president of the National Academy of History of Ecuador, observed during the same gathering that:

> The encounter between [Indians and Spaniards] originated . . . episodes of pain, blood, cruelty . . . exploitation and death; but one cannot deny that there were also cases of comprehension, collaboration, and even love. And

from this encounter . . . emerged a new ethnocultural reality, that of Iberoamerica, to which we belong . . . ; a new [ethnocultural] reality leading the way to progress and evolution for humankind, constituted with a personality [that is] proper to the great current, already universal, of Culture called Christian and Western, with Greco-Roman-Jewish roots which appears to be—to judge by its growing and unrestrainable expansion, development, and progress—the one that advances on the true path of History.[18]

With this we can witness one of the major maneuvers of the ideology of mestizaje: it pits the West against the rest—leaving mestizo America firmly in the former camp.

In these often repeated examples it hardly bears pointing out that the culmination of the colonization of the Americas is believed to be the near disappearance of the indigenes and their world, *not into a brew of Indian-Spanish composition, but into the cultural vortex of the West.* However, some important circumstances have led to the existence of opposing views. For instance, unlike independent India after the loss of Pakistan in 1947, the United States after the battle of Gettysburg in 1863, Canada after the forming of the Confederation in 1867, and Brazil after it declared its independence in 1822, the postindependence Spanish overseas provinces in the Americas failed to create a feeling of nationalism that could override the distinct senses of ethnicity and regional micropatriotism that constituted them. Fragmented culturally and politically at both the interregional and local level, the former imperial holdings fractured into new states, each of which was unable to conflate the sense of nationhood and that of statehood. Once more, hybridity and pluralism, fueled by self-interested prejudice, discrimination, and racialist forms of exclusion, stood in the way of unity.

Not surprisingly, the popular (rather than elite) discourse of many Latin Americans, and of those Latinos in the United States who condemn the "Occidentalizing" narratives,[19] have included a similarly reductive and equally strategic discourse on mestizaje. Some brief examples will suffice.

Seeking to facilitate a collective response to the Mexican-American communities' economically depressed and socially marginalized condition, in the 1960s the Mexican-American ethnic resurgence movement was set in motion as a collective "Chicano" identity began to be woven, among other things, out of the manipulation of primarily "Aztec" symbols.[20] Some particularly creative Chicanos, searching for common roots that could unite the disparate communities, identified Aztlán, the mythical point of origin of the Aztecs, with the U.S. Southwest and consequently—in the imagination of many in the barrios and schools—

symbolically transformed all Chicanos (in spite of their distinct mestizo/ethnic heritages) into the most authentic of Mexicans: the direct descendants of the original Aztecs. This new ethnic myth, which linked all Mexican Americans to the *colonized* descendants of the precontact Nahuatl-speaking peoples, was articulated as a decolonizing discourse in 1969 when, at a conference held in Denver, the participants applauded the authors of the *Plan Espiritual de Aztlán* as the latter affirmed, in the forceful rhetoric of the day, that,

> *[W]e*, the Chicano inhabitants and civilizers of the northern land of Aztlán from whence came our forefathers, reclaiming the land of their birth . . . *declare* that . . .
>
> Aztlán belongs to those who plant the seeds, water the fields, and gather the crops and not to the foreign Europeans. We do not recognize capricious frontiers on the bronze continents. Brotherhood unites us, and love for our brothers makes us a people whose time has come and who struggle against the foreigner "gabacho" who exploits our riches and destroys our culture. With our heart in our hands and our hands in the soil, we declare the independence of our mestizo nation. We are a bronze people with a bronze culture. Before the world, before all of North America, before all our brothers in the bronze continent, we are a nation, we are a union of free pueblos, we are *Aztlán*.[21]

In *Heart of Aztlán*,[22] published after the exuberant phase of the Chicano movement had lost its supportive sociopolitical climate and its contestatory edge, New Mexican novelist Rudolfo Anaya sought to capture metaphorically the redemptive force of this powerful political fiction of displacement and substitution when he wrote, "[Chicanos] are the fruit of the people who wandered from the mythical land of Aztlán, the first people of this land who wandered south in search of a sign." That sign, a sacred heart, was meant to signal the transformation of the (very real) political geography of Aztlán into a subjective space that all Chicanos were said to carry in their blood wherever they might go. In effect, by the late 1970s all of the United States, in the imagination of cultural—as opposed to political—nationalists, was ripe for a Chicano-cum-indigenous reappropriation.[23]

Nevertheless, throughout Latin America, as hinted at by the aggressive Occidentalizing exclamations quoted above, this Indianizing stance would be immediately rejected by the millions of indo-mestizos who have gone to great extremes—abandoning native languages, dress, eating habits, religions, and sometimes kin—to deflect the negative consequences of being identified as *indios*. Even in the United States, in order to counter Anglo-American claims to being the sole foundation of this country, many Mexican Americans in 1992—less willing to lay claim to

an indigenous side in their ancestry—focused on Columbus quincente-
nary commemorations that exalted their "Hispanic" heritage and emphasized Latino contributions to the development of the nation. Still,
Latinos who did this ran the risk of being severely criticized. Antonia
Hernández, then president and general counsel of the Mexican American Legal Defense and Education Fund, accused the Hispanicizers of
hypocrisy, claiming that it was wrong for Latinos to be "so proud of our
Spanish roots without really looking into what our Spanish roots did to
our other half."[24] Echoing this sentiment was Carlos Muñoz Jr., a Chicano professor who in an editorial attacking the five-hundreth anniversary and the use of "Hispanic" as an identifying label for Latinos,
remarked that, although "we cannot . . . deny . . . that Spanish culture
and language are part of us, . . . collectively we must remember from
where the vast majority of us came, in terms of our indigenous racial and
cultural origins."[25]

Here, then, we can observe a second major, but now contestatory,
maneuver of the ideology of mestizaje: it seeks to undermine the negative influence of the West by pitting it against an indigenous rest, this
time locating mestizo America firmly in the latter camp.

The chameleonic nature of mestizaje—Western in the presence of Europeans, indigenous in the native villages, and Indian-like in contemporary United States barrios—is its crucial characteristic.[26] It is the result
of the ambiguous ethnic spaces that appeared in the wake of the demographic decimation of the indigenes, the introduction of enslaved Africans, and the extensive immigration of Europeans. In three centuries
these spaces were filled by an astonishing variety of hybrids, then called
"castas," who, given that those considered "Indians" had little status
and few resources, manipulated their equivocal identities as a tactic in
the struggle to survive in a world dominated by Europeanizers and their
sympathizers. As is well known,[27] by the time the wars of independence
came, with minor exceptions, it was the mestizos, mulattos (often
slaves), Euro-Americans, and Europeans who fought. Therefore, as I
noted above, these contests were in a very real sense civil wars fought
among criollo/hybrid kin, friends, acquaintances, and competitors and,
of course, peninsular enemies. They were not anticolonial struggles for
liberation pitting fragmented, though equally subordinated, colonized
indigenes against privileged indigenous collaborationists and their foreign superiors—as was generally the case, for instance, in India, Africa,
and much of Southeast Asia. They did not result in a postcolonial aftermath that called for postcolonial critics, anxious to rid the masses of
metropolitan influences, to decolonize the minds, souls, and practices of
the indigenous communities. Quite the opposite. The wars of independence not only entrenched the Europeanized criollo sectors in the seats

of power but were prelude to even more devastating civil wars that by the late nineteenth century had nearly destroyed all but the most isolated and resilient of the surviving indigenous communities. How, then, did the Americas come to be spoken about as colonized? And what has been meant by such a characterization?

THE CENTRAL THESIS: PART II

Colonialism, colonization, colonize, and colony are all terms that have varied in meaning over the years and, of course, at any one time these categories have simultaneously referred to a number of practices, events, and things. It is therefore problematic to speak about colonialism as ever meaning one thing. However, this term, and its cognates, have not carried the same semantic weight or been "suspended in the same webs of signification" at each step in their career. Distinguishing among different forms of settlement, acts of political domination, and circumstances of economic dependency, therefore, calls for both the use of more precise terms than has been common practice and for the tracing of semantic genealogies. This is the task before us.

For instance, as historians of early modern Spain and the Americas know, European settlement and political sovereignty in the Western Hemisphere were driven primarily by imperial purposes (which, of course, included economic interests by both the Crown and its supporters). Although frequently ruthless and often destructive (sometimes unintentionally, as in the case of the introduction of lethal germs and viruses), the initiatives had, especially at the official level, a Europeanizing or, in the mind-set of the time, a universalizing ideology. Although not applying to slaves (or only in part, as in the case of Christianization), at some formal level the laws of the Indies sought to promote liberty and equality to the extent these were compatible with the imperial mission to "civilize," "Christianize," and economically exploit. There was no rhetoric of colonialism attendant on these efforts or on those that followed independence in the early nineteenth century.

In contrast, historians of the nineteenth- and twentieth-century non-European Eastern Hemisphere recognize that European settlement throughout this vast area was meager, except in South Africa, and when it took place in significant numbers it was usually focused on places where there were few original natives to contest the intrusion, as in Australia and New Zealand. For the most part, European rule was driven by economic interests and the ideology of liberty and equality was, especially under Protestant monarchs, little concerned with Europeanizing, Christianizing, or, except rhetorically, civilizing. Only marginal official effort was expended on these latter concerns while much went into the systematic exploitation of overseas natives and resources. By the late nineteenth century, as I describe below, the language of colonialism and imperialism became current. And, logically, the anticolonial struggles, by the colonized who, regardless of ethnicity, traced their sense of place only to the local areas they inhabited, were replete with the rhetoric of colonialism and liberation—the very rhetoric that would dominate post-colonial discourses.

It is this latter rhetoric on colonialism, one that identifies the processes primarily with economic servitude, social subjugation, and cultural denigration, instead of with notions of resettlement and the development and spread of new ethnic forms, even under extremely asymmetrical competition, which I believe best applies to the tribute-paying survivors of the devastating epidemics, who continued to live as "Indians" in corporate indigenous communities. It applies as well, perhaps, to the freed descendants of enslaved Africans and indentured Asians, in the Caribbean, Brazil, and other tropical lowland areas on both the Atlantic and Pacific coasts, who were unable to "pass" into the hybrid sectors that were free to pursue their own economic goals or who came to control the reins of government, commerce, and social fashion. Other subalterns, although not under foreign control and nominally free to reside and occupy their time where and as they pleased, were not because of that spared the same or worse sorrows associated with exploitation, abuse, and degradation. Quite the contrary. It is well known that the Americas, from the initial contacts to the present, have been the site of the oppression, torture, rape, and murder of men and women of every physical shade and social caste. In short, because I believe that "colonialism" applies only to some sectors does not mean that all others groupings were left untouched by imperial and local forms of oppression.

Other related points I would like to make include the following. First, the American polities, as imperial overseas provinces, were ultimately subordinated to their respective European monarchs and councils, and nearly all of the extractive sectors and the transatlantic trade, for instance, were dependent on European financial and commercial interests. And although the Americas provided the Old World with important foods and great quantities of precious metals, which greatly transformed the economies and demographies of Europe and its subsequent colonies, the indigenes, first, and the castas, later, were the voluntary or involuntary recipients of even more widespread and penetrating European-introduced forces, such as new technologies, languages, religions, ideologies, diseases, and genes, which had the effect of irreversibly altering their cultures, bodies, and personal lives.

Second, rather than as a result of imperial policies or colonialist machinations, most of the sociopolitical and economic transformations in the indigenous communities were made possible by two nonideological European exports: diseases and genes. Today we know that the rapid depopulation had the effect of removing most of the political and military opposition, weakening the economic and cultural competition (and interindigenous community links), promoting destructive interethnic alliances, and creating new social fields susceptible to immediate Westernization or profound isolation.[28] Within fifty years after the arrival of the Europeans the islands of the Caribbean lost nearly all of their original inhabitants; and most scholars agree that by the beginning of the seventeenth century the indigenous population of central Mexico, for instance, had declined to just over a million.[29] Meanwhile, by the 1640s non-Indians may already have numbered nearly half a million.[30] Although by the second half of the seventeenth century the native populations began to ascend once more, the growing numbers of criollos and castas were such that by the end of the eighteenth century those who identified themselves as non-Indians in Mexico may have represented nearly 40 percent of the population. Though still a minority, throughout Latin America these nonetheless came to control the trades and all the large cities where political and economic power was concentrated, and they owned most of the major commercial establishments, plantations, haciendas, and estancias. The tribute-paying, non-noble indigenes resident in Indian towns, whom I consider to be the colonized subjects, with minor exceptions, served primarily as unskilled laborers and providers of foodstuffs for the mines and for the criollos and castas in the cities. This scenario, with a few adjustments, repeated itself frequently across the formerly densely settled areas of most of the Americas.[31]

Third, the first part of my argument rests on the assumption that the mixing of peoples that began in the sixteenth century became by the end of the seventeenth century a social and cultural commonplace. The ideology of mestizaje—by whatever name—this ultimately created, just before the wars of independence, was promoted by some as a form of nationalism in the nineteenth century as the fissuring of Spanish America into separate countries led to growing micropatriotism. In the case of Mexico, the idea of mestizaje would later be reinforced by the populist anti-Spanish (and anti-French) revolts that culminated with the indigenist-oriented revolution of 1910. By the early 1900s Mexicans on both sides of the border and most Latin Americans from the Andean and Middle American countries were each busily reinscribing their collective histories as epic journeys that charted the course of national unification from an origin of warring peoples. Tragic beginnings, when ethnically and politically distinct native peoples were homogenized into "Indians" and mercilessly transformed into Spanish subjects, became triumphant ends, as contrasting "races" fused into a cultural and genetic mixture expressing a heretofore unknown and, to some, "cosmic" mestizaje. In short, mestizaje, like "Aztlanism" was for Chicanos, is the powerful nation-building myth that has helped link dark to light-skinned hybrids and Euro-Americans, often in opposition to both foreigners and the indigenous "others" in their midst. And it has been effectively used to promote national amnesia about or to salve the national conscience in what concerns the dismal past and still colonized condition of most indigenous peoples of Latin America.

Fourth, in British North America, I suggest, colonialism hardly took place at all. As is frequently observed, in the Thirteen Colonies Europeans merely transplanted themselves to what most, echoing Locke, considered to be empty lands. The Native Americans they encountered, those who survived the epidemics, were killed if they defended themselves aggressively or physically removed if found peacefully obstructing the goals of the Christians. As is to be expected, a few Europeans—those who refused to don the weighty mantle of parochial identity or who were reluctant to keep within established cultural bounds (and norms)—interacted intimately with the locals, trading and reproducing with them. But in the main, few natives were left in the role of mestizos or the exploited colonized; instead, the overwhelming majority, an unnecessary pool of labor for independent Euro-American farmers and craftspersons, saw their communities reduced to impoverished and ignored enclaves.

Not unlike the Spaniards, transplanted Europeans in the English overseas territories of North America succeeded in setting out to create another version of the societies they left behind. Like any other dominion under the political sovereignty of the king, the early Americans were subjects of the monarch and consequently their politics were dependent—drawing their legitimacy from the peaceful recognition of imperial authority. When they sought to remove that dependence, they bid their relatives, friends, and other fellow English speakers a violent adieu, and that was as non-English as the separation scene got. With minor exceptions, neither the Native Americans nor the enslaved Africans profited much from this civil war. As with Latin America, this contest, fought primarily for economic autonomy though necessarily under the guise of political liberation, was not an anticolonial struggle for independence but rather a separatist struggle waged between two parts of the same imperium. Those who fought and won were descended from those who had come and conquered, and their cultural and ideological model, for the most part, remained the imperial motherland. Despite recent claims to the contrary by some Iroquois nationalists, there was no space here for the inclusion of formerly independent then conquered indigenous nations to assert their precontact culture as a model or to wage a war against the empire to reclaim their sovereignty. As with the criollos of Spanish America, the Euro-Americans of British America fought a civil war and won. The descendants of the original inhabitants and the enslaved Africans and their progeny, remained equally colonized, enslaved, or marginalized, but in any event, peripheral to the power struggles being waged within the imperium by Europeans and neo-Europeans.

As this last point makes evident, my argument rests on something more than the rise in the cities and countryside of a highly Westernized mestizo/mulatto hybrid population whose unsettled collective identities ideologues would eventually reinscribe in contemporary nationalist imaginations as *essentially* American. It is also based on what colonialism once meant, what it has come to signify, and on whether the latter meanings are relevant to the preindependence Americas. It is to these questions that I now turn.

HISTORICAL SCHOLARSHIP AND THE POLYSEMY OF COLONIALISM

Colonial Latin America, the charter epoch for most nationalist historians and the testing ground for much speculation about the nature of culture contact and change, has long been studied from a variety of theoretical and methodological perspectives.[32] Prior to the 1960s Latin American colonial history was overwhelmingly dedicated to self-congratulatory studies of conquests and wars; the implantation of European institutions, beliefs, and practices; and the personalities that were believed to have made it all possible. In each case the narrative centered on the ineluctability of the West's march across the American terrain. This was "colonial" history as the term had been understood since Romans sent veteran soldiers to distant lands, that is, as the settlement of one's own people outside the "fatherland." Although the word was rarely used by those who traveled to or wrote about the Americas, this was the primary meaning of the term among the Spaniards before the late eighteenth century. The jurist Juan de Solórzano meant no more by it than that when in 1629 he used it in his *Disputatio de Indiarum Iure* in reference to the laws and political organization of Spanish America.[33] It took until the late eighteenth century for the Spaniards to begin to speak of the Indies as "colonias." And then, according to John Elliott,[34] it was as a result of a borrowing from English usage during the reign of the Bourbon monarch, Charles III.

As is to be expected, in what concerned writings on the conquest itself, the main protagonists and sole victors were the transplanted Spaniards. With regard to the achievements of the colonial societies, a nationalist emphasis on criollos is evident as early as the second half of the sixteenth century. By the next century, unlike the case of British North America, where the colonists were extremely preoccupied with the affairs of Britain, creole culture claimed an overwhelming proportion of criollo/mestizo attention. Thus, after independence, regional nationalisms, based on these local creole concerns, helped give shape to the distinct state histories.[35] Finally, by the early twentieth century, Mexicans, for instance, embroiled in a revolutionary war of class and caste, began to pioneer a radically revisionist history that would permit them to reread their past as the continuous evolution of a mestizo society, "a bronze race," leading the way to a mestizo state. They thereby initiated the erasure of the sense of colony as a transplanting of Europeans by shifting the meaning to one of foreign control—a control overcome only when mestizos (frequently substituting for Indians) arose to wrest control from the always at-all-times "foreign" criollos and Spaniards.[36]

This shift in meaning is not subtle. By signifying control rather than transplantation or resettlement, the concepts connoted by "to colonize" now opened up a fundamentally new set of readings concerning the Spanish presence in the Americas. But not all availed themselves of the opportunity. The early colonial period, in what concerns interethnic encounters, was and continues to be viewed by many "traditionalist" Latin American scholars as the struggle between the triumphant forces of the civilized and the obstructionist opposition of the barbarians. In an ironic twist these authors proclaim ethnoracial and cultural fusion even while asserting—with their detailed descriptions of the many ways in which European institutions, customs, and beliefs replaced those of the natives—that displacement was the rule. This nationalist view is founded on what some of its proponents, such as Samaniego Salazar and Salvador Lara, identify as a "mestizo" perspective: one that feels for the violence suffered by "its Indians" while emphasizing the ways in which the nascent transplanted communities set themselves off from their European roots by creating a colonial variant that gladly integrated native vocabulary, foodstuffs, and genes.[37] For these scholars, I suggest, colonialism has primarily to do with the settling of Europeans elsewhere, with the processes of economic subordination being a necessary but secondary affair, and colonial reality is reconstructed more as a way to be European in America—with cultural variations inspired on American themes and indigenous practices—than as an unsettling period of profound two-way hybridism.[38] The absence of the indigenous communities in any role other than as foil, victim, or parody was promoted by the assumption, based primarily on the study of official records, that little of the indige-

nous world remained viable in the face of Christianity, European technology, and Spanish political and managerial superiority.

   In contrast to this substitution perspective is a vision, common since
the nineteenth century, that took official pronouncements as evidence
that colonialism was the deployment of European political (rather than
ethnoracial) control over non-Europeans. It was founded on the idea—
very fashionable today—that colonialism was about the maintenance of
distinctions through the creation of differences, the propagation of exclusions, and the exercise of cultural controls. Its conceptual framework,
relying especially on the assumed successful implementation of the (un-
feasible) imperial order to maintain the so-called "Indians" and Spaniards in separate "republics," nourished the belief that Spanish-Indian
contacts in the native sectors were rare, limited to some *encomenderos*, a
handful of friars, and occasional intermediaries.[39] Consequently, these
writers argued that the indigenous communities in the sixteenth century
had generally remained isolated from the social and cultural centers of
Spanish American life, and, therefore, much of their culture had survived intact. This perspective mistakenly assumed that, in the main, cities remained Spanish and the countryside was exclusively indigenous.
Beginning in the 1930s anthropologists studying remote indigenous
communities gave support to this conclusion, especially as they interpreted a wide variety of unfamiliar cultural practices and beliefs as being
of precontact vintage, what some still consider to be the social result
of closed, corporate, inwardly oriented, and relatively static cultural
forms.[40]

   In Mexico, the Indianist-Marxist thrust following the revolution of
1910 promoted a more radical perspective based on a version of this
continuity model. In particular, given their anti-Spanish bent, those
who promoted this position argued that the closed native communities
had come to maintain themselves strategically segregated as a defense
against the continuous exploitation of the Spaniards.[41] But before the
New Left's version of the New Social History of the late 1960s turned
this perspective inside out, Charles Gibson,[42] by focusing on the Indian
side through Spanish documents, showed how Spaniards, in order to
succeed in establishing their colonial framework in New Spain, had to
adapt it to the antecedent native structures and institutions. In effect,
Gibson uncovered how the triumphalist—*conquistador*/conquest—perspectives of the past were incorrect to the extent that the successes of the
Spanish institutions (e.g., the encomienda, rural parish, and Spanish-
style Indian town) depended on their adaptation to Nahua ways, rather
than vice versa. James Lockhart, following on the Gibsonian tradition,
but now relying on Nahuatl documents to reconstruct the Nahua side of
the colonial period, as others had long done in Mexico,[43] has argued

convincingly that many precontact institutions, practices, and beliefs continued, not in isolation, but slowly adapting themselves to the changed circumstances precipitated primarily by the demographic collapse and close similarities between Nahua and Spanish modes of organization.[44] Thus, at least in the case of sixteenth-century central Mexico, for which extensive Nahuatl documentation exists, today's indigenous histories have come full circle by putting in question the analytical relevance of such categories as "conquest" and "colonization" as these terms are ordinarily used in the relevant literature; that is, as rubrics for forms of direct and indirect domination of one people by another. After all, the lives of most natives during this early period changed little as a consequence of the Spanish presence. Not until their worlds began to collapse as the epidemics ravaged their communities would colonialism take place, in the sense of domination and control by "foreigners."[45]

In effect, without suggesting, as Sir John Seeley did for Britain, that Spain's American empire happened "in a fit of absence of mind,"[46] I would argue, along with Lockhart and in the light of the experience of the most fully documented area of the New World, that Spain in the Americas created an empire by chance. It was, I believe, an evolving result of the political and demographic opportunities provided by the rampant epidemics that made possible not only the unexpected fall of the Aztec capital, Tenochtitlan, but the subsequent reorganization of the Nahua city-states, and, with this, the exploitation of the natural resources through indigenous labor. In the absence of precious metals and large pools of available native workers the Americas of the early sixteenth century would have been irrelevant to most Europeans except for truly zealous missionaries. Later in the century, however, the resettlement—"colonization"—of the Americas by Spaniards began in earnest. By then the Nahua communities had become productive, "colonized" (dominated and exploited) preserves of laborers serving primarily the growing masses of Spanish/mestizos in the cities, towns, mining centers, and radically transformed country estates. This would now reflect colonization in the style of the British and, to a great extent, the French in late nineteenth- and early twentieth-century Africa. That is, what we had, in all three cases, were small enclaves where capitalist penetration had a direct impact on the people, broader areas where they were only indirectly connected with the international markets (e.g., as producers of food for the miners), and a much larger number of people who were affected only to a degree by the production and payment of tribute, which lasted throughout the entire period of metropolitan control. But even so, the main forms of exploitation continued to be local, focused primarily on families, lineages, and the corporate community; although, in the case of Spanish America, as opposed to sub-Saharan Africa, Western practices and beliefs encoded in Christianity also penetrated deeply at this local level in dramatically transformative ways.

Before turning to the late 1960s readings of colonial experiences, as made possible by the new focus on colonialism as control and exploitation, a few words on how these came about may be useful. Modernity, the five centuries of European global expansion and control, started to unravel when the worldwide process of decolonization went into high gear at the end of World War II. By the mid-1960s the responses to the antihegemonic global disorders then at hand, the effects of misguided development schemes, the diffusion of improved health techniques, and the availability of cheap transportation triggered the unprecedented movement of populations from periphery to core, especially from the previously colonized areas to their official or de facto past metropoles.[47] The nationalist movements, fed by a resurgence of previously inchoate or suppressed ethnic identities and aspirations, the strong criticisms of colonialism during the postwar years, and the need to explain continual poverty and unrelenting subordination, centered discussions about colonialism on the effects of economic domination. It was in this context that the study of colonial Latin America matured in what I prefer to call the "late modern" period.

Although much "traditionalist" colonial history continued to be written, in both Latin America and the United States, by the end of the 1960s the anticolonial intelligentsia had managed to put across the colonial experience as the only category that was appropriate to the historical moments in question. Thus the New Left wing of the New Social History and the Marxist and neo-Marxist political economists—with their strong emphasis on quantitative studies of economic and social history, on bottom-up rather than top-down vectors, and their commitment to mode-of-production narratives as the situs of any discourse on colonialism—began to equate this process with the rise of dependency and underdevelopment, which was either the result of imperialist politics of economic (monopoly) control[48] and/or of peripheralized integration of the colonies into a nascent modern economic world-system.[49] This not only opened the way to the study of colonialism as something other than the control by one group over another inhabiting a separate territory, but as primarily a relation of dependency and as an economic process in which culture is neither fundamental nor determinative but rather epiphenomenal. That is, they managed, for the most part, to elide (or deemphasize) the cultural and social differences between whole sets of peoples—mestizos, indigenes, settlers, sojourners—by privileging the (especially, political) colonial experience above all others and making that a dominant process of unity despite the cultural and social distinctions. This, of course, paralleled and often copied what anticolonial intellectuals in colonized areas had in fact done when they successfully managed to speak on behalf of all people who, though different, were under colonialism's common situation. In this reading "indigenous" peoples, "mestizos," and other subalterns were merely aggregates united under historically constructed labels for subject populations and, as such, were not a central problem for understanding colonialism.

Anthropologists, of course, were less committed to this latter view and sought to articulate the relevance of these distinct aggregates.[50] Nonetheless, with these anticolonial intellectual trends came a series of related social science models that deemphasized the significance of ethnoracial politics and nationalist concerns within metropole-colony relations. When for many scholars colonialism was stripped of its interethnic/interracial composition, and was transformed into primarily a dependency relation leading to underdevelopment of one side (the "periphery") as a consequence of overdevelopment on the other (the "core"), internal colonial models became, de facto, the most effective explanation for poverty within and outside of the metropoles.[51] Stanley and Barbara Stein, for instance, were quite willing to identify the relation between Portugal and western Europe in 1500 as one of "colonial dependency."[52]

Lastly, as I noted earlier, since the late 1970s a profound shift in the character of the study and conceptualization of colonialism has taken root in a number of scholarly communities in Europe, the United States, and Latin America. The transformation has been primarily from a structural perspective, emphasizing economics and politics, to a poststructural one, where the accent is on detailed analyses of local phenomena while highlighting cultural, discursive, and power formations in everyday life. It is also a change that calls for undermining the transcendent pretensions of totalizing theories and narratives, uncovering and rejecting essentialist assumptions, and criticizing reductive dichotomies and binary characterizations.[53] In the introductory section I addressed, in part, some of the significances of these changes to my argument. I will now expand on these.

FROM SIXTEENTH-CENTURY IMPERIALISM TO NINETEENTH-CENTURY COLONIALISM AND BACK

The questions that originally drove my interest in reconsidering the utility of the category "colonial" and the concepts "colonialism" and "postcolonialism" led me to ponder whether the concepts, theories, and methods used to study colonialism in the second half of the twentieth century were inspired by or resulted from research into the colonial experiences of the nineteenth and twentieth centuries. If so, is an error being committed when scholars apply tools and categories of analysis developed in the twentieth century for understanding British colonialism, especially in India and Africa, to make sense of the experiences of sixteenth- to eighteenth-century Latin America? Although I have already made reference to relevant aspects of the history of the terms in question, I now want to be more precise in order to clarify my reading of the shifts in the categories of analysis that took place as we moved both between the Americas and the "Old World," and between the sixteenth to eighteenth centuries and the last two hundred years.

I will begin at the philological starting point. The Latin word *colonia* (from *colonus*: tiller, farmer, cultivator, and later settler in a new [formerly uncultivated] country),[54] originally meant "farm," "landed estate," or "settlement" (the latter meaning is still common in present-day Spanish). This sense expanded with the Roman Empire to include "a public settlement of Roman citizens [especially veteran soldiers] in a hostile or newly conquered country, where they, retaining their Roman citizenship, received lands, and acted as a garrison." This definition comes close to the one Solórzano had in mind when writing his *Política Indiana* in the seventeenth century. However, since the fourteenth century the word had evolved a similar but more generic sense, and even before Solórzano used it in its modern application as the planting of settlements in newly discovered lands, the word was so employed by early sixteenth-century Latin and Italian writers, such as Peter Martyr.[55] However, near the end of the nineteenth century (1883), reflecting the then current predicaments imperial Britain faced, especially in South Asia and South Africa, "colony" began to be defined in England as "a community which is not merely derivative, but which remains politically connected in a relation of dependence with the parent community."[56] I take this definition—an excellent example of the self-interested nature of the changing meanings of these terms—and those that follow, from the *Oxford English Dictionary* because its genealogies of the terms in question evince the history of British colonial/imperial involvement with Ireland, India, and South Africa—the very spaces that I claim provided the conceptual examples for the (mis)understanding and (mis)labeling of the so-called colonial American situation. Because the very distinctions it makes between "colonialism" and "imperialism," which are owed primarily to the contested condition imperial Britain encountered in already colonized South Africa, are critical to my overall argument, I now turn to these.

It is significant for my thesis that the word "colonial" does not appear in a written source in English until the late 1700s, and "colonialism" must await the middle of the following century. Indeed, "colonialism" as used to refer to a colonial system or principle is not attested, as far as the *OED* is concerned, until 1886, when the jurist Albert Venn Dicey, arguing for English control in opposition to Irish rule, smugly asserted that "English colonialism works well enough."[57] This very contemporary use was repeated with precision in 1889 when, in an attempt to distinguish between colonialism and imperialism, an article in the *Standard* of May 20 noted that "there are three competing influences at work in South Africa . . . Colonialism, Republicanism, and Imperialism." The last term, used as "the principle or spirit of empire," is attested for the first time in 1881, when W. R. Greg critically accused some political maneuver of taking place "under the pretext of imperialism" that is, not under the pretext of expanding the power of the Crown within the realm, but having in mind the desire to expand Britain's control over foreign territories. At that time "imperialism"—a term the South African situation called for to describe British intents over an already colonized territory—had only just been coined. Thus the *Western Gazette*, on January 15, 1895, observed that " 'The Expansion of England'—. . . gave a decisive impulse to what may be called in the slang of the day, 'the new Imperialism.' " Three years later, on the eve of the Boer War, the *Daily News* (May 28, 1898) carried a story that confirmed this novelty when a too trendy someone was reproached for having made use of "the tawdry nickname of Imperialism." By 1899 the emblematic and often polemic term "imperialist" was commonly understood to mean an "advocate of 'imperialism' [in the sense noted above] in British or American politics."

Although much needs to be said about the problematically linked ideas of nationalism and patriotism at this time,[58] at stake in our discussion are the distinctions, or lack thereof, then being made between "imperialism" and "colonialism." South Africanist anthropologist Robert Thornton argues[59] that Hobson's magisterial *Imperialism*[60] was responsible for eliding the difference between colonialism and imperialism, which had the effect of leading Lenin to do the same, since the latter relied on this text—which drew heavily from the South African experience—for his own analyses. From him it followed that much twentieth-century theorizing on the subject continued the conflation of the two processes although the predicament in South Africa, which pitted Dutch and British practices, as the *OED* attests, sharpened the distinction between the two related practices and ideologies.

I take the distinction, in what concerns the difference between Spanish America prior to independence and the situation in South Africa at the end of the nineteenth century, to be about a process of colonial (old sense) settlement and imperial expansion of Spain in the New World, transformed, with the dismantling of the city-state governments due to the demographic collapse, into the colonizing (new sense of control and domination by outsiders) of the radically transformed and now disempowered indigenous communities. The practices of power and ideology of imperialism—aimed at transforming the New World into a Catholic New Spain—are here meant to be contrasted to the "pathetic retreat"[61] represented by policies and techniques of "mere" colonialism whose mundane goals were essentially to extract labor and resources from the indigenous communities. When the wars of independence came, long after the rise of a very diversified mestizo world had come into existence—composed of criollos or *gente de razón*, who by this time were mostly well-to-do hybrids, and the castas, mostly Afro-Indo-European subalterns—a set of mestizos, who functioned as mediators between the powerful and the weak, joined with those others powerful enough to be identified as criollos, and together they allied themselves with recently arrived peninsulares whose fundamental interests rested in the Americas. Together they fought their counterparts, primarily other criollos, mestizos, and peninsulares, whose interests were best served by a continuation of imperial power. Many indigenes and enslaved Africans got caught up in the frays—the latter forming a significant force in the struggles in the Caribbean and surrounding areas—but, for the most part, the so-called Indians, genetically pure or mestizo, who continued to live in their corporate communities continued in the colonized state that characterized them before the wars.

Evidently, the specific modern and critical connotations given in the twentieth century to colonialism and imperialism and other interrelated terms come from the experiences of the non-Spanish European colonial powers, Britain in particular, as a consequence of their primarily Old World experiences, especially in India and Africa. As already noted, the changing meanings of colonialism reflect the continually transforming nature of the processes to which they allude. Without exaggerating the too neat and now mostly outdated distinctions between "Old" and "New Empires," popular among many historians until recently, it bears underlining that prior to the Treaty of Paris in 1763—an obviously not arbitrary date—colonialism (as process, principle, and category) was something quite distinct from what it became between the 1760s and the 1870s, when British naval power made possible a global empire. It bears remembering, by the way, that it is during this period of rising British world hegemony, fueled by industrial capital, that the so-called postcolonial age of Latin America takes place. This colonialism, focused primarily on Asia, differed in significant ways, as could be expected, from what came to be called the "new imperialism," found between the 1870s and the beginning of World War I (1914–18), when Africa was

extensively colonized and Britain began to face new challengers seeking
their own colonies. And, of course, the latter phenomenon was unlike
the colonialism of the interwar period (1914–39), at which time colonial rule was at its height with approximately 85 percent of the world
colonized or under neo-European control. Lastly, following World War
II decolonization quickly accelerated and colonialism shifted in meaning
once more as the Left—now fully committed to the use of "colonialism"
to describe any economically or politically dependent condition—re-
christened the predicament of the newly liberated but economically devastated nations as "neocolonialism." (I should add that it is this
problematic postcolonialism, taking place as the British lose hegemony
and capital is internationalized under a U.S. umbrella, which has given
us the current ideology, history, and symbolism that support both subaltern studies and the rhetoric of postcoloniality.)

The Old versus New Empire schema is difficult to use without qualifi-
cation because extensive and revolutionary forms of economic and social
displacement had already taken place in many areas, especially throughout the Americas, prior to the mid-eighteenth century. These had resulted from a number of factors, chief among which were the continuing
need for labor following the preceding decimation of indigenous populations, the rise of plantations in the tropical regions and the accompanying forced movement of large numbers of enslaved peoples, the shifts
in production in numerous places from local subsistence systems to regional commercial agriculture aimed at serving the cities, towns, and
mines, the introduction and broad distribution of livestock, and the successful penetration of both secular organizational and Christian missionization practices and beliefs. Nonetheless, after the second half of the
eighteenth century even more profound and more widespread altera-
tions in the economic role of the overseas provinces took place, thus
helping redefine profoundly the nature of colonialism.

Before this time the metropoles, Spain and England included, were
primarily buyers and consumers of colonial products. Therefore, although complexes of outlying supportive networks existed around productive centers, the metropoles' interest in overseas provinces was primarily focused on the creation and maintenance of enclaves capable of
generating raw materials or precious merchandise. Thus, Portugal, like
the Dutch, needed only forts and trading posts to have an empire. Afterwards, especially after the onset of the Industrial Revolution, the colonies were reorganized as markets and consumers of the goods now
manufactured in the metropoles. These changes implied a shift from a
fundamentally mercantilist perspective to one focused on commerce, industry, and commercial agriculture. In addition, after the 1760s, spices,
sugar, and slaves became less important in comparison to the demand

for either raw materials for industry or food for the industrial areas. All this triggered a radical reconceptualization of colonialism, especially as "colonies" now called for the creation of new needs, the establishment of new loyalties, and the imposition of new identities, hence, irrevocably transforming—more than ever before—the most public and intimate recesses of native life.

Thus, before the 1760s the metropoles primarily exploited areas throughout the world that supplied precious metals, slaves, and tropical products; trading posts and forts dominated the non-Spanish colonies; and European settlers established colonies chiefly along the coasts or in areas previously densely settled by indigenous populations, as was common in the core areas of the Americas. Though all of this was extremely disruptive, most social groupings not fully devastated by epidemics, forced labor, or migration continued their everyday lives following social and economic practices established prior to contact with the Europeans. This is especially the case for those largely self-sufficient communities which, based on subsistence agriculture and domestic production, were poor markets for manufactured goods. But after the mid-eighteenth century European colonies, as was the case for Spanish America under the Bourbons, began to be fundamentally modified to serve the interests of the industrializing core. Among the most profound transformations—many of which, although already familiar in the core areas of Spanish America, had originally been undertaken to satisfy more the interests of transplanted Europeans and castas than those of the metropole—were changes in land ownership and tenure, the implementation of forced and coerced wage labor for commercial agriculture and mining, the introduction of monetary payments, the reduction of home industry, and the restriction of production and exportation by natives. These dramatic reversals encouraged the numerical growth of a cooperative local elite, often mestizo, the spread of rigorous and invasive administrative techniques, the deployment of more effective policing mechanisms beyond those formerly imposed by Roman Catholic missionization, and the systematic imposition of the culture, language, and religion of the dominant powers on those who had previously remained at the margins of these influences.

When indigenes in Latin America were first colonized, this post-mideighteenth-century stage was not yet in place; nevertheless, as I argued above, it is the second and third stages of colonialism, those found in the nineteenth and twentieth centuries, that have defined for Marx, Marxists, and other critical scholars the meanings of colonialism and imperialism in the twentieth century. In turn, these new meanings have been retroactively and anachronistically applied to Latin America. Meanwhile, some critical differences exist not only between one phase of colonialism and another, but between the experiences in the Americas and the Old World. Among the most critical distinctions are the following. The sixteenth-century Spanish mercantilist empire was interconnected primarily by precious metals, leaving the extractive process as the central point of contact. The encomienda, later the repartimiento, and later still the hacienda were focused on local or, at most, regional integration. The metropole, therefore, was generally secondary as a continuing cultural force. All this took place in the light of massive immigration of European settlers coupled with a precipitous decline in the indigenous population. Consequently, by the second half of the sixteenth century widespread intermarriage and cross-cultural mating were generating new ethnic communities without significant metropole connections. Unlike later forms of colonialism throughout the world, in Latin America, especially in those areas where indigenous peoples had previously been organized into city-states, networks of labor and domination developed that were connected to the metropole only to the extent that they participated in providing foodstuffs for the Spaniards and castas in the cities, generated surplus that could be used for tribute, or were part of the extractive structure. In effect, settlers who were not a part of the merchant or official aristocracy were transplanted Europeans or their descendants, natives in the Americas who remained relatively disconnected from the, to them, foreign metropole.

CONCLUSION

As I tried to show in the first two sections, and as is well recognized by many, some meanings of colonialism—dependency, control—are clearly applicable to the past and present relations between the indigenous corporate communities, which were not integrated into either the imperial or, later, the nation-state, and the non-Indian rulers of the two political structures. But if this, and its use as a label in the periodization of Spanish American imperial period art, is all that is meant by colonialism or colonial, then I believe that the terms and their modern derivatives are ultimately not very useful when applied generally to the circumstances lived by the bulk of the population in the core areas of Latin America. A final reason for this is that the transportation and communications technology at the time, the type of economic and political organizations established, and the dynamics of shifting ethnic ratios all conspired to create regional, relatively autonomous sociopolitical and cultural units out of the growing mestizo/criollo worlds. Over the course of the eighteenth century these became more closely linked politically and economically to Spain, but by that time the overwhelming majority of the mainland's populations determining the national cultures were creole, mestizo, or mulatto, not Spanish. These Americans were in the main not transplanted, first-generation *peninsulares*, but literally native peoples, the overwhelming majority of whom did not see themselves as foreign occupiers (like the English in India), but as local natives. When, through the implementation of the Bourbon reforms in the eighteenth century, an attempt was made to transform the Spanish American provinces into colonies in the post-1760s style, by increasing the economic and political links to the metropole, the foreignness of the gesture exploded in the face of Spanish pretensions. Indeed, following the Napoleonic occupation of Spain, the mestizo, mulatto, and especially criollo sectors overcame the last formal vestiges of political dependency on imperial Spain and established their own nation-states in the image of the motherland, tinged by the local color of some precontact practices and symbols, framed by many imperial period adaptations, and suffused with European ideals, practices, and material objects.

The winners were obviously not those who continued their lives as "Indians." It was not those who identified or were identified as indigenes who could now enjoy a postcolonial moment crowded with decolonizing initiatives and the anxious search for their precolonial selves. Instead, those who won were the powerful among the illegitimate and legitimate progeny of the mixtures of former colonialists, Africans, and indigenes, who no longer identified themselves as the latter two. Consequently, neither postcolonialism nor decolonization can be said to have ever taken place in the Americas as it did in South Asia, Africa, or any other part of the Old World, where after liberation the ideal of a precolonial past could at least inspire a newly freed people who ethnically did not identify themselves with their former colonizers. In short, it seems to me that with the exception of peripheral areas, the experience of colonialism, with the senses it has come to have today, primarily as a process of exploitation and dependent subordination to nonlocals, escaped those mestizos who came to form the majority of the population of the preindependence Americas, although these were nonetheless subjugated, abused, exploited, and often killed by other mestizo, mulatto, Indian, and criollo locals who enjoyed hegemony over them. One does not have to be colonized to suffer.

NOTES

I am much indebted to the participants at the Shelby Cullom Davis Center for Historical Studies, Princeton University, whose many valuable comments and challenging observations have been addressed in this essay. I also wish to thank the Getty Center for the History of Art and the Humanities where this essay was written. I dedicate this text to Sergio Klor de Alva, an even more extreme hyperhybrid than his father.

1. Jorge Klor de Alva, "Colonialism and Postcolonialism as (Latin) American Mirages," *Colonial Latin American Review* 1, nos. 1–2 (1992): 3–23.

2. See Patricia Seed, "Colonial and Postcolonial Discourse," *Latin American Research Review* 26, no. 3 (1991): 181–200; and see "Commentary and Debate," *Latin American Research Review* 28, no. 3 (1993): 113–52.

3. Annie E. Coombes, "Inventing the 'Postcolonial': Hybridity and Constituency in Contemporary Curating," *New Formations* 18 (Winter 1992): 39–52; Fernando Coronil, "Can Postcoloniality Be Decolonized? Imperial Banality and Postcolonial Power," *Public Culture* 5, no. 1 (1992): 89–108.

4. For example, Arthur M. Schlesinger Jr., *The Disuniting of America: Reflections on a Multicultural Society* (New York: Norton, 1992); and Peter Skerry, *Mexican Americans: The Ambivalent Minority* (New York: Free Press, 1993).

5. Michel Foucault, *Discipline and Punish: The Birth of the Prison*, trans. Alan Sheridan (New York: Vintage, 1979); and *Power/Knowledge*, trans. Colin Gordon (New York: Pantheon, 1980).

6. Ann L. Stoler, "Sexual Affronts and Racial Frontiers: European Identities and the Cultural Politics of Exclusion in Colonial Southeast Asia," paper presented at Davis Center Seminar, Princeton University, February 7, 1992; Irene Silverblatt, "Family Values in Seventeenth-Century Peru," paper presented at the symposium on Native Traditions in the Postconquest World, Dumbarton Oaks, Washington, D.C., October 2, 1992.

7. See Anthony Pagden, "Fabricating Identity in Spanish America," *History Today* (May 1992): 44–49; Klor de Alva, "Indios y criollos," in *Europa/América 1492/1992: La historia revisada*, ed. John H. Elliot (Madrid: Diario El País, S.A., 1992).

8. Ranajit Guha, Preface in *Selected Subaltern Studies* ed. Ranajit Guha and Gayatri C. Spivak (New York: Oxford University Press, 1988), p. 35.

9. Coronil, "Can Postcoloniality be Decolonized?"

10. Gianni Vattimo, *The End of Modernity: Nihilism and Hermeneutics in Postmodern Culture*, trans. Jon R. Snyder (Baltimore: Johns Hopkins University Press, 1991).

11. Benedict Anderson, *Imagined Communities*, 2d ed. (New York: Verso, 1991).

12. Spivak, "Subaltern Studies: Deconstructing Historiography," in *Selected Subaltern Studies*, pp. 13–15.

13. For example, see Ashis Nandy, *The Intimate Enemy: Loss and Recovery of Self under Colonialism*, (New Delhi: Oxford University Press, 1983).

14. Rolena Adorno, "Reconsidering Colonial Discourse for Sixteenth and Seventeenth Century Spanish America," *Latin American Research Review* 28, no. 3 (1993): 135–45.

15. James Lockhart, *The Nahuas after the Conquest: A Social and Cultural History of the Indians of Central Mexico, Sixteenth through Eighteenth Centuries* (Stanford: Stanford University Press, 1992), pp. 115–16.

16. Klor de Alva, "Indios y criollos."

17. Filoteo Samaniego Salazar, "Identidad Cultural Iberoamericana: Unidad

y Diversidad," paper presented at Symposium of the Americas, Smithsonian Institution, Washington, D.C., September 4–7, 1991, pp. 5–7, and in *American Identities: Traditional, Contested, and Imagined*, ed. J. J. Klor de Alva, A. Gonzalez, and E. J. Stann (Washington, D.C.: Smithsonian Institution Press, forthcoming).

18. Jorge Salvador Lara, "Influencias Hispánicas: Perspectivas sobre los 500 Años," paper presented at Symposium of the Americas, Smithsonian Institution, Washington D.C., September 4–7, 1991, pp. 1–2, and in *American Identities*.

19. See Coronil, "Beyond Occidentalism," in *Critical Inquiry*, forthcoming.

20. Klor de Alva, "Aztlan, Borinquen, and Hispanic Nationalism in the U.S.," in *Aztlan: Essays on the Chicano Homeland*, ed. R. Anaya and F. Lomelí (Albuquerque: El Norte Publications/University of New Mexico Press, 1989); Klor de Alva, "Nahua Studies, the Allure of the 'Aztecs,' and Miguel Leon-Portilla," in *The Aztec Image of Self and Society: Introduction to Nahua Culture*, ed. J. J. Klor de Alva (Salt Lake City: University of Utah Press, 1992).

21. Anaya and Lomeli, eds., *Aztlan: Essays on the Chicano Homeland*, p. 1.

22. Rudolfo Anaya, *Heart of Aztlan* (Berkeley: Editorial Justa, 1976).

23. Klor de Alva, "Atzlan, Borinquen, and Hispanic Nationalism in the U.S."; "La invención de los orígenes y la identidad latina en los Estados Unidos (1969–81)," in *Encuentros interétnicos. De palabra y obra en el Nuevo Mundo*, ed. J. J. Klor de Alva et al. (Madrid: Ediciones Siglo XXI, 1992).

24. *Hispanic* (June 1990).

25. *Vista Magazine* (December 24, 1989).

26. See Klor de Alva, "In Search of the American Chameleon: Mestizaje as Myth, Metaphor, and Mimesis," in *American Identities*.

27. D. A. Brading, *The First America: The Spanish Monarchy, Creole Patriots, and the Liberal State, 1492–1867* (New York: Cambridge University Press, 1991).

28. Steve J. Stern, *Peru's Indian Peoples and the Challenge of Spanish Conquest: Huamanga to 1640* (Madison: University of Wisconsin Press, 1982); Lockhart, *Nahuas after the Conquest*.

29. Woodrow Borah and Sherburne F. Cook, *The Aboriginal Population of Central Mexico on the Eve of the Spanish Conquest*, Ibero-Americana, no. 45 (Berkeley: University of California Press, 1963), pp. 4, 88.

30. Gonzalo Aguirre Beltran, *La población negra de México*, 2d ed. (México: Fondo de Cultura Económica, 1972).

31. See Nicolás Sánchez-Albornoz, *The Population of Latin America: A History*, trans. W.A.R. Richardson (Berkeley: University of California Press, 1974).

32. For a review of the literature, see Lockhart, "The Social History of Colonial Latin America: Evolution and Potential," *Latin American Research Review* 7 (1972): 5–45; idem, "Some Nahua Concepts in Postconquest Guise," *History of European Ideas* 6, no. 4 (1985): particularly pp. 465–68; Benjamin Keene, "Main Currents in United States Writings on Colonial Spanish America, 1884–1984," *Hispanic American Historical Review* 65, no. 4 (1985): 657–82; A.J.R. Russell-Wood, "United States Scholarly Contributions to the Historiography of Colonial Brazil," *Hispanic American Historical Review* 65, no. 4 (1985): 683–723; Eric Van Young, "Mexican Rural History since Chevalier: The Historiog-

raphy of the Colonial Hacienda," *Latin American Research Review* 18 (1983): 5–61; idem, "Recent Anglophone Scholarship on Mexico and Central America in the Age of Revolution (1750–1850)," *Hispanic American Historical Review* 65, no. 4 (1985): 725–43; Linda A. Newson, "Indian Population Patterns in Colonial Spanish America," *Latin American Research Review* 20 (1985): 41–74; Fred Bronner, "Urban Society in Colonial Spanish America: Research Trends," *Latin American Research Review* 21 (1986): 7–72; Lynn K. Stoner, "Directions in Latin American Women's History, 1977–1984," *Latin American Research Review* 22 (1987): 101–34; Ralph Lee Woodward Jr., "The Historiography of Modern Central America since 1960," *Hispanic American Historical Review* 67 (1987): 461–96; John E. Kicza, "The Social and Ethnic Historiography of Colonial Latin America: The Last Twenty Years," *William and Mary Quarterly*, 3d Series 45, no. 3 (1988): 453–88; Elizabeth Anne Kuznesof, "Household, Family, and Community Studies, 1976 1986," in *Women of Latin America: An Interdisciplinary Bibliography and Bibliographic Essay*, ed. K. Lynn Stoner (New York: Academic Press, 1988); Seed, "Colonial and Postcolonial Discourse"; for Mesoamerican ethnohistory, see Robert Wauchope, ed., *Handbook of Middle American Indians*, vols. 12–15 (Austin: University of Texas Press, 1972–75); and Victoria R. Bricker, ed., *Supplement to the Handbook of Middle American Indians*, vol. 4 (Austin: University of Texas Press, 1986).

33. Juan de Solórzano y Pereira, *Política indiana* (Antwerp: Henrico y Cornelio Verdussen, 1703). A modified Spanish edition of *Disputatio de Indiarum Iure* first published in 1647.

34. Personal communication, October 6, 1991.

35. See Brading, *First America*.

36. For example, Guillermo Bonfil Batalla, "Sobre la ideología del mestizaje," in *Decadencia y auge de las identidades*, ed. José Manuel Valenzuela Arce (Tijuana, México: El Colegio de la Frontera Norte, 1992).

37. As I did above, for some of my analyses here I once again draw from the papers, conversations, and notes gathered at the Symposium of the Americas on the Nature of Cultural Identity, Smithsonian Institution, Washington, D.C., September 4–7, 1991. Over fifty well-known historians, anthropologists, literary scholars, and intellectuals in journalism or diplomatic service, from every major area of the Americas, were present.

38. It bears mentioning here that English sources on colonial Latin America during most of this century have generally focused on the age of conquest and early exploration with minimal attention paid to the centuries that followed. The net result has been that, until very recently and then only in certain texts, schools in the United States have tended to skip or gloss over the southwestern colonial period; that is, everything between the initial Spanish explorations in Latin America and the Caribbean and the landing of the English on the Atlantic shores has been elided. This common practice has led to the frequent omission of a full century of Hispanic occupation of the (future) U.S. Southwest, thereby helping to maintain the idea that U.S. history is strictly an east to west phenomenon, with Mexicans playing only a very minor role as (the permanent) foreigners.

39. For example, Clarence W. Haring, *The Spanish Empire in America* (New York: Harcourt, Brace, and World, 1947); Robert Ricard, *The Spiritual Conquest of Mexico*, trans. Lesley Byrd Simpson (Berkeley: University of California Press, [1933] 1966).

40. For example, Eric R. Wolf, *Sons of the Shaking Earth* (Chicago: University of Chicago Press, 1959); Evon Z. Vogt, "The Genetic Model and Maya Cultural Development," in *Desarrollo cultural de los Mayas*, ed. E. Z. Vogt and A. Ruz L. (México: Universidad Nacional Autónoma de México, 1964); idem, "On the Application of the Phylogenetic Model to the Mayas," in *The Social Anthropology and Ethnohistory of American Tribes: Essays in Honor of Fred Eggan*, ed. R. J. DeMallie and Alfonso Ortiz (Norman: University of Oklahoma Press, in press).

41. See Carlos García Mora, ed., *La antropología en México*, 12 vols. (México: Instituto Nacional de Antropología e Historia, 1987–88).

42. Charles Gibson, *Tlaxcala in the Sixteenth Century* (New Haven: Yale University Press, 1952); and *The Aztecs under Spanish Rule* (Stanford: Stanford University Press, 1964); see Lockhart, "Some Nahua Concepts in Postconquest Guise," pp. 466–67.

43. Klor de Alva, "Nahua Studies, the Allure of the 'Aztecs,' and Miguel Leon-Portilla."

44. Lockhart, *Nahuas and Spaniards: Postconquest Central Mexican History and Philology*, UCLA Latin American Studies, vol. 76, Nahuatl Studies Series, no. 3 (Stanford: Stanford University Press, 1991); and *The Nahuas after the Conquest*. Among the most important cultural parallels are densely settled urban centers with monumental architecture, highly stratified social and religious organizations, sedentary agriculture, tribute collection, the use of ritual calendars, the presence of writing and literacy with a fully developed literary and historical tradition, and a widely used system of secular, pragmatic record keeping.

45. See Lockhart, *The Nahuas after Conquest*; S. L. Cline, *Colonial Culhuacan, 1580–1600: A Social History of an Aztec Town* (Albuquerque: University of New Mexico Press, 1986); Robert Haskett, *Indigenous Rulers: An Ethnohistory of Town Government in Colonial Cuernavaca* (Albuquerque: University of New Mexico Press, 1991); Klor de Alva, "Spiritual Conflict and Accommodation in New Spain: Toward a Typology of Aztec Responses to Christianity," in *The Inca and Aztec States, 1400–1800: Anthropology and History*, ed. G. A. Collier et al. (New York, Academic, 1982); idem, "Religious Rationalization and the Conversion of the Nahuas: Some Reflections on Social Organization and Colonial Epistemology," in *To Change Place: Aztec Ceremonial Landscapes*, ed. D. Carrasco (Boulder: University of Colorado Press, 1991).

46. John R. Seeley, *The Expansion of England* (Chicago: University of Chicago Press, 1971).

47. David M. Reimers, *Still the Golden Door: The Third World Comes to America* (New York: Columbia University Press, 1985).

48. Andre Gunder-Frank, *Capitalism and Underdevelopment in Latin America*, rev. and enlarged ed. (New York: Monthly Review Press, [1967] 1969); Stanley J. Stein and Barbara H. Stein, *The Colonial Heritage of Latin America:*

Essays in Economic Dependence in Perspective (New York: Oxford University Press, 1970); Celso Furtado, *La economía Latinoamericana: formación histórica y problemas contemperáneos* (México: Siglo Veintiuno, 1971); Eduardo Galeano, *Open Veins of Latin America*, trans. Cedric Belfrage (New York: Monthly Review Press, [1971] 1973).

49. Immanuel Wallerstein, *The Modern World System I: Capitalist Agriculture and the Origins of the European World-Economy in the Sixteenth Century* (New York: Academic, 1974).

50. Pedro Carrasco, "The Civil-Religious Hierarchy in Mesoamerican Communities: Pre-Spanish Background and Colonial Development," *American Anthropologist* 63 (1961): 483–97; Marvin Harris, *Patterns of Race in the Americas* (New York: Norton, [1964] 1974).

51. Pablo González Casanova, *La democracia en México* (México: Ediciones Era, 1965); English trans. by Danielle Salti, *Democracy in Mexico* (New York: Oxford University Press, 1970).

52. Stein and Stein, *Colonial Heritage of Latin America*, p. 21.

53. Edward Said, *Orientalism* (New York: Pantheon, 1978).

54. This brief survey of terms relies primarily on the *Oxford English Dictionary*, compact edition, 1971. See *OED* for bibliographic details.

55. Pedro Mártir de Anglería, *Décadas del Nuevo Mundo*, ed. E. O'Gorman (México: José Porrua e Hijos, 1964–65).

56. Seeley, *Expansion of England*, p. 38.

57. Albert Venn Dicey, *England's Case against Home Rule* (London: J. Murray, 1886), p. 273.

58. See Eric Hobsbawm, *Nations and Nationalism since 1780* (New York: Cambridge University Press, 1990); Rafael Samuel, ed., *Patriotism: The Making and Unmaking of British National Identity* (London: Routledge, 1989); Partha Chatterjee, *Nationalist Thought and the Colonial World: A Derivative Discourse?* (London: Zed Books, 1986).

59. Personal communication, October 18, 1991.

60. John A. Hobson, *Imperialism: A Study* (London: Unwin Hyman, [1902] 1988).

61. Peter R. Brown, personal communication, October 18, 1991.

Part Three

COLONIAL DISCOURSE AND ITS DISPLACEMENTS

CHAPTER 10

Becoming Indian in the Central Andes of Seventeenth-Century Peru

IRENE SILVERBLATT

THIS ESSAY is about the construction of social categories and social identities—about the making of "Indians" and ideologies of indianness—
which lay at the heart of Spanish empire-building. Spain's colonial enterprise might have sought the New World's wealth and labor, but it was
built through the making of new social relations and social perceptions:
a cultural revolution[1] producing "races" and "nationalities," "bastards"
and "virgins." Yet even with armies of priests, bureaucrats, and soldiers,
colonization's cultural drives often missed their targets, producing un-
foreseen consequences. Here we explore one portion of Peru's unintended cultural history, when Spaniards tried to make "Indians" out of
Andeans.

The cultural work of colonization, of a piece with Spain's state-making projects, took specific forms over time and across the empire's vast
reach. In the Andes that endeavor began with Pizarro's conquest of the
Inca empire in the 1530s and Iberia's intent to convert its descendants
into Spanish subjects. The fact that Andeans (for want of a better term)
had experienced another sort of colony-building as subjects of the Inca
empire, will be crucial to Peru's "Indian" story. Harboring a wide range
of sentiments toward their former masters, Andeans, at the time of the
Spanish conquest, held strong allegiances to their ethnic polities (*ayllus*)
conquered by the Incas. The puzzle I want to explore is the following:
how some Andeans, after about one century of Spanish rule, began to
see themselves—somewhat—as Inca descendants and as "Indian"; or, in
other words, how Andeans, who had primarily identified themselves as
members of ayllus, began, in addition, to conceive themselves by the
social category of political order bequeathed by their Spanish colonizers.

Andeans were preached indianness by Spaniards wanting to ensure
steadfast Indian subjects. This essay, however, also asks us to keep in
mind Hernando Hacas Poma's version. A member of the seventeenth-
century native elite and local minister hounded by the "extirpators of
idolatry" for "dogmatizing" native religion, Hacas Poma's indianness

was in resounding opposition to the colonial spiritual (and temporal) establishment: "Indians, precisely because [we] are Indians, should adore [our] *malquis* (ancestors) since they are the ones who look out for the fertility of fields and the well-being of Indians; and only Spaniards should adore god and the painted saints which are in the church, since they are the gods of the Spanish."[2]

This essay, then, turns on the processes intimated by both Hacas Poma's pleas and by the extirpators' indictments: on the politics of identity-making—the broad contests over definitions of humanness—at the heart of the colonial enterprise. After one hundred years, some Andeans, beginning to take "Indian" to heart, found their imaginations haunted by Spanish categories; yet their self-understandings—along with the novel ways of engaging the world that a sense of indianness inspired— were surely at odds with Spanish intentions.

INTIMATIONS OF INDIANNESS

Andean indianness was a product of Spanish colonialism, yet its meanings were bound to experiences that came before. Spanish colonizers arrived on the heels of the great Inca expansion; and Andeans' experience of subjugation under European rule, and its eventual expression in the seventeenth century as a sense of common indianness, would be colored by memories of Inca pasts.

The Spanish, like the Incas before them, created new social categories of humans—units of "others"—whose possibilities and actions were circumscribed by imperial power structures.[3] Like the Incas, the Spanish derived their great wealth from institutions that tapped the labor of a colonially fashioned peasantry; like the Incas, they attempted to shape Andean senses of self and position—with varying degrees of success—by expanding imperial religion. Like their Inca counterparts, Spanish instruments of government built on systems of indirect rule; and, taking advantage of internal ranks dividing conquered peoples, they promoted local elites (*kurakas*) to middlemen in imperial administration.[4]

However, Spanish colonization—anchored in alien traditions of political economy and political morality, statecraft, and culture—unleashed forces that often proved devastating to Peru's native peoples. Tribute requirements weighed heavily on peasant shoulders, frequently belying Spain's avowed commitment to the material well-being of its subjects. Spanish religion, devoted to a militant cultural/racial purity that expelled Jews and later Moors from its realms, tried to straitjacket Andean customs and beliefs in unknown demands of orthodoxy. And Spanish gender norms, also honed by Counter-Reformation zeal, decried women's participation in Andean public life, while denouncing their fatal attraction to Satan and heresy.[5]

Last, we find a significant contrast in the very categories of colonial relations: Inca government, elaborating long-standing habits of cultural difference in the Andes, inscribed ayllu or "ethnic" distinctions as units of empire. The practices of Inca state-making were particularist; and Andeans did not conceive their experience under Inca rule as a common one.[6] Spanish practices, on the other hand, building on the experiences of an emerging modern European state, imposed broad, universal classifications on their subjects: all natives of the "New World" were "Indian" subjects of Spain; all Spaniards, regardless of social distinctions, were privileged colonists.[7] Spanish legal theory created two "republics," two separate "nations," fusing concerns over "ancestral purity," women's sexuality, and cultural difference with political hierarchy. An uneasy amalgam of racial constructions, gender ideologies, customs, and class—inscribed in law, economic policy, theology, and popular stereotype—established new conditions of living that made indianness a possibility. Thus a sense of common experience, interest, and destiny—transcending internal fractures of privilege, "ethnicity," and gender—became a potential nourishment of Andeans' social selves.

Early hints of "Indian" identities appear in the Andes three decades after the Spanish invasion, when, in 1565, the Taki Onqoy (Dancing Sickness), a movement of nativist redemption, inspired women and men, kurakas and peasants in Peru's central highlands.[8] Signaling both the despair attending European dominion and the hope of being able to abolish it, Andean gods began to take over Andeans' souls. Those possessed by the dancing sickness blamed the deteriorating condition of their lives (impossible labor demands and high mortality) on themselves and other natives for deserting *huacas* (deity, sacred place) for Christian gods. To right the wrongs of this world, the Taki Onqoys argued, would require Andean peoples to return to their sacred traditions, to restore the sacred balance between huacas and mortals, and to renounce Christianity and all things Spanish. Huacas might have been defeated by Christian gods once, but now the tables would be turned. And their promised victory would be a total one: Spanish gods, completely routed, would disappear from the Andes and from native life.[9] Peter Worsley, a scholar of colonial millenarian movements, was struck by their capacity to provoke new loyalties and mobilize alliances across traditional, often hostile, political boundaries.[10] And, as Steve Stern suggests, the Taki Onqoy might mark the beginnings of a pan-Andean consciousness, one that transcended the borders of ayllus and ethnicity.[11] But in certain ways, the Taki Onqoys were not yet "Indian," at least not quite. For this early nativist ideology refused to envision any Andean future (even an oppositional one) in a Spanish-dominated world. Taki Onqoys did not accept—at least in principle—a Spanish presence in the Andes; they would brook no compromise with colonialism (Christian gods would disappear). Nor would they be captured by colonial definitions of their humanness: unlike seventeenth-century nativists, Taki Onqoys do not appear to call themselves by any category analogous to "indios"; nor, interestingly, do Inca gods—with the exception of Huanacauri—appear in their pantheon.[12]

Nevertheless, the Taki Onqoy was steeped in colonial constraints and paradoxes. Its battle cries projected the confrontations of colonial rule onto the heavens. The movement's female champions, organized, in Andean fashion, into gender-specific religious groups, called themselves "sainted Marys." And with all the fears that the movement unleashed, Spaniards found no evidence that its ideological clarions had prompted Ayacucho's natives to arm.[13] However, as an ideology of native position and possibility in the colonial world, the Taki Onqoy set directions of understanding—directions that would be resurrected and transformed during the century to follow.

BECOMING "INDIAN": SOCIAL AND POLITICAL PRACTICES

The Taki Onqoy was one in a series of challenges to Iberian control that pressed Spanish authorities to tighten their grip on the Andean colonies. Spurred by such concerns, Viceroy Toledo, during the last quarter of the sixteenth century, set in motion a series of measures whose goal was to strengthen and consolidate Spain's institutional presence. These reorganizing efforts ushered in what many historians have called the "mature" colonial state—a century and a half long period of relative political stability.[14] They also set the stage for indianism's challenge.

Toledo's reforms, reflecting the growing interests of European absolutism, tried to consolidate the state's control over its colonies and the colonized. The colonial bureaucracy was expanded and its powers increased; its office holders exercised juridical authority over Indians, and oversaw the collection of tribute and the allocation of native labor. As the protector of Indian subjects, the paternalist Spanish state guaranteed the corporate right of Indian communities to land and resources; it also—following Iberian models of municipal government—allowed them significant autonomy with respect to local concerns.[15]

Spain's attempts to engage native living practices to the machinery of colonial rule in Peru were ultimately successful, but it was an achievement that varied dramatically by agenda and region. Plans to forcibly resettle Andeans into compact villages (*reducciones*) were notorious failures in this part of the Andes.[16] And Toledo's efforts to remove kurakas from ayllu government were met with such determined resistance that he was forced to abandon his plans.[17] Colonial state-building was a protracted compromise. For all its "maturity," the colonial state was weak. But it was still hegemonic.

Seventeenth-century Spaniards in Peru explained their political dominion through appeals to a racially tinged paternalism: Indians, as a people, were base, vile, argued one legal scholar; they were simply unfit for governing others.[18] Furthermore, the Incas had also been unfit rulers: through their shrines and huacas, Incas had truck with Satan and, as a result, were both illegitimate sovereigns and condemned to everlasting hell. One of the renowned extirpators of idolatry, Father Avendaño, made it very clear in his sermons just how intertwined satanism, Inca legitimacy, and Christian salvation were. His sermon (published in 1646) also suggests another point: the importance of Inca noblewomen to Cusco's hegemony, as well as to some seventeenth-century memories of Inca authority. "Tell me children (*hijos*). . . . How many Inca kings have gone to hell?—Every one. How many *Coyas* [queens]?—All of them. How many *Ñustas* [princesses, noblewomen]—Every one. Why? . . . because they worshipped the devil in *huacas*."[19]

Although exterminated as a political power, the Incas remained under Spanish attack throughout the seventeenth century. Seventeenth-century Andeans, no less than their European contemporaries, grasped the self-serving implications of Spanish political philosophy. Nevertheless, we would be doing the Black Legend's dirty work to view Spanish ideologies as merely cynical covers for political control. Colonials believed themselves to be moral human beings, acting in the interest of those they colonized and certainly in accord with their God's will. Some were notable defenders of Indians' rights (within a colonial framework) and outspoken critics of the regime's abuses. We run the risk of flattening the knotty sentiments that joined Indians and Spaniards by underestimating the profoundly moral coloring of the colonial endeavor or the ethical seriousness with which (many) colonial authorities undertook their mission. Colonized peoples were not indifferent to the sincerity of Spaniards' beliefs, just as they were not indifferent to their hypocrisy.[20] The powerful feelings of betrayal that indianism voiced were rooted in paternalism's allure as well as in its conflicting and ultimately impossible promises.

Spanish political ideologies and practices riddled Indian/Spanish relations with contradictions. Indians were demeaned by colonial institutions, official policy, and popular prejudice. But, paradoxically, Spanish political theory proclaimed their equality, or nearly: Indians, like Spaniards, were fully human, free vassals of the Crown. As social minors of state paternalism, Indians were guaranteed corporate rights to land and special court protections; and under Spanish law they could fight their very guardian, the state, over abusive labor and tribute demands. Thus Indians learned about the regime's benefits; they also became schooled in its weak points. Catholicism, too, preached conflicting messages. For while instructing Indians in the morality of colonial hierarchies, clerics taught the equality of mortals—Spaniards and Indians—before God. And then, if Christian gods could protect Indians from an eternity in hell, why couldn't they guarantee their welfare in this world, like they seemed to do for Spaniards? The contradictory social relations of the colonial Andes, grasped and experienced ideologically, impressed contradictory Andean/"Indian" selves.

Seeing the colonial endeavor threatened by its own excesses, Spanish policy, with Toledo, attempted to enforce a rigorous division between the Spanish and Indian republics.[21] But Spaniards also feared the cultural challenge that separation might—and did—encourage.[22] In the seventeenth century some Andeans did match Spanish fears and challenge Spanish authority through a renewed sense of collective rights and possibility. While colored by the colonial frame within which it was offered, this movement made use of the promises of Spanish religion, the paternalistic guarantees of Spanish law, and the inconsistencies of Spanish ideology. It also drew on indigenous traditions: nativism, parsed by a logic foreshadowed in the Taki Onqoy, could exalt an ethics of ayllu/ethnic sovereignty and explain Andeans' experiences of degradation in religious terms, while—perhaps encouraged by Spanish preaching—it began to link reconstrued memories of the Inca past to new "Indian" critiques of the colonial present.

BECOMING "INDIAN": TAKING THE SPANISH AT THEIR CATEGORICAL WORDS

A wide range of ideologies, mixing understandings and loyalties, competed for prominence throughout the seventeenth-century Andes; however, during the period of idolatry trials indianism seemed to command a powerful grip over Andeans' imaginings. Along with its promise to transcend ethnic borders, indianism galvanized allegiances across boundaries of gender and privilege. It seized women and men—between whom colonial beliefs and practices had driven a wedge of public legitimacy—by challenging colonial gender "truths," even turning them upside down. And it called to kurakas (local "ethnic" authorities; middlemen in colonial government) and peasants by appealing to a sense of justice, to long-standing ethics of obligation and entitlement between social unequals: to an Andean "truth" that while allegiances across divides of wealth and power might produce ayllu well-being, they could not be taken for granted. Indianism must have been compelling in these difficult times, but it was also fragile. Competing ideologies and allegiances—to ayllus, or kurakas, or even priests—might rip into its strength. And again, with our sources' limitations, there is so much about the movement that we will never know.

In the first half of the seventeenth century, idolatry extirpators discovered that nativist heresies had metastasized. "The reason why "Indians" [are] dying," explained a respected community leader, also condemned as a "witch/dogmatist,"

[is] because they no longer adore their *malquis* [ancestors] and huacas like their elders formerly did, which is why there used to be so many "Indians" who had more fields and clothing and who lived in greater tranquility. It is because they adore the huacas of the Spanish people—no more than a few painted and gilded sticks—that "Indians" keep on dying and losing their lands. Spaniards' gods don't give "Indians" anything. "Indians" because we are "Indians" should adore our huacas and ancestors.[23]

Indianism verbalized Andeans' experience as colonized subjects as a continuous assault on life's fabric—high mortality, loss of lands, insufficient food or clothing, harried and insecure existence. And, like the Taki Onqoy, it fingered Andeans' continued commitment to Christian beliefs as the culprit. In their collective sinning Andeans had abandoned their fundamental obligations to huacas; and, reciprocally, huacas had turned their backs on them. Colonial experience again showed that Spanish gods, governers, and saints had betrayed their promise to protect Andeans' welfare.

Indianism's language was structured by colonial categories: human beings were "Indians" or Spaniards in this imagining of life's prospects—a new way for Andeans to cast themselves and their social universe. Andeans put these classifications into nativism's service, as "Indian" caught some of the spirit of the church-militant and the modern state-categorical, spreading out beyond traditional ayllu boundaries and forging alliances between kurakas and peasants. However, seventeenth-century nativism—perhaps recognizing the limits of Andeans' power and possibilities—did not keep up the uncompromising militancy of the century before. Indianism was willing to defy the church, skirmish the state, and battle Spanish incursions into Andean life—but it had to increasingly do so within colonial bounds. So, even though in vision and in practice, indianness was deeply oppositional, refusing to acquiesce to a way of being defined by colonial authorities and Spanish saints, it nevertheless deferred to Spain's presence. Spain's gods would remain on

Andean soil. This significant change from the belligerency of the Taki Onqoy should not detract from "Indians'" courageous beliefs, beliefs for which many could be brutally whipped, made to labor in colonial sweat shops, or forced into permanent exile.[24] It does suggest, however, some important dimensions in the building of colonial hegemonies and colonial subjects.[25]

Nativist ideology insisted that huacas, the gods of the past, could be kept alive by worship, just as their now-"Indian" descendants could be kept vital and human by returning to "Indian" ways. Reconstituting the ethos of the past in the colonial present was, of course, an impossibility, but it was precisely the tension of impossibility that charged the critical spark on which indianness thrived. And part of that history—the ethos of the past—entailed revitalized memories of Inca rule.[26]

RELATIONS WITH INCA MASTERS
IN THE COLONIAL PRESENT

Unlike the Taki Onqoy, Incas appear in many seventeenth-century nativist understandings of self and place. Andean narratives of social cause and origins, hierarchy and political legitimacy would now also draw on Andeans' Inca experience—reconstrued memories of life as Inca subjects. While difficult to determine the pervasiveness and depth of Inca attachments, Avendaño's fire and brimstone sermon—"How many Incas reside in hell?"—not only hints at colonial fears of Inca memories, but at the broad net these memories cast. In the seventeenth century, ayllus were commemorating past ties with Inca masters. Some envisioned their very existence to be tied to Inca powers, conceptualizing themselves as the descendants not only of local huacas, but of imperial goddesses and gods, Inca queens and kings. Moreover, divine Incas could bring to the provinces the very stuff of life: corn, chili peppers, homes.[27] And as Inca ancestors were cherished well into the seventeenth century, so were rites commemorating Inca conquest and the attendant obligations between Cusco and colonized provinces.

The Incas consecrated political bonds between themselves and conquered peoples through elaborate rituals of human sacrifice. Usually an *aclla* (one of the empire's renowned, chaste, "chosen women") from a newly conquered ayllu would be executed in ceremonies to the Inca and the Sun, the god of conquest. While deifying the victim as a goddess in regional and imperial pantheons, imperial rites celebrated political subordination.[28] Tanta Carhua, for example, an aclla from Peru's north-central highlands, was feted by the Inca king in Cusco and then by her community before she was buried in Inca lands bordering on her ayllu's territory. Tanta Carhua's death commemorated and institutionalized colonial relations between her homeland and Cusco; for with Tanta Carhua's sacrifice, her father and his patriline would become middlemen in Inca administration.[29] Almost ninety years after the Spanish conquest, these ayllus still venerated Tanta Carhua. Over two generations after that, returning extirpators uncovered the same heresy.[30]

So in seventeenth-century rituals, colonial Andeans reenacted the creation of bonds between conquered ayllus and Cusco, bonds pivoting around chaste women and "incanized" kurakas, bonds transforming Andeans into Cusco's subjects. They placed in ceremonial prominence both native elites, as brokers to an imperial power, as well as ayllu dependence on these men fluent in an alien, powerful culture. Colonial ayllus did not merely celebrate the Incas, the "past," but specific qualities of the power relations that had engaged them. The nature of those relations, then, could set the language of Andean expectations and critique, and so, at least in some ayllus, become part of indianness.

Further, by the middle of the seventeenth century, extirpators uncovered that "Inca" might take on novel, expanded meanings. The opposition of Spanish to Indian could be refashioned as a struggle between Spaniards and Incas. Ayllus throughout the highlands were staging ritual battles between what were perceived to be the region's principal political opponents: Spaniards and Incas.[31]

The implications of this novel antagonism for Andean ways of knowing bear thinking about. They suggest that "Inca," as a gloss for "Indian," for the entire indigenous world, was taking on greater discursive and critical prominence, and that "the Inca," as culture hero, was standing for that world. "Inca," then, could envelop a political morality: the image of a legitimate "Indian" kingdom of the past whose sovereignty over the Andes was usurped by Spain. It might suggest future dreams of an Inca utopia, so eloquently analyzed by Flores Galindo,[32] in which the Inca's return to Peruvian soil would signal Spanish defeat and the coming age of "Indian" justice.

Battles of Inca against Spaniard—utopian strands—as moving and provocative as they might prove to be (particularly in the century to follow) murmured hopes and visions at a cost. Casting the Inca as culture hero set certain directions to Andean rememberings. Cusco's noblewomen, queens and princesses, played a prominent role in the empire,[33] and, if Avendaño's sermon is any guide, they were still vital to Andeans' memories of it well into the seventeenth century. Coding Inca (Indian) history as a battleground of kings would weaken their imprint, not to mention that of women in general. It would also wash over the battles

fought between Incas and other Andean ayllus over political sovereignty, the intrusive demands of Inca empire-building, the ambiguous
role of kurakas, and the burdens Cusco's lords placed on peasant
shoulders. "Inca" suggests a common Andean/Indian ground, while,
in reality, that ground was split apart by antagonisms of gender, ethnicity, and privilege. "Inca" might spur remembrances of Cusco's paternalism, notions of imperial obligation, which contrasted so sharply with
Spanish practice. Yet romancing Inca history would also leave in place
visions of social order in which Indian subjects increasingly presumed
their social selves to be anchored in Inca-phrased, politically gendered,
hierarchies.

COMPROMISING RITUALS: EXTIRPATION CAMPAIGNS AND GENDERED FORMS OF RELIGIOUS SUBVERSION

Nativist religious practices, ebulliently anticolonial, were torn by compromise. In the hostile climate of the seventeenth century, Andean nativists—battered by extirpators—could not ignore either the weight of
Spanish institutions or their profound belligerence to Andean beliefs.
Indianism had to be practiced with caution and strategy.

Indianists would worship their huacas under the cover of saints, and
any Christian holiday became a time to celebrate the ancestors. Indianists kept vigilant eyes on the ritual practices that suffused day-to-day Andean life. Whenever huacas were commemorated or ancestors honored,
they would ban the use of Spanish artifacts, keeping Andean purity by
avoiding pork and mutton; or, even more dangerously, by refusing to
attend church services and catechism classes.[34]

Nativist practices were gendered in the colonized Andes, in processes
that joined and countered Andean norms with Spanish "patriarchal" assumptions. As opposed to long-standing Andean traditions, Spanish law
presumed women were innately unsuited to hold public offices. Coming
from the climate of European witch hunts, Spanish theology targeted
native women as the most likely consorts of God's enemies—Peru's
devil/huacas. Colonial irony, however, could turn men's official privileges into indianist women's honor.[35]

Men played key roles in Andean nativism; yet the idolatry trials
abound with references to women witches and to "virgin" priestesses of
"Indian" huacas.[36] Women, like Juana Icha, were accused of a whole
gamut of sorcery, from healing wounds to bewitching colonial bureaucrats, priests, and native tax collectors. Her fury was directed against indigenous and Spanish officials who transgressed what she, and others,
believed to be the legitimate bounds of authority. As an Andean witch,

Juana Icha became an advocate for "Indian morality"; and the standards she represented harkened to pre-Columbian understandings of social justice, of the obligations of those in power to their subordinates or their community. Her support was ayllu-wide. Listen to the testimony of a local official who suffered her wrath:

> and Don Francisco Poma Condor, mayor, apprehended Juana and then let her go . . . and then don Pedro Yauri, an *Indio Principal* (headman or *kuraca*) of this village recaptured her, but she still escaped, and Pedro de Zarate, the priest, ordered her arrest, but to no avail . . . because the Indians of the village support her.[37]

In a similar fusion and countering of gender ideologies, indianism merged the sexual purity of celibate women (and perhaps the political prestige associated with the aclla of Inca times) with efforts to preserve the "purity" of traditional Andean life.[38] Virgin women (often named María; remember the Taki Onqoy), living as "Andean" and hidden a life as possible, were kept from the immoralities, the contaminations, of Spanish civic offices, religious institutions, and Spanish men. The gendered institutions of Spanish colonialism systematically eroded the life possibilities of most Andean women; and in colonial irony, those same ravaging institutions provided them with instruments of challenge. In native eyes, witches and virgins—the devil-inspired subverters of colonial disorder and the pure, uncontaminated ministers of an ordered past—gained a kind of underground legitimacy as the champions of a contentious, anticolonial "Indian" culture.

But when discussing seventeenth-century nativism, its ebullience and limits, we must never forget the toll exacted by the extirpation campaigns—campaigns that at once laid bare the state's ineffectiveness and its abilities to lash out against perceived (or misperceived) threats. Recreating the terrible climate of fear that strangled colonial Peru and peninsular Spain, extirpators, like inquisitors and bureaucrats, believed that heresies—whether of Jews, Protestants, Muslims, witches, or Indians—were gnawing threats to civilization and the colonial enterprise. Indianists met the challenge; and the campaigns against native religion were emblazoned in, even spurred on by, indianist practices: Otuco's indianists spat Father Avendaño's name when they worshiped the charred remains of the huacas he thought he had destroyed twenty years before;[39] some ayllus, at great risk, abandoned colonial settlements to live closer to the hill-top dwellings of their ancestors;[40] others encouraged a more private worship to make indianists less vulnerable to discovery.[41] Nevertheless, even in the most resolutely indianist of ceremonies, the entwined pressures of Christian militancy and colonial authority exacted a price. Ideologies of indianness voiced the toll.

THE SPANISH IN INDIANS

Although the language of indianism was ferociously anti-Spanish, it was, at the same time, pervasively (if unconsciously) hispanified. Some huacas, now, were wearing hispanified clothing, sporting hispanified beards, acquiring hispanified ways. Colonization introduced Spanish figures to Andean idioms of collective sense; and hispanified/Christianized huacas participated in this uneasy, hybridized, ideological terrain shaping judgments of indianness, of where "Indians" came from, who they were, and what their futures might be.

One example is the god Huari, who, in various narratives, brought order, agriculture, and (Andean) "civilization" to ayllu life. An elderly woman, accused of witchcraft and dogmatism, told her young acolyte:

> before there were Incas and *apos* [mountain gods; can also refer to people of rank; Spaniards], when "Indians" would kill one another in order to defend their fields, [huari] appeared in the form of a Spaniard, an old man with a beard, and he distributed all their fields and irrigation canals to them, in every pueblo ... and these are the same [fields] that are now sown, and it was Huari who gave "Indians food" and water.[42]

Extirpators found a similar story in Ocros, a community that remained aggressively anti-Christian despite several idolatry inspections. Called Huari Viracocha, he was also a Spaniard, a powerful Spaniard, who could turn native heroes—the ancestor-founders of ayllus—into stone.[43] Thus in spite of—and along with—resolute anti-Christian sentiments, some Andeans were conceptualizing their foundation as a culture and as a people in hispanified terms. Side by side with indigenous ancestors, local as well as Inca heroes inaugurating social order, lay a Christian-like source of "Indian" society, represented by figures somewhat of a piece with the Spaniard's god.[44]

Perhaps hispanified huaris were nodding to Spain's seemingly unyielding presence and powers; perhaps they also voiced indianism's unavoidable dependency on the Spanish world: for an "Indian" space in the seventeenth century was increasingly dependent on the manipulation of Spanish institutions, on the clever maneuver of Spanish paternalism, its laws, politics, and religion—particularly by hispanified kurakas who, like their incanized predecessors, were fluent in both imperial and local worlds. Kuraka-led victories in court, abetted by the moral force of huacas, could ensure an ayllu's land holdings in the face of outside challenges, moderate forced labor obligations in the mines, curb the abusive behavior of Spanish bureaucrats, or inhibit the ability of priests to set up residence in the countryside.[45] Indianist triumphs on Spanish turf directly shaped the day-to-day terms of colonial living and helped guard the terrain wherein indianists hoped to prosper.

Unlike the enraged huacas of the Taki Onqoy, indianist huacas were prepared to share the Andean heavens with Spanish gods. They also seemed willing to accept (up to a point) the colonial institutions that made Andeans into "Indian" subjects. Kurakas and peasants prayed to their huacas: that colonial labor obligations be moderated, not abolished; that tribute demands be eased, not abandoned; that money (a Spanish introduction) be forthcoming, not eliminated.[46] Indianist militants of the seventeenth century did not seem to question—at least not in entreaties to huacas and ancestors—the legitimacy of the Spanish regime to exact demands on them. They did profoundly challenge, however, the terms of those demands. Kurakas and commoners did not accept colonial calculations of life's rules: indianists were deeply concerned about the nature of Spanish exactions and the genuineness of Spanish commitments; they fought bitterly—in prayers, in court, and in blood[47]—to ensure that colonials' demands were just and that their obligations to Andeans were met. Their militancy notwithstanding, nativists (implicitly? consciously?) understood themselves to be subjects in a larger world of social hierarchies on which their being and welfare depended. Spain, including its caste-like and patriarchal understandings of cosmic order, was finding a place in "Indian" selves.

THE MEANINGS OF "INDIAN"

Contests over social selves, over potential ways of being human, lay at the heart of the colonial enterprise, as Crown and church, in policy and prejudice, struggled to make Andeans—that varied swatch of peoples living under Inca rule—into "Indians." Colonial order turned on this sociological invention, integral to the making of the modern world: the channeling of "New World" humanity into a hierarchy of Spaniards and Indians. One hundred years after forays began, some Andeans started to define their lives, at least in part, by this novel category of "Indian"; but, as this essay has tried to show, "Indians" mobilized by nativist beliefs bore little resemblance to the Indians colonial policy and colonial religion intended to create.

Inspired by a resurgent nativism, men and women, kurakas and peasants, living in different ayllus and worshiping different huacas, galvanized an Andean "common sense" of things, into a sense of indianness, into a critical, anticolonial ethos. What had been the practices of Andean living—the customary ways of burying the dead, praying to ancestors, preparing fields, roofing houses, getting married—became weapons of colonial critique. What had been the ritual practices brought by colonial masters—attending catechism, celebrating saints' days, going to confession—became instruments of ridicule. Praying to huacas for guidance and support, indianist kurakas would engage colonial institutions of government for indianism's benefit. But colonialism's unyielding presence, its relative strength in relation to the ayllus' political weaknesses, along with its guarantees of Indian rights as a community of human beings, pervaded indianist practices and indianism's spirit. Indianism owed much of its character to the colony's structures of power, categories of rule, and entwined ideologies of racial hierarchy, state paternalism, militant Catholicism, and abiding gender differences.

Indianism set certain tones of knowing and could set certain tones of forgetting. Extirpation campaigns—pounding human beings into a polarity of Christian or devil-worshiper, and making all Incas into God's enemies—encouraged some Andeans to recast histories of Inca dominion. Judging colonial predicaments in new lights, they might even construct a notion of "Indian" sovereignty and fuse it with resurrected Inca kings, submerging Cusco's queens, women's participation in Andean public worlds, and Inca incursions into ayllu life. Or, turning Spanish gender norms inside out, indianists might make Andean "witches" into political vigilantes and "virgins," emblems of a new Andean purity, into standards of social legitimacy. All this while indigenous huacas, the standard bearers of indianism, began to take on Iberianish beards and God-like powers. Indianist imaginings were fashioned in, but not reducible to, the antagonisms of colonial life. These novel, sometimes jarring, ways of picturing experience were construing paradoxical "Indian" senses of self and possibility—in intricate dynamic with the compromising practices of Spanish hegemony.

"Indians" battled Spaniards in the seventeenth century; their fights, however, were waged in courts, in small-scale acts of resistance, and principally on religious terrain. The extirpation campaigns, coming in waves throughout the century, seemed to heighten indianist resolve as well as prove the danger and seriousness of Andean religious commitments. Nevertheless, indianist movements, while winning significant cultural victories and some political gains, were ultimately bound by colonial terms of living: they did not directly challenge colonial power. Nativist ideologies, construing "Indian" senses of place and possibility, positioned "Indians" within the confines of the hierarchical colonial world. Politically weak, indianists were born into a world of necessary compromise; and no matter how contentious, fragile, or conditional their loyalties, seventeenth-century "Indians" would appear to be colonial subjects—at least in some part of their contradictory selves. Analyses of hegemony lead us here: to an interpretation of indigenous subjects caught in, disputing, and constructing balances of power. Viewed from the equation's other side, we can see that the consequences (intended or not) of "Indian"/Spanish contests still left colonials in command. With all its demonstrated weaknesses, the colonial regime was able to successfully contain challenges to it. That is what "hegemony" is all about.

Exploring identities through the vantage of "hegemony" opens our analysis to state-making's most intimate dynamics, to ways the social relations of empire—grasped ideologically—impinged on the making of colonial Andeans. Further, it does so humanly, by making us grasp how structures of power limit life's possibilities as well as bridle social imaginings.

Indianism's simultaneous embrace and rejection of the colonial order charted courses of possibility for the years to come. Throughout the next one hundred years, Indian ideologies would galvanize political activities, built upon a growing conviction that the Inca was rightful king of the Indian world. A profound sense of the illegitimacy of the colonial regime—not necessarily a rejection of Crown—could join together ideological descendants of seventeenth-century indianist critics. These were different times, with different possibilities, different configurations of power. Nevertheless, the contradictions borne by Andeans of the 1780s hearken to the ambiguities of indianness of the century before— with Indian allegiances split between royal forces and Tupac Amaru II and with rebel Indian forces split by conflicting ayllu loyalties, gender divisions, and contentions over elite prerogatives.

Finally, "Indians" of the Andes should make us reflect on our own social imaginings. These past decades have witnessed challenges to much of mainstream anthropology's common sense. And terms like "Indian"—an extraordinary catch-all that has mixed together (in various proportions) the juridical categories of states and colonizers, the knowledge-categories of the social sciences, popular stereotypes, and the (some-time) identities of "indigenous" (for want of a better word) peoples—have come under scrutiny. James Clifford,[48] among others,[49] has pointedly reminded us of the term's woeful inadequacies: "Indian" is not a fixed inventory of traits, a thing, making up a bounded identity. Rather, "Indian," like "identity," must be understood in its sociability, emerging in the social relations that engage human beings in time. History is inseparable from social processes of understanding; and this holds for those Andeans who, in seventeenth-century Peru, were mobilized by a consciousness of their indianness as well as for our own attempts to conceptualize the past and present through terms like "Indian."

Swings from noble savage to murderous savage, from shattered victim to heroic resister, from the socialist empire of the Incas to Cusco's totalitarian tyranny,[50] have drained the life and lessons from "Indian." So have similar trends romancing "Indians"/"others" as human ideals before the European invasions or pure challengers of European ways for ever after.[51] Our theoretical biases, echoed in well-known penchants for oppositional thinking, have skirted the compromising social relations making us contradictory selves, part of contradictory worlds. Traditions of critical thinking still direct us to recognize the compromises—the real limits, the unintended consequences, the missed chances, the unrecognized complicities, and the just unknowables—of being part of this, our modern, colony-driven world.

I can imagine Hacas Poma wondering why it has taken us so long to confront our pollutions.

NOTES

This essay has gone through a series of incarnations, and I want to thank participants in the conference, "De mano a obra," held in Trujillo, Spain, 1990, the Department of Cultural Anthropology of Duke University, and particularly the seminarians of the Shelby Cullom Davis Center for Historical Studies, Princeton University, for their welcome comments and critiques. J. Dassin, N. Z. Davis, R. Garner, R. Kirk, J. J. Klor de Alva, C. Martin, E. Mayer, W. Merrill, O. Starn, A. Wightman, K. Warren, and N. Woodruff have been generous with their time and insights, as has G. Prakash—a most thoughtful editor. I first worked in Peruvian archives when conducting dissertation research and was able to do followup studies in Peru's ecclesiastical archives in 1988 and 1989. I am grateful to the Social Science Research Council, the Smithsonian Post-Doctoral Fellowship Program, and the University of Connecticut Research Foundation for their recent support.

1. Philip Corrigan and Derek Sayer, *The Great Arch* (Oxford: Basil Blackwell, 1985), offer important understandings into the cultural politics at the core of state-making. Their study of the constraints placed on social identities in the making of the English nation-state—seen as cultural revolution—animates much of the following discussion. Karen Spalding's essays, collected in *De Indio a Campesino* (Lima: Instituto de Estudios Peruanos, 1974), are crucial touchstones for anyone studying native colonial society.

2. Pierre Duviols, ed., *Cultura Andina y Represión. Procesos y visitas de idolatrías y hechicerías. Cajatambo. siglo XVII* (Cusco: Centro Bartolomé de las Casas, 1986), p. 227. Hernando Hacas Poma preached these words to Andeans living in a wide range of ayllus that dotted what is today called Peru's northern and central sierra. We find them recorded in ecclesiastical court cases that are the prime (and problematic) sources for this essay—seventeenth-century inquisition-like campaigns to "extirpate idolatries" from Peruvians' souls. Note that this quotation of one of Hernando Hacas Poma's "dogmatizing" efforts was entered into court records only in the Spanish; we do not know the actual words he used when preaching in Quechua. While he might have used the Spanish

term "indio" to designate the cultural category, native Andeans, "runa" (people) is another possibility.

Pierre Duviols, *La Lutte contre les réligions autochtones dans le Pérou Colonial: L'extirpation de l'idolâtrie entre 1532 et 1660* (Lima and Paris: Institut Français d'Etudes Andines, 1971), and Lorenzo Huertas, "La religión de una sociedad rural andina: Cajatambo en el siglo xvii" (Tesis para Bachiller, Facultad de Letras, Universidad Nacional Mayor de San Marcos, Lima, 1969), have written pioneering analyses of the extirpation campaigns and of various aspects of native religion that the "idolatrías" section of the Archivo Arzobispal de Lima (AAL) reveal. Subsequent studies include Luis Millones, "Un movimiento nativista del Siglo XVI: El Taki Onqoy," in *Ideología Mesiánica del Mundo Andino*, ed. Juan Ossio (Lima: Prado Pastor, 1973), pp. 83–94; and Karen Spalding, *Huarochirí: An Andean Society under Inca and Spanish Rule* (Stanford: Stanford University Press, 1984), pp. 239–69; and Steve Stern, "The Struggle for Solidarity. Class, Culture, and Community in Highland Indian America," *Radical History Review* 27 (1983): 21–45. I have used this rich documentary source to shed light on the gendered construction of cultural resistance, "Andean" witchcraft, and the participation of women in native religious structures, as well as in a discussion of the making of native colonial religious ideologies. See "Political Memories and Colonizing Symbols: Santiago and the Mountain Gods of Colonial Peru," in *Rethinking History and Myth: Indigenous South American Perspectives on the Past*, ed. J. Hill (Urbana: University of Illinois Press, 1988). I first worked in the Archivo Arzobispal of Lima when conducting dissertation research, and was able to do followup work in the summers of 1988 and 1989.

Pierre Duviols has also edited and published a major collection of trial manuscripts from the Cajatambo region (Cultura Andina, 1986); Ann Sanchez has recently edited a series of "idolatría" documents from Chancay, *Amancebados, Hechiceros y Rebeldes (Chancay, Siglo XVII)* (Cusco: Centro Bartolomé de Las Casas, 1991). See Sabine MacCormack, *Religion in the Andes: Vision and Imagination in Early Colonial Peru* (Princeton: Princeton University Press, 1991), for a study of the intellectual traditions shaping Spanish versions of Andean religion.

3. Irene Silverblatt, "Imperial Dilemmas, the Politics of Kinship, and Inca Reconstructions of History," *Comparative Studies in Society and History* 30, no. 1 (1988): 83–102; John V. Murra, *La Organización Económica del Estado Inca* (Mexico: Siglo XXI, 1978).

4. Charles Gibson, "Indian Societies under Spanish Rule," in *Colonial Spanish America*, ed. Leslie Bethell (Cambridge: Cambridge University Press, 1987); Spalding, *De Indio a campesino*.

5. Irene Silverblatt, *Moon, Sun, and Witches: Gender Ideologies and Class in Inca and Colonial Peru* (Princeton: Princeton University Press, 1987), pp. 159–96.

6. Silverblatt, "Imperial Dilemmas."

7. Gibson, "Indian Societies under Spanish Rule."

8. My principal documentary source for the Taki Onqoy is Millones' edition, *Las informaciones de Cristóbal de Albornoz: documentos para la historia del Taki*

Onqoy (Cuernavaca: CIDOC, 1971). Millones, *El retorno de las huacas. Estudios y documentos sobre el Taki Onqoy. Siglo XVI* (Lima: Instituto de Estudios Peruanos/Sociedad Peruana de Psicoanalysis, 1990), has revised and republished the archival material along with important accompanying essays. See particularly the contribution by Rafael Varon. Christóbal de Albornoz, the priest who was responsible for investigating the Taki Onqoy, also briefly describes the movement in Christóbal Albornoz, "Instrucción para descubrir todas las guacas del Peru y sus camayos y haciendas," *Journal de la Société des Americanistes* 56 (1967): 17-39.

See Stern's *Peru's Indian Peoples and the Challenge of Spanish Conquest* (Madison: University of Wisconsin Press, 1982), pp. 51–70, for an insightful discussion of the Taki Onqoy. He argues that the Taki Onqoy manifested an early pan-Andean, Indian consciousness, one that transcended ethnic boundaries. Other studies include Millones, "Un movimiento nativista del Siglo XVI"; and Wachtel "Rebeliones y milenarismo," in *Ideología Mesiánica del Mundo Andino*, pp. 103–42.

9. Millones, *Las informaciones de Cristóbal de Albornoz*, f.25–149.

10. Peter Worsley, *The Trumpet Shall Sound*, 2d ed. (New York: Schocken, 1968).

11. Stern, *Peru's Indian Peoples and the Challenge of Spanish Conquest*, pp. 51–62.

12. Millones, *Las informaciones de Cristóbal de Albornoz*, f.25–149.

13. It is difficult to determine how widespread the movement actually was and how far it spread beyond the department of Ayacucho. It is also difficult to determine if it was tied to the armed resistance movement of Manco Inca or if its militancy extended to a cache of arms uncovered in Jauja.

14. Spalding, *Huarochirí*, pp. 168–238.

15. John H. Rowe, "The Incas under Spanish Colonial Institutions," *Hispanic-American Historical Review* 37 (1957): 155–99; Spalding, *Huarochirí*, pp. 136–67.

16. Spalding, *Huarochirí*, pp. 179–80, 214–16. However, ayllus of Sarhua and Chuschi in the Rio Pampas region of Ayacucho still live in what had been colonial reducciones.

17. Felipe Guaman Poma de Ayla, *El Primer nueva corónica y buen gobierno [1615]* (critical edition by John Murra and Rolena Adorno, translation and textual analysis of Quechua by J. Urioste, 3 vols. [Mexico, D.F.: Siglo XXI, 1980], 2:415).

18. Juan de Solórzano Pereira, *Política Indiana [1647]* (Madrid: Biblioteca de Autores Españoles, Ediciones Atlas, 1972), 252: 417–32.

19. In Pierre Duviols, *La Destrucción de las religiones andinas (Durante la conquista y la colonia)*, trans. Albor Maruenda (Mexico: Universidad Nacional Autonoma de México, 1977), pp. 42–43.

20. Guaman Poma, *El Primer nueva corónica y buen gobierno [1615]*.

21. See Solórzano, *Política Indiana*, 252:371–83.

22. Anthony Pagden, "Identity Formation in Spanish America," in *Colonial Identity in the Atlantic World, 1500–1800*, ed. N. Canny and A. Pagden (Princeton: Princeton University Press, 1987), p. 66.

23. AAL: Leg. 6, Exp. XI, f.9–9v, f.47.

24. AAL: Leg. 1, Exp. X; Leg. 6, Exp. XI; Duviols, *La Lutte contre les réligions autochtones dans le Pérou Colonial*, p. 385.

25. My argument has been influenced by an extensive literature on "hegemony," including Raymond Williams, *Marxism and Literature* (Oxford: Oxford University Press, 1977), pp. 1–144; Eugene D. Genovese, *Roll Jordan Roll* (New York: Vintage, 1974); Ranajit Guha and Gayatri Spivak, eds., *Selected Subaltern Studies* (New Delhi: Oxford University Press, 1988).

26. Any study of Andean utopian thought, with its ties to beliefs in the Inca's return, is indebted to the pathbreaking work of Flores Galindo, *Buscando un Inca: Identidad y utopía en los Andes* (Havana: Casa de las Americas, 1986). The commemoration of past relations with the Inca empire, while part of a configuration drawing on Inca experience, does not (yet) represent full-blown beliefs in the Inca's coming. However, it could serve as part of the ideological landscape from which an Inca/king figure might be drawn (cf. Flores, *Buscando*).

27. AAL: Leg. 4, Exp. s.n.; Leg. 6, Exp. XI.

28. Silverblatt, *Moon, Sun, and Witches*, pp. 81–108.

29. Rodrigo Hernández Príncipe, "Mitología andina" [1621], in *Inca* 1 (1923): 24–68, 52–63; Silverblatt, *Moon, Sun, and Witches*, pp. 94–100; R. T. Zuidema, "Kinship and Ancestor Cult in Three Peruvian Communities. Hernández Príncipe's Account of 1622," *Bulletin de l'institut français d'études Andines* 2 (1977): 16–23.

30. AAL: Leg. 6, Exp. XI, f.117; Duviols, *Cultura Andina*, p. 169.

31. Duviols, *Cultura Andina*, p. 350.

32. Flores Galindo, *Buscando*.

33. Silverblatt, *Moon, Sun, and Witches*, pp. 40–66.

34. AAL: Leg. 6, Exp. XI, f.33v, f.37, f.39.

35. Silverblatt, *Moon, Sun, and Witches*, pp. 169–96.

36. Ibid., pp. 198–206.

37. AAL: Leg. 4, Exp. XIV, f.3v.

38. See AAL: Leg. 4, Exp. XVIIIa.

39. AAL: Leg. 4, Exp. XVIII, f.5v, f.6.

40. AAL: Leg. 2, Exp. XXVII, f.1, f.8.

41. AAL: Leg. 2, Exp. XIV, f.12v.

42. AAL: Leg. 4, Exp. XVIII.

43. Duviols, *Cultura Andina*, p. 452.

44. For another example of cultural hybridizing, with implications for colonial hegemony, see Silverblatt, "Political Memories and Colonizing Symbols: Santiago and the Mountain Gods of Colonial Peru," an analysis of the merged Lliviac (native god of thunder/lightning) and Santiago (the patron saint of the Spanish conquest). Also see Henrique Urbano, "Dios Yaya, Dios Churi, Dios Espíritu," *Journal of Latin American Lore* 6 (1980): 111–28.

45. AAL: Leg. 4, Exp. XXI; Leg. 6, Exp. VIII; Leg. 6, Exp. XI; Leg. 4, Exp. XVIII; Leg. 2, Exp. XVIII; Leg. 3, Exp. X; Leg. 1, Exp. XII.

46. AAL: Leg. 2, Exp. XVIII; Leg. 4, Exp. XVIII; Leg. 3, Exp. X.

47. For descriptions of violence and acts of rebellion in the Huarochirí region, see Spalding, *Huarochirí*, pp. 203, 247, 248, 270–93.

48. James Clifford, *The Predicament of Culture* (Cambridge: Harvard University Press, 1988).

49. See Kay Warren, *The Symbolism of Subordination: Indian Identity in a Guatemalan Town* (Austin: University of Texas Press, 1978); Michael Taussig, *Shamanism, Colonialism and the Wild Man: A Study in Terror and Healing* (Chicago: University of Chicago Press, 1987); and idem, *The Nervous System* (New York and London: Routledge, 1992).

50. For a particularly glaring example, see Mario Vargas Llosa, "Questions of Conquest: What Columbus Wrought and What He Did Not," *Harper's* 281, no. 1687 (1990): 45–53. Vargas Llosa, in a *Harper's* lead article, describes Peru's Indians as an indistinguishable mass, whose religious fanaticism—blind devotion to an all-powerful "totalitarian" ruler (the Inca)—led to their easy defeat ("disintegra[tion] like ice in water") at the hands of Spanish conquistadores (pp. 49–50).

51. Including myself; see Silverblatt, *Moon, Sun, and Witches*, pp. 3–39, 67–80.

CHAPTER 11

Ethnographic Travesties:
Colonial Realism, French Feminism,
and the Case of Elissa Rhaïs

EMILY APTER

TOWARD A DEFINITION OF COLONIAL REALISM

This essay forms part of a larger project on colonial fiction in France and North Africa. Many of the texts under consideration fall stylistically into a category characterizable as colonial realism. Colonial realism, as distinct from realism *tout court*, is a belated Orientalism of the late nineteenth and early twentieth centuries that may be qualified as both psychological and ethnographic in its painting of modern life. It is perhaps because it is often inexpert in execution or parodic of its more robust Balzacian and Flaubertian predecessors that it emerges as a logical site for examining the literary and visual construction of cultures coded as exotic. Colonial realism's narrative strategies are more technically brittle in their conventional stylizations. Coming apart at the seams, they reveal their fierce competitiveness with the power of the mechanically reproduced image, given mass market appeal by the turn of the century as a result, in part, of the explosion of photographic tourism, ethnography, commercially distributed pornography, national festivals, and world exhibitionism.

Though the problem of realism appears to be of an exclusively literary order, it is also a kind of intellectual vehicle for treating other more difficult political concerns such as how to write on global perspectives in French studies in the context of a fast-growing cultural studies academic industry. It seems that the theoretical and political categories of postcolonialism, even as they burgeon and become increasingly sophisticated, are also becoming more rapidly used up and, in many instances, altogether bankrupt. Preludes and prefaces that take great pains to situate the writer/viewer in a redemptive practice that is ultimately a reenactment of just what she or he is trying to avoid (the voyeurism of "other-gazing"), all these verbal movable markers and narrative devices repeat the colonial gesture of self-authorization. They are rituals of what

Octave Mannoni called "the decolonization of myself," aware upon his return from Madagascar (where he worked in the compromised position of civil servant/ethnopsychiatrist), that even Western anticolonialism inscribes a colonial gesture—specifically, a positioning of the observer in a higher class, a superior seat of power.[1]

In trying to open up certain dead categories and clichés within the framing of culture, realism, a traditional concern within literary criticism, has proved to be surprisingly useful as a source for cultural theory when reconfigured as a genre obsessed with the representation of cultural essentialism, be it physiognomical, characterological, racial, national, ethnic, social, or gender-typed. Anchored since the early 1830s in what might be called the "evidentiary"—specifically, the descriptivist popular culture of fashion journalism, travel writing, political and military press coverage, institutional reports, and so on—realism has always enjoyed a privileged, if highly problematic relation to the "real," for it is virtually impossible to read descriptions of "reality" without awareness of the workings of mimetic fallacies (literary conceits for representing the visual textures of facticity) which condition the conventions of historical novels deemed realist. Recent theoretical work on the "real" has also introduced the problem of how to negotiate analytically between the Lacanian real of our desire and social, historical, or economic reality—the real or "reals" of everyday life.[2] The colonial real, for now, must stand as an experimental term mediating between psychoanalytic and historical accounts of the colonial subject: it refers to a split, ambivalent colonial subject (to adopt Homi Bhabha's framings) whose positionality is a phantasmatic construction of literary texts, themselves firmly anchored in the sociopolitical history of French colonial life in North Africa.

In reexamining realist narrative technique as it evolves from Balzac and Flaubert to the exoticist canon of "minor" colonial novelists, we can begin to grasp some of the shared points of intellectual conservatism between realism and colonialism. Colonial administrations certainly understood the ideological power of colonial fictions, which ordered territorial and psychical conquest into mutually refracting teleological narratives. However, as this analysis of several novels by Elissa Rhaïs shows, the discursive "native" subject that emerges in many of these narratives was often capable of undermining colonial norms either by inadvertently capturing a hostile indigenous gaze, or by displacing the boundaries of the cultural stereotype that the realist genre generally served to put in place, or, finally, by splitting or complicating the very notion of a colonial subject, whether authorial, "native," or metropolitan.

I am certainly not the first to "think colonialism" through realism. Timothy Mitchell, in *Colonising Egypt* (1988), dissected the reality effect of world exhibitions in terms of the problematic scale of their cultural referentiality (at once global and parochial), and their techniques of staging and spectacularity (perspectives ordered by Eurocentric viewing, the optical alienation effect produced by commodified simulations of "Cairo").[3] Antonia Lant has described the "twin realist and fantastic character" of an early cinema infected by "the imperialism of Egyptology."[4] Writing from an Althusserian perspective, John Tagg has noted the socially fixative nature of realism in photographic representation: "Realism sets its subjects in place at the point of intelligibility of its activity, in a position of observation and synthesis which cannot be questioned by the flux of the text and which cannot be thrown into process by the sliding of signifiers that disestablishes social positionality."[5] As a visual codification of the world by a dominant ideology, as a medium that fosters a spirit of surveillance and possessiveness toward the picture, as a mode of image-mediation promising privileged access to (and manipulation of) "truth," (the evidentiary) photographic realism, in Tagg's estimation, also functions historically as a colonization of subjectivity:

> They [photographs] can be taken as evidence. They can incriminate. They can be aids to masturbation or trophies of conquest. They can be emblems of a symbolic exchange in kinship rituals or vicarious tokens of a world of potential possessions. Through that democratized form of imperialism known as *tourism*, they can exert a power to colonize new experiences and capture subjects across a range never envisaged in painting. (T 164)

Tagg traces the way in which photographic realism consolidates historic definitions of typicality, be it "typical" scenes in foreign locales or the physiognomical types of native subjects framed as curiosities. Earlier, in his founding text *Orientalism* (1978), Edward Said had similarly characterized the intransigence of Orientalist tropes and typologies—their ability to sink into consciousness as credible stand-ins for reality itself—as "radical realism." Homi Bhabha, following Said in an essay on stereotype and colonial discourse, made realism the "third term" in a psychoanalytic scheme conjugating fetishism with colonialism.[6] Bhabha's definition of the stereotype as fetish, a reifying fixer that disavows and abjects difference, encourages the use of a deconstructed realism to unbind the coalition of fantasies and identifications agglomerated in the colonial unconscious. Colonially cultured positions, thus critically undone, appear as tenuous as the sexed positions of heterosexual society criticized by Judith Butler in her revisionist account of gender identity.[7] In the context of contemporary postcolonialism, this unfixing effect can have unpredictable consequences, leading, for example, to a more openended politics of the cultural subject, or to a kind of diasporic utopianism of cultural identifications detached from the lived histories of individuals, or to a reactive recathexis with the stereotype—a conservative return to colonial fetishes.

In framing the topic of colonial realism I am trying to approach such problems as the formation of literary stereotype; the phenomenon of what Naomi Schor has recently termed "postcardization"[8] in prose and its attendant poetics of cultural fetishism and visual seduction; the allure of "manners and customs" scenography in popular fiction, theater, opera, and early cinema; the status of formula essential to "the display of peoples" (as when singers, dancers, and kif-smokers in Moorish cafés are trotted out for ritual inspection); the politics of a racial unconscious embedded in the tropes of regional "local color" or the aesthetics of Orientalist colorism; the relationship between caricature and cultural identity; the compenetration of ethnic typology and the essence of genre itself; and, finally, the historic role of colonialism in the perpetuation of literary realism, itself conceivable as a praxis for freeze-framing and hypostatizing cultural attitude.

This essay will be more limited to issues arising from the relationship between the historiography of colonial representation and its destabilization in the context of early First and Third World feminism. This essay will look specifically at the work of Elissa Rhaïs, a popular Algerian novelist of the 1920s, asking to what extent fictions and stereotypes of "real" Muslim life may have motivated feminist struggles in France; to what extent the nomadism, political disenfranchisement, and exploitation of North African women described by Rhaïs served to dramatize what a later generation of feminists (following Luce Irigaray) would characterize as the "homelessness of women in the symbolic order";[9] to what extent Rhaïs's histrionic portraits of passionate, heroically self-destructive North African women formed part of a larger historical pattern in which European women appropriated canonical Orientalist stereotypes for the staging of "new" identities; to what degree these appropriations amounted to yet another form of colonialism; and finally, to what extent ethnographic and gender travesties, typified by the case of Rhaïs's contested authorial identity, operated, and continue to operate at the heart of relations between First and Third World feminism.

ELISSA RHAÏS, THE "NOVEL"

The strange case of Elissa Rhaïs, an Algerian woman writer known in the 1920s in France and North Africa as the author of best-selling Orientalist novels in the realist mode, poses a problem for literature and historiography alike. The principal document concerning her life is a biography ambiguously subtitled "novel," which nonetheless purports to be an authentic, factual account. (*Elissa Rhaïs, roman* was published in 1982 by Paul Tabet, her living executor [he is currently director of a French cultural foundation that protects copyright privileges].)

Elissa Rhaïs was the pen name of Leila Bou Mendil, born in the Algerian resort town of Blidah[10] to a Muslim father and a mother of French Jewish extraction.[11] Tabet maintains that she was married against her will to a wealthy Egyptian spice merchant living in Kabylia, who punished her with neglect and confinement when she attempted to resist his jealousy and sexual despotism. Imprisoned in a harem for fifteen years, treated as a pariah by the other wives, deprived of air and exercise, she became boulemic and virtually ate herself to death. Her "awakening" from this nightmare of moral and physical torpor occurred when her husband died and she was able to return to her native city in 1914. Elissa Rhaïs gradually reclaimed her bodily self from the state of spiritual *mollesse* and psychic nonbeing she had endured for so many years. Using a small inheritance, she created a local salon where intellectuals gathered. She invented herself as a writer, hiring the son of a poor relation who had received a French education as her personal secretary.

Tabet's biographical *roman* continues with the trajectory of Rhaïs's success as a novelist. Her stories recorded the bitter plight of North African women: nomadic mothers disinherited and dispossessed, *café-chanteuses* and *bayadères*, Jewish daughters married against their will, prostitutes and rebellious harem wives. These were her stock characters, and they sold her fiction well at a time when France was preparing to celebrate its centenary of the 1830 conquest of Algeria. *Saâda la Marocaine* (her first novel, published in 1919), *Le Café-chantant, Kerkeb, Noblesse arabe* (1920), *Les Juifs ou la fille d'Eléazar* (1921), *La Fille des pachas* (1922), *La Fille du douar* (1924), *La Chemise qui porte bonheur* (1925), *L'Andalouse* (1925), *Le Mariage de Hanifa* (1926), *Le Sein blanc* (1928), *La Riffaine* and *Petits pachas en exil* (1929), and *La Convertie* (1929) went through multiple printings and were considered to be charming snapshots of North African mores. Reviews in *La Revue des deux mondes, L'Intransigeant,* and *Les Nouvelles littéraires, La Nouvelle revue française,* the *Revue bleue,* and the *Bulletin de l'Afrique française* bolstered her fame and helped garner fans among the French suffragettes. If one trusts Tabet's story, Rhaïs may be seen as occupying a critical juncture between colonialism and feminism; her life-story, imbricated within the plots of her abused, claustrated heroines, functioned as a kind of heroic, allegorical backdrop for global feminist struggles for political enfranchisement and social independence.

Tabet claims that Rhaïs made her first trip to Paris in 1919, and lived there intermittently until her death in 1940. The distinguished roster of visitors to her apartment included Colette, Sarah Bernhardt, Paul Morand, and the Algerian author Jean Amrouche. In 1926, accompanied by her secretary, whom she now called her "son," she made a triumphant voyage to Casablanca where she received an official welcome from the French colonial authorities and was given a stipend of six thousand francs to study the condition of women in Morocco. By the early 1930s an American producer pushed to adapt her novel *La Fille des pachas* for the screen (as a kind of companion piece to *Pépé le Moko*).[12] A novella, *Kerkeb, danseuse berbère*, furnished the material for an opera libretto with music by the composer Samuel-Rousseau. In 1939 the French government decided to award Rhaïs the legion of honor because her novels, in making the colonies seem attractive to French tourists, had performed the invaluable political function of enhancing the "civilizing mission."

There was only one problem: when a background check was ordered, no evidence was found of any kind of formal education in Rhaïs's past. Indeed, Elissa Rhaïs's novels, exemplary for their authenticity of feminine voice, appeared to have been written by a man. This nephew, or "son," known as Raoul Dahan in Tabet's text, was by his own account the sole author of her fiction, despite the fact that after her death no work was ever published under his name. According to the testimony of Rhaïs's domestics, he had become his benefactress's sexual and literary slave, ironically repeating her own sordid tale of psychological and material imprisonment in gender-reverse order. An accomplice in the production of the Elissa Rhaïs myth (itself much publicized by Plon, the publishing house that launched her career), Raoul became a victim of his own success at narrative cross-dressing.

So far we have an extraordinary case history of authorial travesty that doubles as a story of gender and cultural transvestism. In addition to "writing as a woman," Raoul also costumed his prose in the pseudorealist literary style of the French Orientalist/*colon*. But there is still another layer of travesty (in the sense of *supercherie* or hoax): Tabet's biography of his grandmother may itself be a tissue of phantasms anchored with factoids.

When Tabet's *Elissa Rhaïs, roman* appeared in 1982, published by Grasset under the direction of France's editorial superstar Bernard-Henri Lévy (himself a *pied noir*), it received considerable attention from the French press with reviews in *Le Monde*, *L'Express* and *Le Matin de Paris* (this article, "La petite fille juive du harem," by the feminist theorist Catherine Clément). Tabet made a television appearance on the literary talk-show *Apostrophes*, but shortly thereafter a controversy erupted in *Les Nouvelles littéraires* when a piece entitled "Bernard Pivot victime d'une supercherie?" attempted to call Tabet's bluff. The fires were stoked when Rhaïs's newphew, a Parisian lawyer named Richard Dupuy and surviving son Roland Rhaïs entered the fray, claiming that Elissa Rhaïs was indeed the sole author of the works. An "objective" and painstaking account of the whole affair was presented in an article published in 1984 by Jean Déjeux, a well-respected critic and bibliographer of North African and colonial literature. Déjeux punctured many surfaces in the Elissa Rhaïs legend as constituted by Tabet.[13] After acknowledging the difficulty of disconfirming the basic outlines of Tabet's version of the story, Déjeux rectifies certain critical errors in his account. Rhaïs's real name was Rosine Boumendil (not Leila), and she was the daughter of Algerian Jewish parents (on both sides, not just one as alleged by Tabet). Déjeux confirms that she attended the *école communale* in Blida until the age of twelve. She was then married at a young age to a rabbi of Algiers named Moïse Amar, but never incarcerated in a harem as Tabet would have us believe. She had three children by Amar, one of whom died young. Her surviving son, Jacob-Raymond, received a French education and became a staunch supporter of the FLN (National Liberation Front) during the Algerian revolution. A man of letters in his own right who at one time edited an Algerian communist newspaper (coauthoring articles with Algeria's premier postwar authors Mohammed Dib and Kateb Yacine), Raymond Rhaïs has remained, understandably, one of Tabet's most vehement detractors.

According to Déjeux, Rosine married a wealthy businessman named Mardochée Chemouil (who Frenchified his name into Maurice Chemoul) after her divorce from her first husband. It was Chemoul's nephew Raoul-Robert Tabet (not Dahan), only three years her son's senior, who became her amanuensis after he came to live with the family during his studies at the Faculté des Lettres in Algiers. Déjeux confirms that Raoul acted as scribe, but whether he was the lover of his aunt remains a murky matter. Elissa Rhaïs separated from her husband in 1917 and moved to Paris with her two children and adopted "son." In Paris she apparently enjoyed a brilliant social and literary entrée, successfully playing the card of Muslim Arab woman writer. Déjeux speculates that she jettisoned her Jewish origins out of fear of anti-Semitism, though he does point out that other Jewish writers at the time were able to advance their careers without disguising their heritage. (One might interject here that it is hard to believe that there was ever any mystery surrounding her Jewish identity, given the insider's view of Jewish culture offered in her writings.) Déjeux also suggests that some of the Maghrebian literati may have been on to her Orientalist "act," citing as evidence the fact that the "Algerianists"—Robert Randau, Louis Lecoq, Charles Hagel, Charles Courtin—kept her at bay. In the late 1930s she returned to her villa in Blida and died there in 1940 of a sudden illness (not, as Tabet implies, of chagrin over the Foreign Legion debacle). Déjeux makes no mention of any impact she might have had on a burgeoning Third World feminism, but in my own interview with Tabet in 1990 he insisted that her feminist influence was important and cosmopolitan. Tabet was elusive when I tried to press him on questions surrounding Rhaïs's reputation as an author and model for feminism both then and now.

Regardless of whether one can ever ultimately determine the appropriate degrees of fantasy and veracity assignable to the life and legend of Rhaïs, the story itself remains of keen historiographical interest insofar as it highlights ambiguities surrounding the representation of the colonial subject of history. The question of who wrote the novels published under the name of Elissa Rhaïs dovetails with the question of whether Rhaïs's novels "truly" represent North African women subjects (both human and topical). Was Rhaïs's cultural masquerade as vexed as her gender masquerade?[14] Do her novels, read today, amount to an example of textual agency without an agent, that is, articulations of an Imaginary, at once feminist and anticolonial, performed by a "disappeared" colonial subject? Or, to put this another way, to what extent do Rhaïs's writings, for all their ambivalence and bad faith as gender travesties, for all their pandering to a jingoistically colonialist French reading public, operate as "primal scenes" within another historical narrative—namely, the story of French feminism's instrumentalization of Orientalism as a source of enabling feminist myths?

UNFIXING THE COLONIAL STEREOTYPE

It is not surprising that Elissa Rhaïs's novels fall outside the purview of what French arbiters of literary value commonly refer to as the *lisible*. But it is perhaps this very unreadability of Rhaïs's colonial fiction that lends it historical interest as a paradigmatic example of that "forgotten" and rather ignominious genre dubbed *littérature coloniale* by the Lansonists. A motley assortment of authors falls under the rubric of "colonial literature," recently reclassified by Déjeux in his *Bibliographie de la littérature "algérienne" des français.*[15] Déjeux's list, like that of earlier bibliographies in the 1920s and 1930s by Charles Tailliart, Arthur Pellegrin, Jean Pomier, Pierre Mille, Marius-Ary Leblond, and Roland Lebel, subsumes Parisian literati interested in updating exoticism, modernist Orientalists seduced by the spectacular stage-setting of the East, North African authors writing in French (such as Rhaïs), amateur ethnographers with a taste for the tourist sublime, colonial civil servants proselytizing for *la mission civilisatrice*, cross-dressing journalists, and lady travelers.

The authors that might be said to comprise the archive of colonial literature have for the most part fallen into total obscurity, but they were all descendants of Pierre Loti, of Loti's *Aziyadé*, of course, but also of his lesser known works—*Le Roman d'un spahi* (1881); *Les Trois Dames de la Kasbah* (1884) (later subsumed in *Fleurs d'ennui*); *Suleima* (1882), in which a pet monkey is the predominant figure for an Algerian prostitute-criminal; *Au Maroc* (1890); and *Les Désenchantées* (1906). Loti's strongest immediate influences were Flaubert (*Voyage en Egypte*), Gautier (*Voyage pittoresque en Algérie*) Maupassant (*Au Maghreb*), and the Goncourt brothers (those parts of the *Journal* dealing with the Expositions Coloniales); his epigones included Jean Lorrain, Hector France, Robert Randau, Guy de Téramond, Charles Géniaux, Louis Bertrand, Jérôme and Jean Tharaud, Paul Vigné d'Octon, and Michel Vieuchange, among many others. Interestingly enough, a significant number of contributors to the genre were women: Jane Dieulafoy, Marc Elys, Myriam Harry, Clotilde Chivas-Baron, Lucienne Favre, L. M. Enfrey, Lucie Delarue-Mardrus (wife of the French translator of *The Arabian Nights*), and, of course, Elissa Rhaïs.[16]

Rhaïs's novels, though published in the 1920s when modernism, surrealism, and avant-garde experimentation were in vogue, were written in a realist style that for all intents and purposes amounted to a kind of commercialized Flaubertianism.[17] Flaubert, adopting the time-honored literary technique of *ut pitura poesis* in his historical novels, would characteristically evoke exotic urban geography and its "teeming" inhabitants with lapidary, variegated language. In *Salammbô* he adapted the conceits of genre painting (a rubric under which Orientalist subjects continue to be classed), to prose:

> So lay Carthage before the eyes of the soldiers encamped on the plain.
>
> From afar they picked out the markets and crossways, and argued about the positions of the temples. That of Khamon, fronting the Syssitia, had golden tiles: Melkarth, to the left of Eshmun, had branches of coral on its roofing: yonder, Tanit's copper dome bulged among the palm trees: black Moloch was below the cisterns, toward the pharos. At the angles of the pediments, on the tops of walls, at the corners of the squares, they could see gods with hideous heads, either huge or squat, with enormous or immoderately hollowed bellies, opening their jaws, spreading forth their arms, and holding forks or chains or javelins; and the blue of the sea lay below the streets, which in perspective took on an even greater steepness.
>
> These were filled from morning till evening with a tumultuous crowd: young boys rang little bells and shouted before the bathhouse doors; the shops for hot drinks were a-steam; the air echoed with the clangour of anvils, the sacred white cocks of the sun crowed on the terraces; oxen

bellowed in the temples as they were slain; slaves ran about with baskets on their heads; & in the depths of the porticoes a priest could every now and again be seen, draped in a somber cloak, bare-footed, and wearing a pointed hat. Carthage, seen thus, exasperated the Barbarians.[18]

A similar panoptical vertigo, heightened by the spectacle of dead animals (rhopography), anthropological reality effects (place-names, foreign loan words), and splashes of literary technicolor, can be found in the opening of Rhaïs's *Kerkeb, danseuse berbère*:

It was the festival of the Marabout d'Ellouali, on the neighboring heights of Fez. Around the white cupola of the great saint, between the rocks and aloe, innumerable tents raised their banners. The black, red or green burnouses of the men swarmed, among the gandourahs of the women which were white, fringed in shadow. Everyone pushed at the threshold of the funerary kiosk to make their offering to the marabout. . . . Sharp voices intoned the *Fatiha*. . . . On the edge of the closest oasis, hundreds of sheep were being immolated. Their hacked cadavers hung on carab trees, the oasis ran bloody, clouds of incense rose above the trees. Everywhere there were joyous fires, music. . . . Women let forth their you-you and called out to each other in song. . . . [. . .] Around a waterfall, soldiers equipped themselves for the ritual fantasia. The crowd of pilgrims swelled without end. New groups arrived, scaling the rocky pathways, preceded by flute-players and standard-bearers, and yaouleds holding multicolored wax candles destined for the marabout's bier. . . . And over all this, the torrid heat of July, the blinding light of the great Moroccan sky.[19]

Rhaïs thus updated Romantic Orientalism for an age of mechanical reproduction, aping, in this opening passage, the "you are there" sensation conveyed by the moving camera, replacing the image petrifaction of Flaubertian genre painting in prose with a mobile (though equally formulaic) display of peoples, manners, and customs. In his *Histoire de la littérature coloniale en France* (1931), Roland Lebel, distinguishing colonial fiction from its fin-de-siècle forebears, stressed its reliance on a politically motivated visuality—an optical, nationalistic projection of élan vital. Lebel argued that colonial literature was not to be summed up by its treatment of colonial subject matter, but rather, by its *optique nouvelle*: "The colonial spirit," he wrote, "is an affirmation of moral energy which affirms itself against decadentism and pessimism, it is a doctrine of action, a school of energy, an act of faith." Where Loti and his successors treated foreign topographies as mere frameworks for description, the colonial writers, according to Lebel, "opted for the colony, assimilating to it as object, as a *milieu naturel*." No longer did it suffice to *faire beau*, he claimed; now it was necessary to *faire vrai*.[20]

Rhaïs's novels were marketed as representations of "true" Muslim life in contradistinction to the "false" Orientalism of an earlier tradition of literary exoticism. Writing in *Le Journal des débats* in 1920, Jean de Pierrefeu noted that the "obsessional" aura generated by the vivid colorism of *Sâada la Marocaine* was so strong that the reader would see vestiges of Oriental decor upon looking up from the book. Consistently praised for their *puissance de vérité*, that is, their ability to purvey with seeming authenticity the essential(ist) "Arab" character (with its putative penchants for violence, jealousy, and self-destruction), Rhaïs's writings did indeed "faire vrai" by filling in the larger-than-life characterological cut-outs of Orientalism ascribed by Said to the "radical real."

Whether filled in or not, one could say that the culturally essentializing stereotype grounded colonial fiction (regardless of the author's political persuasions), imposing itself through a variety of devices, from the naming of characters to the description of physiognomies. In *Le Café-chantant* for example, the name of the singer ("Fouad El Begri"— "Lungs of an Ox") or that of her cohort ("Fathma Calyptus"—"Fathma long-waisted as the Eucalyptus tree") functions like a concentrate of essentialism, metonymizing her character throughout, enhancing its typicality. There is even a didactic, self-reflexive intervention at this moment in the text, where the narrator explains this essentializing process, informing the reader that the assignment of epithets to famous entertainers was an unvarying practice in the café-chantants, a custom inspired by both malice and admiration.

A great deal of work has been done on the impact of physiognomical theory, fostered by Gall and Lavater, on French realism. The commensurability between facial characteristic and charactological profile, between body type and historic destiny, between physical aberration and psychic flaw, between national costume and cultural identity, forms the bedrock of readerly expectations and has been dissected in the works of canonical realist authors from Balzac to Zola.[21] Rather than rehearse these ideas, it is sufficient to point out the extent to which Rhaïs's use of physiognomy catered to the marketable stereotype. In *Kerkeb*, for instance, the domestic patriarch is described as follows:

> Sid Hafid, the master, is there on the threshold in his white gandourah and yellow leather slippers. He gives orders to the servants in a brutal tone of voice. Sid Hafid is representative of the evolved Moroccan. Long, thin, nervous, a bony face with a beard trimmed into a necklace that trembles at the slightest command, piercing eyes, made up with khol, a hooked nose which bespeaks his sensual egoism, trickiness, and hard pride of race. It is essential that everyone bend to his every word like the camel under the *flissa* of the guide. (K 72)

Here the strokes of the literary brush—a bony face, a beard that quivers with the issuance of a command, piercing eyes, a hooked nose—serve to "harden and hook" the outlines of this character into the type. The mastery of this tyrannical sidi is emphasized not only by the repetition of the phrase "he is the master" and the relentless predictability of adjective, but also by glimpsed vignettes of his servants rushing to obey orders, of a camel sinking to its knees at the switch of its rider. This use of stereotype recalls Roland Barthes' definition in *The Pleasure of the Text*:

> The stereotype is the word repeated without any magic, any enthusiasm, as though it were natural, as though by some miracle this recurring word were adequate on each occasion for different reasons, as though to imitate could no longer be sensed as an imitation: an unconstrained word that claims consistency and is unaware of its own insistence. Nietzsche has observed that "truth" is only the solidification of old metaphors. So in this regard the stereotype is the present path of "truth," the palpable feature which shifts the invented ornament to the canonical, constraining form of the signified.[22]

Bearing down inexorably on the signifier, the chain of words that coagulates into the type, produces, according to Barthes, a nausea that comes whenever "the liaison of two words follows of itself." Though it is this queasiness of the sign that the stereotype evokes in the reader, this is precisely what the reader wants in consuming stereotypical literature— the nausea of certainty, of semantic finitude, of what psychoanalysis has described as the fatal attraction of the death drive.

The deathly aspect of the type is eroticized in Rhaïs's tales through an almost photographic realism of costume in which the body is arrested in space, materialized in its sartorial envelope, embalmed, as it were (to use an Orientalist analogy), like a prose mummy in an Egyptian tomb. Take, for example, her description of Kerkeb, a quintessentially dissolute harem wife, posed on a red satin couch in the shadow of a sumptuous apartment:

> Of all his wives she was the preferred one, a splendid creature with a saffron complexion, black eyes circled in khol, a chiselled nose, amorous lips half-open to accommodate her ardent breathing. She held on her knees a coffer filled with perfume bottles and aromatic sweets, one of those cases of meticulous, elaborate carving which disciplined sculptors worked on for years in the slums of the upper city. And with no concern for her master's presence, she gazed at herself in a gold-handled, silver encrusted mirror. [. . .] She took a diadem of brilliants out of the box and placed it in her hair glossy with cumin oil. She admired herself for the last time, satisfied, smiling in the mirror, and lazily got up from the sofa. She was ready. Under the

white gandourah her strong body moved freely, her firm breasts, her volup-
tuous hips around which had just been tied a belt embroidered in black
silk, pinned with a giant emerald. (K 73)

Kerkeb's palpitating belly-dancer's body (the guiding trope of the
whole story), weighed down beneath piles of *clinquant* that "tie" her
identity in place, matches up with many of the 1920s postcards analyzed
by Malek Alloula in his book *The Colonial Harem*. Commenting on the
native finery insisted upon by the colonial photographers in their female
models (usually prostitutes), Alloula speaks of the "ethnographic alibi"
that adds, paradoxically not to the effect of authentic otherness but
rather to the "feigned realism" or faked up, trompe l'oeil cultural verisi-
militude marketed by the colonial gaze.[23] These simulacral images of
colonial subjects, constituting pictures already adjusted for readability
and purchase by an Occidental eye, may be seen as visual correlates of
textual stereotypification.

Alloula's notion of the "ethnographic alibi" points up the element of
potential self-parody in colonial representation by emphasizing the
juncture where the alibi risks revealing itself as just that, as a sham fac-
simile used to account for the absence of the real thing. Like the colonial
stereotype, the ethnographic alibi comes dangerously close to overplay-
ing itself to the viewer, thereby relinquishing its ability to persuade the
unconscious of its truth value. We can see this breaking point occur
most clearly in Rhaïs's fiction when the type veers into caricature and
more is revealed about the complex process of "native" self-representation and self-marketing under the conditions of colonial image-produc-
tion than about the "local color" of authentic autochthonous experi
ence. We can identify the most obvious instances where this occurs in
Rhaïs's writing when excessive Orientalism is used, as when in *Le Café-
chantant*, the singer Fouad El Begri is introduced wearing a profusion of
necklaces, a heavy costume in mauve silk embroidered in gold, a silver-
lamé mauve scarf, mauve slippers embossed with emeralds, and heavy
gold ankle bracelets. The Moorish café where she works, depicted as a
gaudy stage set projecting "the fascinating splendor of a vision from *A
Thousand and One Nights*," is home to a bevy of singers "languishing in
nonchalant poses" and "buried under an orgy of satin, ribbons, lace and
jewels," "Their vaporous costumes, of sequined muslin and delicate silk
stripes, allowed furtive glimpses of matte flesh and sumptuous, undulating limbs to shine through."[24]

Here costume and decor suggest the Hollywoodized vamp image of
Oriental women that many entertainers of the 1920s and 1930s were
incorporating into their stage personas. As Sarah Graham-Brown has
noted with respect to the changing image of Egyptian belly-dancers:

"This chic, westernized image was curiously mingled with what seemed to be parodies of "Orientalist" poses and costumes. Usually these were costume photographs taken to advertise the appearance of a performer in a particular role. But they add a strange twist to the imagery of women, apparently internalizing some Western ideas of how Middle Eastern women looked."[25]

Extrapolating from Graham-Brown, one begins to see how Rhaïs may have undermined the ethnographic alibi at the very moment of relying upon it in full. Her colonial subjects may be interpreted as dialectical performative identities, posing and masquerading as themselves "under western eyes." What emerges as "real" in her realism is the way in which this destabilizing reciprocity of First World and Third World "looked-at-ness" (the expression is Laura Mulvey's) is captured in prose at an oblique angle, almost as if by accident. Thus, while freeze-framing and essentialist stereotyping form an integral part of the literary technique with which she begins, the net effect is of another kind of realism entirely—the real of colonial image-making and its commercial conditions in the context of French colonialism of the 1920s.

We begin to see how different realisms converge and clash within colonial representation. In the case of Rhaïs's fiction, the tensions are complicated by her ambivalent positionality as a North African woman author writing in French for a largely European audience. Though in some sense she clearly subscribed to the flattening, mummifying techniques of exotic stereotypification, she also inadvertently fractured the moorings of the type by recording the otherwise "invisible" traces of Westernization on native self-representation. Moreover, unlike many of her European realist predecessors, she avoided aggregating all Maghrebians in a blurry, diasporic miasma of otherness. A perfect example of this miasma effect can be found in Théophile Gautier's *A Winter in Russia* (*Voyage en Russie*, 1867), where the interchangeability of ethnic stereotypes results in a multicultural salad, each national silhouette blurring into the other:

> Russia, with its immense territory, includes many different races and the type of feminine beauty varies much. One may, however, indicate as characteristic, an extreme fairness of complexion, grayish-blue eyes, blonde or chestnut hair, and a certain *embonpoint*, (emph. in text) arising from the lack of exercise and the life in-doors, which is compelled by a winter lasting seven or eight months. They suggest the idea of odalisques, whom the Genius of the North keeps confined in the tropical atmosphere of a hot-house. They have complexions of cold-cream and snow, with tints from the heart of a camellia—like those over-veiled women of the Seraglio whose skin the sunlight has not touched. By this extreme fairness, their delicate

features are rendered even more delicate; and the softened outlines form faces of Hyperborean sweetness and polar grace.

At this very moment, as if to contradict my description, in the sledge which has just drawn up by the side of my troika, shines a radiant Southern beauty; the eyebrows black and velvety, the aquiline nose, the lengthened oval of the face, the brunette complexion, the lips as red as pomegranates, all betray the pure Caucasian type;—a Circassian, and, for all I know, a Mahometan. Here and there, eyes long and narrow, and rising a little at the outer angle, remind us that, at one extreme, Russia touches upon China; charming little Finns with eyes of turquoise blue, pale golden hair, and tint, pure red and white, contrast well with those handsome Greek women from Odessa, whom you recognize by the straight nose and great black eyes, like those of the Byzantine madonnas. It makes a charming picture,—these lovely heads emerging, like winter flowers, from a mass of furs, which is itself covered by white or black bear-skin thrown over all.[26]

Here the physiognomical pile-up technique ultimately risks slipping away from its author's control. Gautier's Russian woman melts into a "pale" Arabian concubine, who metamorphoses into a "dark" southern European, who glides into a "possibly Mahometan" Circassian, with affinities to Finnish, Chinese, Greek, and Byzantine models. Having so relinquished the power to classify discrete identities, Gautier seems to have defeated the point of the exercise.

In contrast to Gautier, Rhaïs remained more "true to her types." On the one hand, it could be argued that by doing so she avoided the potentially incendiary topic of racial mixing that constitutes the historical "truth" behind Gautier's description of Russian women. On the other hand, it may be said that Rhaïs paid more attention to "critical differences." Unlike French travelers who went from region to region sampling ethnic body-types much like local cuisines or markets, Rhaïs signaled the differences within North African culture. In *Saâda* she noted Algerian racism toward Moroccan immigrants. In *Les Juifs ou la fille d'Eléazar* she alluded to Muslim anti-Semitism. In *Le Mariage de Hanifa* she dramatized the risks of unmarriageability and cultural alienation to Muslim girls who attended French schools. In *La Fille du pacha*, she focused on a noble Arab girl condemned to death for daring to fall in love with a Jewish officer (a triple oppositional play among Arab-Jew, Arab-Westerner, Westerner-Jew). In *Le Café-chantant* she explored the way in which Berber entertainers operated as the ethnic "other" for Arab audiences. In *Noblesse arabe* she described the rivalry between a local Bedouin girl, in love with the son of her aristocratic landlord, and his designated fiancée brought in from "outside"—a beautiful "lalla de harem, un modèle de la race andalouse."[27] *Noblesse arabe* is a particularly complex work insofar as it examines the renomadization of a Bedouin family living in the Algerian city of Tlemcen. It is a Moroccan rather than a French landlord who expropriates their cherished settlement. In this case, Rhaïs explores the sociology of economic, class, and cultural conflict among North African ethnicities, while at the same time implicitly alluding to the history of French territorial and cultural self-implantation.

Though Rhaïs drew heavily on clichés, she gave them a social realist cast when she revealed the harsh conditions under which North African communities suffered. Seeming to follow Frederick Engels, who wrote, "Realism, to my mind, implies, besides truth of detail, the truthful reproduction of typical characters under typical circumstances," Rhaïs, in a sense, redeemed her complicity with the commercialized, patriotic genre of colonial fiction by painting scenes whose "true-to-life-ness" could only arouse the reader's social conscience.[28] The opening paragraphs of *Saâda* provide an arresting picture of Spanish and Moroccan immigrants displaced from their homelands and brought to Algeria to work as domestics for the settler bourgeoisie.

> On a freezing afternoon in January 1915, all along the rue du Bey, one of the most tranquil in Blidah, streamed a procession of strangers arriving at the hour of the trains. They were Spaniards for the most part. Women, short and heavy, with an oily complexion, dressed in yellow shawls and loose dresses embellished with dirt-encrusted flounces. Under their arms they carried enormous brown packets, rusty buckets full of cooking utensils, which they supported against their wide hips. Around their skirts, clusters of children squalled, miserable, jaundiced human rejects whose black eyes glittered. (S 1)

It will be useful to compare this passage, rich in compassionate human observation undercut by a note of contempt, with the opening passage of an earlier study of *Les Femmes arabes en Algérie* published by the French suffragette Hubertine Auclert in 1900:

> On entering the terrestrial paradise of Algiers, the first that strikes one immediately, under the blue sky, sparkling on the pavement like steel, is the sight of shocking packets of dirty laundry.
>
> These packets move, advance; only then does one discern that they are carried along on dirt-encrusted feet and topped by heads so frayed, decrepit, creviced and streaked that one hardly recognizes them as human faces; it is the statue of suffering, personifying a race tortured by hunger.
>
> These creatures without age or sex, jostling and exploding in this fairy-tale space, in their no longer white rags and tatters, have just become mothers. An adorable baby is perched on their hips, swaddled in the fold of a *haick*.

> Wives of the dispossessed, a mouth too many in their tribes, they wander, poor females, everywhere rejected, brutally hunted, insulted in every language by the settlers of all races who installed themselves on their fathers' land.[29]

One wonders, reading this passage, to what extent Auclert was using the spectacle of feminine injustice afforded by Algeria as a spur to institute legal and social reforms in Algeria itself, or to what extent she saw the plight of impoverished, disenfranchised North African women as symbolic reflections of the condition of women in France. The dehumanizing gaze of the narrator is ambiguous: while images of "packets of dirty laundry," ravaged faces, and "statues of suffering" are clearly intended to move the reader, they also exemplify First World feminism's symptomatic (and ultimately self-centered) tendency to construct "Third World Woman" as a flattened, or in this case, negated, subjectivity.[30]

Chandra Talpade Mohanty has pointed out that "colonization almost invariably implies a relation of structural domination, and a suppression—often violent—of the heterogeneity of the subject(s) in question." She articulates the way in which contemporary First World feminism recolonizes the other (despite good intentions to do otherwise) by constructing for theoretical purposes "a composite, singular 'third world woman'—an image which appears arbitrarily constructed, but nevertheless carries with it the authorizing signature of Western humanist discourse."[31] Though we are comparing Rhaïs's novel to Auclert's political essay, it is still possible to measure the "essential difference" between them by comparing the two titles: Rhaïs chose a proper name, which individuates the subject of her social critique, whereas Auclert's generic "Arab women" refers to a culturally undifferentiated mass.

Saâda shares with Auclert's *Les Femmes arabes* a use of stereotype in the name of humanism, but *Saâda* nuances social typicality through psychical realism, thereby destabilizing the fixed representations of native subjects commonly found in the works of metropolitan authors of *littérature coloniale*. Uprooted from their native Moroccan soil, Saâda and her family are forced to live in a dark hovel. Her husband Messaoud fails to find work and becomes an alcoholic. Saâda turns to prostitution and develops a taste for vice. Worst of all, by the standards of the text's Islamic normative frame, is her studied indifference to the stigma of social shame:

> Saâda thus did nothing to hide her crime. . . . she refused even to pull her djellbala over her shameless nudity. [. . .] Every day she would go with another client. She sold herself to whomsoever came along, without hesitating or haggling over the price, tasting in her debasement a bitter pleasure, as if drunk on vengeance. She was happy to let the jet of filth fall back on those she considered to be the authors of her fall. (S 139)

A marked strain of exoticized sadomasochism runs through Rhaïs's exploration of the "inner life" of prostitution. In a fit of crazed lust and dejection, Saâda's husband rapes a child and is taken away for punishment. Poverty, prostitution, and rape—this chain of depredations set against the backdrop of Oriental nomadism becomes a universalized allegory for woman's oppression and psychic homelessness.

FRENCH FEMINISM AND THE COLONIAL STEREOTYPE

Though Saâda's story read today from a postcolonial perspective seems to call for interpretation as an allegory of France's political "rape" of North Africa, French feminism in the 1920s chose to ignore this reading in favor of the universalistic one. At one level it can be argued that this universalism was justified insofar as French women in their failure to obtain the vote in the postwar period became the political "Third World" not only of the West, but also, as Steven Hause and Anne Kenney have shown, of the Third World:

> Of the five European "great powers" that went to war in August 1914, only France had not given women the vote by 1919. With the enactment of integral suffrage laws in the United States and Canada in 1920, the equal political rights of women (at least in the law) had become an unmistakable characteristic of Western civilization. Indeed, Western imperialism exported this equality. The British soon implanted it in East Africa and South Asia. Ataturk encompassed it in his westernization of Turkey. By the 1930s, while the French Senate stood intransigent, women were voting in Palestine, parts of China and several Latin American republics. Women voted in Estonia, Azerbaijan, Trans-Jordan, and Kenya but not in the land of Jeanne d'Arc and the Declaration of the Rights of Man. This contrast was widely noted in France. The Buisson Report covered it in detail and the Barthélemy Report reiterated the argument. By 1919, suffragists found it "humiliating to think that a daughter of the country of the Revolution" still had to beg rights granted to women in "backward" countries.[32]

Hause and Kenney alert us once again to the uneasy relationship between French feminism and the colonies.[33] Not only was there the unpleasant mirror effect of political "backwardness" that complicated the identification of First World feminism with Third, but there was also the fact that First World feminism simply could not see how women of the colonies might define their liberatory struggles in a path conflicting with the goals of European empire. This is not to suggest that all French feminists, whether on the left or right, wholeheartedly endorsed la mission civilisatrice, but it is probably safe to say that in this period of invoking Enlightenment principles in the service of the rights of women, it was assumed that what was in the best interest of French feminists would be in the best interest of women of all nationalities. And of course, in many instances, this is often how North African feminists presented the matter themselves. Tabet notes the voluminous correspondence that Rhaïs received from Tunisian, Algerian, and Moroccan women, many of them indicating their solidarity with Western feminism's stand against a patriarchal social order. It hardly mattered that Rhaïs's representation of pashas and sultans nourished Western clichés about Oriental despotism; the bottom line for many North African (and Middle Eastern) feminists of the 1920s was release from the oppressive strictures of family, religion, marriage practices, the veil, and so on.[34]

This said, it is hard to imagine that First World feminism's instrumentalization of colonial typologies fully masked the significant political contradictions between global pan-feminism and colonialism. Just as the World War II vocabulary of democracy, resistance, and liberation helped fuel the FLN on the eve of the Algerian revolution, so the rhetoric of feminism led logically to the questioning of colonial domination. And it must be remembered here that the interwar period during which the majority of Rhaïs's fictional works were written was a volatile period in colonial history, one in which nascent Algerian nationalisms burgeoned. The Jeunes Algériens movement (anti-Muslim, assimilationist, in favor of extending suffrage to pro-French Algerians) emerged after the 1919 Jonnart reforms alongside the Islamic, pan-Arab, nationalistic Reformist party of Ben Badis, which competed in its turn with the Etoile Nord Africaine, an ancestor party of the FLN advocating secular nationalism.

Not surprisingly, First World feminism's vision of nationalism was highly selective in its myopic Eurocentrism. Whether in fiction or in the staging of political demonstrations, indigenous self-determination movements simply failed to figure. As Lisa Tickner notes with respect to the suffragette pageants in Britain (themselves "colonially mimetic" of official state ritual), there was a profound ambivalence surrounding the staging of the colonies, a potentially destabilizing semiotic of insurgency that seemed paradoxically to have been ignored. There was also a profound (though once again ill-perceived) irony attached to the spectacle of colonial and commonwealth unity, whereby the suffragettes unwittingly recolonized the world through images that sought to decolonize women worldwide:

> In order to give substance to their claim for international representation the suffragists were obliged to draw on the rhetoric of national identity. All the national costumes, tokens, music and assorted cultural signifiers that

could be mobilized (some of them of fairly recent origin) were pressed into service. Scottish pipers, Welsh choirs, Irish harps, joined the fern tree (New Zealand), the kangaroo (Australia), the maple leaf (Canada), the springbok (South Africa) and the elephant (India) among the colonial and international contingents. In lieu of a history of their own, women turned to an accumulated language of symbolic identities, much of it claiming ancient authority but in fact a fairly recent development along with the nation-state. Boadicea was for them not the embodiment of "an ancient past beyond effective historical continuity" as she was for British nationalism, but like Joan of Arc a type of militant femininity. If all invented traditions attempt to use history as the cement for group cohesion as Eric Hobsbawm has argued, then the women's use of historical components was no more and no less selective that those of the discourses to which they were opposed.[35]

Tickner highlights the political dimensions of cultural masquerade whereby European feminists embodied the mythic personas of nation-states or impersonated the larger-than-life inspirational identities of legendary women (Mary Queen of Scots for the royalists, Joan of Arc for the militants in both England and France). Writing in 1898 in his antifeminist tract *La Femme dans les colonies*, Pétrus Durel inveighed against the French woman who neglected her duties as wife and mother, choosing instead to "reread history" with an eye to resurrecting Joan of Arc or Jeanne Hachette as icons of imminent feminist victory.[36]

Though suffragette demonstrations in Britain tended to be more visually arresting than their counterparts in France, one could say that in France a less explicitly politicized and more sexually underground use was made of symbolic identity-performance. From the scandalous pantomime of 1907, *Rêve d'Egypte*, in which Colette and Missy (arabized on the playbill as "Yssim") "offered the spectacle of a prolonged, passionate kiss," through to the plethora of plays, operas, ballets, cabaret, and music hall shows that coded sapphism and/or unbridled female desire through Orientalism (*Cléopâtre, Salomé, Thaïs, Sémiramis, Schéhérazade*), one could say that the ethnographic alibi acquired new layers of meaning within the Parisian "city of women."[37] Orientalist performativity was also at work in the cult of Isabelle Eberhardt[38] on the part of women writers who were themselves involved in "acting out" Orientalism (Lucie Delarue-Mardrus, Myriam Harry, Henriette Célarié). Henriette Célarié, in her book *Nos Soeurs Musulmanes: scènes de la vie du désert* (1925), describes her arduous pilgrimage to one of Eberhardt's temporary dwelling-places in El-Oued. After interrogating the landlord about her physical appearance and taste for cross-dressing, she gave herself over to expansive prosopoeia. Like Célarié, Lucie Delarue-Mardrus,

wife of the French translator of *Mille et une nuits,* lover of Ida Ruben-
stein (celebrated for her role in *Schéhérazade*), and author of plays, stories, and memoirs that drew on her travels through the Middle East and
North Africa, persevered as far as the Kabylian town of Aïn-Sefra in
order to depose (in the words of her admiring biographer Myriam
Harry) "a bouquet of withered roses plucked from the Queen's Pavillion
onto the tomb of the mysterious islamic Isabelle Eberhardt."[39] In her
verses dedicated to Eberhardt, Delarue-Mardrus, much like Célarié,
evoked her "bedouin coat" as a kind of sacred mantle of transvestism
sanctioning future feminist explorations into the shadowy regions of bisexual biculturalism.[40]

Though cultural masquerade can be seen quite easily as being of a
piece with gender travesty, it hyperbolizes the histrionics of difference
and focuses attention on the utopian dream of a transhistorical, geographically global female colony. This colony could be invented next
door to the mythic isle of Lesbos, as when Rénée Vivien, favored muse
of Colette, Delarue-Mardrus, and Natalie Barney, among others, purchased the island of Mytilene in the hopes that it would become a requi-
site stop on the itinerary of the lesbian tourist-traveler. It could also be
incarnated in the amateur theatricals that took place in private salons in
which women supplemented the habitual frisson of drag by donning the
costumes of legendary female sinners of antiquity and Byzantium.[41]
From 1900 to the 1920s one encounters a striking instrumentalization
of Orientalism in the cultural productions, both high and low, of transgressive female sexuality.[42] There are obviously many reasons why cultural masquerade was paired with gender masquerade: each deployed
the other as a cover for surreptitious erotic and political ends. But what
remains less clear is the "value" of the exoticist costumes and mise en
scènes. Were they simply new strains of Orientalism, nexes of essentializing mythologies and stereotypes, theme parks for Western identity-
staging? Or were they, in fact, contestatory practices constituting a vital
chapter of French feminist history?

Though these questions form the basis of another discussion, I will
conclude by emphasizing the extent to which this kind of gender masquerade was encrypted within Rhaïs's own ethnographic travesty, displacing a confession of "bitextuality" (or double-gendered copyright)
into the ethnographic alibi provided by colonial realism. In a café scene
in *Saâda,* an unknown youth who goes by the name of "Sid Moussa" is
introduced by the sheik into the male circle of hashish smokers
(*haschaïschïa*):

> Blushing "Sid Moussa" advanced toward the assembly, extending a hand
> to each one, pronouncing not a word, hardly looking up.

This did not prevent them for a second from guessing that "Sid Moussa" was a woman. The light touch of the fingers alone sufficed in averting them. Closer up, physically, they smelled the *odor di femina*.

Despite this, not one of them flinched or signalled their protest to Sid Kaddour with an indiscrete allusion. They respected their sheik. They also knew him to be experienced, and wondered whether he might not have had some secret reason for daring an initiative that would otherwise seem imprudent.

This woman whom he had introduced among them was certainly out of the ordinary. The very fact that she had asked or consented to penetrate here testified to that. In any case, she possessed a splendid body, which their instinct ferreted out beneath the burnous, and eyes to drive you mad. (S 193)

We might have guessed: Saâda has entered the text (much like Eberhardt in "real life") disguised as a young man. As she "penetrates" the inner sanctum of male privilege for some "secret reason," it becomes, of course, just too tempting not to see this secret reason as linked to the riddle of authorship surrounding the name of Rhaïs. Was Raoul merely the scribe, transmitting the oral tradition of harem tales told to Rosine Boumendil, or was he a consummate ventriloquist of female voice? Was Rhaïs a bisexual narrator? Did it matter that the novels may have been written by a man if, for female readers at the time, they rang true as the creations of an authentic Third World, feminine voice? The splitting of Rhaïs into a s/he ultimately leads one to read this scene from *Saâda* as a message in a bottle, a "sign" sent by Raoul to the reader alerting her to the fact that the appearance of gender identities should never be trusted. The hashish smokers choose to ignore the travesty, naturalizing it as part of a motivated cultural ritual. In the process, one could say, they dupe the reader into taking this cultural masquerade at face value as a "true" performance of the colonial real.

But the colonial real fails to preserve its veracity when resituated in the "new" literary history of narrative styles and belletristic travesties. Read critically, the strange case of Elissa Rhaïs turns into a parable about the interpretation of the colonial stereotype in which cultural masquerade uses gender masquerade to deflect attention from its strategies and conceits. Once the focus is turned back on the artifice of culturalist typologies, Rhaïs's Moorish temptresses, obdurate sidis, and nomadic Berber women become detached from their costumes and rhetorical props, seen as tenuous ontologies: reactive, defensive, projective, phantasmatic, and politically performative (mythic go-betweens mediating the distribution of colonial power). At this point, suspicion falls more on the genuine "North African-ness" of Rhaïs's authorial signature than on her gender identity. For all we know, the novels were written by a French colonial officer. The mere fact that such doubts prove difficult to dispel on the basis of the writing alone points to the fundamental unreliability of time-honored notions of historical narration, authentic voice, and national literature. Without such notions, the historiography of literary history will have to be rewritten, but do we have any choice? Just as traditional gender terminology recedes under the onslaught of challenges to "compulsory heterosexuality," to be replaced by more tentative articulations of performative sexual identities or by nothing at all, so the language of culture and type becomes increasingly impossible to employ in good faith. What remains for the critic is the search for a lexicon that defines itself self-reflexively as a symptom of cultural vision: parodic, provisional, and historically posed.

NOTES

I would like to thank Professors Natalie Zemon Davis, Homi Bhabha, and Gyan Prakash for their comments and suggestions on an earlier version of this essay. All translations unless otherwise noted are my own.

1. Octave Mannoni, *Prospéro et Caliban: Psychologie de la colonisation* (Paris: éditions universitaires, 1984), pp. 207–15.

2. On the relationship between the real and reality, see Slavoj Zizek, *Looking Awry: An Introduction to Jacques Lacan through Popular Culture* (Cambridge, Mass.: MIT Press, 1991), chaps. 1–2. See also Elizabeth Grosz, *Jacques Lacan: A Feminist Introduction* (New York: Routlege, 1990). In evoking the category of the "colonial real" I am aware of the multiple slippages and ambiguities surrounding the notion of the real in Lacanian theory. Definable as a term that marks the haunting of the subject by a dream of subjective plenitude or nonseparation with the maternal body (the "lack of the lack," in Lacan's words); immersed in the traumatic moment of the splitting of the subject; identified in its retroactive function in fantasy as the "object-cause of desire" (Lacan) or the "psychic reality of desire" (cf. Slavoj Zizek), the real in psychoanalytic terms presents itself linguistically and visually on the sly. Intruding itself on the subject at a moment least expected, the real is that sudden and terrifying flash when the subject perceives the gaping hole in subjectivity tenuously papered over by repression.

3. Timothy Mitchell, *Colonizing Egypt* (Cambridge: Cambridge University Press, 1988).

4. Antonia Lant, "The Curse of the Pharaoh, or How the Cinema Contracted Egyptomania," *October* 59 (Winter 1992): 86–112. Lant writes:

The configuring of Egypt and the cinema expressed cinema's twin realist and fantastic character. By mining the pharaonic archive, the disturbing potential of the cinema to produce pornography through extremely realistic representations of the human body could be diffused, safely channeled, into a distant yet compelling culture, claimed through the imperialism of Egyptology. Roman Egypt, contemporary Arabian Egypt, and the ideas about the harem, the sheik, Arabian nights, and the vamp could then ride into the cinema on the back of pharaonic Egypt, as it were. (p. 109)

5. John Tagg, *The Burden of Representation: Essays on Photographies and Histories* (Amherst: University of Massachusetts Press, 1988), p. 101. All further references to this work will appear in the text abbreviated T.

6. Edward Said, *Orientalism* (London: Routledge and Kegan Paul, 1978), p. 72; Homi K. Bhabha, "The Other Question—The Stereotype and Colonial Discourse," *Screen* 24, no. 6 (1983): 23.

7. Judith Butler, "Phantasmatic Identification and the Question of Sex," lecture delivered at UC Berkeley, Feb. 13, 1992.

8. Naomi Schor, "Cartes *Postales*: Representing Paris 1900," *Critical Inquiry* 18, no. 2 (Winter 1992): 188–244.

9. I take this phrase from Margaret Whitford's account of Irigaray (*The Ethics of Sexual Difference*) in her excellent book, *Luce Irigaray: Philosophy in the Feminine* (London: Routledge, 1991), p. 125. Whitford writes:

one could put her position like this. In imaginary and symbolic terms, theory, like language, constitutes a house or a home for men: "men continually seek, construct, create for themselves houses everywhere: grottoes, huts, women, towns, language, concepts, theory, etc." (E: 133).

We could say, then, that the theory of the male philosophers is equivalent to the maternal body, the body-matter of woman which forms the imaginary infrastructure of metaphysics. But this still leaves women "homeless" in the symbolic order, and it is this homelessness and dereliction with which Irigaray is concerned.

10. By a coincidence of fate, Blidah was also the place where André Gide "came out" in 1894. Espying the names of Oscar Wilde and Lord Alfred Douglas on the hotel register, he felt compelled to erase his own name. Afterwards he felt ashamed of his timidity, changed his itinerary, and returned to the hotel, where he awaited them in the lobby.

11. Paul Tabet, *Elissa Rhaïs, roman* (Paris: Bernard Grasset, 1982). Part "talking cure," part factual biography, this book is the highly problematic source of much of my information about Elissa Rhaïs's life and reception. The author, by his own account, is Raoul Tabet's (alias Dahan) son. In the book's opening pages he recounts how he came by Rhaïs's story on his father's death-bed. When I interviewed Tabet in Paris a year ago, he confirmed the factual basis of his autobiographical narrative, but did not offer access to family papers or archives. He has never replied to my subsequent letters requesting factual verifications and precisions.

Natalie Davis has pointed out that a great deal more might be found out about the "real" Rhaïs and her family if one were to investigate records in Algeria on the Jewish community of Blida. She has also suggested that we might read Rhaïs's novel *Le Mariage de Hanifa* semiautobiographically insofar as it treats the theme of female literacy (at the heart of the enigma surrounding Rhaïs's legitimacy as a writer). Hanifa's sad fate in the novel seems to be rooted in a moral economy that makes social retribution the logical outcome of a Western education.

12. For more on the role of women in French colonial literature and cinema, see Yvonne Kniebiehler and Régine Gontalier, *La Femme au temps des colonies* (Paris: Stock, 1985).

13. Jean Déjeux, "Elissa Rhaïs, Conteuse Algérienne (1876–1940)," *Revue de l'Occident Mousulman et de la Mediterranée* 37 (1984): 47–79.

14. In using the expression "cultural masquerade" I am deliberately experimenting with the transfer of a term from gender studies to cultural studies. Joan Riviere's 1929 essay "Womanliness as a Masquerade" implied a critique of femininity as a compensatory feint deployed by intellectual women to disguise their "masculinity complex." Riviere also argues that insofar as the masquerade involves coquetting and seducing the father, it may also cover up a sadistic, castrating intent. Obviously to graft this idea onto cultural masquerade involves adjusting the definition. In this essay I use the term to underscore the performativity of cultural identity, its tenuous anchor in historical reality.

15. Jean Déjeux, *Bibliographie de la littérature "algérienne" des français* (Paris: Éditions du Centre National de la Recherche Scientifique, 1978).

16. I have examined a number of harem texts by these women authors in terms of their projection of an "other" eroticism in "Female Trouble in the Colonial Harem," *Differences* 4 (Spring 1992): 205–24.

17. Predominant literary influences on Raoul/Leila's style included, according to Paul Tabet, Racine, Chateaubriand, Flaubert, Loti, and the Tharaud Brothers.

18. Gustave Flaubert, *Salammbô*, trans. E. Powys Mathers (New York: Hart, 1976), p. 55.

19. Elissa Rhaïs, *Kerkeb, danseuse berbère*, in *Le Café chantant* (Paris: Plon, 1923), pp. 71–72. All further references to this work will appear in the text abbreviated K.

20. Roland Lebel, *Histoire de la littérature coloniale en France* (Paris: Librairie Larose, 1931), pp. 211–13 and p. 86.

21. See Graeme Tytler, *Physiognomy in the European Novel: Faces and Fortunes* (Princeton: Princeton University Press, 1982).

22. Roland Barthes, *The Pleasure of the Text*, trans. Richard Miller (New York: Farrar, Straus and Giroux, 1975), pp. 42–43.

23. Malek Alloula, *The Colonial Harem*, trans. Myrna Godzich and Wlad Godzich (Minneapolis: University of Minnesota Press, 1986), p. 18.

24. Elissa Rhaïs, *Le Café-chantant* (Paris: Plon, 1923), pp. 35–36. All further references to this work will appear in the text abbreviated C.

25. Sarah Graham-Brown, *Images of Women: The Portrayal of Women in Photography of the Middle East 1860–1950* (London: Quartet Books, 1988), pp. 180, 185.

26. Gautier's *Winter in Russia*, trans. M. M. Ripley (New York: Henry Holt, 1877) pp. 117–18.

27. Elissa Rhaïs, *Noblesse arabe*, in *Le Café-chantant*, p. 206. Future references to the work will appear in the text abbreviated N.

28. As cited by Tagg, *Burden of Representation*, p. 178.

29. Hubertine Auclert, *Les Femmes arabes en Algérie* (Paris: Société d'Editions Littéraires, 1900), pp. 1–2.

30. David Prochaska situates this problem of flattening in relation to post-cardization. In *Making Algeria French* (Cambridge: Cambridge University Press, 1990) p. 215, he refers to the photographic genre of

> *scènes et types*, generic representations of certain kinds of people (Arabs, Berbers, Jews, Mozabites), practicing certain kinds of occupations (barbers, musicians, shoeshine boys), participating in certain kinds of activities (*fantasias*, making *couscous*), and depicted in certain kinds of environments (in front of *gourbis*, "under the tent"). The processes whereby individuals are transformed into collectivities, abstracted from three-dimensional flesh and blood people living down the street into two-dimensional consumer goods suitable for mailing to friends in the *métropole*, is a subject full of fascinating possibilities for future research.

31. Chandra Talpade Mohanty, "Under Western Eyes: Feminist Scholarship and Colonial Discourses," in *Third World Women and the Politics of Feminism*, ed. Chandra Talpade Mohanty, Ann Russo, and Lourdes Torres (Bloomington: Indiana University Press, 1991), pp. 52, 53.

32. Steven Hause with Anne R. Kenney, *Women's Suffrage and Social Politics in the French Third Republic* (Princeton: Princeton University Press, 1984), pp. 253–54.

33. For a critically nuanced, informed discussion of how the representation of Maghrebian feminism has fared in the postcolonial period (particularly as articulated by contemporary North African women writers such as Fatima Mernissi, Homa Hoodfar, Rachid Boudjedra, Nabile Farès, Assia Djebar, and Leïla Sebbar), see Winifred Woodhull, *Transfigurations of the Maghreb: Feminism, Decolonization and Literatures* (Minneapolis: University of Minnesota Press, 1993). Her chapter, "Wild Femininity and Historical Countermemory," is both urgent and relevant on the issue of North African feminism's task of negotiating between a bigoted anti-Islam in the West and the hard line fundamentalist restriction of women's rights in the name of a return to traditional Islam.

34. For a vivid picture of Arab feminist concerns as they evolved from country to country from the 1880s to the present, see the excellent anthology of selected writings edited by Margot Badran and Miriam Cooke, *Opening the Gates: A Century of Arab Feminist Writing* (Bloomington: Indiana University Press, 1990).

35. Lisa Tickner, *The Spectacle of Women: Imagery of the Suffrage Campaign 1907–14* (London: Chatto and Windus, 1987), pp. 126–27.

36. Pétrus Durel, *La Femme dans les colonies françaises* (Paris: J. Dulon, 1898), p. 154.

37. For masculine counterparts in Britain and France, I am indebted to Joseph Boone's as yet unpublished paper, "Vacation Cruises: Male Homoeroticism and the Near East."

38. The sensational life of Isabelle Eberhardt (1877–1904), a journalist of Slavic descent who cross-dressed as an Arab youth and "went native" in North Africa, has been the subject of many biographies and a feminist film by Leslie Thornton. She was killed in a freak flood at the age of twenty-seven (after having already survived an assassination attempt); her death, like her life, lent itself to violent fantasies, both colonial and postcolonial. Her writings, which explored the outlaw margins of cultural and erotic identity, also came to stand at the heart of a "new order" of lesbian theatricality that coded itself through Orientalism.

39. Myriam Harry, *Mon Amie Lucie Delarue-Mardrus* (Paris: Ariane, 1946), p. 57.

40. For a lively, anecdotal discussion of Orientalist cross-dressing, see Marjorie Garber's chapter, "The Chic of Araby: Transvestism and the Erotics of Appropriation," in *Vested Interests: Cross-dressing and Cultural Anxiety* (New York: Routledge, 1992), pp. 304–52.

41. See Sue-Ellen Case, *Feminism and Theatre* (New York: Routledge, 1988), for a discussion of the British suffragette revival in 1914 of Hrotsvit von Gandersheim's mid-tenth-century play *Paphnutius*. Hrotsvit, according to Case, may be considered "the first known woman playwright of written texts" (p. 57). Her play focuses on the dancer and courtesan Thaïs (for whose soul the priest Paphutius struggles, even as he falls in love with her) (pp. 32, 34). In the suffragette version, the role of Thaïs was played by Ellen Terry. Case also describes Colette's legendary encounter with Mata Hari in Natalie Barney's private theatricals (p. 53).

42. For a detailed study of twentieth-century appropriations of Cleopatra, see Lucy Hughes-Hallett, *Cleopatra: Histories, Dreams and Distortions* (New York: Harper and Row, 1990).

CHAPTER 12

In a Spirit of Calm Violence

HOMI K. BHABHA

A great disaster like the massacre at Vellur, acts
like iodine upon, hidden writings in rice water.
(*Sir John Kaye*, History of the Indian Mutiny)

for some of us the principle of indeterminism is
what makes the conscious freedom of
man unfathomable
(*Jacques Derrida*, My Chances/Mes Chances)

AT THE MAGISTERIAL END of Michel Foucault's *The Order of Things*, when the section on History confronts its uncanny doubles—the countersciences of anthropology and psychoanalysis—the argument begins to unravel. It happens at a symptomatic moment when the representation of cultural difference attenuates the sense of History as the imbedding, domesticating "homeland" of the human sciences. For the finitude of History—its moment of doubling—participates in the conditionality of the contingent. An incommensurability ensues between History as the "homeland" of the human sciences—its cultural area, local chronologies, and specific geographical boundaries—and the claims of Historicism to a more universalist perspective. At that point "the subject of knowledge becomes the nexus of different times, foreign to it and heterogeneous in respect to one another." In that contingent doubling of History and nineteenth-century historicism the time-lag in the discourse enables the *return* of historical agency: "Since *time* comes to him from somewhere other than himself he constitutes himself as a subject of history only by the superimposition of . . . the history of things, the history of words. . . . But this relation of simple passivity is immediately reversed . . . for he too has a right to a development quite as positive as that of beings and things, one no less autonomous."[1]

As a result the *heimlich* historical subject that arises in the nineteenth century cannot stop constituting the *unheimlich* knowledge of itself by compulsively relating one cultural episode to another in an infinitely repetitive series of events that are metonymic and indeterminate. The

grand narratives of nineteenth-century historicism on which its claims
to universalism were founded—Evolutionism, Utilitarianism, Evangel-
ism—were also, in another textual and territorial time-space, the technologies of colonial and imperialist governance. It is the "rationalism"
of these ideologies of progress that increasingly come to be eroded in
the encounter with the "contingency" of cultural difference. Elsewhere
I have explored this historical process, perfectly caught in the picturesque words of a desperate missionary in the early nineteenth century as
the colonial predicament of "sly civility."[2] The result of this colonial encounter, its antagonisms and ambivalence, has a major effect on what
Foucault beautifully describes as the "slenderness of the narrative" of
history in that era most renowned for its historicizing (and colonizing)
of the world and the word.

"History now takes place on the outer limits of subject and object,"
Foucault writes, and it is to probe the uncanny unconscious of history's
doubling that he resorts to anthropology and psychoanalysis. It is in
these disciplines that the cultural unconscious is spoken in the slenderness of narrative—ambivalence, catachresis, contingency, iteration,
abyssal overlapping. In the agonistic temporal break that articulates the
cultural symbol to the psychic sign, we shall discover the postcolonial
symptom of Foucault's discourse. Writing of the history of anthropology as the "counterdiscourse" to modernity—as the possibility of a
human science *post*modernism—Foucault has this to say: "There is a certain position in the Western *ratio* that was constituted in its history and
provides a foundation for the relation it can have with all other societies,
even with the society in which it appeared" (my emphasis).[3]

In a massive forgetting Foucault fails to name that "certain position"
and its historical constitution. By disavowing it, however, he names it in
a negation in the next breath. "Obviously this does not mean that the
colonizing situation is indispensable to ethnology."[4]

Are we demanding, from the postcolonial position, that Foucault
should rehistoricize colonialism as the missing moment in the dialectic
of modernity? Do we want him to "complete" his argument by appropriating ours? Definitely not. I want to suggest that the postcolonial is
metaleptically present in his text in that moment of contingency that
allows the contiguity of his argument—thought following thought—to
progress. Then, suddenly, at the point of its closure, a curious indeterminacy grips the chain of discourse. This becomes the space for a new
discursive temporality, another place of enunciation that will not allow
the argument to expand, to include and surmount what is said in opposition to it. We could call this the catechrestic moment in all critical elaboration; or the incommensurable time/space of contingency in all forms
of closure.

I want to suggest a departure for the postcolonial text in the Foucauldian forgetting. In talking of psychoanalysis Foucault is able to see how knowledge and power come together in the enunciative "present" of transference: the "calm violence," as he calls it, of a relationship that constitutes the discourse. By disavowing "the colonial moment" as an *enunciative present* in the historical and epistemological condition of Western modernity, Foucault can say little about the transferential relation between the West and *its* colonial history. He disavows precisely the colonial text as the foundation for the relation the Western *ratio* can have *even with the society in which it historically appeared*.

Read from this perspective we can see that in insistently spatializing the "time" of history Foucault constitutes a doubling that is strangely collusive with its dispersal, equivalent to its equivocation, uncannily self-constituting, despite its game of "double and splits." Read from the transferential perspective, the "Western" *ratio* of (post)modernity encounters itself *contingently* in the liminality of cultural difference. If we introduce this "transferential" perspective where the Western *ratio* returns to itself from the time-lag of the colonial relation, then we see how modernity and postmodernity are constituted from the marginal perspective of cultural difference. They encounter themselves *contingently* at the point at which the "internal difference" of their own societies are reiterated in terms of the difference of the cultural otherness, the alterity of the postcolonial site. The question of *postcolonial* agency returns, in a spirit of calm violence, to interrogate Foucault's fluent doubling of the figures of modernity.

Why does Foucault anxiously play with the folds of Western modernity, fraying the finitudes of man, obsessively undoing and doing up the threads of that *slender narrative* of nineteenth-century historicism? This nervous narrative illustrates and attenuates his own argument: like the slender thread of history, it refuses to be woven in, menacingly hanging loose from the margins. What stops the narrative thread from breaking is Foucault's concern to introduce, at the nexus of his doubling, the idea that "the man who appears at the beginning of the nineteenth century is *dehistoricized*."

The dehistoricized authority of man and his doubles produces, in the same historical period, those forces of naturalization that create a modern Western disciplinary society. The invisible power that is invested in this dehistoricized figure of Man is gained at the cost of those "others"—women, natives, the colonized, the indentured and enslaved—who, at the same time but in other spaces, were becoming "the peoples without a history."

How is historical agency enacted in the slenderness of narrative? How do we historicize the event of the dehistoricized? If, as they say, the past is a foreign country, then what does it mean to encounter a past that is your own country reterritorialized, even terrorized, by another?

It is just such reverberations that the Indian scholar Veena Das elaborates in her fine essay, "The Subaltern as Perspective." She demands a historiography of the subaltern that displaces the paradigm of social action as defined primarily by rational action. She seeks a form of discourse in which affective and iterative writing develops its own language. History as a writing that constructs the moment of defiance emerges in the "magma of significations," for the "representational closure which presents itself when we encounter thought in objectified forms is now ripped open."[5] Instead we see this order interrogated, she writes, in transgressive agency that effects a "splitting of the various types of speech produced into statements of referential truth in the indicative present."[6]

The emphasis on the disjunctive present of utterance enables the historian to get away from defining subaltern consciousness as basically binary, as having positive or negative dimensions. It allows the articulation of subaltern agency to emerge as relocation and reinscription. Gayatri Spivak has usefully described the "negotiation" of the postcolonial position "in terms of reversing, displacing, and seizing the apparatus of value-coding,"[7] constituting a catachrestic space: words or concepts wrested from their proper meaning, "a concept-metaphor without an adequate referent" that perverts its imbedded context. In the seizure of the sign there is neither dialectical sublation nor the empty signifier: there is a contestation of the given symbols of authority that shifts the terrain of antagonism. The synchronicity in the social ordering of symbols is challenged within its own terms, but the grounds of engagement have been displaced in a "supplementary" movement that exceeds those terms.

In "Where is speech? Where is language?" Lacan describes this moment of negotiation of agency in relation to the production of the subject of utterance in the realm of social knowledges.

> It is the temporal element . . . or the temporal break . . . the intervention of a scansion permitting the intervention of something which can take on meaning for a subject. . . . There is in fact a reality of signs within which there exists a world of truth entirely deprived of subjectivity, and that, on the other hand there has been a historical development of subjectivity manifestly directed towards the rediscovery of truth which lies in the order of symbols.[8]

The process of reinscription and negotiation—the insertion or intervention of something that takes on new meaning—happens in the temporal break *initiated through* the sign, deprived of subjectivity, in the realm of the intersubjective. Through this time-lag—the temporal break in representation—emerges the process of agency both as a historical development and as the narrative agency of historical discourse. What comes clearly in Lacan's genealogy of the subject is that the agent's intentionality, which seems *manifestly directed* toward the truth of the order of symbols in the social imaginary, is also an effect of the rediscovery of the world of truth denied subjectivity (because it is intersubjective) at the level of the sign. It is in the "contingent" tension that sign and symbol overlap and are indeterminately articulated through the "temporal break." Where the sign deprived of the subject—intersubjectivity—returns as subjectivity directed toward the rediscovery of truth, then a (re)ordering of symbols becomes possible in the sphere of the social.

The catachrestic activity of postcolonial agency is made possible because the fixity of the signifer or the subject opens up a space that "displaces the value-coding." The Lacanian "voice" that speaks outside the sentence is itself the voice of an interrogative, calculative agency: *Che vuoi?—You are telling me that, but what do you want with it, what are you aiming at?*[9] What speaks in the place of this question, Lacan writes, is a "third locus which is neither my speech nor my interlocutor."[10]

Such a disjunctive space structures the intersubjective realm, the realm of otherness and the social, where "we identify ourselves with the other precisely at a point at which he is inimitable, at the point which eludes resemblance."[11] And it is my contention, elaborated elsewhere in my concepts of mimicry, hybridity, sly civility, that it is this liminal moment of identification—eluding resemblance—that produces a subversive strategy of subaltern agency that negotiates its own authority through a process of an iterative "unpicking" and relocating. Agency requires a grounding but it does not require a totalization of those grounds; it requires movement and maneuver but it does not require temporality of continuity or accumulation; it requires direction and contingent closure, but not teleology and holism.[12]

Is this structure of agency not similar to what Fanon describes as the knowledge of the practice of action?[13] Fanon argues that the primitive Manicheanism of the settler—black and white, Arabs and Christians—breaks down in the "present" of struggle for independence. Polarities come to be replaced with truths that are only partial, limited, and unstable. Each local ebb of the tide reviews the political question from the standpoint of all political networks. The leaders should stand firmly against those within the movement who tend to think that shades of meaning constitute dangers and drive wedges into the solid block of popular opinion.

SIGNS OF VIOLENCE IN THE MID-1800S

I have suggested earlier that the process of historical revision—new forms of political and cultural agency—emerges through a discursive time-lag, in the contingent tension between the social order of symbols and the "desubjectified" scansion of the sign. This temporality finds its spirit of place in the "not-there" that Toni Morrison memorializes in her fiction and uses, interrogatively, to establish the presence of a black literary work. The act of "rememoration" (her concept for the re-creation of popular memory) turns the present of narrative enunciation into the haunting memorial of what has been excluded, excised, evicted, and for that very reason becomes the *unheimlich* space for the negotiation of identity and history. "A void may be empty but it is not a vacuum." Toni Morrison writes, "Certain absences are so stressed [that] they arrest us with their intentionality and purpose, like neighborhoods that are defined by the population held away from them. Where . . . is the shadow of the presence from which the text has fled? Where does it heighten, where does it dislocate?"[14]

Intentionality and purpose—the signs of agency—emerge from the "time-lag," from the stressed absence that is an arrest, a caesura of time, a temporal break. In so specifying slave history, through an act of communal memory, Morrison negates narrative continuity and the cacophonous comfort of words. In *Beloved* it is the cryptic *circulation* of number as the very first word, as the displacement of the "personalized" predication of language, which speaks the presence of the slave-world: "124 was spiteful. Full of baby's venom. The women in the house knew it and so did the children."[15]

In the habitus of death and the demonic, reverberates a form of memory that survives in the sign—124—which is the world of truth deprived of subjectivity (Lacan). And then suddenly from the space of the *not-there* emerges the remembered historical agency "manifestly directed towards the rediscovery of truth which lies in the order of symbols." *124 was spiteful.* The act of predication and intention effected by numbers is Morrison's attempt to constitute a form of address that is personalized by its own discursive activity, "not the pasted on desire for personality"[16] (what I have called individuation, *not* individualism). And this creation of historical agency produces the subject from out of the temporality of the contingent: "snatched as the slaves were from one place to another, from any place to another, without preparation and without defense. . . . The reader is snatched, yanked, thrown into an environment completely foreign."[17] It is the caesura of the sign—124—which constitutes the "first stroke," Morrison writes, of the communal, inter-subjective experience of the slave world.

I want to link this *circulation* of the sign from the mid-1800s in Sweet Home, Kentucky, the world of *Beloved*, to the circulation of other signs of violence in the 1850s and 1860s in northern and central India. I want to move from the tortured history of abolitionism to the Indian mutiny. My reckless historical contingency is based not on a sense of the contiguity of events, but on the temporality of repetition that constitutes those signs by which marginalized or insurgent subjects create a collective agency. I am interested in cultural strategy and political confrontation constituted in obscure, enigmatic symbols, the manic repetition of rumor, panic as the uncontrolled, yet strategic affect of political revolt. More specifically, I want to tease out the slenderness of narrative that, in the midst of the major agrarian and political causes of the Indian mutiny tells the story of those *chapatis* (unleavened flat bread) that were rapidly circulated across the rural heartlands of the mutiny, just after the introduction into the native infantries of the Enfield rifle and its notorious "greased" cartridge. In *Elementary Aspects of Peasant Insurgency*, Ranajit Guha uses the chapati story as one of his main illustrations of the "symbolic" transmission of rebel agency. He also provides the most illuminating account of the various genealogies and antecedents of such occurrences within insurgent peasant cultures.

The indeterminacy of rumor constitutes its importance as a social discourse. Its intersubjective, communal adhesiveness lies in its enunciative aspect. Its performative power of *circulation* results in a contagious spreading, "an almost uncontrollable impulse to pass it on to another person."[18] It is this iterative action of rumor, its *circulation* and *contagion*, which links it with panic—as one of the *affects* of insurgency. Rumor and panic are, in moments of social crisis, double sites of enunciation that weave their stories around the disjunctive "present" or the "not there" of discourse. My point here is close to Ashis Nandy's strictures on Western historicism in his essay "Towards a Third World Utopia." The suffering of "Third World" societies creates an attitude to its history that shares some of the orientations of semiotics and psychoanalysis, "for the dynamics of history, according to these disciplines, is not an unalterable past moving towards an inexorable future; it is in the ways of thinking and in the choices of present time . . . antimemories at that level . . . allow greater play and lesser defensive rigidity."[19] It is at the point of the omen's obscurity, not in the order of the symbol but in the temporal break of the sign that the interrogative *che vuoi* of agency emerges: What is the vertiginous chapati saying to me? The "indeterminate" circulation of meaning as rumor or conspiracy, with its perverse, psychic affects of panic constitutes the intersubjective realm of revolt and resistance. What kind of agency is constituted in the circulation of the chapati?

Let us take Sir John Kaye's narrative of the phenomenon in his monumental *History of the Indian Mutiny* written in 1864, based on the most extensive research in contemporary sources, drawn widely from the correspondence with participants in the mutiny:

> It fixed, too, more firmly in the mind of Lord Canning, the belief that a great fear was spreading itself among the people, *and that there was more danger in such a feeling than in great hatred.* Thinking of this he also thought of another strange story that had come to him from the North-West, and which even the most experienced men about him were incompetent to explain. From village to village, brought by one messenger and sent onward by another, passed a mysterious token in the shape of those flat cakes made from flour and water, and forming the common bread of the people, which in their language, are called chapatis. All that was known about it was that a messenger appeared, gave the cake to the headman of one village, and requested him to despatch it, onward to the next; and that in this way it travelled from place to place; no one refusing, no one doubting, few even questioning in blind obedience to *a necessity felt rather than understood.* . . . The greater number looked upon it as a signal of warning and preparation, designed to tell the people that something great and portentous was about to happen, and to prompt them to be ready for the crisis. One great authority wrote to the Governor-general that he had been told that the chapati was the symbol of men's food, and that its circulation was intended to alarm and to influence men's minds by indicating to them that their means of subsistence would be taken from them, and to tell them therefore, to hold together. Others laughing to scorn this notion of the fiery cross, saw in it only a common superstition of the country. It was said that it was no unwonted thing for a Hindu, in whose family sickness had broken out, to institute this transmission of chapatis, in the belief that it would carry off the disease. Then, again, it was believed by others . . . that the purpose attaching to the circulation [of the chapatis] was another fiction that there was bone dust in them, and that the English had resorted to this supplementary method of defiling the people. . . . But whatsoever the real history of the movement, it had doubtless the effect of keeping alive much popular excitement in the districts through which the cakes were transmitted. . . . Some saw in it much meaning; some saw none. Time has thrown no new light upon it. Opinions still differ. And all that history can record with certainty is that the bearers of these strange missives went from place to place, and as ever as they went new excitements were engendered, and vague excitements were raised.[20]

It is the indeterminacy of meaning, unleashed by the contingent chapati, which becomes the totem meal for historians of the mutiny. They bite the greased bullet and circulate the myth of the chapati, and in so doing they pass on the contagion of rumor and panic into their own serial, sensible narratives that become unsettled in that very act of repetition.

The discursive figure of rumor produces an infectious ambivalence, an "abyssal overlapping," of too much meaning and a certain meaningless-ness. What is customary and commonplace becomes archaic, awesome, terrifying. This reinscription of a traditional system of organization through the disturbance, or interruption, of the circulation of its cultural codes whereupon "new excitements were engendered, and vague expectations were raised," has a marked similarity to the conjunctural history of the mutiny.

The slender narrative of the chapati, with its performative rhetoric of circulation/panic, enacts those wider contextual conditions of the 1857 rebellion that Eric Stokes has suggestively described as a "crisis of dis-placement"[21] in his fine essay on the agrarian context of the 1857 rebel-lion. The obsessive fear of religious contagion and the extreme suspicion of the government are symptomatic of a desperate soldiery clinging to its own traditions with a renewed fervor in the face of new regulations for the control and modernization of the native army, of which the En-field rifle was only the most obvious symbol. The leveling zeal of the government to liberate the peasant from the *taluqdar* (landlord) and the infamous annexation of the kingdom of Oudh, among other smaller principalities, created a sense of social dislocation that had its effects within an army consisting mainly of high-caste peasant mercenaries. The 20th Bengal Native Infantry that raised the rebellion in Meerut in May 1857 consisted mainly of rajput and brahmin petty landholders from southern Oudh. The influx of lower castes and outsiders into their ranks as a result of the radical "leveling" policies of the government—as Philip Mason has described it[22]—led to such a widespread sense of the confu-sion of status and reference that in the midst of the mutiny, in October 1857, an officer wrote to the *Lahore Chronicle* warning that "a ploughman is not a subadar because he is styled so, and an indian noble-man or gentleman is not the less so because we treat him as a trades-man."[23]

I have pried open, once more, the space between the symbol of the chapati and the sign of its circulation in order to reveal rumor *affect*. It is "panic" that speaks in the temporal caesura between symbol and sign, politicizing the narrative; the agency of politics obscurely contained in the contagion of chapati flour, or in the more revealing castratory phan-tasies of the former governor-general Ellenborough "to emasculate all the mutineers and to call Delhi Eunuchbad."[24] If we read Kaye's account from its space of undecidability we find that panic mounts in its phrases, producing the kinetic tension of the contingent. His narrative attempts to relate the chapatis contiguously to historical or cultural events in a metonymic series: common-bread: potentious event: deprivation of subsistence (reorganization of army, land resettlement, abrogation of *taluqdars'* rights and privileges: fiery cross: passing on the malady (ritual peasant practice of *chalawa* or scapegoating an animal in order to rid the community of epidemics): religious defilement (Enfield rifle, greased bullet paper). However, the articulation of these sites of cultural difference and social antagonism—what connects them in the absence of the validity of interpretation—is a discourse of panic. Citing Canning, Kaye writes that "there was more danger in such a feeling [of the *spreading* of fear] than in great hatred"; that the circulation of the chapatis was "a necessity *felt* rather than understood"; the circulation was intended to influence *through alarm* and thereby hold together the people; and whatsoever the *real history*, the political purpose of the circulating chapati was to "keep alive much popular excitement."

Panic spreads. It does not simply hold together the native people but binds them—through the process of projection—affectively and ambivalently with their masters. In Kaye's rendering of Canning's account it is the passages of panic that are written neither simply from the native point of view, nor from the superior interpretative, "administrative" perspective of Lord Canning. While he largely attributes fear and panic to a "preliterate" native mind, its superstition and misapprehensions, its "preformed" psychological and political pliability, the *genre* of "intelligence gathering" that constitutes the discourse is proof of the fact that the fear was not limited to the peasants. The indeterminacy of the event reveals the panic among the bureaucrats, and within the army, which can be read in the anxious, conflicting opinions that Canning musters.

By projecting the panic and anxiety on native custom and ethnic particularity, the British attempted to contain and "objectify" their anxiety by finding a ready "native" reference for the undecidable event that afflicted them. This is clearly seen in the rhetorical split in Kaye's passage where the subjects of the discourse are natives, but the subjects of the act of enunciation—experienced men, one great authority, others laughing, others believing—are "British" authorities whether they are part of the administration or Indian spies. It is at the enunciative level that the humble chapati circulates both a panic of knowledge and power. The great spreading fear, more dangerous than anger, is equivocal, circulating wildly on both sides. It spreads beyond the knowledge of ethnic or cultural binarisms and becomes a new, hybrid space of cultural difference in the negotiation of colonial power-relations. Beyond the barracks and the bungalow opens up an antagonistic, ambiguous area of engagement that provides, in a perverse way, a common battleground that gives the Sipahi a tactical advantage.

What lesson does the circulation of panic—the "time" of the chapati—have for historical agency?

To see the chapati as an "internal," orderly transformation from the symbol of pollution to politics, reproduces the binary between the peasant and the raj, and denies the particular historical agency of the sipahi, which as Stokes has repeatedly shown, succeeded by "stratagem not arms." In disavowing the politics of indeterminacy and panic the collective agency of the insurgent peasant would be given a simplistic sense of intentionality. The mutineers are located in a semifeudal time-warp, the playthings of religious conspiracies. Rewriting Kaye's splendid account of Canning twenty-five years later, in the fifth volume of the *History*, his prosaic successor Malleson produces the interesting myth of Mohamedan conspiracy and, unwittingly "authorizes" the chapatis. The treacherous tracery of the chapatis across the Northwest provinces follows the path of the Maulvi of Faizabad, one of the few conspirators known by name. Like the chapati, he traveled extensively in the Northwest after the annexation of Oudh, "on a mission which was a mystery to the Europeans." Like the chapati, the Maulvi's circulation had its ramifications "at Delhi, at Mirath, at Patna, and at Calcutta"![25]

If, however, we follow the discourse of panic, the *affectivity* of historical understanding, then we encounter a temporal "speed" of historical events that leads to an understanding of rebel agency. The chapati's circulation bears a contingent relation to the time-lag or temporal break in-between sign and symbol, constitutive of the representation of the intersubjective, collective realm of meaning and action. Contemporary historical accounts stress a similar temporality in suggesting that the spread and solidarity of insurgency were effected with an almost "timeless" speed, a temporality that cannot be represented except as "repetition" or uncertainty or panic.

Lieut. Martineu, the musketry inspector at Umballa Rifle Depot, was responsible for training native infantrymen in the use of the Enfield. Having been terrorized by an occurrence of the chapati-flour omen in his own ranks, he writes in desperation to General Belched about the state of the army on May 5, 1857, just five days before the mutiny broke at Meerut. His apprehensions have largely been ignored and his demand for a court of inquiry to investigate the unusual agitation in the ranks has been turned down. His is an obscure but representative voice and bears a fine witness to the link between the circulation of panic and its representation as a "cut" in time or an instant shock:

> Everywhere far and near the army under some maddening impulse are
> looking out with strained expectation for something, some unseen, invisi-

ble agency has caused one *common electric thrill* to run through all. . . . I don't think they know what they will do, or that they have any plan of action except of resistance to invasion of their religion and their faith.[26]

In retelling the chapati tale as a major instance of the transmission of insurgency, Ranajit Guha associates the speed of the transmission of rebellion with the "psychosis of dominant social groups"[27] confronted suddenly with the rebellion of those considered loyal.

The link I am attempting to make between the speedy time of panic and the break-up of a binary sense of political antagonism resonates with an important insight of psychoanalyst Wilfrid Bion on the place of panic in the fight-flight group, of which war and the army are examples. The psychosis of the group consists in the reversibility or interchangeability of panic and danger. This ambivalence is part of the group structured within a time-lag similar to the process I described as the "individuation" of agency: "His inalienable inheritance as group animal gives rise to a feeling in the individual that he can *never catch up* with a course of events to which he is always, at any given moment, already committed."[28] It is this disjunctive structure within and between groups that prevents us from representing oppositionality in the equivalence of a binary structure. Where anger and panic arise they are stimulated by an event, Bion writes, which always falls outside the functions of the group.

How are we to understand this notion of falling "outside" in relation to the discourse of panic? I want to suggest that we understand this "outside" not in simple spatial terms but in terms of the time-lag constitutive of meaning and agency. The "outside event" could also be the unacknowledged liminality of "margin" of the discourse, the point where it contingently touches the other's difference *as itself.* In this sense, those passages of panic in Kaye's account of the chapati, which occupied a space in his narrative where meaning was undecidable and the "subject" of discourse split and doubled between the native informer and colonial "enunciator," represent this "outside." The moment when we realize that what is being represented and fixed as native panic is, at the level of enunciation, the spreading, uncontrolled fear and fantasy of the colonizer, then a contingent borderline experience opens up *in between* the two. This is the space of cultural and interpretive undecidability that is being produced in the "present" of the colonial moment. Such an outside is also visible in my insistence that the chapati's meaning *as circulation* only emerges in the time-lag, or temporal break, *in between* its social-symbolic ordering and its iterative repetition as the sign of the undecidable, the terrifying. Isn't this Kaye's very predicament when he says that "all that history can record with any certainty is that these strange missives went from place to place," and yet it is this temporal process of the transmission of rebel agency about which he chooses to say nothing? So the moment of political panic as it is turned into historical narrative is a *movement* that breaks down the stereotymy of inside/outside and reveals the contingent process of the inside turning into the outside and producing another hybrid site or sign. Lacan calls this kind of inside/out/outside/in space a moment of *éxtimité*: a traumatic moment of the "not-there" (Morrison) or the indeterminate or the unknowable (Kaye) around which the symbolic discourse of human history comes to be constituted. In that sense, then, the extimate moment would be the "repetition" of rumor in the seriality of the historical event (1857), the "speed" of panic at the site of rebel politics, or indeed, the temporality of psychoanalysis in the writing of history.

The margin of hybridity where cultural differences "contingently" touch becomes the moment of panic that reveals the borderline experience (in the political and psychoanalytical sense of that term). It resists the binary opposition of racial and cultural groups, sipahis and sahibs, as homogeneous polarized political consciousness. The political psychosis of panic constitutes the boundary of cultural hybridity across which the mutiny is fought. The native order of Indian symbols, their indigenous ethnic reference "inside," is displaced and turned inside-out; they become the circulating signs of an "english" panic, impenetrable to the official discourse of imperial history, represented in the language of indeterminacy. The chapati, then, is also a displacement of and defense against the Enfield rifle; the chapati flour contaminated with bone-meal and shaped like "english ships-biscuits" are a heterogeneous, hybrid sign that suggest, according to the advocate-general, that the conspirators were imputing that army chaplains were trying to impose "one food one faith."[29] In these sudden, slender signs of panic, we see complex cultural writing of rebel agency in 1857 that Eric Stokes has expanded into a wider, more traditional argument:

> Much of what passes for primary resistance occurs at the onset of "local crisis" when the first phase of collaboration has gone sour. The internal configuration of society has already been altered by the yeast of modernity, so that the "local crisis" is as much an internal as an external one and reflects the strains of dislocation and displacement.[30]

It is this notion of the historical as much an internal (psychic, affective) as an external (political, institutional, governmental) event, and vice versa that I have been trying to explore within the wider dialectic of the Sipahi and the Raj. Again, it has been my argument that historical agency is no less effective because it is disjunctive or displaced. Would such an ambivalent borderline of hybridity prevent us from specifying a political strategy or identifying a historical event?

On the contrary, it would enhance our understanding of certain forms of political struggle. After all my mad talk about group-psychosis and flying chapatis let us take a sober, historical example. In one of the last chapters that Stokes wrote on the Indian mutiny before his death— "The Sepoy Rebels"—he displays an almost hyperreal sense of the contingency of time and event caught like a slow motion replay of the mutiny itself. Stokes came "increasingly to emphasize the importance of the contingent events of military action in his account of the incidence and spread of the revolt," writes Christopher Bayly in his afterword to *The Peasant Armed*. He came to see the importance of the "human drama and the mythology of revolt . . . those contingent, almost accidental features of the revolt that also help to explain the puzzle of its timing in relation to longer-term trends in north Indian history."[31] This new emphasis on the contingent and the symbolic is particularly visible in a fine passage where Stokes writes:

> An Army wore out like clothing and needed frequent renewal. Its tatterde-malion appearance was also of more than symbolic significance. In the hour of desperation the British might dispense with regular uniform and strict punctilio, but once the crisis was passed and their regiments multiplied, their military practice tightened rather than relaxed. For the sepoys the abandonment of shakos and jackets might have been sensible for ease of fighting, but it helped obliterate distinction of company and regiment and turned them increasingly from regular soldiers into civil insurgents.[32]

Seen from the perspective of the outcome of the rebellion, Stokes is surely right to assert, as he does repeatedly, that the defeat of the rebels came from the "absence of a tactical plan or *controlling mind* and of disciplined organisation to press home the assault."[33] Stokes is impeccable in his understanding of the disciplines of the regular soldier and the guerrilla tactics of the civil insurgent, but his adherence to a certain notion of the "controlling mind" does not permit him to see the doubled, displaced strategy of sepoy-as/and-civil insurgent. With my taste for in-between states and moments of hybridity, I shall briefly attempt to describe that inside-out movement when the sepoy and the civil insurgent are two sites of the subject in the same moment of historical agency.

Of the very few contemporary "native" narratives available about the scene of battle, Munshee Mohan Lal's account of a conversation overheard between a Mohamedan trooper of the influential 3rd Cavalry and Sir William Nott's sepoy orderly is the best. Despite his function as a spy with an obvious interest in suggesting a Mohamedan conspiracy, his account provides valuable corroborative evidence. In the attorney-general's account of Mohan Lal's evidence the drama and the "controlling mind" of the rebel action have been reduced to treachery and conspiracy. If we return to Mohan Lal's original letter written in November 1857, we read quite a different story.

It was on the release of their friends and comrades from the Meerut Prison that the mutineers decided on the siege of Delhi. The famous cry of "*Chalo Delhi—Onwards to Delhi*" does not simply provide "an immediate loose-knit unity to excited and distracted men" as Stokes describes it.[34] The rebel account makes quite clear that it was only after they tested their strength as a fighting body, and burned the houses of the "saheb logue" that they called a meeting to decide what their next move would be. They decided against Rohilcund in the direction of Agra, because they could not take enough defensive positions on the way. "After clam [sic] and deliberate consideration Delhi was named and resolved to make the headquarters"[35] for tactical military and political reasons: "the annihilation of the few English and Christian residents . . . the possession of the magazine, and the person of the King."

It is the "person" of the king that constitutes the most interesting rebel strategy. To centralize the rebellion in Delhi—a tactic that was to fail in the long run—was a way of providing an affective focus for the mutiny, to establish it as a public political sphere. "The name of the King will work like a magic and induce the distant states to mutiny," the soldiers reason. This public affirmation of power is necessary because they (the natives!) are aware of the problems of conspiratorial communication. "The sepoy said the *he* had witnessed the artful modes of General Nott to conceal and forward his letters during the Cabool disasters to Sindh and Cabool, such acts of ours will not escape *their* attention"— which is to say, of course, that General Nott's secret letters were bazaar talk, just as the chapatis became the staple fare of Government House.

The body of the king has another destiny in the political strategy of the mutineers. They contrived to bring out Bahadur Shah in a royal procession to "restore confidence in the citizens." Then surrounded by "disciplined troops" and "respectable residents," whether jagirdars or merchants, the king as spectacle becomes that name that can work like magic. This magic is worked by a deliberate narrative strategy—rumor. When the king assumes his public persona then the mutineers "excited his ambition" by exaggerated stories of ranged regiments bearing treasures from various stations; that all European troops were engaged in Persia; that the unsettled state of European politics would hardly permit the home authorities to reach any reinforcement to India. This magic of narrative made the king assume his name, not the other way round, "made Bahadur Shah to believe that he had been born to restore the lost realm of the great Taimoor in the last days of his life. *He now threw off the mask and took interest in encouraging the rebellion.*"

The sepoy as civil insurgent, that tatterdemalion figure, creates his hybrid narratives from a number of slender tales: the political secrecy of the saheb logue; the late medieval inscription of the body of the king; the Mughal durbar ritual of *khelat*, a gift of clothing through which loyal subjects are "incorporated"[36] into the body of the king; rumors of English politics; and, of course, the vanity of human wishes and the messianic desires of crowds. I want to tug once more at the ragged coat of the rebel and draw a tattered thread that takes my story from this public political moment to its other slender narrative, psychic panic. From the body of the Mughal I want to move back to the body of the Sipahi, by way of a time-lag; from the mutiny of 1857 and its chapatis to the Vellore mutiny of 1806 and its *topi*.

After the reorganization of the Madras army in 1796, all the traditional accoutrements of the native soldier's appearance were effaced. Ear-rings and caste-marks were obliterated, the turban forbidden. The sipahi was shaved and dressed "in a stiff round hat, like a pariah drummer's with a flat top, a leather cockade and a standing feather."[37] In the eyes of his countrymen the soldier became a *topiwalla*, a hat-wearer, synonymous with being a *feringhi* or Christian. Rumors began to circulate about an imminent conversion of Hindus and Muslims to Christianity through the contagion of the leather hat. In those anxious times wandering mendicants "with the odor of sanctified filth about them" told strange stories and incredible fables, within the military lines. The unmistakable stirrings of panic could be heard, swiftly carried on the wings of anger, through the bazaars, the countryside, the barracks. Just before the great massacre at Vellore of July 10, 1806, of which the history books tell us, an event occurred that was so common that recent historians seem to have forgotten it.

As the soldiers in their new *firinhi* topis and uniforms mingled with the palace servants and retainers of the Mysore princes, their traditional protectors, they were jeered and humiliated:

> The different parts of their uniform were curiously examined amidst shrugs and other expressive gestures, and significant "Wah wahs!" and vague hints that everything about them in some way portended Christianity. They looked at the Sipahi's stock and said, "What is this? It is leather! Well!" Then they would look at his belt and tell him that it made a cross upon his person. But it was the round hat that most of all was the object of the taunts and warnings of the people of the palace. "It only needed this to make you altogether a Faringhi. Take care or we shall soon be made Christians . . . and then the whole country will be ruined."[38]

When the body of the sipahi comes to be hybridized in the circulation of cryptic omens, then new faringhi uniforms become the sources of primal fears. The fiery cross turns into a high hat or a flat, unleavened bread. The "yeast of modernity" causes archaic fears to arise; political signs and contagious portents inhabit the body of the people. Is this panic, written on the sipahi's skin, the omen that sends rumor and rebellion on their flight? Is this the narrative of hysteria? Beyond these questions you can hear the storm break in Vellore on July 10, 1806. The rest is History.

NOTES

1. Michel Foucault, *The Order of Things* (London: Tavistock, 1970), p. 369.

2. Homi K. Bhabha, "Sly Civility," *October* 34 (1985): 71–80.

3. Foucault, *Order of Things*, p. 52.

4. Ibid., p. 377.

5. Veena Das, "Dubaltern as Perspective," in *Subaltern Studies, VI*, ed. Ranajit Guha (Delhi: Oxford University Press, 1989), p. 313.

6. Ibid., p. 316.

7. G. C. Spivak, "Postcoloniality and Value," in *Literary Theory To-day*, ed. P. Collier and H. Gaya Ryan (Cambridge: Polity, 1990), p. 228.

8. *The Seminar of Jacques Lacan, Book 11: 1954–55*, ed. J. A. Miller, trans. Sylvana Tomaselli, with notes by John Forrester (Cambridge: Cambridge University Press, 1988), pp. 284–85.

9. For a clear, recent explanation of this process, see Slavoj Zizek, *The Sublime Object of Ideology* (London: Verso, 1989), pp. 104–11.

10. Jacques Lacan, "Agency of the Letter in the Unconscious," *Ecrits* (London: Tavistock, 1977), p. 173.

11. Zizek, *Sublime Object of Ideology*, p. 109.

12. For a related discussion that elaborates some of these concepts, see my essays: "The Commitment to Theory," *New Formations* 5 (Summer 1988), reprinted in *Third Cinema Reader*, ed. J. Pines and P. Willemen (London: British Film Institute, 1989); and "DissemiNation: Time, Narrative and the Margins of the Modern Nation," in *Nation and Narration*, ed. Homi K. Bhabha (London and New York: Routledge, 1990).

13. F. Fanon, *The Wretched of the Earth* (Harmondsworth; Penguin, 1969), pp. 117–18. I have used some of Fanon's phrases, and changed the order of the argument to give an efficient summary of his argument.

14. Toni Morrison, "Unspeakable Things Unspoken," *Michigan Quarterly Review*, 28, no. 1 (Winter 1989): 11–12.

15. Toni Morrison, *Beloved* (London: Chatto and Windus, 1987), p. 4.

16. Morrison, "Unspeakable Things Unspoken," p. 31.

17. Ibid., p. 32.

18. I am deeply indebted to Ranajit Guha's reading of the chapati story in his classic account of rebel politics in *Elementary Aspects of Peasant Insurgency in Colonial India* (Delhi: Oxford University Press, 1983), see chap. 6, in particular, pp. 239–46. Although my analysis of the event differs from his in ways that will become clearer as the argument proceeds, his splendid reading produces an important framework for all successive readings.

19. A. Nandy, *Traditions, Tyranny and Utopias* (Delhi: Oxford University Press, 1987), pp. 47–48.

20. J. W. Kaye and G. B. Malleson, *History of the Indian Mutiny of 1857–58* (London: W. H. Allen, 1888), 1:416–20.

21. Eric Stokes, "The Context of the 1857 Rebellion," *The Peasant and the Raj* (Cambridge: Cambridge University Press, 1978), see p. 130 *et passim*.

22. P. Mason, "Fear and Its Causes," in *A Matter of Honour: An Account of the Indian Army, Its Officers and Men* (London: Jonathan Cape, 1974), pp. 247–57.

23. India Office Library and Records (London), Kaye Papers: Home Misc. 725, p. 421.

24. Eric Stokes, *The Peasant Armed* (Oxford: Clarendon, 1986), p. 92.

25. Kaye and Malleson, *History of the Indian Mutiny*, 5:292.

26. Kaye, Home Misc. 725.

27. Ranajit Guha, *Elementary Aspects of Peasant Insurgency* (Delhi: Oxford University Press, 1983), p. 225.

28. Wilfrid Bion, *Experience in Groups* (London: Tavistock, 1983), p. 91.

29. Kaye and Malleson, *History of the Indian Mutiny*, 5:341.

30. Stokes, "Context of the 1857 Rebellion," p. 124.

31. In Stokes, *Peasant Armed*, pp. 240–41.

32. Ibid., p. 66.

33. Ibid., p. 82.

34. Ibid., p. 50.

35. Kaye Papers: Home Misc. 725, pp. 399–407.

36. F. W. Buckler, "The Oriental Despot," quoted in B. S. Cohn, "Representing Authority in Victorian India," in *The Invention of Tradition*, ed. E. Hobsbawm and T. Ranger (Cambridge: Cambridge University Press, 1983), p. 168.

37. Kaye and Malleson, *History of the Indian Mutiny*, vol. 5.

38. Ibid., p. 164.

Notes on the Contributors

EMILY APTER is professor of French and comparative literature, University of California, Los Angeles. She is the author of *Feminizing the Fetish: Psycho-analysis and Narrative Obsession in Turn-of-the-Century France* (1991), and has recently coedited *Fetishism as Cultural Discourse* (1993).

HOMI K. BHABHA is reader in English, Sussex University, and the author of *The Location of Culture* (1994).

LEONARD BLUSSÉ is secretary of the Institute for the History of European Expansion, Leiden. He has edited several volumes on trade in east and southeast Asia, and is the author of *Strange Company: Chinese Settlers, Mestizo Women and the Dutch in VOC Batavia* (1986).

JOAN DAYAN is professor of English and African-American studies, University of Arizona, Tucson. Her books include *Fables of Mind: An Inquiry into Poe's Fiction* (1987) and *Rene Depestre* (1994).

STEVEN FEIERMAN is professor of history at the University of Florida, Gainesville and the author of *The Shambaa Kingdom* (1974). His recent publication is *Peasant Intellectuals: Anthropology and History in Tanzania* (1990).

J. JORGE KLOR DE ALVA is professor of anthropology, Princeton University. He is editing a several-volume series on culture contact and change in the Americas, entitled *De palabra y obra en el Nuevo Mundo* (1992–), translated as *Discourse and Practice in the New World*.

ZACKARY LOCKMAN is fellow, Woodrow Wilson International Center for Scholars, Washington, D.C., and the coauthor of *Workers on the Nile* (1987). He is currently working on popular culture and social change in Egypt, 1882–1919.

ANTHONY PAGDEN is fellow, King's College, Cambridge, and the author of several books on early modern Europe and the New World, including *Colonial Identity in the Atlantic World, 1500–1800* (1987) and *European Encounters with the New World from Renaissance to Romanticism* (1993).

RUTH B. PHILLIPS is professor of art history, Carleton University, Ottawa. She has curated several museum exhibitions of North American Indian art, and is the author of the forthcoming *Representing Woman: The Sande Society Masquerades of the Mende* (1994).

GYAN PRAKASH is associate professor of history, Princeton University. He is the author of *Bonded Histories: Genealogies of Labor Servitude in Colonial India* (1990), and is currently preparing a manuscript on the cultural authority of science in the imagination of modern India.

EDWARD SAID is University Professor at Columbia University. His many publications include *Orientalism* (1978), *The World, the Text and, the Critic* (1983), and *Culture and Imperialism* (1993).

IRENE SILVERBLATT is associate professor of cultural anthropology, Duke University, and the author of *Moon, Sun, and Witches: Gender Ideologies and Class in Inca and Colonial Peru* (1987). Her current project is on the cultural work of state-making and colonization.

GAURI VISWANATHAN is associate professor of English and comparative literature, Columbia University, and the author of *Masks of Conquest* (1989). She is completing a book on conversion and cultural change in British colonialism.

Index

PRINCETON STUDIES IN
CULTURE/POWER/HISTORY